BLACKSTONE'S GUIDE TO

The Serious Crime
Act 2007

Rudi Fortson

OXFORD
UNIVERSITY PRESS

OXFORD

UNIVERSITY PRESS

Great Clarendon Street, Oxford ox2 6DP

Oxford University Press is a department of the University of Oxford.
It furthers the University's objective of excellence in research, scholarship,
and education by publishing worldwide in

Oxford New York

Auckland Cape Town Dar es Salaam Hong Kong Karachi
Kuala Lumpur Madrid Melbourne Mexico City Nairobi
New Delhi Shanghai Taipei Toronto

With offices in

Argentina Austria Brazil Chile Czech Republic France Greece
Guatemala Hungary Italy Japan Poland Portugal Singapore
South Korea Switzerland Thailand Turkey Ukraine Vietnam

Oxford is a registered trade mark of Oxford University Press
in the UK and in certain other countries

Published in the United States
by Oxford University Press Inc., New York

© Rudi Fortson 2008

The moral rights of the author have been asserted

Database right Oxford University Press (maker)

Crown copyright material is reproduced under Class Licence
Number C01P0000148 with the permission of OPSI
and the Queen's Printer for Scotland

First published 2008

All rights reserved. No part of this publication may be reproduced,
stored in a retrieval system, or transmitted, in any form or by any means,
without the prior permission in writing of Oxford University Press,
or as expressly permitted by law, or under terms agreed with the appropriate
reprographics rights organization. Enquiries concerning reproduction
outside the scope of the above should be sent to the Rights Department,
Oxford University Press, at the address above

You must not circulate this book in any other binding or cover
and you must impose the same condition on any acquirer

QM LIBRARY
(MILE END)

British Library Cataloguing in Publication Data

Data available

Library of Congress Cataloging-in-Publication Data

Fortson, Rudi.
Blakstone's Guide to the Serious Crime Act 2007 / Rudi Fortson.
  p. cm.
Includes bibliographical references and index.
  ISBN-13: 978-0-19-954304-5 (pbk. : alk. paper) 1. Racketeering—
Great Britain. 2. Restraining orders—Great Britain. 3. Inchoate
offenses—Great Britain. 4. Forfeiture—Great Britain—Criminal
provisions. 5. Crime prevention—Great Britain.
I. Title: Serious Crime Act 2007. II. Title.
  KD8006.F67 2008
  345.411'02—dc22

                                                                    2008011111

Typeset by Cepha Imaging Private Ltd., Bangalore, India
Printed in Great Britain
on acid-free paper by
Ashford Colour Press Limited, Gosport, Hampshire

ISBN 978–0–19–954304–5

1 3 5 7 9 10 8 6 4 2

Preface

The SCA2007, which received Royal Assent on the 30 October 2007, is a major measure in respect of which many of its provisions apply to all offences and not just to instances of 'serious crime'. The Act makes provision to abolish the Assets Recovery Agency (ARA) and to transfer its functions to other agencies. The powers of Accredited Financial Investigators are widened, and provision is made to enable law enforcement agencies to investigate the origins of 'cash' that has been seized by them under Chapter 3 to Part 5 of the Proceeds of Crime Act 2002. The sharing and matching of data, by public authorities, for the purpose of preventing fraud or a particular kind of fraud, is put on a statutory footing. A new injunctive civil order, called the 'Serious Crime Prevention Order', is created under Part 1 of the Act. Inappropriately labelled by the media as 'the super ASBO', the Serious Crime Prevention Order has the potential to be a draconian instrument.

The most complex Part of the 2007 Act is Part 2 (encouraging and assisting crime). Although Part 2 consists of a mere 24 sections it creates an intricate set of rules that builds on the work of the Law Commission in its Report No 300 'Inchoate Liability for Assisting and Encouraging Crime' and, to a lesser extent, Report No 305 ('Participating in Crime'). Part 2 SCA 2007 creates three inchoate offences in respect of acts of encouragement or assistance in circumstances where the anticipated offence was not committed (for whatever reason). Unhappily, Part 2 SCA 2007 does not enact a complete legislative code with respect to complicity in the commission of a criminal offence: Part 2 of the Act needs to be considered with that fact in mind.

The aim of this book is to give practical assistance and insight into the operation of the Act. Some readers will want no more than an overview of the relevant provisions of the Act, while other readers will be looking for a more detailed discussion of them. The book has been written in a way that is intended to allow readers to focus on aspects of the legislation that is of greatest interest to them and at a level that meets their requirements.

Although this book is written in a style that assumes that the Act is fully in force it must be noted that—apart from a few general provisions—the Act will come into force on such dates as the Secretary of State may by order appoint. At the time of writing this preface (14 February 2008), one commencement order has been made, namely, SI 2008/0219 which, on 15 February 2008, brought into force s 85 (disclosure of information by Revenue and Customs); s 88 and Sch 12 (extension of investigatory powers of Revenue and Customs); and s 92 (repeals and revocations) in so far as it relates to the entries in Sch 14 (repeals and revocations), that is to say, the entries relating to s 108(1) of the Police Act 1997, ss 56(1) and 81(1) of the Regulation of Investigatory Powers Act 2000; and paras 1 and 11 of Sch 2 to the Commissioners for Revenue and Customs Act 2005.

SI 2008/0219 also brought into force, on 1 March 2008, the following provisions, namely, s 24(9) and (10) (order making powers relating to appeals procedure); s 37 (functions of applicant authorities) in so far as it relates to paras 4 and 18 of Sch 2 (Code for Crown Prosecutors and Code for Public Prosecutors); s 40(1), (2), and (4) (order making powers relating to authorised monitors); s 68(8) (interpretation and power to specify an anti-fraud organization); s 71(1), (2), (4), and (5) (code of practice for disclosure of information to prevent fraud); s 73 (data matching) in so far as it relates to three sets of provisions. First, the provisions in paras 1 and 2 of Sch 7 in so far as they insert new s 32G(1), (3), and (4) of the Audit Commission Act 1998 (code of data matching practice), secondly, the provisions in para 4 of Sch 7 that inserts new s 64G(1), (3), and (4) of the Public Audit (Wales) Act 2004 (code of data matching practice), and thirdly provisions in para 6 of Sch 7 in so far as it inserts new Article 4G(1), (3), and (4) of the Audit and Accountability (Northern Ireland) Order 2003 (code of data matching practice); s 74(1) (order making power relating to the abolition of the Assets Recovery Agency); s 74(2)(d) and (g) (transfer of investigation functions and amendments to other enactments) in so far as it relates to the provisions in para 115 of Sch 8 that inserts new s 377A(1) to (5) and (10) of the Proceeds of Crime Act 2002 (code of practice of Attorney General or Advocate General for Northern Ireland) and para 169 of Sch 8 (new s 2A of the Serious Organised Crime and Police Act 2005) for the purpose of the preparation of the Serious Organised Crime Agency's annual plan under s 6 of the Serious Organised Crime and Police Act 2005 for the financial year commencing 1 April 2008; and s 74(3) together with Sch 9 (transfers to the Serious Organised Crime Agency and the National Policing Improvement Agency).

The publication of this book has involved a considerable amount of work on the part of the production team at Oxford University Press. With true professionalism, they make their work look easy whereas it certainly is not. I am immensely grateful to all of them—with particular thanks to Jane Kavanagh, Faye Judges, and Jodi Towler and to the proofreaders for their painstaking work. I am also immensely grateful to Rock Tansey Q.C., to my colleagues, clerks, and staff, at 25 Bedford Row, London, for their unswerving support and assistance. Thanks are also due to Professor David Ormerod for all his time, invaluable comments, and thought-provoking discussions: he has assisted me greatly. I am also very grateful to the School of Law, Queen Mary, University of London. If there are errors in the text, the fault is entirely mine. My wife is to be afforded special praise. Long-suffering and patient, her support has been unfailing, and her secretarial skills much appreciated. This book is dedicated to my parents and to my sister: all have moved on to a better world but they are missed nonetheless.

Rudi Fortson
25 Bedford Row, London

14 February 2008

Contents—Summary

Contents—Detailed

Table of Cases

Table of Primary Legislation

Table of Secondary Legislation and Codes of Practice

1

INTRODUCTION

A. PROGRESS OF THE SERIOUS CRIME
BILL IN PARLIAMENT

The Serious Crime Bill was a government Bill that was introduced in the House of   1.01
Lords by Baroness Scotland of Asthal on 16 January 2007. The Bill was considered
by Parliament on the dates shown in the table below. The Serious Crime Act 2007
consists of 95 sections in four Parts, and 14 Schedules.

Date	Event	Place
16 Jan 07	1st reading	HL
7 Feb 07	2nd reading	HL
7–27 Mar 07	Committee	HL
25–30 Apr 07	Report	HL
9 May 07	3rd reading	HL
10 May 07	1st reading	HC
12 Jun 07	2nd reading	HC
26 Jun–10 Jul 07	Committee	HC
22 Oct 07	Report and 3rd reading	HC
24 Oct 07	'Ping-pong' (amendments)	
30 Oct 07	Royal Assent	

Explanatory Notes relating to the Serious Crime Bill were printed on 17 January 2007 and on 11 May 2007. A final set of Explanatory Notes was printed on 7 November 2007, following Royal Assent. An informative 86-page Research Paper 07/52 was published by the Home Affairs Section on 8 June 2007,[1] and complements the House of Lords Library Note 'The Serious Crime Bill'.[2] The aforementioned documents of course reflect the contents of the measure as then drafted but, nonetheless, the documents do provide useful background material. Research Paper 07/52 is particularly informative in its treatment of Serious Crime Prevention Orders. It only briefly discusses Part 2 of the Act (encouraging and assisting crime)—which is understandable—given the complexity of a topic that is the subject-matter of two detailed Reports by the Law Commission (Nos 300 and 305). Some 13 pages of that paper are taken up with the 'admissibility of intercept evidence in criminal proceedings', and were written at a time when the Serious Crime Bill included a clause (clause 4) to 'enable covert investigatory material, including intercept material, to be used in the High Court in connection with the making of serious crime prevention orders'. Clause 4 came to be known as the 'Lloyd amendment'[3] which was first moved on 7 March 2007 (but later withdrawn). It was moved again on 25 April, when the clause was added to the Bill. The government opposed the amendment on both occasions, and it got its way in General Committee on 26 June 2007 when clause 4 failed to stand part of the Bill (by a majority of one).[4] By that time, the then Home Secretary, Dr John Reid, had published a 'Government Discussion Document Ahead of Proposed Counter Terror Bill 2007' (Home Office 2007) in which he stated that the government's position was that the law would only be changed to permit the evidential use of intercept material, if safeguards can be put in place to protect sensitive techniques and if the benefits of using such material outweigh the risks of doing so. On 24 October 2007, the House of Lords agreed with the amendment made by the House of Commons to remove clause 4 from the Bill.[5]

1.02　　A number of amendments were made in October 2007, and the Bill 'ping-ponged' on the 24th of that month. Examples of amendments that were made to the Bill, at that stage, include: (a) ss 39 and 40 of the SCA 2007 (compliance with SCPOs: authorised monitors, and costs); (b) s 82 of the SCA 2007, which makes provision with respect to powers of management receivers and enforcement receivers; (c) s 83 of the SCA 2007, which creates a new receiver for the purpose of civil recovery under Part 5 of the Proceeds of Crime Act 2002, namely, the 'civil recovery management receivers'; and (d) s 87 of the SCA 2007, which amends s 60 of the Criminal Justice and Public Order Act 1994 in relation to specified circumstances in which

---

[1] Miriam Peck, Alexander Home and Grahame Danby; Home Affairs Section, House of Commons Library, 07/52.

[2] By Patrick M. Vollmer (2 February, 2007); LLN 2007/001.

[3] It was moved by a former Law Lord: Lord Lloyd of Berwick.

[4] Ayes 7, Noes 8; *Hansard*, General Committee, 26 June 2007, col 86.

[5] *Hansard* 24 Oct 2007, col 1082

powers of stop and search may be carried out with respect to dangerous or offensive weapons.

B. 'SERIOUS CRIME' OR JUST 'CRIME'?

Despite the reference in the short title of the 2007 Act, to 'Serious Crime', a significant number of provisions of that Act apply to *all* crimes of varying gravity. This is particularly true of Part 2 of the 2007 Act (encouraging and assisting crime). 1.03

The provisions enacted in Part 3 of the SCA 2007, concerning data sharing and data matching, are not confined to cases of serious fraud: there are no words of limitation in that Part of the Act, and there are no monetary thresholds. In its Report for 2004/05, the Audit Commission's National Fraud Initiative stated that the value of detected 'fraud and overpayments' rose from £83 million in 2002/03, to £111 million in 2004/05—an increase of 33 per cent.[6] If this figure relates to some 16,577 cases (as would seem to be the case) then the mean average is approximately £6,700. No doubt, some cases involved substantial sums of money, while other cases did not. 1.04

Amendments made by ss 75–77 of and Sch 10 to the SCA 2007 to chapter 3 of Part 5 of the Proceeds of Crime Act 2002 (POCA 2002), in relation to the civil summary process for the recovery of 'cash' that constitutes 'recoverable property', apply to all cases where the amount of cash exceeds the threshold amount (currently £1,000). However, the principal amendments made to POCA 2002—insofar as they relate to detained cash—concern the creation of the 'detained cash investigation' by which the provenance or intended destination of cash that has been seized under POCA 2002, can be investigated. In practice, the investigatory powers that are now made available with respect to a detained cash investigation (eg production orders, search and seizure orders) are likely to be exercised only in cases where the amount of cash detained is large, if not substantial. 1.05

C. SERIOUS CRIME PREVENTION ORDERS

Part 1 of the 2007 Act (ss 1–43) creates a new kind of civil order called the 'Serious Crime Prevention Order'. In the popular press, these orders have been styled 'Super ASBOs' but this is to mis-describe their effect. Anti-Social Behaviour Orders (ASBOs), and Serious Crime Prevention Orders (SCPOs) are civil orders but, whereas an ASBO is imposed on a person to prevent him/her carrying out antisocial acts that are likely to cause harassment, alarm or distress to another person, an SCPO is directed against persons (including bodies corporate, partnerships or unincorporated 1.06

---

[6] Page 2. It is not entirely clear whether the words 'fraud and overpayments' are to be read conjunctively or disjunctively.

associations) who are 'involved in serious crime'. The power of the High Court to make an SCPO is not confined to cases where the proposed subject of the order has been *criminally* involved in serious crime—it is enough that he/she has *facilitated* the commission of a 'serious offence', or that his/her conduct was *likely to facilitate* the commission of an offence (intentionally or otherwise).

1.07 The provisions contained in Part 1 of the 2007 Act were foreshadowed in the government's Consultation Paper 'New Powers Against Organised and Financial Crime' (July 2006, Cm 6875). The background to the enactment of this Part of the Act is described in this book and little would be gained by repeating that description here. Suffice to say that the government believes that the SCPO fills a gap in the law to deal with persons who are involved in serious crime and who, for one reason or another, cannot be satisfactorily controlled by way of other judicial or administrative processes.

1.08 An SCPO may be made in the High Court or in the Crown Court. An SCPO may only be made in the Crown Court if the subject appears to be sentenced in that Court for a 'serious offence' or for an offence under s 25 of the SCA 2007. A 'serious offence' is an offence specified in Sch 1 to the Act (eg drug trafficking, people trafficking, money laundering, corruption and bribery, and various fraud offences). A 'serious offence' may also be one which, in the particular circumstances of the case, the court considers to be sufficiently serious to be treated by the Court as if it were specified in Sch 1 to the Act.

1.09 The procedure for making an order, either in the High Court or in the Crown Court, is set out in the SCA 2007. The standard of proof is expressed to be the 'civil standard' but the government anticipates that the courts will apply, in effect, the criminal standard of proof. This is a topic that is discussed in detail in this book.

1.10 The intensity of control that the court can exert over the subject of an SCPO, is left to the judgment of the court. The court may include in an SCPO any condition that it considers necessary and proportionate to prevent, restrict, or disrupt, that subject's 'involvement in serious crime'. It is when we come to look at s 5 of the SCA 2007 that the potential power of the SCPO becomes clear. Section 5 contains examples of the kinds of conditions that may be included in an SCPO but 'it does not limit the type of provision that may be made by such an order'. The order can include prohibitions, restrictions, or requirements, in connection with: (a) an individual's financial, property, or business dealings or holdings; and/or (b) an individual's working arrangements; and/or (c) the means by which an individual communicates or associates with others, or the persons with whom he communicates or associates; and/or (d) the premises to which an individual has access; and/or (e) the use of any premises or item by an individual; and/or (f) an individual's travel (whether within the United Kingdom, between the United Kingdom and other places or otherwise). An SCPO can also include a requirement that the subject answers questions, or provides information, or produces documents specified or described in an order.

1.11 It is an offence under s 25 of the 2007 Act to fail to comply with the terms of an SCPO and, by virtue of s 26, the court has the power to forfeit anything in the offender's possession at the time of the offence, which the court considers to have been involved in the offence. The court has the power under s 27 of the SCA 2007 to wind up companies, partnerships, or a 'relevant body' (defined by s 27(12)) in the event that the subject of an SCPO commits an offence contrary to s 25.

D. ENCOURAGING AND ASSISTING CRIME

Part 2 of the SCA 2007 (ss 44–67) builds on the Law Commission's Report 'Inchoate 1.12 Liability for Assisting and Encouraging Crime',[7] as well as the draft Bill appended to that report. However, a number of significant differences exist between the Law Commission's draft Bill and Part 2 of the Act.[8]

It is important to note that Part 2 of the Act is intended to hold a person crimi- 1.13 nally liable *on an inchoate basis*, if he/she (with the requisite *mens rea*) helps another person to commit an offence (the 'anticipated offence') by encouraging or assisting its commission in circumstances where, for whatever reason, the offence is not committed. For example, D sold a ladder to D2 knowing that D2 would use it to commit burglary, but the offence was not committed because D2 was arrested for something else. D's motive in supplying the ladder was to make a profit, it was not his motive that D2 should commit burglary. Under Part 2 of the SCA 2007, D might now be liable for the commission of an inchoate offence of encouraging or assisting the commission of the anticipated offence, namely burglary. Strange as it may seem, there can be circumstances in which a person can be held liable under Part 2 of the SCA 2007 even if the anticipated offence *has been* committed (s 49(1), SCA 2007). The reasoning behind s 49(1) is discussed in Chapter 6 of this book.

Part 2 of the 2007 Act creates three inchoate offences. The first offence concerns 1.14 cases where a person *intends* to encourage or to assist another person to commit an offence (s 44, SCA 2007). The second offence deals with cases where a person *believes* that the anticipated offence will be committed (not 'might be' committed), and he *believes* that his act will encourage or assist its commission (s 45, SCA 2007). The third offence concerns cases where a person does an act that is capable of encouraging or assisting the commission of *one or more of a number of offences* and he *believes*: (a) that one or more of those offences will be committed (but he has no belief as to which); and (b) that his act will encourage or assist the commission of one or more of those offences (s 46, SCA 2007). The inchoate offences are potentially wide in their reach—arguably, too wide.

The common law offence of incitement is repealed by s 59 of the SCA 2007, but 1.15 many statutory offences of incitement, assisting, encouraging, conspiring, or attempting the commission of a crime, are retained. These offences are set out in Parts 1, 2, and 3 of Sch 3 to the SCA 2007 (England and Wales), and Parts 1, 4, and 5 of that Schedule (Northern Ireland). The offences include: solicitation of murder,

---

[7] Law Com No 300.
[8] These differences are identified and discussed in Ch 6 of this book.

attempting an act calculated or likely to cause sedition or disaffection,[9] assisting unlawful immigration to a member State,[10] inciting the commission of an offence contrary to the Misuse of Drugs Act 1971,[11] statutory conspiracy under s 1(1) of the Criminal Law Act 1977,[12] and criminal attempts under s 1(1) of the Criminal Attempts Act 1981.[13]

1.16   Part 2 of the SCA 2007 does not repeal, or replace, s 8 of the Accessories and Abettors Act 1861. Part 2 does not alter the position where D and D2 act as 'joint principals', ie where both parties participate in the *actus reus* of the offence, and share the requisite fault element for the offence in question. Moreover, Part 2 of the SCA 2007 does not alter rules relating to secondary liability for a collateral offence that is committed by the principal offender (eg a joint venture to assault V, but D2 goes on to kill V). Those three areas of the law are the subject of another detailed Law Commission Report (Law Com No 305, 'Participating in Crime'). Put briefly, Law Com No 300 deals with instances where a person encourages or assists another person to commit an anticipated offence that was *not* committed, whereas Law Com No 305 deals with instances where a person participates in a crime that *was* committed. It follows that Part 2 of the SCA 2007 does not enact a comprehensive statutory code relating to complicity in crime, incitement, and innocent agency. One might well wonder whether it was sensible for Parliament to enact measures that only deal with part of this complex subject.

1.17   One can only praise the Law Commission for its skill and industry in producing the aforementioned Reports, it was a Herculean task. But the Law Commission has also exposed the extent of the conceptual and practical difficulties that exist when endeavouring to enact a statutory code in this area of law. The Explanatory Notes, being only Notes, are therefore of limited assistance. For reasons that are set out in this book, the reader would be well advised to read the Law Commission's Report 'Inchoate Liability for Assisting and Encouraging Crime' (Law Com No 300)—or at least to read the Draft Bill appended to that Report and the accompanying commentary[14]—and, if time permits, to read Law Com 305 ('Participating in Crime').

1.18   It is submitted that the language of Part 2 of the SCA 2007 does not fully reveal the reasoning of the Law Commission (or Parliament, insofar as there is divergence) behind the enactment of that Part. There are several potential traps in Part 2. Three examples suffice to make that point. First, on an initial reading of Part 2, it is not strikingly obvious that its provisions are primarily concerned with *inchoate* acts of encouraging or assisting the commission of an offence. But even here, one has to keep in mind s 49(1) which reads that 'a person may commit an offence under this

---

[9] Contrary to s 3(1) of the Aliens Restriction (Amendment) Act 1919; see para 5, Part 1 of Sch 3 to the SCA 2007.

[10] See s 25 of the Immigration Act 1971; para 11, Part 1 of Sch 3 to the SCA 2007.

[11] s 19, MDA 1971.

[12] para 32, Part 2 of Sch 3, SCA 2007.

[13] para 33, Part 2 of Sch 3, SCA 2007.

[14] App A, Law Com No 300.

Part *whether or not any offence* capable of being encouraged or assisted by his act *is committed*' (emphasis added). Secondly, some phrases in Part 2, such as 'doing an act' and 'an act', are not used in a consistent fashion throughout Part 2. Thus, in some sections, those expressions refer to the anticipated perpetrator but, in other sections, they refer to the person who gave encouragement or assistance *to* the perpetrator (or the intended perpetrator). Thirdly, it is not entirely clear what the position is when dealing with cases where D has allegedly 'procured' the commission of an offence. In Law Com No 300, the Law Commission states that whilst 'counsel' means to 'encourage', the expression 'procure' is 'an anomalous "niche" form of secondary liability'.[15] At para 2.22 of Law Com No 305 ('Participating in Crime'), the Law Commission states '[it] is doubtful if all cases of "procuring" can be described properly as involving the provision of assistance or encouragement'. If that is so, does that mean that some cases of 'procuring' fall outside (or might fall outside) the language of Part 2 of the SCA 2007? If the answer is in the affirmative, then a potential gap remains in the law that is not filled by the wording of Part 2. How significant that gap is (if a gap exists) is debatable.

Chapter 6 of this book examines Part 2 in detail. It attempts to put the new provisions into the wider context of complicity for a crime committed. Part 2 requires practitioners to revisit concepts that are all too often taken for granted because (understandably) practitioners tend to treat as whole, the words 'aid, abet, counsel, or procure' as they appear in s 8 of the Aiders and Abettors Act 1861. These concepts are also discussed in this book.   1.19

E. DATA SHARING AND DATA MATCHING

Chapter 1 to Part 3 of the SCA 2007 is one of three chapters under the heading   1.20 'Other Measures to Prevent or Disrupt Serious and Other Crime'. The provisions of chapter 1 are timely given the number of highly publicized reports concerning the loss of confidential personal data that had been collected and held by one public authority or another. The measures enacted in ss 68–72 of chapter 1 of the SCA 2007 are presently confined to disclosures that may be made by 'public authorities' to each other, or to third parties, for preventing fraud or a particular kind of fraud, but it is foreseeable that these measures will be extended to prevent, and to detect, the commission of other crimes.

The provisions in chapter 1 of Part 3 were enacted following publication of the   1.21 Performance and Innovation Unit's Report 'Privacy and Data Sharing: The Way Forward for Public Services',[16] and the government's Green Paper 'New Powers Against Organised and Financial Crime'[17] which proposed the use of data sharing

---

[15] Law Com No 300; para B.7, fn 6.
[16] April 2002.
[17] Cm 6875.

to investigate and prevent fraud. The proposals in the Green Paper also build on the experience of the Audit Commission's National Fraud Initiative (ACNFI)—an initiative that has run since 1996—and which utilizes 'data matching' techniques to detect and to prevent fraud in the public sector. One effect of the measures enacted under the SCA 2007 is to empower the Audit Commission to prevent and to detect fraud beyond the public sector, albeit that its work in this regard will, presumably, be limited to the fraudulent use of public funds.

1.22   The sharing of data—particularly sensitive personal data—raises obvious concerns about data security, the use to which data can be put, the interests of privacy and confidentiality, and the steps that must be taken to install adequate and effective safeguards with respect to data handling.

1.23   The provisions enacted in ss 68–72 should be read in the context of s 73 of, and Sch 7 to, the SCA 2007. Schedule 7 makes detailed (but separate) provision with respect to data matching in England, Wales, and Northern Ireland. The difference between data sharing and data matching is explained later in this book, and the significance of chapter 1 of Part 3 is discussed in detail.

1.24   For the purpose of data matching exercises that are carried out in England, the Audit Commission Act 1998 is amended to empower the Audit Commission to conduct such exercises or to arrange for them to be conducted on its behalf, for assisting in the prevention and detection 'of fraud'. The word 'fraud' is not defined in the SCA 2007. The Public Audit (Wales) Act 2004, and the Audit and Accountability (Northern Ireland) Order 2003 (SI 2003/418 (NI 5)) are similarly amended in connection with data matching exercises that are carried out in Wales and in Northern Ireland (respectively).

1.25   Some people might be surprised to learn that the Audit Commission is engaged in data-handling exercises of this kind. Indeed, during a debate in the House of Lords, it was said that the Audit Commission would appear 'in a new guise as spymaster general'.[18] But another view is that the Audit Commission is doing no more than using established data analysis techniques (albeit with modern technological aids) to carry out its statutory duties under Part II of the Audit Commission Act 1998. Regardless of what might be said about its role, it is respectfully submitted that both the Audit Commission and the Information Commissioner's Office are to be given considerable credit for installing safeguards with respect to the Commission's own processes. The Audit Commission's National Fraud Initiative was up-and-running for about three years before the Data Protection Act 1998 came into force on 1 March 2000 (at which point the DPA 1984 was repealed). The Commission published a Code of Data Matching Practice (1997) shortly after the NFI was launched, in order to deal with issues that encompass an individual's right to privacy with respect to the processing of personal data. In 2006, the Audit Commission, in consultation with the Information Commissioner, revised the 1997 Code and the Code was again revised in November 2007. In the foreword to the 2006 Code,

---

[18] Lord Thomas of Gresford, Liberal Democrat Shadow Lord Chancellor, 7 February 2007, *Hansard*, House of Lords.

the Information Commissioner welcomes its provisions 'to ensure that National Fraud Initiative data matching activities take place in accordance with the requirements of the law', and noting that most of the information drawn together is about people who are not engaged in fraudulent activities.

During the second reading debate in the House of Lords,[19] Baroness Scotland   1.26
said that data shared under Chapter 1, Part 3, of the SCA 2007 would be done in accordance with the provisions of the Data Protection Act 1998. That issue is discussed in this book, as well as the offence of disclosing 'protection information'—an offence created by s 69 of the SCA 2007. There are a number of circumstances (specified in the 2007 Act) in which the s 69 offence does not apply. Parliament has enacted two defences to the s 69 offence, by virtue of s 69(4), which places a burden on the accused to prove that he reasonably believed (a) that the disclosure was lawful, or (b) that the information had already and lawfully been made available to the public. The Act does not specify whether the burden on the accused is evidential or persuasive. This aspect of the legislation is discussed in this book.

F. THE DEMISE OF THE ASSETS RECOVERY AGENCY

From 1 April 2008, s 74 of the SCA 2007 (Chapter 2 of Part 3) abolishes the Assets   1.27
Recovery Agency (ARA) and redistributes its functions to other agencies, chiefly to the Serious Organised Crime Agency (SOCA). The ARA's functions with respect to (a) the making of confiscation orders, and (b) restraint orders[20] are repealed (Sch 8, Part 1, SCA 2007). Restructuring is discussed in Chapter 8 of this book: see SI 2008/575, and note SI 2008/574.

The plan to transfer the functions of ARA to SOCA was announced in the House   1.28
of Lords by way of a written statement made by Baroness Scotland of Asthal on 11 January 2007. The ARA was set up in February 2003 under the POCA 2002, with statutory powers to recover the proceeds of 'criminal conduct' by way of: (a) confiscation proceedings following a person's conviction for a criminal offence; or (b) by taxation; or (c) the civil recovery regime enacted under Part 5 of the POCA 2002 (regardless of whether the person holding 'criminal property' had been convicted of a criminal offence or not). Although the ARA did reach a number of its targets for the year 2004/05, it did not meet its target for collecting the value of recoverable property, or becoming self-financing by 2005/06. A 'Report by the Comptroller and Auditor General', identified a number of weaknesses in the processes of the ARA including a lack of referrals, a high turnover of staff, and receivership costs. That said, the ARA did have several notable successes, and it is arguable that the root problem was overstated optimism about what this new agency could realistically achieve by the target dates.

---

[19] *Hansard* 7 Feb 2007, col 731 (House of Lords).
[20] Part 2, POCA 2002, with respect to confiscation proceedings in England and Wales; Part 4, POCA 2002, for Northern Ireland.

G. DETAINED CASH INVESTIGATIONS

1. Use of production orders and warrants

(a) *Accredited financial investigators*

1.29   Sections 75–77 and 79–80 of and Schs 10 and 11 to the SCA 2007, amend the 'cash forfeiture' provisions in chapter 3 of Part 5 of the POCA 2002 in two key ways. First, the powers of a customs officer or a constable to seize and to detain 'cash' under chapter 3 of Part 5 of the POCA 2002, are extended to certain 'accredited financial investigators' (ss 79–80). Secondly, amendments are made to the POCA 2002 by ss 75–77 of the SCA 2007, which create a new type of investigation, namely, a 'detained cash investigation', for investigating the provenance or intended destination of cash that has been seized under chapter 3 of Part 5 of the POCA 2002. According to the Explanatory Notes, '[these] new investigation powers will assist in the preparation of a case for forfeiting the cash before the magistrates' court in England and Wales and Northern Ireland or the Sheriff in Scotland'. The SCA 2007 extends the use of production orders, and search and seizure warrants (under Part 8 of POCA 2002) for detained cash investigations. The expression 'cash forfeiture' is actually a misnomer because the POCA 2002 substantially widened the pre-existing definition of 'cash' to include: (a) notes and coins in any currency; (b) personal orders; (c) cheques of any kind including travellers' cheques; (d) banker's drafts; and (e) bearer bonds and bearer shares.

1.30   The reader would derive little assistance from a text that merely listed, or identified, amending provisions to the POCA 2002, without trying to put those amendments into context. Accordingly, Chapter 9 of this book gives a short history of the 'cash forfeiture' legislation, and identifies defects in earlier statutory schemes which subsequent legislation has sought to rectify. The scheme enacted under chapter 3 of Part 5 of the POCA2002, is described in this book as if the amendments made to the 2002 Act by the SCA 2007 were in force.

1.31   'Accredited Financial Investigators' (AFIs) are specialist investigators who exercise the powers conferred upon them under the POCA 2002. Those powers include the power to seize 'realisable property', to apply for restraint orders with respect to property that is specified in the relevant part of the 2002 Act, and to exercise powers in connection with a 'confiscation investigation'. Such investigators are accredited under s 3 of the POCA 2002, and they need not be constables or officers of HMRC. The range of powers that may be exercised by an AFI under the POCA 2002, has been extended by the SCA 2007. It becomes an offence to assault an AFI (new s 453A(1) POCA 2002), or to resist such an investigator (new s 453A(2), POCA 2002), or to wilfully obstruct an AFI (new s 453A(2), POCA 2002), when he/she is acting in the exercise of a relevant power (s 81(2), SCA 2007 that inserts new s 453A into POCA 2002). Changes made to the POCA 2002 with respect to AFIs are dealt with in Chapter 10 of this book.

H. RECEIVERS

1. Management receivers and enforcement receivers

(a) *Management receivers in civil recovery proceedings*

Sections 49 and 51 of the POCA 2002 empower a Crown Court to appoint a   1.32
Management Receiver (s 44, POCA 2002), or an Enforcement Receiver (s 51,
POCA 2002) in relation to assets that are the subject-matter of a restraint order
made by that Court. For the position in Northern Ireland, see ss 197 and 199 of the
POCA 2002. The difference between the two types of receiver is that a 'management receiver' preserves assets, in respect of which a defendant has an interest, pending the outcome of criminal proceedings. The aim of the management receiver is to
ensure that the assets will be realized for their best value in the event that a confiscation order is made against the defendant in criminal proceedings. An Enforcement
Receiver may be appointed by the Crown Court, following the conviction of a
defendant, in order to realize the value of his interest in the receivership estate and
to satisfy the payment of a confiscation order that has been made against the defendant. Even before s 82 of the SCA 2007 was enacted, it had been open to a receiver
to sell perishable goods, or to sell assets that were diminishing in value, but only if
the Court made an order to that effect after giving interested parties the opportunity
to make representations pursuant to subs (8) of the relevant section (ss 49, 51, 197,
199). Section 82 of the SCA 2007 inserts a new subs (8A) into ss 49, 51, 197, and
199 of the POCA 2002, which *disapplies* subs (8) in each of the aforementioned
sections in respect of perishable property, or in respect of property that ought to be
disposed of before its value diminishes.

In civil proceedings for the recovery of 'criminal property' without conviction   1.33
(pursuant to Part 5, POCA 2002), the High Court may appoint an 'interim receiver'
under s 246 of the POCA 2002. Such a receiver not only has power to manage the
property in question, but he/she may also exercise investigative functions under the
POCA 2002 with respect to it. Section 83 of the SCA 2007 amends the POCA
2002 by creating yet another type of receiver in civil recovery proceedings (to be
known as a 'civil recovery management receiver'), whose function is to manage
property that has been made subject to a 'freezing order' under the POCA 2002
(see new s 245E of the POCA 2002). These provisions are discussed in Chapter 11
of this book.

I. EXTENSION OF INVESTIGATORY POWERS OF REVENUE AND CUSTOMS

Section 88 of and Sch 12 to the SCA 2007 make a large number of amendments to   1.34
various enactments, the thrust of which is to make powers that are available to

HMRC exercisable with respect to revenue functions as well as ex-customs functions. Section 93 of the Police Act 1997, is amended so that references to an 'officer of HMCE' become references to an 'officer of revenue and customs'. Intrusive surveillance powers are also widened under the SCA 2007 so that regardless of whether the matter in question relates to a revenue function or a customs function, an 'authorising officer' may authorize action to 'interfere with property'—eg to place a listening device in a property, or in a car, or elsewhere; or to take action with respect to wireless telegraphy—if the 'authorising officer' believes such action to be necessary for the purpose of preventing or detecting serious crime, and it is proportionate to take that action (s 93(2), Police Act 1997). Other powers which have been modified or extended relate to: (a) interception warrants; (b) the power to obtain traffic data relating to both postal services and telecommunications systems; (c) powers in respect of data protected by encryption; and (d) the disclosure of information by (or with the authority of) the Commissioners of Revenue and Customs, to the Criminal Assets Bureau in Ireland ('CAB'), or to any specified public authority in the United Kingdom or elsewhere, for purposes that include the identification of 'proceeds of crime', and/or the bringing of civil proceedings for enforcement purposes in relation to proceeds of crime; and/or the taking of other action in relation to proceeds of crime (see s 85, SCA 2007). These, and other amendments, are set out in Chapter 12 of this book.

J. STOP AND SEARCH AMENDMENT (s 87, SCA 2007)

1.35 Section 87 of the SCA 2007 adds a further circumstance to s 60 of the Criminal Justice and Public Order Act 1994, in which powers of stop and search that are specified in s 60 of the 1994 Act can be used, namely, that an incident involving serious violence has taken place in England and Wales in the relevant police area; and a dangerous instrument or offensive weapon used in the incident is being carried in any locality in that area by a person; and it is expedient to give an authorization under s 60 of the CJPA 1994 to find the instrument or weapon.

2

SERIOUS CRIME PREVENTION
ORDERS: GENERAL MATTERS

A. GENERAL MATTERS

1. What is a Serious Crime Prevention Order (SCPO)?

An SCPO is an order that aims to protect the public by preventing, restricting, or disrupting a person's involvement in serious crime in England and Wales (or in Northern Ireland, if proceedings are initiated there) (see s 1(3), SCA 2007). Section 1(6) states that, for the purposes of Part 1 of the 2007 Act, references to the person who is the subject of an SCPO 'are references to the person against whom the public are to be protected'. For ease of reference, this chapter tends to use the expression 'the subject' to denote the person against whom an SCPO is sought, or in respect of whom such an order has been obtained.

2. Rationale for SCPOs

In its Green Paper, 'New Powers Against Organised and Financial Crime' Cm 6875, the government suggested that its earlier White Paper 'One Step Ahead, a 21st Century Strategy to Defeat Organised Crime' (Cm 6167) had exposed a gap in the criminal law for catching those who are involved 'at the edges of organised crime'. This is a rather enigmatic statement, given that 'One Step Ahead' had much to say about the incidence of serious crime, which is committed nationally and internationally by accomplished criminals. The expression 'at the edges of organised crime' appears to have been used to encompass two groups of persons: (a) those who encourage or assist the commission of crime; and (b) perpetrators who avoid prosecution for one reason or another. Part 2 of the 2007 Act (inchoate offences of assisting or encouraging crime) addresses the first group. Part 1 of the SCA 2007 encompasses both groups.

2.01

2.02

2.03   Rather than leaving law enforcement authorities with a 'stark and unproductive choice' between 'prosecution or no action when dealing with organised crime', the Green Paper saw a place for 'something in between', namely, the Serious Crime Prevention Order (SCPO). The Green Paper envisaged that SCPOs might be used in cases where there was insufficient evidence to secure a conviction but the evidence would meet the civil standard of proof. This not the best example to give because, although the standard of proof under Part 1 of the SCA 2007 is expressed in ss 35 and 36 to be the civil standard, the government went out of its way to state, in Parliament, that it anticipates that the courts will apply a standard of proof that is equivalent to the criminal standard. Other examples, set out in the Green Paper, include cases where: (a) evidence that would be admissible in civil proceedings is not admissible in criminal proceedings; (b) crimes have been committed overseas that cannot be prosecuted in the UK; or (c) a person has been released after conviction overseas 'in circumstances where we would expect them in the UK to be subject to strict licence conditions'.[1] The government also envisages SCPOs being used as 'an additional option in the run up to a criminal prosecution, imposed to restrict the harm the subject can do while the case is being prepared' perhaps (according to the Green Paper) as part of a deal to turn Queen's Evidence to ensure that the subject is bound to conditions of good behaviour.[2]

2.04   The government was of the view that pre-existing rules were insufficient to deal with criminal ventures that have 'many of the characteristics of a business and may depend on a range of facilitators with varying degrees of culpability in the underlying criminality' (Cm 6875, p 9).

2.05   The government considered, and rejected, the idea of introducing laws modelled on the Racketeer Influenced and Corrupt Organisations Act (RICO; enacted in the United States in 1970). Part 1 of the 2007 Act is capable of applying to any person who has connections with 'serious crime' regardless of whether that crime is 'organised' or not, and regardless of whether the person who is the subject of a proposed 'serious crime prevention order', has been convicted of a 'serious offence' or not.

2.06   In the popular media, the SCPO has been described as 'the super ASBO'. In reality, and for reasons that are given in this chapter, the SCPO is in a league of its own.[3]

3. Against whom might an SCPO be made?

2.07   The Green Paper specified two main potential target groups for the making of an SCPO:

(i)   *As against 'known criminal individuals'*—to make crime more difficult to carry out, for example by imposing restrictions on travel or the means by which the

---

[1] Green Paper, p 31.
[2] Green Paper, p 31.
[3] For a useful summary of the history leading up to the enactment of this Part of the Act, see Research Paper 07/52, Home Affairs Section, House of Commons Library.

subject of an SCPO communicates or associates with others, or to restrict the persons with whom the subject of an SCPO communicates or associates. The government believes that even if these restrictions failed in their primary aim of deterring continuing criminal activity, 'they would either force the subject to change his way of working, leaving himself open to easier law enforcement scrutiny, or in the case of a stubborn refusal to follow the order's provisions at all, the subject would become vulnerable to breach proceedings'.[4]

(ii) *As against companies and 'other organisations facilitating organised crime'*. The procedure for making an SCPO is intended to be 'flexible and risk based, imposing no burdens at all on legitimate companies but a proportionate and highly targeted burden on specific organisations for which there is already good evidence of complicity in criminal activity'. An example of how this might be done was given by the Government in the Green Paper:

> [A] company making concealed compartments supposedly to enable drivers to hide their valuables, but which in practice have been used to conceal drugs. Making the compartments is not in itself illegal, but an order could impose a requirement on the business to notify law enforcement of the details of all such compartments which have been fitted and the details of the customers.

4. Potential effect of an SCPO

The intensity of control that can be imposed by way of an SCPO can range from treading lightly over the affairs of the subject (as well as those of third parties) or, at their most extreme, an SCPO can devastate them. The intensity of control is set by the court having regard to all the circumstances of the case. The court may attach such conditions to an SCPO as the court believes are necessary and proportionate in order to protect the public from the subject's involvement in serious crime in England and Wales (or in Northern Ireland, as the case may be). The powers exercisable by the High Court or by the Crown Court are subject to safeguards set out in ss 6–15 of the 2007 Act. It follows that SCPOs are not orders that Parliament intends should be made routinely, or lightly, by the courts.

2.08

5. Routes for obtaining an SCPO

There are two routes by which an SCPO may be obtained. First, an SCPO may be obtained in the High Court (which need not be contingent upon the subject having been convicted of a 'serious offence' or of an offence under s 25 of the SCA 2007 (breaching an SCPO)). Secondly, an SCPO may be made in the Crown Court following a person's conviction for a 'serious offence' or for an offence under s 25 of the 2007 Act.

2.09

---

[4] 'New Powers Against Organised and Financial Crime' Cm 6875, p 10.

2.10   Proceedings in the High Court, or in the Crown Court, can only be made on an application by the Director of Public Prosecutions, the Director of Revenue and Customs Prosecutions, or the Director of the Serious Fraud Office (England and Wales); or, in Northern Ireland, by the Director of Public Prosecutions (s 8, SCA 2007). It follows that a sentencing judge of the Crown Court has no power under the 2007 Act to initiate proceedings to make an SCPO once a person falls to be sentenced by the Court for a 'serious offence'.

2.11   The procedure for obtaining an SCPO is civil in nature regardless of whether the proceedings are in the High Court (s 35(1), SCA 2007) or in the Crown Court (s 36(1)). The standard of proof is the civil standard. However, for reasons that will be explained, it seems likely that proceedings will entail an application of a 'heightened' standard of proof, making the distinction between the criminal and civil standards barely visible.

2.12   The structure of Part 1 of the SCA 2007 is somewhat confusing in that it is not immediately apparent that some of its provisions are common to the jurisdiction of the High Court and the Crown Court. The provisions in common are ss 2–8 and ss 11–15 (information safeguard) and s 16 (duration of orders).

6. The potential for 'forum shopping': differences in jurisdiction

2.13   An initial reading of s 22 (inter-relationship between different types of orders) might convey the impression that for the purposes of making, varying, or discharging an SCPO, a party to the proceedings (including a third party) can switch between the jurisdiction of the High Court and the Crown Court in a manner that is tantamount to 'forum shopping'. In fact, the rules enacted under Part 1 of the SCA 2007, in connection with proceedings before the High Court and before the Crown Court, are very different. Thus:

(1) Proceedings for an SCPO in the High Court are not triggered by the fact that the subject has been convicted in criminal proceedings in England and Wales (or Northern Ireland as the case may be). By contrast, the Crown Court only has jurisdiction to *make* an SCPO in respect of a person who appears at the Crown Court to be sentenced for a 'serious offence',[5] or for an offence under s 25 of the 2007 Act. The defendant may appear before the Crown Court for sentence having been (a) convicted in summary proceedings and committed for sentence to the Crown Court, or (b) convicted on indictment (see s 19, SCA 2007).

(2) The High Court may *vary* SCPOs that were made either by the High Court or by the Crown Court. By contrast, the power of the Crown Court to vary an SCPO is limited to cases where (a) the defendant falls to be sentenced in the Crown Court for a 'serious offence' in England and Wales (s 20), or for an offence under s 25 for breaching an SCPO (see s 21), *and* (b) at the time of his

---

[5] As defined by s 2, SCA 2007.

conviction, the defendant was then the subject of an SCPO[6] (and note Para 4.12). The reasons for this appears to be that there would be no point in making a fresh SCPO if one exists, and therefore the Crown Court is empowered to vary the existing SCPO on application by 'the relevant authority'. The order, as varied, takes effect in addition to (a) a sentence imposed in respect of the offence, or (b) in addition to an order discharging the person conditionally (s 20(6)). If the Crown Court varies an SCPO, the court may include an extension of the period during which the SCPO (or any part of it) is in force (s 20(7)). Despite the 'tone' of s 20, it would seem that the Crown Court could vary an SCPO to make it more or less onerous, depending on the circumstances of the case.

(3) There is no power under Part 1 of the SCA 2007 for the Crown Court to discharge an SCPO (eg on the grounds that the defendant will be imprisoned for a substantial period of time) and this seems to be the position even in connection with SCPOs that were made by the Crown Court. Only the High Court has the power to discharge an SCPO. This point is reinforced by the wording of s 22(1)–(4), which refers to the power of the Crown Court to *make*, or to *vary*, an SCPO, but the section says nothing about discharging an order.

Section 22 permits the 'relevant applicant authority' to make an application to   2.14
the High Court for an SCPO should the Crown Court decline to do so (s 22(3)). The High Court also has the power to vary an SCPO in the event that the subject is convicted of a 'serious offence' or an offence under s 25 of the SCA 2007, and this is so notwithstanding that the Crown Court declined to vary an SCPO (s 22(4)).

Part 1 of the SCA 2007 provides a route of appeal to the Court of Appeal from   2.15
the High Court and/or from the Crown Court (with leave of the Court of Appeal or the judge at first instance) (ss 22 and 23, SCA 2007). However, notwithstanding the existence of this route of appeal, a 'relevant applicant authority' that is not content with a decision of the Crown Court, has a choice whether to make an application to the High Court for the order that it seeks, or it may appeal to the Court of Appeal. Unless a 'brake' is applied by the High Court to restrict that Court from being used as an avenue of appeal (in all but name), the likelihood is that the first 'port of call' following a decision by the Crown Court, will be to the High Court rather than to the Court of Appeal.

---

[6] Para 62, Explanatory Notes to SCA 2007, reads: 'This section, together with section 21, makes provision for the two cases in which the Crown Court can vary the terms of an order, namely on the conviction for a serious offence of a person already subject to an order (section 20), or the conviction of a person for breach of an order (section 21). The Crown Court cannot discharge an order. This can only be done by the High Court. Section 20 provides the Crown Court with the power to vary an order where the person before it is the subject of an order and has been found guilty of a serious offence in England and Wales, either having been committed from the magistrates' court or having been convicted in the Crown Court (subsection (1)).'

7. The notion of 'serious crime'

2.16 In Part 1 of the SCA 2007, the legislature has wisely resisted the temptation to use the expressions 'organised crime', or 'serious organised crime'. It is a temptation that was not resisted when Parliament enacted the Serious Organised Crime and Police Act 2005. The expression 'organised crime' is misleading because a significant amount of serious crime is committed in an elementary fashion, or even haplessly, and it can be perpetrated by a person acting alone but who succeeds in inflicting considerable damage nonetheless.[7] The reasons why Parliament plumped for the expression 'serious crime' were explained by Baroness Scotland in the House of Lords (emphasis added):[8]

> . . . the term has already been acknowledged and used in other ways in our legislation. One main reason that we rejected the term 'organised crime' was that the term is widely used, both in this country and abroad, and there are so many different understandings of what it is . . . at Second Reading it was made plain that many of the serious offences and crimes are now, regrettably, not purely national; they have become international, and often we have to rely on other agencies in the international community working with us to interdict serious criminals' activity in our various countries. *The term 'serious' has an existing definition in our jurisdiction; in other countries, there are a number of different definitions of 'organised crime'. Given the international nature of these crimes, we wanted to avoid any confusion, and we believe that it is appropriate to focus on the seriousness of the crime concerned as opposed to whether two, three, four or more people are engaged in the activity. The concept of serious crime, as I have said, is already understood and applied in related legislation;* for example, the Proceeds of Crime Act. While the definition provided by [ss 1, 2, and 3], together with Schedule 1, is not identical to that in the Proceeds of Crime Act, since they are for different purposes, its basic similarity will make it familiar to practitioners and the courts. That related jurisprudence will greatly assist us.

B. MATTERS COMMON TO THE HIGH COURT AND THE CROWN COURT

1. Meaning of 'serious crime' under Part 1 of the SCA 2007 (proceedings in England and Wales)

2.17 References in Part 1 of the SCA 2007 to 'serious crime' are references to the commission of a 'serious offence' as defined in s 2 of the SCA 2007 (England and Wales) and in s 3 (Northern Ireland).

2.18 Conduct that is relevant for the purposes of Part 1 of the SCA 2007 falls into three categories:

(1) Conduct which is specified, or described, in Part 1 of Sch 1 to the 2007 Act (see s 2(2)(a), SCA 2007). For Northern Ireland, the relevant Part is Part 2 of

---

[7] See the commentary to the 2005 Act, by this author, in *The Serious Organised Crime Act 2005*, Current Law Statutes (Sweet & Maxwell).

[8] House of Lords, Serious Crime Bill, 7 March 2007, col 233.

Sch 1 (eg drug trafficking, people trafficking, armed robbery, fraud).[9] That Schedule may be amended by an order made by the Secretary of State.

(2) Conduct which, in the particular circumstances of the case, the court considers to be sufficiently serious to be treated for the purposes of the application or matter as if it were so specified in Part 1 of Sch 1 (s 2(2)(b), SCA 2007; s 3(2)(b) for Northern Ireland).

(3) A serious offence that is committed in a country outside England and Wales (or Northern Ireland as the case may be). For the relevant definition see s 2(5) of the SCA 2007 (England and Wales) and s 3(5) (Northern Ireland). The third category relates only to proceedings for an SCPO conducted in the High Court (England, Wales, or Northern Ireland).

For the purposes of Part 1 of the SCA 2007, it is therefore necessary to know where the relevant criminal acts were done. So far as proceedings in the Crown Court are concerned, the Court is only required to have regard to serious offences committed in England and Wales (or Northern Ireland as the case may be) (see s 19, SCA 2007).

2. Meaning of 'involved in serious crime'

If proceedings for an SCPO are conducted in England and Wales (either in the High Court or in the Crown Court), the meaning of the expression 'involved in serious crime' is that which appears in s 2(1) (with respect to crimes committed in that jurisdiction), or in s 2(4) (in connection with offences committed *elsewhere*). For the purposes of proceedings conducted in Northern Ireland, the relevant section is s 3. The meaning of 'involved in serious crime' is examined in detail below but at its core are three forms of conduct:

2.19

(a) That X *committed* a 'serious offence'. By 'committed' is meant 'convicted' (at least in respect of offences committed in England and Wales) (s 4(1)(a)(i)).

(b) That X *facilitated* the commission of an offence. 'Facilitated' is not defined by the SCA 2007, but the Explanatory Notes confidently state (probably correctly) that 'facilitation here takes its natural meaning of "to make easier"'.[10]

(c) That X, by his conduct, was *likely to facilitate* the commission of an offence.

For the purpose of High Court proceedings, it is immaterial whether a person's involvement in serious crime is direct or indirect, for example, by actually *committing a crime* or by conducting him/herself 'in a way that was *likely to facilitate*' the

---

[9] The list of offences is quite short, and not as long as the 'lifestyle offences' for the purposes of the POCA 2002.

[10] Paragraph 16, Explanatory Notes to the 2007 Act.

commission of a serious offence (see s 2(1), and (4), SCA 2007 or s 3 (in the case of Northern Ireland)).

(a) *Is the threshold set too low?*

2.20 The intention of the government concerning persons who facilitate the commission of serious crime was made clear when Baroness Scotland said in the House of Lords:[11]

> . . . We are dealing with groups of criminals who have previously been convicted of offences and whom we wish to prevent adopting a similar modus operandi and committing future crimes. We are also dealing with individuals—quite often third-party—used by those criminals to undertake legitimate activity for an iniquitous purpose. For example, there may be an arrangement whereby a criminal buys vehicles with false bottoms in which to transport people and/or drugs. The third party involved never sees the criminal or has an explicit conversation with that individual, but it is clear that the use to which the vehicles are being put, such as people-trafficking or drugs, is iniquitous. At present, there is a difficulty because such third parties will seek to rely on the fact that the activity is legal, commercial and cannot be interfered with. The orders would enable us to prevent that continuance in order to prevent serious crime being facilitated.

2.21 Concern has been expressed that, for the purposes of High Court proceedings, the threshold is set too low. Thus, the organization 'Justice' said:[12]

> It is easy to think of all kinds of third parties who, in all innocence, can facilitate the commission of a serious offence: the taxi driver who drives passengers to a destination, unaware that they plan to assassinate someone there; the computer retailer who sells a computer to a person who uses it to run a human trafficking syndicate; the landlord who rents premises to a tenant not knowing that they will be used for the manufacture and storage of controlled drugs. The orders are, in part, aimed at commercial/business activity, and it is particularly easy to see how businesspeople may innocently facilitate crime, in circumstances where they are either deceived by the criminal or are under no legal duties to make enquiries as to the criminal's plans for the goods, premises, etc, in question. The court must disregard activity that the defendant shows to be reasonable—however, this criterion is both vague, and subject to a reverse burden of proof.

2.22 It is submitted that although Part 1 is capable of being read as 'Justice' has construed it, it is unlikely that the High Court would make an SCPO unless it was shown that the proposed subject was, at the very least, blatantly indifferent about whether his actions facilitated the commission of a serious offence or not, *and* that there are reasonable grounds to believe that the subject will continue to act as he did unless an SCPO was made in his case.

3. The civil standard of proof: SCPO, a 'criminal charge'?

2.23 Sections 35(2) and 36(2) of the SCA 2007 state that the standard of proof is the civil standard.

---

[11] House of Lords, Serious Crime Bill, *Hansard*, 7 Mar 2007, col 244.

[12] See, for example, Justice: 'Serious Crime Bill (HL) Part I Briefing for House of Lords Second Reading'; February 2007.

A question that will quickly arise once Part 1 of the Act comes into force is   2.24
whether the application of the civil standard of proof is compatible with the
European Convention on Human Rights (ECHR). This is not a point to be lightly
disregarded as a number of authoritative individuals, groups, and committees, have
voiced their concern about this aspect of the legislation.

(a) The government's stance

It should be stressed at the outset that when Part 1 was debated in Parliament (as part   2.25
of the Serious Crime Bill) the government made it clear that notwithstanding that
the proceedings are civil in nature, and that ss 35(2) and 36(2) of the SCA 2007
explicitly state that it is the 'civil standard of proof' which is applicable, the government anticipates that the courts will determine the question of whether a person has
been involved in serious crime by applying (in effect) the *criminal* standard of proof.
This was forcefully asserted by the Minister for Security, Counter Terrorism and
Police (Tony McNulty MP) during the Bill's second reading in the House of Commons
on 12 June 2007.[13] It would appear that the organization Liberty had asserted in a
briefing note that 'the Government may hope that these orders are a way of getting
round the presumption of innocence because the applicable standard of proof will
be the lowest civil standard of "on the balance of probabilities"'. The Minister rejected
that assertion in the following terms (emphasis added):

That is absolutely wrong. My noble and learned Friend Baroness Scotland stated categorically in
the other place that, in keeping with the House of Lords judgment in the case of *McCann, we
expect that the standard of proof required in relation to the question of whether a person has been
involved in serious crime will be the same as in criminal cases, namely 'beyond reasonable doubt'.*
Liberty's assertion is thus entirely unfounded—a bit of a shame. Contrary to the statement in the
briefing, *the purpose of the orders is not to avoid the full rigours of criminal prosecution; they are aimed
at preventing future behaviour, not punishing past behaviour. If a criminal prosecution is possible, it
will be brought* . . . the orders will contain only conditions that prevent the subject from further
involvement in serious crime. That is set out clearly in the Bill and goes against Liberty's assertion
that the conditions that can be put in place would amount to criminal sanctions. The conditions
will be decided by the High Court, or the Crown Court in the case of an order made immediately
on conviction, and can and will act only in a way that is compatible with convention rights.

(b) SCPO: a 'criminal charge'?

In considering whether proceedings for an SCPO constitute a 'criminal charge', for the   2.26
purposes of Article 6 of the ECHR, three criteria come into play, namely, (i) the
classification of proceedings in domestic law, (ii) the nature of the proceedings/
offence, and (iii) the severity of any penalty which may be imposed (*Engel v Netherlands*
1 EHRR 647). The classification of proceedings as 'civil' is not determinative but it
is a starting point. An SCPO is not a conviction and the existence of an SCPO
cannot be entered on a defendant's record as a conviction (any more than an ASBO

---

[13] *Hansard*, 12 June 2007, col 664.

under the Anti-Social Behaviour Act 2003). An order under Part 1 of the 2007 Act is not a 'recordable offence' for the purposes of the Police and Criminal Evidence Act 1984.

2.27   Although the effect of an SCPO can be severe, the purpose of such an order is 'preventing, restricting, or disrupting involvement by the person concerned in serious crime in England and Wales or (as the case may be) Northern Ireland' (see eg s 1(3)). The stated aim of the legislation is not conclusive of the issue but it will doubtless enable the argument to be advanced that the order is not intended to be punitive or disciplinary.

2.28   Section 25 of the SCA 2007 creates an offence of failing to comply with an SCPO. It is an offence punishable, on summary conviction, to imprisonment not exceeding 12 months,[14] or on conviction on indictment, to a term not exceeding five years.[15] The existence of the s 25 offence does not, by itself, go far enough to characterize the proceedings for making an SCPO as 'criminal proceedings'. This is because the proceedings which must be brought in the event of a breach of an SCPO are discreet from those that must be brought when applying for such an order, see *R v Crown Court at Manchester ex p McCann and others* [2002] UKHL 39, in which the offence under s 1(10) of the Crime and Disorder Act 1998, for failing to comply with an ASBO made under that Act, was held (by the House of Lords) not to characterize the process for making ASBOs as 'criminal proceedings' (consider too the judgment of Lord Bingham in *B v Chief Constable of Avon and Somerset Constabulary* [2001] 1 WLR 340, 352B, para 25, in the context of the making of sex offenders orders). On the other hand, although it was said in *McCann* that the making of an ASBO was not a condemnation that the subject of an ASBO was guilty of an offence (on the grounds that the process for obtaining an ASBO was directed at antisocial acts likely to cause harassment, alarm or distress), the same cannot always be said about SCPOs. It will be seen that SCPOs are not aimed at preventing localized acts of antisocial behaviour that cause alarm and distress to persons who live and work in close proximity to the person in respect of whom an ASBO has been imposed. SCPOs operate at a macro level. In 'Legislative Scrutiny: Fifth Progress Report', the House of Lords/House of Commons Joint Committee on Human Rights, said (emphasis supplied):[16]

1.11 The Government also relies on the decision in the case of *McCann* in which the House of Lords upheld the Government's argument that proceedings leading to the making of an ASBO do not involve the determination of a criminal charge for the purposes of Article 6 ECHR.[17] *ASBOs generally concern relatively low-level anti-social behaviour which may not even be criminal. We consider serious crime prevention orders, however, to be a different matter, more analogous to control orders*

---

[14] And/or a fine, not exceeding the statutory maximum.
[15] And/or an unlimited fine.
[16] Twelfth Report of Session 2006/07.
[17] *R (McCann) v Manchester Crown Court* [2002] UKHL 39, [2003] 1 AC 787.

in terms both of the seriousness of the conduct in which the subject of the order is alleged to have been involved and in the severity of the possible restrictions which can be imposed . . .

. . . In our view, however, a combination of the implication that a person has been 'involved in' serious crime, the severity of the restrictions to which they may be subject under a SCPO, and the possible duration of such an order (up to 5 years and indefinitely renewable) means that in most cases an application for a SCPO is likely to amount to the determination of a criminal charge for the purposes of Article 6 and therefore to attract all the fair trial guarantees in that Article.

1.14 . . . the House of Lords Select Committee on the Constitution reached a very similar conclusion as a matter of UK constitutional principles, concluding that SCPOs represent an incursion into the liberty of the subject and constitute a form of punishment that cannot be justified in the absence of a criminal conviction.[18]

1.15 In our recent work on counter-terrorism policy and human rights we have drawn attention to the unsustainability in the long term of resort to methods of control which are outside of the criminal process and which avoid the application of criminal standards of due process. We are concerned that the introduction of SCPOs represents a similar step in relation to serious crime generally. In our view, the human rights compatible way to combat serious crime in the long run is not to sidestep criminal due process, but rather to work to remove the various unnecessary obstacles to prosecution, for example by relaxing the current prohibition on the admissibility of intercept material, lowering the charging threshold, allowing post-charge questioning and the drawing of adverse inferences (with appropriate safeguards), and enhancing the incentives to give evidence for the prosecution.

2.29 By definition, the making of an SCPO involves a finding that the subject has been involved in serious crime (see s 1(1)(a)),[19] but it is not a requirement for making an SCPO that the subject was himself *criminally* involved in that activity. Although it is likely that the majority of SCPOs will be made against persons who have been convicted of a 'serious offence', not all subjects of an SCPO will fall into that category. This aspect of the legislation is considered further below.

(c) *Is an enhanced standard of proof needed?*

2.30 In cases where the issue is whether (for the purpose of ss 2(1)(a)[20] and 3(1)(a), SCA 2007[21]) the proposed subject 'committed a serious offence', the position is clear. Section 4(1)(a)(i) explicitly states that the expression is established only by proving that the person 'has been convicted of the offence'.[22] In this situation, any discussion about the appropriate quantum of proof for the purposes of Part 1 of the SCA 2007 has to have regard to the fact that a conviction returned in the United

---

[18] (footnote 15 in the original text): 'House of Lords Select Committee on the Constitution, Second Report of Session 2006–07, Serious Crime Bill, HL Paper 41, at para.17'.

[19] s 1(2)(a) for Northern Ireland.

[20] England and Wales.

[21] Northern Ireland.

[22] It is less clear whether s 4(1)(a)(i) also applies in connection with offences that have been committed 'elsewhere' (see s 3(4)(a) and s 4(1)(a)), but it is submitted that it does.

Kingdom is presumably the result of a trial conducted in accordance with criminal rules of evidence and procedure, and where the standard of proof was the criminal standard with respect to the matters that the prosecution had to prove. It is submitted that by 'conviction' the 2007 Act is plainly not including cautions.

2.31   In its Report, the House of Lords/House of Commons Joint Committee on Human Rights, said that SCPOs amount to the determination of a criminal charge, and that the standard of proof should be the criminal standard, not the civil standard. It added (emphasis supplied):[23]

> 1.20 . . . Even on the Government's approach, however, *we note that it is accepted that the criminal standard of beyond reasonable doubt is appropriate when the court is determining whether a person has been 'involved in serious crime'*. In our view, *if this is the case in relation to ASBOs, as has been held by the House of Lords, it is even more strongly the case in relation to an order premised on an even more serious allegation of involvement in criminality.* We therefore recommend that the Bill be amended to make explicit that the appropriate standard of proof in relation to this part of the test for a SCPO be the criminal standard, in accordance with the decision of the House of Lords in *McCann*. It should be spelt out on the face of the Bill that before making a SCPO the court must be satisfied beyond reasonable doubt that the person has been involved in serious crime.

2.32   However, the provisions of Part 1 of the SCA 2007 encompass persons who *either* (a) have 'facilitated' criminal conduct, *or* (b) their conduct 'was likely to have facilitated the commission of a serious offence', whether by himself, or by another (s 2(1), (b), and (c)). It is not necessary to prove that such persons have been convicted of an offence with respect to that conduct. The 'relevant applicant authority' need only adduce evidence to establish, to the civil standard of proof, that the subject had conducted himself as alleged. But what does 'facilitated' or 'likely to have facilitated' mean in the context of Part 1 of the 2007 Act? The Act does not tell us, but the Explanatory Notes state that 'facilitation here takes its natural meaning of "to make easier"'.[24] However, not every act of 'facilitation' is a criminal act (not even under Part 2 of the SCA 2007), and not all conduct that is 'likely to facilitate the commission of a criminal offence' constitutes a criminal offence. Part 1 appears to embrace situations where: (a) there is evidence that the 'subject' acted as a secondary party to a crime; or (b) that he acted as a joint principal; or (c) that he acted inchoately, for example having encouraged ('incited') the commission of an offence; or (d) that he assisted in the commission of an offence (see now ss 44–46, SCA 2007); or (e) that although he did not act 'criminally' in the aforementioned senses at all, his conduct (objectively determined) did facilitate the commission of an offence, or that it was likely to have done so.

2.33   If it is said that the standard of proof applicable is the enhanced standard (effectively the criminal standard), must the same quantum of proof be applied with respect to every issue that falls to be decided under Part 1 of the SCA 2007, or may a different quantum be applied, depending on what the issue is? For example, if it is

---

[23] The Legislative Scrutiny: Fifth Progress Report.
[24] Paragraph 16, Explanatory Notes to the 2007 Act.

alleged that X's conduct facilitated the commission by Z of a serious offence, *and* that his own actions constituted a criminal offence (albeit that no charges were brought), is the court required to apply the enhanced civil standard of proof when deciding (a) whether X's conduct was criminal, and (b) whether X had facilitated the commission of the offence by Z? If it is alleged that X did facilitate the commission of serious crime but it is not alleged that X acted criminally, is it open to the court to apply the usual civil quantum of proof when deciding that issue? It would be an odd result if the respondent against whom an SCPO is sought, and who is alleged to have acted criminally, must have his case determined on the basis that the allegation constitutes a 'criminal charge' (for the purposes of Article 6, ECHR) and therefore that the enhanced standard of proof should apply to him, whereas the person who incompetently allowed himself to be exploited by criminals, and who unwittingly facilitated the commission of crime, does not face a 'criminal charge' and he is therefore to be treated differently. In each case, an SCPO might have serious adverse consequences on the subject of the order, and on third parties.

Parliament did not amend the Bill to make explicit that the standard of proof is 2.34 the criminal standard. Given what was said in Parliament and by the Joint Committee on Human Rights (referred to above), one might wonder why not. The courts might decide that the quantum of proof cannot be determined purely on a construction of Article 6 of the ECHR. On the other hand, having regard to what is at stake, and the intrusive nature of SCPOs, the courts might take the view that a heightened civil standard of proof will usually be necessary (see *R v Manchester Crown Court ex p McCann*). If this step is taken, the result might be that the civil standard of proof will 'for all practical purposes be indistinguishable from the criminal standard' per Lord Bingham, *B v Chief Constable of the Derby Constabulary* [2001] 1 WLR 340; per Lord Phillips MR, *Gough v Chief Constable of Derbyshire Constabulary* [2002] 3 WLR 289; and see the *McCann case*, per Lord Hope, para 83.

4. An SCPO is not a 'sentence'

An appeal against the making of an SCPO lies to the Court of Appeal pursuant to 2.35 s 24(1) of the SCA 2007, presumably to the Civil Division. Had the route of appeal been specified in the SCA 2007 as an appeal against 'sentence', it could have been argued that this characterized an SCPO as a 'penalty'. However, regardless of the merits of such an argument, it is simply not available because s 24(11) explicitly provides that an appeal lies to the Court of Appeal by virtue of s 24 and not pursuant to s 9 of the Criminal Appeal Act 1968 (appeal against sentence following conviction on indictment) (see s 24(11), SCA 2007).

3

SERIOUS CRIME PREVENTION ORDERS: JURISDICTION OF THE HIGH COURT

A. OVERVIEW

1. Introduction

The following flowchart is for ease of reference only, it is not intended to be definitive 3.01
of all matters which the High Court is required to consider.

By s 1(1) of the 2007 Act, the High Court may (not 'must') make a Serious Crime 3.02
Prevention Order (SCPO) if two requirements are satisfied:

(1) That the court is satisfied, to the civil standard of proof, that a person 'has been
    involved in serious crime'. The 'serious crime' in question may have been carried
    out in England and Wales, or elsewhere (s 1(1)(a)). The reason why the legisla-
    ture has split up 'England and Wales' and 'elsewhere' is because different rules
    (set out in Part 1) apply for determining whether the court should include in its
    reckoning conduct performed 'elsewhere'.

(2) The court must be satisfied that there are 'reasonable grounds to believe' that an
    SCPO *would* (not might) protect the public by preventing, restricting, or dis-
    rupting 'involvement by the person in serious crime in England and Wales'.

Corresponding provisions exist in relation to Northern Ireland (s 10(2)). Note 3.03
that the requirements of s 1(1)(b) (or s 1(2) (b)), and s 1(3), do not operate if the

HIGH COURT JURISDICTION TO MAKE AN SCPO

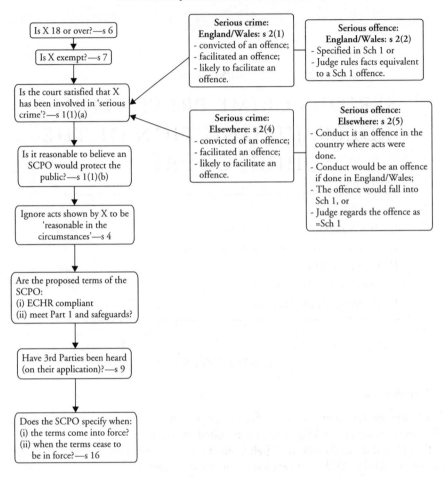

Figure 3.1

SCPO contains terms for the provision of 'monitoring services' pursuant to s 39 in relation to a body corporate, a partnership, or an unincorporated association.

(a) *Judging outcomes: setting the intensity of control under an SCPO*

3.04 The High Court must not make an SCPO unless it has reasonable grounds to believe that the order would protect the public by preventing, restricting, or disrupting involvement by the person in serious crime in England and Wales. No court can ever know that the measures it takes will protect the public from any form of peril. Accordingly, the criterion set out in s 1 of the 2007 Act, namely, that the Court has 'reasonable grounds to believe' that an SCPO 'would protect the public', is the best that can be hoped for. But how confident does a judge have to be before concluding that an SCPO '*would* protect the public'? The answer, it is submitted, is that the judge need only believe on reasonable grounds that the terms of the SCPO would at least disrupt, if not prevent, the subject, or any of his/her associates who are involved in serious crime, from continuing to be so if, to that extent, the public would be protected.

2. Persons against whom an SCPO may be made under Part 1 of the SCA 2007

No order may be made under Part 1 of the 2007 Act unless the person who is the proposed subject of an SCPO is 18 years of age or more (s 6, SCA 2007). A person who falls 'within a description specified by order of the Secretary of State' (the Home Department) is exempt from the provisions of Part 1 (see s 7, SCA 2007). No exemptions are specified in the Act. **3.05**

Section 1(6) of the SCA 2007 makes it clear that references in the Act to the person 'who is the subject of' an SCPO are references 'to the person against whom the public are to be protected'. Part 1 of the 2007 Act does not define 'person' but, when that Part is read as a whole (and particularly, having regard to ss 30–33), it is apparent that an SCPO may be made and enforced against any individual, body corporate (s 30), partnership (ss 30 and 31), unincorporated association (s 32), and (if an order has been made by the Secretary of State) an overseas body formed under the law 'having effect outside the United Kingdom' (s 33). **3.06**

In the case of bodies corporate, including limited liability partnerships, nothing in s 30 of the SCA 2007 prevents an SCPO from being made against an officer or employee of a body corporate or against any other person associated with a body corporate. Similarly, if an SCPO is made against a partnership, other than a limited liability partnership, the order must be made in the name of the partnership, and not in the name of any of the partners (s 31(1)), but nothing in s 31 prevents an SCPO from being made against (a) a particular partner, or (b) a senior officer or employee of a partnership or any other person associated with a partnership. If the order is to be made against an unincorporated association it must be made in the name of the association, and not in that of any of its members (see s 32(1)). In an appropriate case, an SCPO can be made against (a) a member, or officer or employee of an unincorporated association, or (b) any other person associated with an unincorporated association (s 32(9)). **3.07**

References in Part 1 of the Act to 'the public' includes a section of the public or a particular member of the public (s 42). **3.08**

3. Who may apply for an order?

Section 8 of the SCA 2007 provides that four authorities may apply for an SCPO: **3.09**

(1) the Director of Public Prosecutions;
(2) the Director of Revenue and Customs Prosecutions;

(3) the Director of the Serious Fraud Office;

(4) in Northern Ireland, the Director of Public Prosecutions for Northern Ireland.

Each of these officeholders is described as the 'relevant applicant authority' for the purpose of Part 1 of the 2007 Act (s 10(4)).

4. Notice requirements

(a) *Generally*

3.10　Notice requirements are set out in s 10 of the SCA 2007. It is important to observe that the notice provisions in s 10 relate to the stage *after* an order has been made. The provisions are not designed to put the proposed subject, or third parties, on notice of a contemplated application to obtain, or to vary, an SCPO. This construction is supported by the Home Office Research Paper (07/52), which states that the Act 'does not require that a serious crime prevention order be made or varied in the presence of the person to whom it relates'. Paragraph 39 of the Explanatory Notes to the 2007 Act is to the same effect. Furthermore, the subject of an SCPO is only bound by the order if he/she is either represented at the proceedings (whether 'in person or otherwise'), or a notice setting out the terms of the order (or variation of the order) has been served on the subject (s 10(1)). Part 1 of the 2007 Act makes no provision at all for an application for an SCPO to be made on notice (and this is so with regards to applications to vary or to discharge an order). Presumably, this might be something that will be dealt with in the Civil Procedure Rules.

3.11　　Having regard to the foregoing, it would seem to be open to a 'relevant applicant authority' to apply for an SCPO, without prior notice being given to the proposed subject of the order. However, in practice, this is unlikely to happen, save in exceptional circumstances.

(b) *Third party interests*

3.12　Although s 9(1) of the SCA 2007 states that the High Court 'must' give a third party an opportunity to make representations in the proceedings 'about the making' of an SCPO, this requirement is conditional on (a) the third party making an application to be heard, and (b) the court considers that the making of an SCPO would be likely to have a 'significant adverse effect' on that person. In the House of Lords, Lord Henley enquired of the government how it intended the word 'significant' to be interpreted. Would people have to be facing bankruptcy because of the order, or would their personal liberty have to be severely infringed?[1] The government's response was that it wished to set limits on the rights of third parties, 'so that the proceedings are not tied up with spurious or frivolous applications'; that the court should hear only those 'who genuinely need to be heard'.[2] The government did not

---

[1] *Hansard*, House of Lords, 14 Mar 2007, col 794.

[2] *Hansard*, House of Lords, 14 Mar 2007, col 795, Baroness Scotland.

think that it would be sensible to allow people who have been 'negatively affected only in a very minor way to make such representations or applications to the court'. However, the government also made it clear that the Civil Procedure Rules would require the applicant authority to bring the potential impact of the proposed terms of an order on third parties *to the court's attention*.

5. Service of the SCPO/Notice

The 'notice' (in reality the notice constitutes the order) may be served on the 'subject' personally, or by sending it (recorded delivery) to the subject's last-known address (s 10(2)). The last-known address need not be the subject's last known residential address; it seems to be sufficient to send it to the last-known business address, or hotel, hostel, or other address. The notice may be served on the subject by a constable, or by a person 'authorised for the purpose by the relevant applicant authority' (eg the director of public prosecutions) (s 10(3), SCA 2007).   3.13

Note that for the purposes of s 10 a notice may be served on 'persons' other than individuals in accordance with the following provisions of the 2007 Act: 3.14

(1) *Body corporate and limited liability partnerships.* A notice is served if:
    (i) it is delivered to the body corporate in person, ie if it is delivered to an officer of the body corporate in person; or
    (ii) it is sent by recorded delivery to the body corporate at its last-known address, ie if it is so sent to an officer of the body corporate at the address of the registered office of that body or at the address of its principal office in the United Kingdom (s 30(1)(a));

(2) *Other partnerships*: a notice is served if:
    (i) it is delivered to the partnership in person, ie if it is delivered to any of the partners in person or to a senior officer of the partnership in person; or
    (ii) it is sent by recorded delivery to the partnership at its last-known address, ie if it is so sent to any of the partners or to a senior officer of the partnership at the address of the principal office of the partnership in the United Kingdom (s 31(4)(a));

(3) *Unincorporated associations*: a notice is served if:
    (i) it is delivered to the association in person, ie if it is delivered to an officer of the association in person; or
    (ii) it is sent by recorded delivery to the association at its last-known address, ie if it is so sent to an officer of the association at the address of the principal office of the association in the United Kingdom (s 32(3)(a)).

(a) *Entry and search of premises to effect service*
The expression 'a person authorised for the purpose [of delivering the notice]' in s 10(3) is not to be treated lightly because both the authorised person, and a constable, have power under s 10(3) to enter any premises (if need be by force), and to search   3.15

the premises for the subject in order to serve the notice on him. The power conferred by s 10(3) is modified in respect of bodies corporate, limited liability partnerships (s 30(1)(a)), other partnerships (s 31(4)(b)), and unincorporated associations (s 32(3)(b)).

3.16 'Premises' is defined by s 5(7) to include any land, vehicle, vessel, aircraft, or hovercraft. The constable or authorised person, must have reasonable grounds for believing that the person to be served with the notice is on the premises (s 10(3)(a)).

3.17 The Act does not suggest the circumstances in which it would be necessary, or proportionate, to effect service by the use of force in order to enter and to search the premises, rather than by merely sending the notice by recorded delivery to the subject's last-known address. The legislature's thinking may have been that in cases where the terms of the order are to be of immediate effect, or the order is likely to have far-reaching consequences for the subject or a third party, then the circumstances justify the use of force to enter premises in order to serve the order.

B. 'HAS BEEN INVOLVED IN *SERIOUS CRIME*'

1. Proving involvement in 'serious crime' (in England and Wales)

3.18 Section 2 of the SCA 2007 deals with the position in relation to proceedings in England and Wales. Section 3 of the SCA 2007 deals with the position as it concerns Northern Ireland. However, given that both sections are framed in almost identical terms, it is proposed in these pages to focus on the provisions of s 2 of the 2007 Act. The concepts are the same in each case.

3.19 By virtue of s 2(1) of the SCA 2007, a person will be found to have been 'involved in serious crime' in England and Wales if he has:

(a) *committed* a serious offence in England and Wales;

(b) *facilitated* the commission by another person of a serious offence in England and Wales; or

(c) conducted himself in a way that was *likely to facilitate* the commission by himself or another person of a serious offence in England and Wales (whether or not such an offence was committed).

3.20 Note that by s 31(3), a partnership is 'involved in serious crime' in England and Wales, Northern Ireland, or elsewhere, if the partnership, or any of the partners, is so involved.

3.21 The structure of s 2 of the SCA 2007 is liable to mislead if it is read in haste. It will be recalled that, for the purposes of s 1(1)(a), the Court must be satisfied that the subject has been involved in serious crime in England/Wales, *or elsewhere*. Thus:

(a) If the allegation is that the 'subject' has been involved in 'serious crime' *only* in England and Wales, the court looks to s 2(1)–(3).

(b) If the allegation is that the subject has been involved in serious crime '*elsewhere*' then the court must look to s 2(4), (5), and (7).

(c) If the allegation is that the subject has been involved in serious crime *both* in England/Wales, and elsewhere, then the court must look to the place (i) where the relevant offence was committed, or (ii) where the relevant Acts were done and which constitute 'facilitating the commission' of an offence, or (iii) whether conduct was performed that was 'likely to facilitate' the commission of an offence, etc.

A 'serious offence' is one specified in Part 1 of Sch 1 (eg drug trafficking, people 3.22 trafficking, armed robbery, fraud),[3] or it 'is one which, in the particular circumstances of the case, the court considers to be sufficiently serious to be treated for the purposes of the application or matter as if it were so specified [in Part 1 of Sch 1]' (s 2(2)(b)).

2. Meaning of 'sufficiently serious'

By virtue of s 2(2)(b) of the SCA 2007, an offence is a 'serious offence' if it is one 3.23 which, in the particular circumstances of the case, the court considers to be sufficiently serious to be treated for the purposes of the application or matter, as if it were specified in Part 1 of Sch 1 to the 2007 Act. What does the phrase 'sufficiently serious' mean, for the purposes of Part 1 of the 2007 Act? Does it mean that the offence must be no less serious than the offences that are specified in Sch 1, or is it open to the court to contextualize the offence with respect to the wider question of whether it would be appropriate to make an SCPO for the purpose of protecting the public (ie either preventing the subject's involvement in serious crime in England and Wales having regard to the risk that the defendant poses to the public)? If the latter construction is the correct one, then it may be that a court would be entitled to take into account an offence which, although not specified in Part 1 of Sch 1 to the 2007 Act, had been committed in circumstances which caused or posed a significant social problem.

Although a decision made under s 2(2)(b) is one susceptible to review by a higher 3.24 court, it is an open question whether that court would state a general principle that it will not interfere lightly with the decision made by a judge of first instance if the judge applied the correct tests when deciding whether the offence was 'sufficiently serious'. On the other hand, having regard to the potentially draconian effects of the making of an SCPO (particularly in circumstances where an SCPO does not follow a conviction for a 'serious offence'), there is much to be said for the reviewing court making its own determination of 'seriousness', on the facts as the judge (at first instance) found them to be.

3. 'Committed a serious offence in England and Wales' (ss 1(1)(a), 2(1)(a))

Section 2(1)(a) is to be read together with s 4(1)(a)(i) which provides that the court 3.25 may conclude that the subject has 'committed a serious offence' if he has been

---

[3] The list of offences is quite short, and not as long as the 'lifestyle offences' for the purposes of the POCA 2002.

convicted of the offence in question and the conviction has not been quashed (s 4(1)(a)(ii)). In order to prove that a person has 'committed a serious offence', it is not open to the court to receive evidence/information, other than the fact of conviction. The definition of a 'serious offence in England and Wales' appears in s 2(2) of the Act.

4. 'Committed a serious offence' elsewhere (ss 1(1)(a), 2(4)(a))

(a) *General principles*

3.26 For the purposes of s 1(1)(a), a person has been involved in 'serious crime' *elsewhere* if he has committed a serious offence in a country outside England and Wales (s 2(4)(a)). The expression 'outside England and Wales' would seem to include Scotland and Northern Ireland. Section 2(4)(a) must be read together with s 2(5) (which defines 'a serious offence in a country outside England and Wales') and s 2(7).

3.27 Section 2(5) requires proof of two conditions before an offence committed elsewhere can be taken into account by the High Court. First, it must be shown that the conduct constituted an offence under the law of a country outside England and Wales, and which had it been performed in England and Wales would also be an offence there (ie a dual criminality requirement) (s 2(5)(a)). Secondly, the offence must be a 'serious offence', that is to say, had the conduct been performed in England and Wales, it would have constituted an offence specified in Part 1 of Sch 1 to the SCA 2007, or it is conduct which, in the particular circumstances of the case, the High Court considers to be 'sufficiently serious' to be treated as if it came within Part 1 of that Schedule (s 2(5)(b)). Note that by s 2(7) an act punishable under the law of a country outside the UK constitutes an offence under that law for the purposes of s 2(5), *regardless of how it is described in that law.*

(b) *Is proof of a conviction essential?*

3.28 It is not clear whether, for the purposes of s 2(4)(a), it must be proved that the subject was *convicted* of a serious offence committed elsewhere. Section 4(1) of the SCA 2007 states that, for the purposes of Part 1, the court is obliged to decide that the person has committed the offence if he has been convicted of the offence, and the conviction has not been quashed on appeal, nor has the person been pardoned of the offence. Section 4(1)(b) goes on to state that the court 'must not otherwise decide that the person has committed the offence'. Unhappily, the section does not state whether s 4 applies to convictions in England and Wales and/or elsewhere: a rather important loose end.

5. 'Facilitated the commission' of a serious offence: England and Wales (ss 1(1(a), 2(1)(b))

3.29 Section 2(1)(b) is to be read together with s 2(2) (definition of a 'serious offence'), s 2(3)(b), and s 4(2) (reasonable acts). There are a number of interesting, and potentially problematic issues.

(a) *What does 'facilitate' mean?*

The 2007 Act does not define the expression 'facilitated the commission [of an offence]'. The Explanatory Notes say that that 'facilitation here takes its natural meaning of "to make easier"'.[4] There clearly is no difficulty if a person has been convicted of a 'serious offence' on the basis that he 'facilitated' its commission in the sense that he acted as a secondary party (s 8, Accessories and Abettors Act 1861). The conviction would be sufficient to satisfy s 2(1)(a). In order to satisfy s 2(1)(b) the court will have little difficulty deciding that the subject did 'facilitate' the commission of a serious offence if it is proved that he aided, abetted, counselled, or procured the commission of the offence, sharing a common intention that the offence would be committed. It might also be sufficient to show, to the civil standard of proof (perhaps a 'heightened' standard), that the subject intentionally (ie deliberately) encouraged or assisted the commission of the offence even if it was not his purpose to do so, for example by selling a car to P, believing that P would use it to commit a robbery (which he did). The subject's purpose was to make a profit from the sale of a car, but he was indifferent about whether P would commit the offence or not. But would it be permissible for the court to construe the word 'facilitating' as amounting to no more than indifference on the part of the subject (or a lack of awareness) that his/her acts had facilitated the commission of an offence? For example, if the subject routinely sold cars to persons whom he knew had a propensity to rob, or to steal, is the subject to be regarded as 'facilitating' the commission of an offence merely because a customer decided to use one of the cars to commit a major bank robbery? The answer would appear to be in the affirmative having regard to s 4(2) (this provision is discussed below).

(b) *Matters to be disregarded: mental health: reasonable acts*

Section 4(2)(a) (and see s 4(3)(a)) provides some protection for a subject when deciding whether a person facilitated the commission of a serious offence by another. It is open to the subject to show that any act of his was 'reasonable in the circumstances'. Such acts will be left out of the reckoning. However, s 4(2)(b) provides that the court must ignore, ie disregard, his 'intentions' or 'any other aspect of his mental state' at the time the act was done.[5] The Explanatory Notes state that this means that 'it does not matter if the respondent did not, for example, intend to facilitate the commission of a serious offence, or had no knowledge that he was conducting himself in a way that was likely to facilitate serious crime'.[6] Section 4(2)(b), as well as its corresponding provision in relation to conduct that is 'likely to facilitate the commission of a serious offence' (s 4(3)(b)), caused disquiet in the House of Lords.

3.30

3.31

---

[4] Paragraph 16, Explanatory Notes to the 2007 Act.

[5] In other words, to quote Baroness Scotland: '... while the court will ignore the mental state of the proposed subject, it will also ignore any action which the proposed subject can show was reasonable', *Hansard*, House of Lords, 25 Apr 2007, col 700.

[6] Paragraph 25.

3.32   Two issues need to be separately considered. The first relates to the meaning of the words 'mental state' as they appear in s 4(2)(b). When the House of Lords considered this provision as part of the Serious Crime Bill, Baroness Scotland said (on behalf of the government) that 'mental state' includes, for example, knowledge or recklessness.[7] The second issue concerns acts that can be regarded by a court as 'reasonable in the circumstances'. Baroness Anelay of St Johns enquired how a court should approach a person's 'mental health or mental incapacity' concerning their actions.[8] Would evidence that a person acted through fear, or under duress, or acted whilst depressed, satisfy s 4(2)(a)? Would a person's lack of an intention to facilitate the commission of a serious offence be sufficient to satisfy s 4(2)(a)? The point is clearly of some importance because if mental health is a matter that comes within s 4(2)(b) (or s 4(3)(b)) then a person's mental health is *immaterial* when the court is considering whether a person's act facilitated (or was likely to facilitate) the commission of a serious criminal offence. If, on the other hand, his mental health is a relevant consideration for the purposes of s 4(2)(a) (or s 4(3)(a)) a court must ignore the act in question if, in the circumstances of the case, his act was 'reasonable'. Baroness Scotland pointed out that Part 1 of the Act was deliberately drafted so as not to include a mental element for the purposes of determining whether a person had facilitated serious crime, or had acted in a way that was likely to facilitate it. Baroness Scotland gave three broad reasons for that decision being taken (emphasis added):[9]

> . . . *prevention will be occasioned by terms that are reasonable and proportionate.* In that context, there will be instances when the need to prevent this considerable harm will mean that an order would be appropriate where it would be almost impossible to show the suggested element of intention or recklessness; for example, where a person who owns a string of lodging houses that have been found on several occasions to contain individuals who have been trafficked or smuggled, with the accommodation paid for by others. A first option for law enforcement might be to approach the owner and make him aware of the problem. But when it continued to happen he could potentially successfully argue that he had no knowledge that these people were being trafficked or smuggled, and so could not have the requisite element of intention . . . In such a situation it would be difficult to prove an element of recklessness if the person could argue that he had no means of checking whether the person was or was not an illegal immigrant. Therefore, an order which required the owner to provide law enforcement for a limited period with a list of those staying in the houses, or where people's stay was paid for by a third party, would be a reasonable and proportionate response to prevent those houses being used as stepping stones on the way to people trafficking.
>
> . . . Secondly, *it would be inappropriate to import into a civil order concepts of intention and recklessness*, which are essentially criminal in nature.
>
> Finally, and perhaps most importantly . . . *any action which* the potential subject of the order can show was *reasonable cannot constitute either facilitating, or acting in a way which was likely to facilitate, serious crime* for the purposes of this legislation . . . [As for] those who may lack capacity and may not be able to understand . . . I am sure that these issues would be raised. If the authority

---

[7] *Hansard*, House of Lords, 14 Mar 2007, col 764.
[8] *Hansard*, House of Lords, 14 Mar 2007, col 760.
[9] *Hansard*, House of Lords, 14 Mar 2007, col 762.

bringing the order did not have the sense to do that, I am relatively confident that the judiciary would.

Section 4(2) reinforces a point made elsewhere in this book that it appears to be   3.33
immaterial that the subject's actions *not only* did not result in a conviction, *but also*
that his action could not have resulted in a conviction (eg although his conduct did
facilitate the commission of an offence, it was not his purpose that it should do so).

6. 'Facilitated the commission'—elsewhere (ss 1(1)(a), 2(4)(b))

Section 2(4)(b) must be read together with s 2(5), (7) and s 4(2) and (3). For a dis-   3.34
cussion of the meaning of the word 'facilitated', see para **3.30**. For a discussion
of the expression 'a serious offence in a country outside England and Wales', see
paras **3.26–3.27**.

7. 'Likely to facilitate' crime in England and Wales (ss 1(1)(a), 2(1)(c))

For the purposes of Part 1 of the SCA 2007, s 2(1)(c) provides that a person has been   3.35
involved in serious crime in England and Wales 'if he has conducted himself in a
way that was *likely to facilitate the commission* by himself or another person of a serious offence in England and Wales (whether or not such an offence was committed)'.
Section 2(1)(c) must be read together with s 4(3) (reasonable acts). A number of issues
relating to these provisions have already been discussed (see paras **3.29–3.33**).

Section 2(1)(c) is particularly widely drawn. Whether the subject of the proceed-   3.36
ings 'was likely to facilitate' the commission of a serious offence is a matter that must
be objectively determined. Many different situations are capable of being encompassed by s 2(1)(c), but it would seem that both s 2(1)(c) (England and Wales) and
s 2(4)(c) (conduct elsewhere) are intended to deal with cases where a person
or organization turns a 'blind eye' to conduct which, if performed, constitutes a
'serious offence'. In the House of Lords, Baroness Scotland said (emphasis added):

> The sort of behaviour that we are talking about here is where a person or organisation *turns a blind eye* to the likely outcome of their actions . . . *They may not specifically intend to facilitate serious crime*, but they are *not taking the precautions that we would expect reasonable people to take to ensure that their actions cannot facilitate serious crime*, and so their actions help to bring real harm to others.

> . . . the applicant authority would have to show that the behaviour was 'likely' to facilitate serious crime, but we do not believe that that is an easy test to meet. We think that the authorities would have to have cogent evidence to satisfy the court that they fell within this criterion. *I believe that the test set out in McCann[10] would apply to these provisions.* The court would have to be satisfied that the condition was met, and that would mean that the probable outcome of their actions would have to be the facilitation of serious crime. The vast majority of people are able to appre-hend the risk of something being the result of their actions where it is probable. This, combined

---

[10] This is a reference to the House of Lords' decision in *McCann and others* [2002] UKHL 39.

with the exclusion contained in Clause 4(3)(a), under which any action which is reasonable cannot be the basis for an order, provides strong safeguards to those who might inadvertently facilitate serious crime.

3.37   If the above statement correctly describes the effect of s 2(1)(c) (England and Wales), and s 2(4)(c) (elsewhere), then the reach of Part 1 is broad indeed. The use of the expression 'blind eye' is not particularly helpful because it is an expression that is often used to describe a state of mind that ranges from choosing to ignore what one knows or believes to the case—to indifference—or even choosing not to enquire into the circumstances lest the truth about what is occurring causes a sense of unease about the legitimacy of a person's conduct. For an interesting discussion regarding the 'blind eye' concept see a decision of the Court of Appeal of Singapore in *Tan Kiam Peng v Public Prosecutor* [2007] SGCA 38.

3.38   Section 2(1)(c) states (in terms) that it is *immaterial* whether or not the offence, which was likely to be facilitated by the subject, was actually committed by him or by another. If the crime was committed, then it is sufficient to show that the subject's conduct was likely to have contributed to the commission of the offence (ie that the subject was likely to have 'made it easier' for the offence to have been committed).[11]

3.39   By virtue of s 4(3), the court must ignore (a) any act that the respondent can show to be reasonable in the circumstances, and (b) subject to this, his intentions, or any other aspect of his mental state, at the time. The wording of s 4(3)(a) and (b) is identical to that in s 4(2)(a) and (b). Section 4(2) is discussed at paras **3.31–3.33**.

8. 'Likely to facilitate': elsewhere (ss 1(1)(a), 2(4)(c))

3.40   Section 2(4)(a) must be read together with s 2(5) and (7), and s 4. Many of the issues and concepts relating to these provisions have been discussed elsewhere in this chapter (see para **3.30–3.33**).

C. CONDITIONS THAT MAY BE ATTACHED TO AN SCPO

1. Power of the Court to impose any condition that is necessary to protect the public

3.41   Section 1(3) of the SCA 2007 confers a general power on the High Court to attach such terms to an SCPO as it 'considers appropriate' for protecting the public by preventing, restricting, or disrupting involvement by the subject in 'serious crime' in England and Wales or Northern Ireland (as the case may be). Just as prohibitions and restrictions in Anti-Social Behaviour Orders should be clear and unambiguous,

---

[11] See para 16 of the Explanatory Notes to the 2007 Act, which suggests that 'facilitation here takes its natural meaning of "to make easier"'.

there is no reason to think that the position in relation to SCPOs will be any different (consider *Director of Public Prosecutions v T* [2007] 1 WLR 2009, para 41, and see *R v McGrath* [2005] 2 Cr App R (S) 85). During the Serious Crime Bill's passage through Parliament, s 5 was modified to remove a provision that would have permitted SCPOs to include prohibitions, restrictions, or requirements 'that are not specified in the orders but are determined in accordance with provision made by the orders (including provision conferring discretion on law enforcement officers)'. Its removal had been recommended by the Joint Committee on Human Rights Legislative Scrutiny (*Fifth Progress Report* (para 1.30). It is therefore left entirely to the judgment of the Court to decide the degree of control to be imposed on the subject of an SCPO, and how that level of control is to be effected.

The legislature has made it clear that the Act does not limit the type of provision 3.42 that may be made under an SCPO (s 5(1), SCA2007). Section 5 merely provides *examples* of the kinds of terms that can be attached to an order. The terms can have far-reaching consequences, and they may relate to *places*, including where an individual may reside including their private dwelling (s 5(6), SCA 2007). Other conditions may be imposed with respect to *individuals, body corporates, partnerships, unincorporated associations*. The conditions are not limited in their reach to the person against whom proceedings have been initiated but include, for example, 'partners in a partnership' (s 5(3)).

The examples set out in s 5 fall into two groups: (a) prohibitions, restrictions or 3.43 requirements that may be imposed on individuals (see s 5(3)); and (b) prohibitions, etc, that may be imposed on body corporates and other legal entities (s 5(4)). Further examples of requirements that may be imposed by way of an SCPO on any person are set out in s 5(5).

An SCPO may not include terms which restrict the freedom of a service provider 3.44 (s 34(8))[12] who was established in an EEA state (s 34(7)) other than the United Kingdom to provide 'information society services' (s 34(8))[13] in relation to an EEA state, unless the conditions specified in s 34(2) and (3) met (see s 34, SCA 2007).

(a) *Authorised monitors*
An SCPO may also make provision that entitles a 'law enforcement agency' as defined 3.45 by s 39(10) to appoint an 'authorised monitor' (s 39(1) and (2)) to monitor compliance of an SCPO by a body corporate, partnership, or unincorporated association. The SCPO may require the body corporate (etc) to pay some or all of the costs of

---

[12] A person providing an information society service.

[13] '(a) has the meaning given in Article 2(a) of the E-Commerce Directive (which refers to Article 1(2) of Directive 98/34/EC of the European Parliament and of the Council of 22 June 1998 laying down a procedure for the provision of information in the field of technical standards and regulations); and (b) is summarised in recital 17 of the E-Commerce Directive as covering "any service normally provided for remuneration, at a distance, by means of electronic equipment for the processing (including digital compression) and storage of data, and at the individual request of a recipient of a service".'

the monitoring service, unless it would not be appropriate in all the circumstances of the case to do so (s 39(4) and (7)). Section 39 of the SCA 2007 (and the accompanying s 40) was added to the Serious Crime Bill on 22 October 2007.[14] In the House of Commons, concern was expressed that a person might be required to pay costs even if the subject of the SCPO had not been 'knowingly' involved in serious crime. In dealing with that issue, the Parliamentary Under-Secretary of State for the Home Department (Mr Vernon Coaker) said that where, for example, a business has been proved to be involved in serious crime, an order can require it to provide its accounts or other information to an authorised monitor, to ensure that it complies with a requirement not to conduct its business in a particular way:

That will be effective where the information is particularly complex and where someone such as a forensic accountant will be able to make a far better assessment than a law enforcement agency of the way in which the business is conducting itself. If the court authorises a law enforcement agency to employ a monitor, it can go on to provide, as a term of the order, that the organisation that is the subject of the order must pay the costs that the law enforcement agency incurs in employing the authorised monitor. That effectively increases the regulatory burden on a business because it has been proved to be involved in serious crime. The provisions target regulation in a risk-based manner, and mean that burdensome regulatory approaches do not have to be taken to deal with the few bad apples in any business area. Regulation does impose a cost on business, but we can all agree that this is better than the results of no regulation at all.

3.46   The Minister pointed out that s 39 includes a safeguard whereby the courts will impose a requirement to pay costs only where it considers it appropriate to do so:

In reaching that decision, it will have regard to the means of the body corporate, partnership or unincorporated association concerned; to the expected size of the costs; and to the effect of the terms on the ability of any body corporate, partnership or unincorporated association that is carrying on business to continue to do so. That provides a strong steer to the courts to ensure that the orders are used only where the overall effect on the business is not such as to cause damage to it as an ongoing concern.

2. Requirement to furnish information

3.47   One of the more striking features of the process for making an SCPO concerns s 5(5) of the SCA 2007, which provides by way of 'example' that it is open to the Court to require 'any person'—not just the subject of the order—to answer questions at a time, place, and in a form and manner, to a 'law enforcement officer' (as defined by s 5(7)). A power of this type is increasingly being enacted to enable law enforcement agencies to carry out their functions. Although the power given in s 5(5) resembles that seen in the context of 'disclosure notices', for example s 2 of the Criminal Justice Act 1987,[15] there is a significant difference, namely, that s 5(5) of

---

[14] *Hansard*, House of Commons, 22 Oct 2007, col 44.
[15] See also the Financial Services and Markets Act 2000, s 65; the Enterprise Act 2002, s 193; and more recently, the SOCPA 2005, ss 60–70; and see the Money Laundering Regulations 2007, reg 37.

the SCA 2007 confers a power *on a judge of the High Court* to require a person to answer questions, or to provide information or documents (specified or described in the order); or to determine which agency or law enforcement authority shall be responsible for dealing with the material to be provided by the subject under an SCPO. It would seem that it is for the court to specify the questions that the person is required to answer (perhaps by way of a questionnaire) and to specify in the SCPO the information and documents that the subject is required to furnish.

Section 5(7) of the SCA 2007 defines a 'document' to mean 'anything in which   3.48
information of any description is recorded'—whether or not in legible form. If a document is held by a person in illegible form, the court/official/agency can specify that a copy of it shall be produced in legible form (s 5(8)). It is not entirely clear whether this would include encrypted/coded material.

Note that a person is not to be required to answer questions, or to provide infor-   3.49
mation, orally (s 11, SCA 2007). Information safeguards are set out in ss 11–15 of the SCA 2007. These include: (a) restrictions for legal professional privilege (s 12) (considered below at para **3.50**); (b) excluded material, see para **3.54**; (c) banking information (s 13; and see para **3.55**); (d) disclosures prohibited by statute (s 14); and (e) the privilege against self-incrimination (s 15; and see para **3.56**). A brief explanation of these safeguards appears below. Subject to ss 11–14, a person who complies with a requirement imposed by an SCPO to answer questions, or to provide information or to produce documents, does not breach (a) any obligation of confidence, or (b) any other restriction on making the disclosure concerned (however imposed) (s 38(1), SCA 2007).

3. Legal professional privilege (s 12)

Section 12 of the SCA 2007 provides that a person is not required to answer any   3.50
'privileged question', or to produce 'privileged information' or a 'privileged docu-
ment'. In each case, the 'privilege' is legal professional privilege (LPP) in proceedings in the High Court. Unlike s 10 of the Police and Criminal Evidence Act 1984 which was thought to reflect the position of common law (and perhaps it did in 1984),[16] it is arguable that s 12 is narrower, in that it clearly embraces litigation privilege, but it is less certain whether s 12 covers legal advice privilege in circumstances where adversarial legal proceedings are neither pending nor contemplated. There is no better description of 'litigation privilege' and 'legal advice privilege' than that given by Mr Justice Aikens in *Winterthur Swiss Insurance Company v AG (Manchester) Limited* [2006] EWHC 839 (Comm):

67. The cases have developed a distinction between two sub-types, or 'sub-heads'[17] of 'legal professional privilege'. In the earliest cases, the privilege from compulsory production was confined to information (principally documentary) that was created where legal proceedings were

---

[16] *R v Central Criminal Court ex p Francis & Francis* [1989] AC 346.
[17] The phrase of Lord Carswell in *Three Rivers DC v Bank of England (No 6)* [2005] 1 AC 610 at para 105.

in contemplation. That type of legal professional privilege has become known today as 'litigation privilege'. But, in two landmark cases in 1833, Lord Brougham LC held that legal professional privilege extended to communications where legal advice was sought and given when no litigation was contemplated.[18] That sub-type of legal professional privilege has become known today as 'legal advice privilege'.

68. The rationale for the first sub-type (i.e. 'litigation privilege') rests, in modern terms, on the principles of access to justice, the proper administration of justice, a fair trial and equality of arms. Those who engage in litigation or are contemplating doing so may well require professional legal advice to advance their case in litigation effectively.[19] To obtain the legal advice and to pursue adversarial litigation[20] efficiently, the communications between a lawyer and his client and a lawyer and a third party and any communication brought into existence for the dominant purpose of being used in litigation must be kept confidential, without fear that what is said or written might be disclosed. Therefore those classes of communication are covered by 'litigation privilege'.[21]

69. The rationale for the second sub-type of privilege, (i.e. 'legal advice privilege'), is that it advances the rule of law.[22] Citizens, corporations and other legal entities need to know what the law is so that they can decide what they can and cannot do and so manage their affairs according to law. If a citizen or corporation is to obtain advice on his legal rights and obligations, the lawyer consulted must be given all the relevant facts so as to give effective advice. Many cases have concluded that all the relevant facts will not necessarily be given unless they are imparted in confidence to the lawyer and the lawyer is under a duty to keep that information and his advice confidential. To protect that confidentiality and so advance the rule of law, the cases have developed the rule that communications between lawyers and clients[23] that are generated even when no litigation is contemplated, will not be subject to compulsory production, unless a statutory power expressly or by implication requires it.[24] But 'legal advice privilege' does not extend to communications obtained from third parties that are to be shown to the lawyer for the purpose of obtaining legal advice.[25]

3.51   A significant feature of the distinction between litigation privilege and legal advice privilege relates to the position of third parties. Thus, at common law if a definite

---

[18] *Greenough v Gaskell* (1833) 1 M&K 98 at 103; *Bolton v Liverpool Corporation* (1833) 1 M&K 88 at 94.

[19] Several cases have quoted Dr Johnson's description of the function of lawyers as a 'class of the community who, by study and experience, have acquired the art and power of arranging evidence, and of applying to the points at issue what the law has settled. A lawyer is to do for his client all that his client might fairly do for himself if he could'. Boswell (ed), *Life of Johnson, Birkbeck Hill* (1950) vol 5, p 26.

[20] 'Litigation privilege' cannot be relied on in legal proceedings that are not 'adversarial', per the majority of the House of Lords in *In re L (A Minor) (Police Investigation: Privilege)* [1997] AC 16.

[21] *Three Rivers DC v Bank of England (No 6)* at para 27, per Lord Scott of Foscote.

[22] Ibid at para 34 per Lord Scott of Foscote, referring to paras 15.8–15.10 of Professor Adrian Zuckerman's book: *Zuckerman's Civil Procedure* (LexisNexis/Butterworths 2003).

[23] In *Three Rivers DC v Bank of England (No 5)* [2003] QB 1556, the Court of Appeal held that, in the case of a corporate client, in relation to 'legal advice privilege' the privilege could not attach to communications to the legal adviser by either employees who were not part of the directing mind and will of 'the client' or by others who were not 'the client'.

[24] *R (Morgan Grenfell & Co Ltd) v Special Commissioner of Income Tax* [2003] 1 AC 563.

[25] *Waugh v British Railways Board* [1980] AC 521 at 541–542, per Lord Edmund-Davies. See also *Three Rivers DC v Bank of England (No 5)* [2003] QB 1556 at paras 19 and 21 per Longmore LJ, giving the judgment of the court. The House of Lords dismissed a petition to appeal this decision and refused to consider its correctness in *Bank of England (No 6)*.

prospect of litigation is not contemplated, *legal advice privilege* (LAP) protects only communications between lawyer and client. Even if litigation is contemplated, the communication to/from a third party must have been made, and/or the document created, for the purpose of advising or acting with regard to the litigation. Thus, in relation to third parties, LAP does not 'apply to documents communicated to a client or his solicitor for advice to be taken upon them but only to communications passing between that client and his solicitor . . . and documents evidencing such communications' (*Three Rivers DC No 5* [2003] EWCA Civ 474, CA, per Longmore LJ). In relation to organizations and corporate entities, this state of affairs may cause difficulties for several reasons. First, it is not always easy to identify who the 'client' is (see now *Three Rivers DC No 5* [2003] EWCA Civ 474, CA).[26] Secondly, it may be difficult to determine whether a person is the 'agent' of a client, or a 'third party'. Thirdly, the communication or document might have more than one purpose—in which case, one looks to the 'dominant purpose'.

The problem is compounded by the fact that the relationship between the legal   3.52 adviser and the client begs the question 'who is the client?' And, in the context of organizations and corporations, the 'client' might not extend to employees (or even to the officers) of the organization or firm in question (see *Three Rivers District Council (No 5)* [2003] QB 1556; and see the interesting article by Ho Hock Lai 'Legal Advice Privilege and The Corporate Client', Singapore Journal of Legal Studies (2006) 231–63). Documents communicated or produced to a legal adviser by a third party, for the purpose of giving legal advice, and where adversarial litigation is not even contemplated, are not protected (consider *Wheeler v Le Marchant* (1881) 17 Ch D 675). In other words, source material, or pre-existing material (eg reports, invoices, contracts) provided to a legal adviser, or obtained by him, would not be privileged. This is in marked contrast with 'litigation privilege' by which both the information given, and the identity of the person supplying it, are confidential and privileged (*China National Petroleum Corp* [2002] EWHC Ch 60, and see *Kelly v Warley JJ* [2007] EWHC 1836 (Admin)).

It follows from the above that practitioners need to be careful not to assume that   3.53 once legal advice has been given with respect to a document, information, or to a topic raised orally or in writing by client, that the material is thus protected by legal professional privilege.

4. Excluded material and banking information (s 13)

The protection relating to 'excluded material' (as defined by s 11 of the Police and   3.54 Criminal Evidence Act 1984 or, in the case of Northern Ireland, Article 13 of the Police and Criminal Evidence (Northern Ireland) Order 1989), is set out in s 13 of the SCA 2007 without any conditions or restrictions attaching to it.

---

[26] See Ho Hock Lai, 'Legal Advice Privilege and the Corporate Client'; Singapore Journal of Legal Studies [2006] 231–63.

3.55   The protection enacted in s 13, regarding material in respect of which a person 'owes an obligation of confidence by virtue of carrying on a banking business', resembles the protection enacted, for example, in s 2(10) of the Criminal Justice Act 1987 (serious fraud). But whereas s 2 of the Criminal Justice Act 1987 (and similar provisions in other enactments) confers a power on the Director of the Serious Fraud Office to require the production of material (effectively overriding the obligation of a duty of confidence), s 13 empowers a judge of the High Court to include a term in the SCPO requiring a person to disclose specified information or documents.

5. Self-incrimination (s 15)

3.56   Section 15 of the SCA 2007 provides that a statement made by a person in response to a requirement imposed by an SCPO may not be used in evidence in criminal proceedings against him unless: (1) the offence in question is that he failed to comply with an SCPO, contrary to s 25 of the SCA 2007; or (2) that whilst giving evidence in criminal proceedings for an offence other than that enacted in s 25, the person in question made a statement which is inconsistent to a statement that he made in response to the request imposed under the terms of the SCPO.

3.57   Without s 15 of the SCA 2007, an SCPO that includes a term of the kind set out in s 5(5) (eg to answer questions or to produce information) and which overrides the privilege against self-incrimination (PSI), would be at risk of being struck down for not being ECHR compliant (see *Saunders v the United Kingdom* 23 EHRR 313). A number of statutes were amended by s 59 of and Sch 3 to the Youth Justice and Criminal Evidence Act 1999 to give effect to the decision of the ECrtHR in *Saunders*, but the decision did not have retrospective effect in the United Kingdom (ie prior to the HRA 1998 coming into force, and which incorporated much of the ECHR) and see *Lyons, Saunders and others* [2003] Cr App R 24, HL per Lord Bingham:

> In response to this decision the Attorney General issued guidance to prosecutors, referring to section 434(5) of the [Companies Act 1985] and other statutory provisions to similar effect and indicating that, save in certain situations not relevant for present purposes, prosecutors should not normally use in evidence as part of the prosecution case or in cross-examination answers obtained under compulsory powers. Statutory effect was given to this guidance by section 59 of and Schedule 3 to the Youth Justice and Criminal Evidence Act 1999.

3.58   It is sometimes said that to compel a person to make a statement, or to produce documents or information, conflicts with the concept/notion of the 'right to silence'. This is a complex and controversial subject, a discussion of which falls outside the scope of this book.[27] What is settled is that in criminal proceedings, the privilege

---

[27] Interesting contributions have been made by Professor Richard Helmholz *The Privilege Against Self Incrimination*, University of Chicago Press, 1997. See also, 'The Privilege Against Self-Incrimination: a historical tour of the privilege as we know it' 2005; Sally Ramage <http://www.indymedia.org.uk/en/2005/09/323584. html>; Michael Redmayne 'Rethinking the Privilege Against Self-Incrimination' Oxford Journal of Legal Studies (2007), Volume 27, Issue 2 (209).

against self-incrimination does not apply to 'freestanding' documents or to information that was not brought into existence (ie created) under compulsion. Until recently, it seemed to be the law that, in relation to pre-existing documents, PSI operated differently in civil and criminal law. The traditional view was that *in civil proceedings*, PSI applies to pre-existing freestanding documents, and therefore a person could assert the privilege when served with a civil 'search order' (formerly an *Anton Piller* order[28]) and thereby keep the material confidential.[29] The privilege is not available if the same person is faced with a search warrant issued pursuant to statute (eg PACE 1984). In his textbook on *Civil Procedure* (2003), Adrian Zuckerman described the difference (if it exists) as 'absurd'.[30] However, the current law of England and Wales appears to be that the privilege against self-incrimination (PSI) is limited to testimonial evidence (oral and written). Excluded from its application is self-standing evidence, which was not produced under compulsion.[31]

In Strasbourg jurisprudence, PSI does not extend to self-standing/independent evidence. Thus, in *Saunders v UK*,[32] the Court said: 3.59

69. The right not to incriminate oneself is primarily concerned, however, with respecting the will of an accused person to remain silent. As commonly understood in the legal systems of the Contracting Parties to the Convention and elsewhere, it does not extend to the use in criminal proceedings of material which may be obtained from the accused through the use of compulsory powers but which has an existence independent of the will of the suspect such as, inter alia, documents acquired pursuant to a warrant, breath, blood and urine samples and bodily tissue for the purpose of DNA testing.

Even before the HRA 1998 came into force, recent judgments of UK domestic courts have chimed with those of the Strasbourg Court. Thus, in *R v Kearns* [2002] EWCA Crim 748, the Court said: 3.60

(*Attorney-General's Reference (No 7 of 2000)*) [33] came to the conclusion that the *Saunders case* (at paragraphs 68 and 69) recognised a distinction between a statement of a defendant that had been made under compulsion and the production of pre-existing documents or other evidence under compulsory powers.

52. The Court concluded (in paragraph 59) that this distinction was valid; jurisprudentially sound and should be followed. In the Court's view legitimate objection might be made to evidence that a defendant had been forced to create by the use of compulsory powers. However if the

---

[28] See *Anton Piller K.G. v Manufacturing Processes Limited* [1975] EWCA Civ 12.

[29] The *Anton Piller* jurisdiction was put on a statutory footing by s 7, Civil Procedure Act 1997, but the Act offers the following protection: 'This section does not affect any right of a person to refuse to do anything on the ground that to do so might tend to expose him or his spouse to proceedings for an offence or the recovery of a penalty'.

[30] See too the submissions to like effect made on behalf of the Attorney General in *In The Matter of OTL* [2006] EWHC 1226 (Ch); and see now *C Plc v P* [2007] EWCA Civ 493.

[31] See *In The Matter of OTL* [2006] EWHC 1226 (Ch); and see now *C Plc v P* [2007] EWCA Civ 493, following *Attorney General's reference (No 7 of 2000)* [2001] 1 WLR 1879—having regard to the judgment of Justice La Forrest in *Thompson Newspapers Ltd v Director of Investigation and Research* (1990) 54 CCC 417—and see *R v Kearns* [2002] 1 WLR 2815.

[32] 43/1994/490/572, (1996) 23 EHRR 313.

[33] [2001] EWCA Crim 888, [2001] 2 Cr App R 286.

evidence was already in existence and the only effect of the use of the compulsory powers was to bring such evidence to the attention of the court, then its production could not be so objectionable. That is because the existence and quality of such evidence are independent of any order to produce it that is made against the will of the accused person. Therefore the production of such pre-existing and 'independent' evidence could not render a trial unfair and so breach Article 6.

53. What conclusions can be drawn from the Strasbourg cases and the UK cases on the scope of the right to silence and the right not to incriminate oneself? In our view the following is clear:

. . . .

(4) There is a distinction between the compulsory production of documents or other material which had an existence independent of the will of the suspect or accused person and statements that he has had to make under compulsion. In the former case there was no infringement of the right to silence and the right not to incriminate oneself. In the latter case there could be, depending on the circumstances.

3.61   Note also *R v Hundal and Dhaliwal* [2004] EWCA Crim 389, CA, which concerned a prosecution under s 11 of the Terrorism Act 2000. The Court, in dismissing the appeal, approved the passage at para 53(4) in the judgment of Mr Justice Aikens in *Kearns* (above).

3.62   In *C Plc v P* (2007) EWCA Civ 493:

C alleged intellectual property infringements by P. C obtained a civil search order (formerly known as an '*Anton Piller* Order') which authorised a computer expert to take charge of the material seized from P's premises. Before the search was carried out, P obtained the advice of a solicitor who attended the premises. The solicitor informed the parties and the Supervising Solicitor, that P would assert PSI in respect of incriminating material which the search might disclose. The search went ahead, and computers were seized and delivered to the computer expert who discovered the allegedly 'offending material' stored on one of the computers.

3.63   The question arose whether P lacked PSI in material that existed *before* the search order was executed and whether, in any event, he lacked that privilege once the offending material was discovered. At first instance,[34] Evans-Lombe J held that P had effectively claimed PSI in respect of the material to be produced pursuant to the search order, before the search started, and an objective consideration of the events occurring after the execution of that order did not result in the conclusion that he lost the benefit of it. By so holding, the case of *C Plc* was distinguishable from *O v Z*.[35] Although the facts of the two cases were very similar, in *O v Z* no claim to PSI was made by the Respondent to the search order before the search started, in the course of which the offending material was passed to the independent computer expert for imaging. On that basis, Mr Justice Lindsay held that the suspect had lost his PSI and directed that the offending material be handed over to the police (para 53). A claim to PSI was made by Z after the offending material had been discovered by the computer expert and after the adjourned return date of the

---

[34] The case was then styled *OTL*.
[35] [2005] EWHC 238 (Ch).

application for the search order. In *C Plc*, P's solicitor had at least raised the prospect that PSI might be an issue. Evans-Lombe J also held that PSI does not extend to material *which constitutes freestanding evidence* not brought into existence by him under compulsion and which could have come to public notice otherwise than as the result of the exercise of some statutory power to require disclosure enforceable by a court (para 24).[36] Mr Justice Evans-Lombe[37] summarized the effect of the judgment of Justice La Forest in *Thompson Newspapers Ltd v Director of Investigation and Research* (1990) 54 CCC 417 in these terms:

Whereas a compelled statement is evidence that would not have existed independently of the exercise of the powers of compulsion, evidence which exists independently of the compelled statements could have been found by other means and its quality does not depend on its past connection with the compelled statement. Accordingly evidence of the latter type is in no sense 'testimonial' and PSI ought not to attach to it. [38]

The Court of Appeal dismissed the appeal but on different grounds.[39] Longmore   3.64
LJ said that the court was bound by *Attorney-General's Reference (No 7 of 2000)* (2001) 1 WLR 1879, and since in that case the privilege was held not to extend to documents which were independent evidence then the same must apply to 'things' which are independent evidence. Longmore LJ added that even if that were not so, the words 'or thing' does not apply to a 'thing' discovered in execution of a court order as distinct from a 'thing' that is compelled to be produced:

[the] privilege can be invoked to refuse to answer interrogatories or to refuse to disclose matters which are ordinarily discoverable; those matters may be documents or other 'things', but independent matters coming to light in the course of executing a proper order of the court are in an altogether different category.

Longmore LJ said: 3.65

36. I would, therefore, conclude in the present case that, although the offending material had to be disclosed to the Supervising Solicitor and the computer experts by virtue of the order originally granted by Peter Smith J, there is no privilege in the offending material itself which is material which existed independently of the order. This is essentially the position maintained by Professor Adrian Zuckerman in the first (2003) edition of his work on Civil Procedure, paras 17-9 to 17-13. These paragraphs are repeated in his second edition (2006) where he welcomes the decision of Evans-Lombe J in this case at para. 17-12A.

37. It follows that even before the enactment of the Human Rights Act 1998, there was no privilege in the material and there could be no bar to the disclosure of the material to the police if it is otherwise right to do so.

38. It is necessary to emphasise that the only issue before the judge and on this appeal is whether W should have the leave of the court to disclose the offending material to the police. It is in this

---

[36] [2006] EWHC 1226 (Ch)
[37] Ibid.
[38] Note *Attorney General's reference (No 7 of 2000)* [2001] 1 WLR 1879.
[39] [2007] EWCA Civ 493.

context that I would hold that no privilege exists in the material itself which is itself 'real' and 'independent' evidence and is not itself 'compelled testimony' from P.

3.66   In *C Plc v P*, Collins LJ did not think that it was necessary to rule on the wider question whether it is open to the Court of Appeal to find as a general rule that there is no privilege in respect of what has been described as pre-existing or independent material, but he accepted that there is a powerful case in policy terms for there being no privilege with respect to disclosure of free-standing documents or other material not brought into existence under compulsion (see Professor Adrian Zuckerman, *Civil Procedure*, 2nd edn, 2006, ch 17). Sir Martin Nourse agreed with the judgment of Longmore LJ.

3.67   The impact of *C Plc v P* is likely to be profound, but both the Strasbourg jurisprudence and domestic case law has moved ever closer to the position set out in *C Plc v P* (see also *R v Kearns* [2002] EWCA Crim 748).

D. DURATION OF ORDERS

3.68   An SCPO must specify when the order is to come into force and when it will cease to be effective (s 16(1), SCA2007). In theory, it would be possible for a court to stipulate that the order shall be of immediate effect, but this would surely only occur if there was compelling reason for that to happen. One consequence of s 16(1) is that in the event that the court should fail to specify a 'start' date, the order has no effect at all. An SCPO cannot be enforced for a period longer than five years (s 16(2)). Although a court will be acting beyond its powers were it to make an order that exceeded five years, it seems to be open to the court to make a 'new order to the same or similar effect' (s 16(5)). A party need not wait until one SCPO has ceased to be in force before applying for another one (s 16(6)). Different terms can be brought into force at different times and for different periods (s 16(3)). If terms are 'staggered', ie to come into force at different times, the court must specify the dates on which each term comes into force, and ceases to be in force (s 16(4)).

E. VARIATION OF AN SCPO (s 17)

3.69   Section 17 of the SCA 2007 sets out (in general terms) the procedural steps that are to be followed in respect of applications for the variation or discharge of an SCPO. Applications are heard in the High Court. An application to vary an SCPO may be made by the 'relevant applicant authority', or by any other person (s 17(3)). The test that is to be applied by the court when deciding whether to vary an SCPO is set out in s 17(1), namely:

it has reasonable grounds to believe that the terms of the order as varied would protect the public by preventing, restricting or disrupting involvement, by the person who is the subject of the order, in serious crime in England and Wales.

Note that if the subject of an SCPO is a body corporate, a partnership, or unin- 3.70
corporated association, the test in s 17(1) and (2) does not apply if the SCPO contains terms relating to the provision of 'monitoring services' in accordance with
s 39 of the SCA 2007.

In cases to which s 17(1) applies, the question arises whether the court, when 3.71
deciding upon the terms of an SCPO, must aim for the greatest level of protection,
or the least, or somewhere in between. The short answer is that the court must
comply with the Human Rights Act 1998, and therefore the concept of proportion-
ality is engaged. The court has to weigh the interest of the public against the interest
of the person (or persons) affected by the order. Section 17(4) provides that the
court must *not* entertain an application made by the person who is the subject of
the order unless it considers that there has been a change of circumstances affecting
the order. Similarly, a third party must show a change of circumstances if they had
made representations to the High Court under s 9 of the SCA 2007 or to the Crown
Court, at the time that the making of an SCPO was being considered (s 17(5), (6)).
The court may hear from a third party if he/she had not made representations when
the making of an SCPO was being considered and it was reasonable in all the
circumstances for the person not to have done so (s 17(5), (7)).

F. DISCHARGE OF AN SCPO (s 18)

The High Court may discharge an SCPO (England and Wales) on an application by 3.72
'any person' to do so (s 18(2)), but only if there has been a change of circumstances
since the SCPO was made or varied (s 18(3)). A third party who is 'significantly
adversely affected' by the SCPO must also show a change of circumstances if he/she
had been heard in proceedings (pursuant to s 9, SCA 2007) before the High Court
or Crown Court (s 18(4) and (5)), *unless* the third party had not been previously
heard (and it was reasonable in all the circumstances for the third party not to have
made representations at an earlier time) (s 18(4) and (6)).

4

SERIOUS CRIME PREVENTION ORDERS: JURISDICTION OF THE CROWN COURT

A. INTRODUCTION

The reader is invited to read the commentary at paras **2.17–2.33**. This is because a 4.01 number of provisions in Part 1 of the SCA 2007 are common to proceedings in the High Court and in the Crown Court. These are ss 2–8, 11–15 (information safeguards), and 16 (duration of orders). Although an initial reading of Part 1 of the 2007 Act might convey the impression that interested parties can switch, or 'forum shop' between the jurisdiction of the High Court and the Crown Court (and, to some extent, that is possible), para **2.13** describes the differences in jurisdiction between the two courts, and the relationship between them.

Part 1 of the 2007 Act confers a power on the Crown Court to make an SCPO in 4.02 respect of a person who falls to be sentenced following his/her conviction for a 'serious offence' or an offence under s 25 of the SCA 2007 (whether that person was convicted in the magistrates' court and committed to the Crown Court for sentence, or convicted on indictment). The court has a limited power to vary an SCPO, but it has no power to discharge an SCPO. Proceedings in the Crown Court can only be made on an application by the Director of Public Prosecutions, the Director of Revenue and Customs Prosecutions, or the Director of the Serious Fraud Office (England and Wales); or, in Northern Ireland, by the Director of Public Prosecutions (s 8, SCA 2007). No power is conferred on the Crown Court by the 2007 Act to initiate proceedings under Part 1 of the Act.

B. MAKING AN SCPO—REQUIREMENTS (s 19)

4.03   Where a person aged 18 years or over[1] has been convicted of a 'serious offence', or convicted of an offence under s 25 of the SCA 2007 (whether convicted by a magistrates' court and committed for sentence to the Crown Court, or he/she has been convicted on indictment), the court has the discretionary power to make an SCPO (s 19(1)). A 'serious offence' is defined by s 2(2) of the SCA 2007.

4.04   The Crown Court may make an SCPO if it has 'reasonable grounds to believe that the order would protect the public by preventing, restricting, or disrupting involvement by the person in serious crime in England and Wales' (s 19(2), SCA 2007). The nature of this test has been discussed at para **3.04** in relation to the power of the High Court to make an SCPO: the test is identical in both jurisdictions. By s 19(2), an SCPO may be made 'in addition' to dealing with the offender in relation to the offence, and not as an alternative to impose a sentence (see s 19(7)). There is nothing in Part 1 of the SCA 2007 to prevent a Crown Court from imposing an absolute discharge, or a conditional discharge, if the circumstances of the offence merited such an outcome, as well as imposing an SCPO. On the other hand, given that an SCPO is, by definition, an order that is directed at the defendant with respect to his involvement in serious crime, such an outcome would be exceedingly rare.

4.05   Proceedings for an SCPO in the Crown Court are civil in nature (s 36(1)). The standard of proof is the civil standard (s 36(2)). However, for the reasons given in paras **2.23–2.34**, Parliament enacted this provision in the belief that an enhanced quantum of proof would be applied by the courts (one Minister said that he anticipated that the standard would be 'proof beyond reasonable doubt'[2]). Note that s 36(4) provides that when the Crown Court exercises its jurisdiction to make an SCPO under Part 1 of the SCA 2007, the Court remains a 'criminal court' for the purposes of Part 7 of the Courts Act 2003 (procedure rules and practice directions).

4.06   Note that, pursuant to s 9(4) of the SCA 2007, a third party has a right to be heard in proceedings before the Crown Court when the court is exercising its powers under ss 19–21 of the 2007 Act. However, the burden is on the third party to apply to be heard before the court. The court appears to be under no obligation to notify the third party that it has been asked to consider making an SCPO against the defendant. An order made under s 19 may run for a period not exceeding five years in any one period (s 16(2), SCA 2007), but it is open to the court to make a new order 'to the same or similar effect' (s 16(5)).

4.07   Note that an SCPO is not a 'sentence' for the purposes of the Criminal Appeal Act 1968 (see s 24(11)(a), SCA 2007).

---

[1] s 6, SCA 2007.
[2] *Hansard*, 12 June 2007, col 664.

C. ATTACHING TERMS TO AN SCPO

An SCPO that is made by the Crown Court may contain prohibitions, restrictions, or requirements (or other terms) as the court considers appropriate, for protecting the public by preventing, restricting, or disrupting the defendant's involvement in serious crime (s 19(5), SCA 2007). 4.08

The expression 'serious crime in England and Wales' is defined by s 2(3) of the SCA 2007. In cases where a defendant is acquitted of an offence that would fall within the definition of a 'serious offence in England and Wales' (s 2(2)), but he/she is convicted of the lesser offence, there appears to be no power for the Crown Court to make an SCPO, even if the trial judge/sentencer is satisfied that the defendant has been involved in serious crime 'elsewhere'. In such cases, the power to make an SCPO rests with the High Court, pursuant to its powers under s 1(1) or (2) in the case of Northern Ireland. 4.09

The terms and requirements that may be imposed on the defendant by the Crown Court are illustrated by s 5 of the SCA 2007. These include the power to require a person to answer questions, or to provide information, that is specified or described in the order. The reader might query whether s 5 applies at all to Crown Court decisions made pursuant to s 19 of the SCA 2007. This is because s 19 does not refer to s 5 of the 2007 Act. However, s 5 is one of the provisions which appears under the heading 'General' to Part 1 of the 2007 Act, and therefore s 5 applies to Crown Court proceedings. Note that s 5 contains only 'examples' of the type of conditions that may be included in an SCPO. The Crown Court is free to make such provision in the order as it considers appropriate subject to: (a) satisfying the test set out in s 19(2), namely, to protect the public by preventing, restricting, or disrupting involvement by the person in serious crime in England and Wales;[3] (b) the terms of the order being compatible with 'convention rights', and (c) the powers having been exercised subject to ss 6–15 of the SCA 2007 (general safeguards and information safeguards (see s 19(6), and see paras **3.49–3.67**). 4.10

D. VARIATION OF AN SCPO IN THE CROWN COURT

Sections 20 and 21 of the SCA 2007 cater for two situations in which the Crown Court may vary the terms of an SCPO. The first is described in s 20 and concerns cases where a defendant is convicted of a 'serious offence' when he was already subject to an SCPO. The second situation is where the defendant is convicted under s 25 for breaching an SCPO (s 21). The thinking of the legislature appears to be that in each situation the fact of conviction constitutes a change of circumstances that entitles the court to review the terms of an existing SCPO imposed on the defendant. 4.11

---

[3] For Northern Ireland, see s 19(4), SCA 2007.

The court may therefore vary the order in the light of the information before it, by imposing such conditions that the Court considers necessary and proportionate to prevent, restrict, or disrupt the defendant's involvement in serious crime. It is to be noted that only a 'relevant applicant authority' (eg the DPP) may apply for a variation of an SCPO.

4.12   Although Part 1 of the SCA 2007 does not make the point clear, it is submitted that the Crown Court has no power to vary an SCPO which *it* has made under s 19 of the SCA 2007.

5

SERIOUS CRIME PREVENTION ORDERS: APPEALS AND ENFORCEMENT

A. APPEALS

An appeal lies to the Court of Appeal from a decision of the High Court relating to the making, varying, or discharging of an SCPO (s 23, SCA 2007).   5.01

An appeal from the Crown Court may be initiated by (a) a defendant, (b) the 'relevant applicant authority', or (c) a third party who made representations in proceedings before the Crown Court. An appeal against a decision of the Crown Court is to the Court of Appeal. Subject to any rules of court that may be made under s 53(1) of the Senior Courts Act 1981,[1] an appeal from the Crown Court in either England or Wales will be to the Criminal Division of the Court of Appeal (s 24(5), SCA 2007).   5.02

An appeal requires the leave of the Court of Appeal (s 24(3), SCA 2007) or the leave of the judge who made the decision in the court below (s 24(4)). An appeal also lies from the Court of Appeal to the Supreme Court, but only with leave to appeal, and leave will be refused unless (a) the Court of Appeal certifies that a point of law of general public importance is involved in the decision, and (b) that either the Court of Appeal, or the Supreme Court, decides that the point is one which ought to be considered by the Supreme Court (s 24(8)).   5.03

---

[1] The 1981 Act is concerned with the distribution of business between the Civil and Criminal Divisions of the Court of Appeal.

B. OFFENCE OF FAILING TO COMPLY WITH AN SCPO (s 25)

1. The offence

5.04   A person who, without reasonable excuse, fails to comply with an SCPO commits an offence under s 25 of the SCA 2007, punishable (a) on summary conviction, for a term of 12 months' imprisonment and/or a fine (not exceeding the statutory maximum), or (b) on indictment, to imprisonment for a term not exceeding five years and/or an unlimited fine (s 25(1) and (2)). A fine imposed on a partnership for an offence under s 25 is to be paid out of the partnership assets.[2] In the case of an unincorporated association, any fine must be paid out its funds.[3] In Northern Ireland the maximum term of imprisonment on summary conviction is six months' imprisonment (s 25(3)). The offence is not to be regarded lightly because not only can it administer the 'sting' of imprisonment and/or a fine, but it can also trigger the power of forfeiture under s 26, or trigger confiscation proceedings if 'benefit' has been obtained by the defendant as a result of, or in connection with, the offence (see s 76(4), POCA 2002). The court is also conferred with the power to wind up companies, partnerships, or other relevant bodies (ss 27–29, SCA 2007).

5.05   A copy of the original order, or any variation of it, which has been certified as being a copy of the original by the proper officer of the court which made it, is admissible as evidence of its having been made and of its contents 'to the same extent that oral evidence of those things is admissible' in proceedings for an offence charged under s 25 of the SCA 2007 (see s 25(4)).

5.06   A body corporate can commit the s 25 offence as well as any of its officers or persons who purport to act as its officers and who connive or consent to the commission of the offence (s 30(2)). Note that a 'body corporate' includes a limited liability partnership (s 30(4)). Proceedings for an offence under s 25 which is alleged to have been committed by an unincorporated association, or by a partnership (other than a limited liability partnership), must be brought in the name of the association[4] or partnership[5] (and not in that of any of its members/partners).

2. Defence of 'reasonable excuse'

5.07   It is submitted that whether the facts are *capable* of amounting to a reasonable excuse is a matter of law. Whether the facts *do* amount to a reasonable excuse is a question of fact.

5.08   Section 25 of the SCA 2007 is one of many statutory offences that declares what is forbidden, and then provides that no offence is committed if the defendant has a

---

[2] s 31(5), SCA 2007.
[3] s 32(6), SCA 2007.
[4] s 32(4), SCA 2007.
[5] s 31(5), SCA 2007.

'reasonable excuse' for his conduct. Where the statute is silent as to the incidence and standard of proof (and s 25 is silent on this point) the usual effect is that the defendant shoulders an evidential burden to raise the issue which, when discharged, places the legal burden on the prosecution to disprove it to the criminal standard of proof (consider eg s 7(6) of the Road Traffic Act 1988: failure to provide an evidential specimen; and see *R v Harling* [1970] RTR 441). Other statutory provisions expressly provide that the incidence of proving a 'reasonable excuse' shall lie on the accused (eg s 1, Prevention of Crime Act 1953, and s 19 Firearms Act 1968: 'the proof whereof shall lie on him'). Provisions of the latter type usually impose a persuasive burden on an accused, but not always, and regard must always be had to Article 6(2) of the ECHR and the Human Rights Act 1998 (see *Davis v Alexander* [1970] 54 Cr App R 398; *Petrie* [1961] 1 WLR 358; *Brown* (1971) 55 Cr App R 478; and note *Lambert* [2002] 2 AC 545). When it comes to summary proceedings, a complicating feature is s 101 of the Magistrates' Courts Act 1980, which provides that 'where the defendant to an information or complaint relies for his defence on any exception, exemption, proviso, excuse or qualification . . . the burden of proving the exception, exemption, proviso, excuse or qualification shall be on him'. It is submitted that an invaluable approach was that provided by Lord Nicholls in *Johnstone* [2003] 1 WLR 1736 (concerning s 92(5) of the Trade Marks Act 1994):

A sound starting point is to remember that if an accused is required to prove a fact on the balance of probability . . . this permits a conviction in spite of the fact-finding tribunal having a reasonable doubt as to the guilt of the accused . . . This consequence of a reverse burden of proof should colour one's approach when evaluating the reasons why it is said that, in the absence of a persuasive burden on the accused, the public interest will be prejudiced to an extent which justifies placing a persuasive burden on the accused. The more serious the punishment which may flow from conviction, the more compelling must be the reasons. The extent and nature of the factual matters required to be proved by the accused, and their importance relative to the matters required to be proved by the prosecution, have to be taken into account. So also does the extent to which the burden on the accused relates to facts which, if they exist, are readily provable by him as matters within his own knowledge or to which he has ready access.

C. POWERS OF FORFEITURE FOR FAILING TO COMPLY (s 26)

A person convicted of an offence under s 25 of the SCA 2007 may be ordered to forfeit 'anything in his possession at the time of the offence which the court considers to have been involved in the offence' (s 26(1)). The court may make such provision as it considers necessary for giving effect to the forfeiture of the item (s 26(4)). It may, in particular, include provision relating to the retention, handling, destruction, or other disposal of what is forfeited (s 26(5)). 5.09

An order under s 26(1) may not be made 'so as to come into force at any time before there is no further possibility (ignoring any power to appeal out of time) of the order being varied or set aside on appeal' (s 26(3)). The wording is seen in some recent enactments that have made provision for a power of forfeiture (eg the Terrorism Act 2006). 5.10

5.11   It is easy to see how a car, which is used as a getaway vehicle in a robbery, has been 'involved in the offence'. But the 'offence', for the purposes of s 26, is a breach of an order. Much will turn on the nature of the breach. For example, if the defendant had been required to disclose the extent and whereabouts of his assets, and he failed to mention the existence of a boat in France, the question arises whether that item of property is one which has been 'involved in the offence'.

5.12   It is not clear why, in s 26, the legislature employed the phrase 'involved in the offence' given that other forfeiture provisions in other enactments use the expression 'relate to the offence' (eg s 7(3) of the Forgery and Counterfeiting Act 1981; s 27(1) of the Misuse of Drugs Act 1971).

5.13   Was it necessary to enact s 26 at all given the existence of the forfeiture provisions of s 143 of the Powers of the Criminal Courts (Sentencing) Act 2000? Section 143 of the 2000 Act applies to any property which was lawfully seized from the offender, or which was in his possession or under his control at the time when he was apprehended, and which had been used for the purpose of committing an offence, or facilitating the commission of any offence, or the property was intended by him to be used for that purpose. According to the Minister of State for the Home Office (Baroness Scotland), s 26 was needed to avoid getting 'some pretty perverse results'. The example that the Minister gave to the House of Lords (when s 26 was debated as part of the Serious Crime Bill) was that of multiple telephones used in trafficking cases:[6]

> One of the provisions that the court makes is that the individual involved should have possession of only one mobile to prevent the widespread use of clean and dirty mobiles for personal and criminal business respectively. After the person's arrest for breach of the order of having more than one mobile and the subsequent disposal of the offence, the police would have to return the other mobiles which the subject had been using to breach the order, as the breach would be having in his possession other mobiles. Not only would the vast majority of people think that this was a rather unusual outcome, it would also mean that the subject of the order was immediately in breach of it again because the police were not able to remove from him the mobiles or the article that caused the breach.

D. THE POWER TO WIND UP COMPANIES (s 27)

5.14   Section 27 of the SCA 2007 confers a power on the Director of Public Prosecutions, the Director of Revenue and Customs Prosecutions, or the Director of the Serious Fraud Office to petition the court for the winding up of a company (s 27(12)), partnership, or a 'relevant body' eg a building society (s 27(12)). The power under s 27 is available only if:

(a) the company, partnership, or relevant body has been convicted of an offence under s 25 of the SCA 2007; and

---

[6] *Hansard*, House of Lords, 14 Mar 2007, col 808.

(b) the Director concerned considers that it would be in the public interest for that body to be wound up.

The 'Director concerned' does not have the last word, that rests with the court. 5.15 During debates in the House of Lords, the Minister of State for the Home Office (Baroness Scotland) made it clear that a petition under s 27 of the SCA 2007 would be presented 'only if it is in the public interest for the winding-up to happen and the court can make an order for winding-up only if it would be just and equitable to do so. To provide for this, we have tapped into the Insolvency Act 1986, which . . . already provides an established framework for the winding-up of a company'.

The court must apply a modified test in relation to companies, arguably an addi- 5.16 tional test, namely, whether it is 'just and equitable for the company to be wound up' under s 125 of the Insolvency Act 1986 (see s 27(4), SCA 2007). For the position concerning partnerships and 'relevant bodies', see s 27(5) and (6) respectively. Similar powers exist in relation to proceedings in Northern Ireland (see s 28).

Note that a petition for winding-up a company etc, may not be presented and 5.17 it is not open to a court to order the winding-up of such a body (pursuant to s 27, SCA 2007) if: (a) an appeal against conviction for the offence concerned has been made and not finally determined; or (b) the period during which such an appeal may be made has not expired (s 27(9)). Similarly, no such petition or order can be presented or made if the relevant body is already in the process of being wound up by the court (s 27(10)).

6

ENCOURAGING AND PARTICIPATING IN CRIME: OVERVIEW AND FUNDAMENTAL PRINCIPLES

A. OVERVIEW

1. Part 2 of the SCA 2007 fills a gap in the law where the anticipated offence was not committed

Under pre-existing law, if for whatever reason the anticipated offence was not com- 6.01
mitted, and it could not be proved that D either (i) incited D2 to commit an offence,
or (ii) conspired with D2 to commit it, the likely result was that D would escape

61

criminal liability. The pre-SCA 2007 position was concisely described by Professor Glanville Williams in *The Textbook of Criminal Law*:[1]

> . . . the mere supplier of an instrument of crime does not commit any offence at common law if the crime is not committed. It is true that, by a somewhat anomalous extension of the law of complicity, he will become a party to the crime if it is committed, unless after supplying the instrument he makes quite strenuous attempts to prevent it being used.[2] But even if he makes no effort to prevent the crime, he escapes liability if it happens not to be committed, unless he happens to be guilty of some specific statutory offence, or unless the would-be perpetrator attempts to commit the crime—in which case the supplier will be an accessory to the attempt. The analysis appears to be the same where a person upon request gives information helpful for the commission of a crime.

6.02   Part 2 SCA 2007 changes that state of affairs.

Example 1[3]

D lent a van to D2, *believing* that D2 would use it to commit a robbery.

Prior to Part 2 of the SCA 2007, D was not criminally liable if D2 was arrested by the police before he could commit the offence. But if D committed the robbery, D stood to be charged, indicted, and punished as a principal offender by virtue of the operation of s 8 of the Accessories and Abettors Act 1861.

D might now be convicted of an inchoate offence (ss 44–46, SCA 2007) of assisting or encouraging the commission of a crime, even if the crime was not committed.

Example 2

D supplies a cricket bat to D2, believing or intending that D2 will use it to hit V. D2 is arrested before he could carry out the attack.

D might now be guilty of an offence under Part 2 of the SCA 2007.

If D2 succeeds in hitting V, and he does so with the requisite fault element for an offence, D might incur *secondary liability* (albeit treated as a principal) pursuant to s 8 of the Accessories and Abettors Act 1861, *or* D might be liable under Part 2 of the SCA 2007 for an inchoate offence, if the prosecution cannot prove whether D acted inchoately (contrary to ss 44–46, SCA 2007) or as a secondary party pursuant to s 8 of the 1861 Act.

2. Three inchoate offences of encouraging or assisting a crime

6.03   Part 2 of the 2007 Act creates three inchoate offences to deal with cases where a person (D) does an act, which is *capable* of encouraging or assisting another person (D2), to commit a crime (the 'anticipated offence'). The offences are set out in ss 44, 45, and 46 of the SCA 2007:

(1)   The first offence concerns cases where D *intends* to encourage or to assist another to commit an offence (s 44).

---

[1] 1978, published by Stevens, p 387; and see Smith & Hogan, *Criminal Law*, 11th edn, pp 349–50.
[2] *R v Curr* (1968) 2 QB 944.
[3] Based on an example given by the Law Commission (Law Com No 300, para 1.3).

(2) The second offence deals with cases where D *believes* that the anticipated offence will be committed (not might be committed) and he *believes* that his act will encourage or assist its commission (s 45).

(3) The third offence concerns cases where D does an act that is capable of encouraging or assisting the commission of *one or more of a number of offences* and he *believes* (a) that one or more of those offences will be committed (but has no belief as to which), and (b) that his act will encourage or assist the commission of one or more of them (s 46).

3. Part 2 of the SCA 2007: a major piece of reform

The rules relating to encouraging and participating in crime constitute a major   6.04
area of reform introduced by Part 2 of the SCA 2007. Part 2 of the Act builds on the Law Commission's Report (Law Com No 300, 'Inchoate Liability for Assisting and Encouraging Crime'). Although the provisions in Part 2 are few in number, they are conceptually difficult to understand without some knowledge of the Law Commission's reasoning as set out in Law Com No 300 and Law Com No 305. That reasoning has been summarized at various places within this chapter, and it appears in a numbered list at paras **6.25–6.28**.

The inchoate offences enacted under Part 2 of the SCA 2007 now bring into   6.05
focus concepts which many criminal law practitioners tend to apply intuitively, such as the notion of 'joint enterprise', or 'aiding, abetting, counselling or procuring'. It is submitted that Part 2 requires practitioners to keep well in mind the different categories of parties who may be held culpable for acts performed in circumstances that make those acts 'criminal', for otherwise there is a danger that the offences created under Part 2 will be charged inappropriately, or not charged when they ought to be. It is therefore important to understand the principles that underpin the notions of a person's liability as (a) a principal offender, or (b) a secondary party, or (c) a party incurring inchoate liability under Part 2. When construing Part 2 of the Act, the reader will be assisted by having to hand a copy of Law Com No 300 and the Law Commission's draft Bill (appended to that Report). This is because Part 2 draws upon the reasoning of the Law Commission. The Law Commission's commentary to its draft Bill is particularly useful (Appendix A, Law Com No 300). However, a number of significant differences exist between the draft Bill and Part 2 of the Act.

4. Statutory offences of incitement, conspiracy, attempts, are retained

The common law offence of incitement has been repealed by s 59 of the SCA 2007,   6.06
but many statutory offences of incitement, assisting, encouraging ('inciting'), conspiring, or attempting the commission of a crime have been retained. These offences are set out in Parts 1, 2, and 3 of Sch 3 to the SCA 2007 for England and Wales, and Parts 1, 4, and 5 of that Schedule for Northern Ireland. The offences include: solicitation of murder, attempting an act calculated or likely to cause

sedition or disaffection,[4] assisting unlawful immigration to a member State,[5] inciting the commission of an offence contrary to the Misuse of Drugs Act 1971,[6] statutory conspiracy under s 1(1) of the Criminal Law Act 1977,[7] and criminal attempts under s 1(1) of the Criminal Attempts Act 1981.[8] For the purposes of ss 45 and 46 of the SCA 2007, those offences are to be disregarded but not for the purposes of the s 44 offence. One practical effect of this is that whereas a person can commit a s 44 offence by *intentionally* encouraging another person to *conspire* to commit an offence (conspiracy being, in this instance, the anticipated/principal offence), it is not possible for a person to be convicted under either s 45 or s 46 of the SCA 2007, if he/she gave encouragement or assistance merely *believing* that a conspiracy (or some other inchoate crime) would be committed. The same point applies in relation to attempts to commit the anticipated offence under the CCA 1981 and, indeed, with respect to all the aforementioned statutory offences listed in Sch 3 to the 2007 Act.

5. What Part 2 of the SCA 2007 does not do

6.07 Note that Part 2 of the SCA 2007 does not:

(1) Repeal or replace s 8 of the Accessories and Abettors Act 1861. In other words, Part 2 of the SCA 2007 does *not* give statutory force to the Law Commission's recommendations and draft Bill in its Report No 305 (Participating in Crime), ie secondary liability where the principal offender commits the offence anticipated by D.

(2) Alter the position where D and D2 act as 'joint principals', ie where both parties participate in the *actus reus* of the offence, and share the requisite fault element for the offence in question.

(3) Alter rules relating to secondary liability for a collateral offence that is committed by the principal offender (eg a joint venture to assault V, but D2 goes on to kill V), see the *Chan Wing Siu, Rahman, Rafferty*, line of cases. Nevertheless, in order to put the rules enacted by Part 2 into their wider context, a brief description of the rules relating to secondary liability, and joint principals, is included within these pages.

6. Charging an inchoate Part 2, SCA 2007 offence, notwithstanding that the full offence was committed

6.08 An offence under ss 44–46 of the 2007 Act will typically be charged in circumstances where, for whatever reason, the anticipated offence was not committed by

---

[4] Contrary to s 3(1) of the Aliens Restriction (Amendment) Act 1919; see para 5, Part 1 of Sch 3 to the SCA 2007.

[5] See s 25 of the Immigration Act 1971; para 11, Part 1 of Sch 3 to the SCA 2007.

[6] s 19, MDA 1971.

[7] para 32, Part 2 of Sch 3, SCA 2007.

[8] para 33, Part 2 of Sch 3, SCA 2007.

the perpetrator. However, even if it is proved that the anticipated offence was committed, a person who gave encouragement or assistance to the perpetrator (principal) may be convicted of an inchoate offence under ss 44–46 of the SCA 2007 (s 49(1), SCA 2007). The reasoning seems to be that the fact that the principal offence is committed by P has no bearing on the criminal act D intended or expected:

D is liable in relation to the (hypothetical) criminal act he intended or expected, rather than the actual offence committed by P. This will be the position even if the offence committed by P is the same in all respects as the principal offence in relation to which D is charged under (Part 2). Accordingly, it is not necessary to include provisions in the Bill[9] to take into account matters such as a change in the way the offence was committed, or a change in the identity of the perpetrator or victim (Law Com No 300).[10]

7. Inchoate liability under the SCA 2007 might put a person in a worse position than the principal offender

There are some situations in respect of which Part 2 of the SCA 2007 operates more harshly against a secondary party than the principal offender. This is because D could be inchoately liable for encouraging or assisting D2 to commit an offence (which D2 does not, or cannot, commit) whereas D2 escapes criminal liability if he does not attempt to commit it, or if he cannot be convicted of conspiring to commit the full offence (see Law Com No 300, paras 4.22–4.26). When dealing with that issue, the Law Commission said: 6.09

. . . If D sells P a weapon that D correctly believes P will use to murder V, D has done everything that he or she intends to do. Nothing more turns on D's subsequent conduct whereas P has yet to take the step of attempting to commit the offence (para 4.25).

However, for the reasons given by the Law Commission, the principal offender will often be in a position no better than D:[11] 6.10

. . . if P approaches D for assistance in committing an offence, P will incur criminal liability . . . if P asks D to supply him or her with an article so that P can commit an offence, P is doing an act capable of encouraging D to do an act capable of assisting P to commit an offence. In other words, if D supplies the article to P, not only is D committing the (s 45) offence but, by encouraging D to commit the (s 45) offence, P is committing the (s 44) offence.

8. Does Part 2 of the SCA 2007 go too far?

Under s 8 of the Accessories and Abettors Act 1861, a person incurs liability as a secondary party even if he/she did not share the principal's *intention* that the offence 6.11

---

[9] That is to say, the Law Commission's proposed draft Bill (see Law Com No 300).
[10] para A.5.
[11] para 4.26.

would be committed (see paras 1.7–1.9, Law Com No 305). Thus, where a shop-keeper (D) sells a torch to D2, believing that the latter is likely to use the torch to commit burglary, D will be criminally liable in the event that D2 commits that offence even if D did not intend, desire, or agree that the offence should be committed. If the supply of items by the helper could give rise to secondary liability in circumstances where the principal offence is committed, then it can be argued that a person should not escape liability for encouraging or assisting the commission of an offence merely because the offence was not committed, or in circumstances where it cannot be proved whether the defendant was a perpetrator or an encourager (see s 56, SCA 2007). On the other hand, inchoate offences have often been criticised for punishing thoughts rather than deeds; Part 2 of the SCA 2007 is open to the same objection.

6.12   It is foreseeable that Part 2 of the 2007 Act could have effects not anticipated by Parliament. For example, if D sold cannabis seeds in the belief that the purchasers *would* use them to unlawfully cultivate cannabis plants,[12] would he be guilty of an inchoate offence, contrary to Part 2 of the 2007 Act, even if it cannot be proved that the seeds were planted, still less that cannabis plants were cultivated? There has been some discussion about whether an offence of 'using' a controlled drug should be enacted. Were that to happen, some consideration would have to be given to the inchoate offences enacted in ss 44–46 of the 2007 Act. For example, a person who supplied a syringe or any part of one, to another for the self-administration of an illicitly obtained controlled drug, would not have committed an offence contrary to s 9A of the Misuse of Drugs Act 1971. But, in the absence of further statutory protection (in the interests of public health and harm reduction) the question arises whether the supply of a syringe to a person for the purpose of enabling the latter to *use* illicitly obtained heroin would constitute an offence under ss 44–46 of the SCA 2007 (if the user was arrested before he could self-inject)? It would seem that the answer would be the same even if the anticipated offence had been committed because s 49(1) provides that a person may commit an offence under Part 2 whether or not any offence capable of being encouraged or assisted by his act, is committed.

B. CATEGORIES OF PERSONS WHO ARE PARTIES TO A CRIME

1. Joint perpetrators, perpetrators, and accessories

6.13   Once Part 2 of the SCA 2007 comes into force, practitioners will need to exercise care to establish whether the case is one to which (a) Part 2 of the SCA 2007 applies (or might apply), or (b) it is a case governed by s 8 of Accessories and Abettors Act 1861, or (c) it is governed by rules relating to conspiracy or attempts, or (d) it is a case where the defendant can be charged with a statutory offence of 'incitement' (eg s 19 of the Misuse of Drugs Act 1971) or with a statutory offence of 'assisting'.

---

[12] Contrary to s 6, Misuse of Drugs Act 1971.

Accordingly, when considering Part 2 of the 2007 Act, it is important to distinguish between different categories of persons who can be parties to a crime.

There has been an understandable tendency for practitioners to speak loosely   6.14
about 'joint principals', 'joint ventures', and 'accessories'. It is understandable for the reasons given by the learned authors of *Blackstone's Criminal Practice* (2008),[13] namely, that the statutory expression 'aid, abet, counsel, or procure' tends to be used *as a whole* even though the accused's conduct may be properly described only by one of the four constituent words. Advocates, as well as judges when directing juries, tend not to refer to the terms of the 1861 Act at all. There usually is no need to explain to juries any of the constitute terms in s 8 of the 1861 Act. It is submitted that Professor William Wilson is correct to say that 'at a practical level there are obvious procedural and evidential advantages in collapsing the distinction between perpetrators and other participants'—which is the practical effect of s 8 of the 1861 Act.[14]

There are times when the expressions 'joint enterprise' and 'joint venture' are used   6.15
exceedingly loosely to describe cases where persons have assisted or encouraged others to perform the *conduct element* of an offence, notwithstanding that the intention, desire, or aim, of each person differed, or each person had a different level of awareness of the essential matters that constitutes the offence in question. Two situations need to be distinguished:

(1) *Joint principals*: An offence can be committed by two or more principals (perpetrators). For example, if D and D2 unlawfully wound V, and each intended to cause V grievous bodily harm, both D and D2 are guilty as joint principals *provided* that each defendant caused or contributed to the harm inflicted upon V. Although in everyday speech it is natural to describe D and D2 as having acted 'jointly', each participant performed the *actus reus* necessary for the commission of the offence, and each had the requisite *mens rea*. Secondary liability does not arise. Each person is liable as a principal offender of the offence charged.

(2) *Accessory and principal (perpetrator) acting 'jointly'*: A person who encourages or assists another person to commit an offence is sometimes described as acting 'jointly' with the other (particularly if both persons were present at the scene of the crime), although only one person performed the *actus reus* of the offence and the parties 'either agree to commit an offence, or share with each other an intention to commit an offence and the offence is subsequently committed'.[15]

Example
D3 stabbed V, assisted by D who provided the knife, encouraged by D2 who shouted, 'stab him'.

---

[13] Chapter A.5.1.
[14] See 'A Rational Scheme of Liability for Participating in Crime' (2008) Crim LR 3.
[15] See Law Com 305, para 1.10.

6.16   Part 2 of the SCA 2007 is not concerned with joint principals (1 above) but it is concerned with the role of accessories and perpetrators.

6.17   In his celebrated *Textbook of Criminal Law*,[16] Professor Glanville Williams provided a useful diagram of the parties to a crime. It is reproduced here (with some modification):

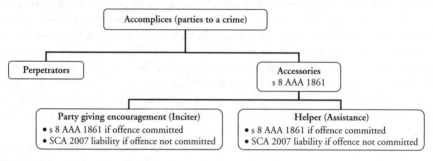

Figure 6.1

2. Expressions used to describe accomplices

6.18   In his textbook, Professor Glanville Williams was critical of the use of the expression 'principal', and he preferred the term 'perpetrator' to denote the person who commits the offence (and see Professor Williams' article 'Complicity, Purpose and the Draft Code-1' (1990) Crim LR 4). This is because the words 'principal offender' tend to convey the impression that the offender was the 'brains' behind the venture, and not the 'doer' whereas the converse is often the case. However, it is customary to adhere to the expressions 'principals' and 'accessories' and that custom has largely been followed in this book.

C. THE CASE FOR INCHOATE LIABILITY: THE ANTICIPATED OFFENCE IS NOT COMMITTED

1. Distorting offences to deal with inchoate acts of assisting/encouraging

6.19   Except for the offences of conspiracy[17] and incitement, in any other situation where D assists D2 to commit an offence, which D2 neither commits nor attempts to

---

[16] Stevens, 1978, p 285.

[17] s 1 of the Criminal Law Act 1977, or the common law offence of conspiracy to defraud (consider *Hollinshead* [1985] AC 975; and consider *GG and others* [2007] EWCA Crim 2659). Charges of conspiracy are popular with prosecutors because: (a) the ambit of the offence is broad; (b) evidence is perceived to be more readily admissible; (c) pre-trial severance of defendants is less likely; and (d) the charge can embrace, in a single

commit, D incurred no liability at common law. Conspiracy is apt to deal with many cases where D has encouraged or assisted D2 to commit an offence, which the latter ultimately did not commit. But such a charge might not be possible in circumstances where D lacked the fault element for conspiracy (eg where D gives a torch to D2 but D does not share a common intention with D2 that the latter shall commit burglary).

Professor Spencer QC has argued that some offences, notably conspiracy, have   6.20
been distorted in order to fill a gap in the law, which has been created by the absence of inchoate liability for assisting crime:

> . . . the lack of an inchoate offence of facilitation creates a theoretical gap in the criminal law
> through which undeserving rogues threaten to escape, and (which) the courts regularly plug . . .
> by bending other offences, with baleful side effects.[18]

The argument runs that the House of Lords in *Anderson* [1986] AC 27 distorted   6.21
the offence of conspiracy when it held that there could be a criminal conspiracy *which none of the conspirators intend to carry out.* This is based on the words of Lord Bridge who said 'I am clearly driven by consideration of the diversity of roles which parties may agree to play in criminal conspiracies to reject any construction of the statutory language which would require the prosecution to prove an intention on the part of each conspirator that the criminal offence or offences which will necessarily be committed by one or more of the conspirators if the agreed course of conduct is fully carried out should in fact be committed'. In an earlier decision (by three weeks), the House of Lords held in *Hollinshead* [1985] AC 975, that is was possible 'to convict of conspiracy to defraud those who contemplate that the execution of their agreement will facilitate a third party to perpetrate a fraud' (Law Com No 300, para 3.17).[19] In that case, D made a number of electrical devices known as 'black boxes' the object of which was to connect them up to electricity meters to make it appear that less electricity had been consumed that was in fact the case. The decision has been criticised on two grounds. First, that in carrying out the agreement to manufacture and to sell the boxes, the appellants had not defrauded anyone. Secondly, that the *purpose* of the accused was not to perpetrate a fraud by, for example, causing loss to an electricity board, but to make a profit (ie by manufacturing and selling devices that were intended to under-record the amounts of electricity used) (see para 3.16, Law Com No 300). It is arguable that the 'distortion' complained of has been minimized in practice because the courts have tended to step around *Anderson* (see Law Com No 300, footnote 14, para 3.13, and the cases

---

count, criminal acts that otherwise could only be reflected in multiple substantive charges and some of those might attract an application 'to sever'.

[18] per Professor Spencer QC; and see para 3.9, Law Com No 300.

[19] The Law Commission cite Professor Spencer QC as saying that the House of Lords made that possible by making 'an offence which was already vague and amorphous even more so' (*'Trying to help another person commit an offence'* in P Smith (ed) Essays in Honour of JC Smith (1987) 148, 156). The need to do so would have been obviated had there been an inchoate offence of assisting crime.

there cited, namely, *McPhillips* [1989] NI 360; *Yip-Chiu-Cheung* [1995] 1 AC 111; *Edwards* [1991] Crim LR 45; *Saik* [2006] UKHL 18; [2006] 2 WLR 993;[20] and see Smith & Hogan, *The Criminal Law*, 11th edn, pp 374–7.

6.22   The Law Commission identified a number of other arguments in support of its recommendations for 'inchoate liability for assisting'. These are (para 4.4):

(1) combating serious crime;
(2) preventing harm before harm arises;
(3) eliminating the element of chance;
(4) imposing criminal liability where a conduct is sufficiently culpable to warrant it;
(5) deterrence;
(6) coherence;
(7) labelling and punishment;
(8) restoring the proper boundaries of offences.

6.23   The arguments against inchoate liability are (para 4.12):

(1) liability for otherwise lawful conduct;
(2) premature intervention;
(3) disparity in the liability between D and P;
(4) vagueness and uncertainty.

6.24   The Law Commission concluded that the objections to a general inchoate liability for assisting crime do not withstand scrutiny (para 4.28), but they do raise important issues as to what should be the appropriate fault element for the offences now enacted in Part 2 of the SCA 2007.

2. Reforms proposed by the Law Commission: anticipated offence not committed

(a) *Inchoate liability*

6.25   In Law Com No 300 (Inchoate Liability For Assisting And Encouraging Crime), the Law Commission made the following recommendations (among others) where a person assists or encourages another person to commit an offence which the latter (for whatever reason) fails to carry out:

1. That two offences should be created, namely:
    (a) Encouraging or assisting the commission of a criminal act *intending* that the criminal act should be committed (the s 44 offence).
    (b) Encouraging or assisting the commission of a criminal act *believing* that the encouragement or assistance will encourage or assist the commission of

---

[20] Lord Nicholls said, 'The conspirators must intend to do the act prohibited by the substantive offence'.

the criminal act and *believing* that the criminal act will be committed (s 45 offence).

2. That the conduct element of each offence should consist of 'do[ing] an act capable of encouraging or assisting the doing of a criminal act' (para 5.22) and this includes:
    (a) threatening or pressurizing another person to do a criminal act (para 5.43); or
    (b) failing to take reasonable steps to discharge a duty (para 5.65).

3. That the fault element in relation to 1(a) above is that D *intends* that the criminal act should be done, or that a person be encouraged or assisted to do it (para 5.89).

4. That the fault element in relation to 1(b) above is that D, in order to be guilty of the (s 45) offence, need not intend that the criminal act should be done, but he must *believe* that the criminal act *will* be done and that his or her own act *will* encourage or assist the doing of the criminal act.

5. That the following rules should apply in cases where D's acts are capable of encouraging *more than one* criminal act (see s 46):
    (a) D must believe:
        (i) that at least one of those acts *will* be done but without having any belief as to which it will be; and
        (ii) that his or her conduct *will* encourage or assist the doing of at least one of those acts.
    (b) But D, at the discretion of the prosecuting agency, may be prosecuted for only one offence (para 5.96).

6. That in respect of each offence:
    (a) D must *believe* that, were another person to do the criminal act, that person *would* do it with the fault required for conviction of the principal offence;

    Example
    D must *believe* that D2 would take property belonging to another, but D must also *believe* that D2 intends to 'steal it'.

    or

    (b) D's state of mind must be such that, were he or she to do the criminal act, he or she *would* do it with that fault. D is to be assumed able to do the criminal act in question. This ensures that where D is, for example, physically incapable of committing the offence himself/herself, D is judged on the basis of his/her state of mind (para 5.104).

7. Where the principal offence includes a 'circumstance element' and/or a 'consequence element', D cannot be guilty of assisting or encouraging its commission unless D intended or believed that it would be done in those circumstances always or with those consequences (para 5.118).

8. D should only be guilty of inciting D2 to incite X if D *intended* that D2 should do so, or that D2 should be encouraged to incite X (para 7.11).

(b) *Defences and exemptions*

6.26 The Law Commission recommended that it should be a defence to either offence (now ss 44–46) if D proves:

(1) that D acted for the purpose of preventing the commission of either the offence that he or she was encouraging or assisting, or that D acted to prevent the commission of another offence (para 6.16); *or*

(2) that D acted to prevent or limit the occurrence of harm; *and*

(3) that it was reasonable to act as D did in the circumstances.

6.27 In relation to the s 45 offence—rooted in D's belief—the Law Commission recommended that it should be a defence for D to prove that his/her conduct was reasonable in the circumstances as he/she knew or reasonably believed them to be (para 6.26).

3. Reforms proposed by the Law Commission: anticipated offence actually committed

(a) *Secondary liability—where D2 commits an offence*

6.28 In Law Com No 305 (Participating in Crime), the Law Commission recommended:

1. That s 8 of the Accessories and Abettors Act 1861, and s 44(1) of the Magistrates' Courts Act 1980 should be repealed (para 3.10).

2. 'Encouraging' should include acts designed to embolden, threaten, or to pressurize another person to carry out a criminal act (para 3.15).

3. To prove liability as a secondary party (where D assists D2 to commit an offence, and D2 does commit it):
   (i) D must intend D2 to commit the *conduct element* of the principal offence (para 3.91); but
   (ii) D need not intend that it should be D2 who commits the principal offence (para 3.95);
   (iii) D must either (para 3.122):
      (a) believe that D2 in committing the conduct of the offence would be committing the offence; or
      (b) have it in mind that were he to commit the conduct element of the offence, he would commit the offence.

4. In respect of an alleged 'joint criminal venture'
(1) D must either (para. 3.59):
      (a) agree with D2 to commit an offence;
      (b) share with D2 a common intention to commit an offence.

(2) The fault element is satisfied if:
      (a) D intended that D2 (or X) should commit the conduct element;
      (b) D believed that D2 (or X) would commit the conduct element; or

(c) D believed that D2 (or X) might commit the conduct elements (para 3.151).

(3) D is not liable if D2's actions fall outside the scope of the joint enterprise (para 3.166).

D. EXTERNAL ELEMENTS OF AN OFFENCE

1. Understanding Part 2 of the SCA 2007 by understanding the elements of an offence

The Law Commission approached the issue of secondary liability, and inchoate liability, with reference to the 'essential elements' of an offence (consider *Johnson v Youden* [1950] 1 KB 544). It is helpful to follow the approach of the Law Commission when considering Part 2 of the SCA 2007.[21]   6.29

The *actus reus* of an offence can consist of one, two, or three external elements: 6.30

(1) the *conduct element* (which D must know), eg appropriating property;

(2) the *circumstance element* (which D must know), eg that the property belongs to another; and

(3) the *consequence element* (which D must know except in respect of 'constructive liability offences' eg murder, manslaughter, s 18 of the Offences Against the Person Act 1861; see Law Com No 305, para 2.60; and see *Rook* [1993] 97 Cr App R 327.

The *mens rea* of a secondary party is that D must: 6.31

(i) *intend* to encourage or assist D2 to commit an offence (or, in the case of 'procuring', to bring about the commission of the offence); and

(ii) when D encouraged or assisted D2 to perform the *conduct element* of the offence, D must 'know' that D2 *would* (not might) perform that element.

In relation to (i) above, it will be seen that s 44 of the SCA 2007 is based on an intention to encourage or to assist another to commit an offence. Thus, for the purposes of s 44 there must be (a) an intention on the part of the accused to do the act which is *capable* of encouraging/assisting, eg by deliberately supplying a jemmy to D2, and (b) an intention that his acts will encourage or assist, eg knowing that D2 will use the jemmy to commit burglary. It seems that it need not be proved (for the purposes of secondary liability at least) that it was D's purpose to encourage or to assist the perpetrator to commit the offence but that D's knowledge that his act will assist is sufficient.[22] It is arguable that the law should be the same with respect to the s 44 offence.   6.32

---

21 And see Smith & Hogan, *The Criminal Law*, 11th edn, p 179.

22 See Smith & Hogan, *The Criminal Law*, 11th edn, p 179; and see 'Participating in Crime', Law Com No 305, paras 2.63–2.69.

6.33   In relation to (ii) above, the word 'know' must be qualified because, as the Law
Commission points out, the courts have diluted 'the stringent fault requirement of
knowledge' with regard to the *conduct element* of an offence. The case law, said the
Law Commission, reveals at least four levels of awareness that constitute 'something less
than a belief that P will commit the *conduct element*' of an offence. The tests are:[23]

(1) *Belief* that P might commit the conduct element (*Blakely and Sutton v DPP*
[1991] RTR 405).
(2) *Foresight of the risk* of a strong possibility that P will commit it (*Reardon* [1999]
Crim LR 392).
(3) *Contemplation of the risk* of a real possibility that P will commit it (*Bryce* [2004]
EWCA Crim 1231, (2004) 2 Cr App R 35); and
(4) *Foresight that it is likely* that P will commit it (*Webster* [2006] EWCA Crim 415,
(2006) 2 Cr App R 6).

2. Must D encourage or assist a 'criminal act' (Law Com), or 'an offence' (Part 2, SCA 2007)?

6.34   The approach of the Law Commission and Parliament differs significantly in relation
to what it is that D must do in order to be guilty of encouraging or assisting an
offence that D had anticipated D2 would commit.

6.35   At the heart of the Law Commission's proposed offences (see cls 1 and 2 of the
Draft Bill, Law Com No 300, p 147) is the element that D 'does an act capable of
encouraging or assisting the doing of a *criminal act*'. The Law Commission chose
the expression 'criminal act' having regard to the three external elements that make
up an offence, namely (a) the conduct element, (b) the circumstance element, and
(c) the consequence element. Thus, references made by the Law Commission to a
'criminal act' are references to the *conduct element* of the offence, without reference
to the *circumstance* or *consequence* elements (if any) of that offence.[24]

Example 1
D assists D2 by giving the latter a knife believing that D2 will use it to stab V (conduct), but
V dies (consequence).

Example 2
D supplies D2 with a hammer knowing that the latter will use it to smash a window belonging
to another. Wielding a hammer (conduct) which results in damage to property (consequence)
belonging to another (circumstance), are all matters relevant to the actus reus of the offence of
criminal damage.

6.36   By contrast, ss 44–46 of the SCA 2007 refer to acts that are capable of encouraging
or assisting the commission of '*an offence*'. The key word here is 'offence'. This is

---

[23] 'Participating in Crime', Law Com No 305, para 2.65.
[24] See cl 17(2), Draft Bill, Law Com No 300.

wide enough to embrace acts which are referable to *all* the elements of an offence, including the fault element. It might be said, reasonably enough, that the wording of Part 2 of the SCA 2007 has the advantage of limiting the number of arguments that might be advanced regarding whether an act is 'criminal' or not. However, for reasons that will be explained in this commentary, that does not mean that legal practitioners can disregard any consequence element, or any circumstance element, that exists with respect to the anticipated offence.

E. TERMS AND CONCEPTS FOR THE PURPOSES OF PART 2 OF THE SCA 2007

1. Several key words and phrases are not defined in Part 2 of the SCA 2007

A number of key words are not defined in the Act, notably 'capable of', 'act', 'encourag-   6.37
ing', and 'assisting'. The Explanatory Notes that accompany the Act are helpful but they give only a brief description of the operation of the provisions to this Part of the Act. The reader is strongly recommended to read the Law Commission Report No 300 as an aid to construction. However, for reasons that are set out in this chapter, there are a number of differences (intended by Parliament or otherwise) between the Law Commission's proposals and the measures enacted in Part 2 of the SCA 2007.

2. Encouraging

The word 'encouraging' is not defined by the 2007 Act, so it will be left to the courts   6.38
to define it. Presumably, Parliament is confident that the courts, like the Law Commission, will conclude that 'encouraging' should have the same broad meaning which 'inciting' had acquired at common law (Law Com 300, para 5.37; *Goldman* [2001] Crim LR 822). In *Invicta Plastics Limited v Clare* [1976] RTR 251, the Divisional Court adopted the definition of 'incitement' given by Lord Denning MR in *Race Relations Board v Aplin* [1973] 1 QB 815, namely, 'to spur on by advice, encouragement or persuasion' but it is not every encouragement which necessarily amounts to incitement.[25] For a wider discussion about the current preference for 'encourage' over 'incite', see the article by Professor William Wilson, 'A Rational Scheme of Liability for Participating in Crime' (2008) Crim LR 3.

It is not entirely clear whether, for the purposes of ss 44 and 45 of the 2007 Act,   6.39
it must be proved that the 'perpetrator' (D2) heard, or was aware of, the words of encouragement that were spoken to him by the defendant, or that D2 was aware that he/she was being assisted. The Law Commission was of the view that it is immaterial if no one was aware of the defendant's words of encouragement

---

[25] See Smith & Hogan, *The Criminal Law*, 11th edn, p 351.

(Law Com No 300, para 5.29). This is to be contrasted with the position at common law and under statute in relation to the offence of incitement (the common law offence has been abolished by s 59 of the SCA 2007, but the statutory offences have been preserved). For incitement, it is necessary that the incitement should have been communicated (*Banks* (1873) 12 Cox CC 393, and see Smith & Hogan, *The Criminal Law*, 11th edn, p 352). The learned editors of *Blackstones' Criminal Practice* suggest that 'a total failure to communicate, as where written incitement is intercepted by the police, arguably amounts only to an attempt to incite (*Ransford* (1874) 13 Cox CC 9; *Krause* (1902) 66 JP 121)'.[26]

6.40   The Law Commission also recommended[27] that the word 'encouraging' should include 'instigating', 'persuading', 'threatening',[28] and 'coercing', as well as embracing conduct which 'emboldens a person who has already decided to commit an offence'. There need not be actual encouragement—this is apparent from the fact that the 'act' need only be 'capable of' encouraging or assisting another person to commit an offence.

3. Assisting

6.41   The word 'assisting' is not comprehensively defined by the Serious Crime Act 2007, but the expression includes acts that are designed to reduce the possibility of criminal proceedings being brought in respect of that offence (s 65(2)(a), SCA 2007). A person may also 'assist' by failing to take reasonable steps to discharge a duty (s 65(2)(b), SCA 2007). But a person does not do an act that is 'capable of encouraging or assisting the commission of an offence' merely by failing to respond to a constable's request for assistance in preventing a breach of the peace (s 65(3), SCA 2007).[29] The Law Commission's Consultation Paper said that assisting in its normal sense 'extends to any conduct on the part of D that, as a matter of fact, makes it easier for P to commit the principal offence' (Consultation Paper No 131, para 4.48; para 5.46, Law Com No 300). For a wider discussion about the use of the word 'assist' in the context of secondary liability, see the article by Professor William Wilson, 'A Rational Scheme of Liability for Participating in Crime' (2008) Crim LR 3.

6.42   The assistance need not be substantial. As the Law Commission pointed out:[30]

Inchoate liability is not dependent on the commission of a substantive offence. D's liability turns not on what P does but on what D intends or believes will be the impact of his or her conduct. We think that to introduce such a requirement would lead to uncertainty and difficulty. It would require juries and magistrates to 'seek to assess how extensive a contribution the assistance would have been (or was) in bringing about the principal offence'. Accordingly, D should be liable if his

---

[26] (2008), para A.6.5.
[27] See Law Com No 300, para 5.37; adhering to its view expressed in the Consultation Paper.
[28] See s 65(1), SCA 2007.
[29] See the recommendations of the Law Commission (Law Com No 300, para 5.46); and see *Attorney-General v Able* (1984) QB 795.
[30] Law Com No 300, para 5.5.

or her act is capable of assisting (or encouraging) another person to any extent. The marginal nature of any assistance or encouragement can be reflected in the sentence.

The Commission added:[31]   6.43

We think that to introduce such a requirement [that assistance is substantial] would lead to uncertainty and difficulty. It would require juries and magistrates to 'seek to assess how extensive a contribution the assistance would have been (or was) in bringing about the principal offence'. Accordingly, D should be liable if his or her act is capable of assisting (or encouraging) another person to any extent. The marginal nature of any assistance or encouragement can be reflected in the sentence.

4. Indirect encouraging/assisting

Note that a person may indirectly encourage (or assist) a person to commit an   6.44
offence. Section 66 of the SCA 2007 has been enacted to ensure that indirect
encouragement or assistance is encompassed by ss 44–46 of the SCA 2007:

If a person (D) arranges for a person (D2) to do an act that is capable of encouraging or assisting the commission of an offence, and D2 does the act, D is also to be treated for the purposes of this Part as having done it.

Section 66 of the SCA 2007 mirrors cl 16 of the Law Commission's draft Bill.   6.45
The Law Commission explained the purpose of that provision by way of the following example (para A.95, Law Com No 300):

. . . if D arranges for another person (D2) to do something which has the capacity to encourage or assist another person to commit a criminal act, then D is also to be regarded as having done D2's act. Thus, a person such as a gang leader can be held liable for the encouragement or assistance provided by a member of his gang in carrying out his instructions.

5. When is 'procuring' not 'encouraging' or 'assisting'?

In Law Com No 300, the Law Commission states that whilst 'counsel' means to   6.46
'encourage', the expression 'procure' is 'an anomalous "niche" form of secondary
liability'.[32] At para 2.22 of Law Com No 305 ('Participating in Crime'), the Law
Commission states that '(it) is doubtful if all cases of 'procuring' can be described
properly as involving the provision of assistance or encouragement'. The Law
Commission points out that in *A-G's Reference (No 1 of 1975)*[33] the Court of Appeal
said 'To procure means to produce by endeavour . . . Causation here is important.
You cannot procure an offence unless there is a causal link between what you do and
the commission of the offence.' This case is treated as firm law, although it is not
without interest that Professor Glanville Williams in his textbook, *Criminal Law,*

---

[31] Law Com No 300, para 5.51.
[32] Law Com No 300, para B.7, footnote 6.
[33] (1975) QB 773.

thought there might be 'doubt whether the decision was put on the right basis'. For him, the proper basis of the decision was that of 'aiding and abetting'.[34] However, the decision of the Court in *A-G's Reference (No 1 of 1975)* is now well established. The view of the Law Commission seems to be that some cases of 'procuring' cannot be aptly described as involving the provision of 'assistance' or 'encouragement'. If that is so, does that mean that some cases of 'procuring' fall outside (or might fall outside) the language of Part 2 of the SCA 2007? If the answer is in the affirmative, then a potential gap remains in the law that is not filled by the wording of Part 2 of the SCA 2007. How significant that gap is (if it does exist) is debatable.

6. Meaning of an 'act', 'doing of an act', and related expressions in Part 2 of the SCA 2007

(a) *Exercise care with the expressions 'the act', 'his act', 'does an act', 'doing of an act'*

6.47 Care needs to be taken over the expressions, 'the act', 'his act', 'an act', 'does an act', and 'doing of an act' as they appear in Part 2 of the SCA 2007. This is because the expressions are not used consistently throughout Part 2. In some places, an expression (eg 'an act') refers to the alleged offender ('D'), but in other places, the same expression refers to the perpetrator of the anticipated offence. Three important instances where this occurs are considered below.

(1) First, in ss 44–46 of the SCA 2007, references to 'an act', and 'his act' are clearly references to the acts of the person who gave encouragement or assistance. But when one looks at s 47 (proving an offence under the Act), the words 'an act' now refer to the acts of the perpetrator. For example, s 47(3) states that if D 'believed . . . that his act would encourage or assist its commission . . . it is sufficient to prove that he believed . . . that *an act* would be done which would amount to the commission of an offence.' Suppose D assists D2 by giving him a jemmy. D intends or believes that D2 will use the jemmy to gain access to a building. D's act of assistance is 'an act' for the purpose of ss 44–46. But in the context of s 47(3), the use of the jemmy by D2 to commit burglary is 'an act . . . which would amount to the commission of that offence' (in this instance, burglary).

(2) A distinction must be noted between the expression 'does an act' (ss 44–46) and 'doing of an act' (s 47). It will be seen that references in ss 44–46 to the person who 'does an act', are references to the person who gives encouragement or assistance (D). However, and somewhat confusingly, s 47(8) states that reference in s 47 to the 'doing of an act' includes reference to:
   (a) a failure to act;
   (b) the continuation of an act that has already begun;
   (c) an attempt to do an act (except an act amounting to the commission of the offence of attempting to commit another offence).

---

[34] *Textbook of Criminal Law*, p 291, Stevens, 1978; and see the commentary to *Sutton v DPP* [1991] Crim LR 763.

It is easy to fall into the trap of thinking that s 47(8) means that D can encourage or assist the commission of an offence in one of the three ways mentioned in (a)–(c) above. However, when s 47 is read in full, it is plain that the phrase 'doing of an act' for the purpose of that section, refers to an act performed by the perpetrator and not by D. It is further submitted that the 'doing of the act' refers to the *conduct element* of the *actus reus* of the anticipated offence. For example, under s 47(2), it must be proved that D intended to 'encourage or assist the *doing of an act* which would amount to the commission of that offence', ie an act done by the anticipated perpetrator, for example entering premises as a trespasser.

(3) Note that s 47(8)(a) must not be confused with s 65(2)(b) of the SCA 2007. This is because both provisions refer to the 'doing' of an act, and both provisions relate to a 'failure' to act. But whereas s 47(8)(a) is directed at the inaction of the perpetrator, s 65(2)(b) is referring to the helper! It will be seen that s 65(2)(b) states that a reference in Part 2 of the 2007 Act to a person '*doing an act* that is capable of encouraging or assisting the commission of an offence' includes '*failing to take reasonable steps* to discharge a duty'.[35]

(b) An act of encouragement or assistance need not be inherently illegal

The 'act' performed by D need not itself be illegal (eg supplying a torch, or a ladder to another). Relevant acts would include, for example, written and oral communications, the placing of material on the Internet, or distributing leaflets. Context is all-important. If D supplied D2 with bolt croppers to cut the shackle of a padlock, D's actions may well be lawful if the padlock belonged to D2 but not if D1 knew that D2 would use the bolt croppers to break into a warehouse to steal therein.   6.48

(c) Acts as a 'course of conduct'

An 'act' includes a 'course of conduct' (s 67) (mirroring cl 17(1) of the Law Commission's draft Bill). The Law Commission state that D could be liable under Part 2 of the SCA 2007 'if he does a number of acts, none of which would be regarded as having the capacity to encourage or assist the doing of a criminal act, if the cumulative effect of D's course of conduct would be regarded as having the capacity to encourage or assist'.[36]   6.49

7. Meaning of an act 'capable of encouraging or assisting'

(a) Actual encouragement/assistance need not be proved

The act need not actually encourage or assist. It is enough that it is *capable* of doing so. This reflects the provision in relation to the offence of incitement (at common   6.50

---

[35] The Law Commission believed that confining liability to positive acts 'would result in D incurring no criminal liability in situations where he or she ought to, for example D, a disgruntled security guard, who fails to turn on a burglar alarm with the intention of assisting P to burgle the premises of D's employer'.

[36] Law Com No 300, para A.101, footnote 108.

law or under statute) (see eg *Higgins* (1801) 2 East 5, 102 ER 269). Whether an act is capable of assisting or encouraging is question of fact and degree. If D, knowing that D2 intends to escape from prison, sends a game card to D2 marked 'get out of jail free', D cannot sensibly be said to have done anything that was capable of assisting D2 in his criminal venture and, on that basis, it would be fanciful to allege that D, by so acting, had 'encouraged' D2!

(b) *Perpetrator may be unaware of the fact of encouragement/assistance*

6.51 It is submitted that an actor is capable of assisting even if the perpetrator is unaware of that fact (see para 5.29, Law Com No 300). For example, where a person distributes leaflets which are capable of encouraging others to commit criminal damage (with the requisite fault element), it is immaterial that all the leaflets are gathered up and destroyed by litter attendants who have not read any of them.

(c) *Acts capable of encouraging, contrasted with 'inchoate-upon-inchoate' conduct*

6.52 There may be circumstances in which a distinction needs to be drawn between an act that is 'capable of encouraging or assisting' the commission of an offence (and which gives rise to inchoate liability under Part 2 of the SCA 2007) and an act that constitutes only an attempt to 'encourage or to assist' the commission of an offence (ie inchoate-upon-inchoate). However, the words 'capable of encouraging or assisting' are broad, and it will surely be rare for anyone to be tried on the basis of an attempt to contravene s 44 or s 45 of the SCA 2007.

(d) *There must be an act and a state of mind specified in s 47*

6.53 The SCA 2007 requires D to act with one of the states of mind described in s 47(2), (3), or (4), and s 47(5). Typically, the prosecution will be required to prove that D intended or believed that the perpetrator *will* (not might) commit the anticipated offence (or, more accurately, that he will commit the *conduct element* of the offence), and D *believes* that the act will be carried out (or he is *reckless* as to whether the act will be carried out) by the perpetrator, with the fault/circumstances/consequences that must exist in order for the full offence to be committed.

(e) *Acts specified in s 65 as being capable of encouraging/assisting the commission of an offence*

6.54 Section 65(2) of the SCA 2007 makes specific provision to include three situations that constitute acts 'capable of encouraging or assisting' the commission of an offence, namely:

(1) by threatening another person 'or otherwise putting pressure on another person' to commit the offence (s 65(1));

80

(2) by taking steps to reduce the possibility of criminal proceedings being brought in respect of that offence (s 65(1)(a));

(3) by failing to take reasonable steps to discharge a duty (s 65(2)(b)).

The third situation is discussed further below.

(f) *Failing to take reasonable steps to discharge a duty (s 65(2)(b))*

Section 65(2) gives effect to the Law Commission's recommendation that the incho- 6.55
ate offences enacted in ss 44–46 of the SCA 2007:

should be capable of being committed by virtue of inaction on the part of D that consists of refraining from taking steps to discharge a duty. Confining liability to positive acts would result in D incurring no criminal liability in situations where he or she ought to.[37]

It is submitted that s 65(2)(b) is intended to deal with cases where D *deliberately* 6.56
failed to take reasonable steps to discharge a duty (and thereby gave encouragement
or assistance), but it does not apply where D failed to discharge a duty through inad-
vertence or forgetfulness (eg D a disgruntled security guard, fails to turn on a burglar
alarm with the intention of assisting P to burgle the premises of D's employer).[38]
Whether a duty existed is a matter of law to be decided by the judge. Whether there
had been a failure to take reasonable steps to discharge a duty, is a question of fact.

The Law Commission and Parliament drew the line at holding a person culpable 6.57
where he/she fails to respond to a constable's request for assistance to prevent a
breach of the peace.[39] Accordingly, s 65(3) provides:

But a person is not to be regarded as doing an act that is capable of encouraging or assisting the commission of an offence merely because he fails to respond to a constable's request for assistance in preventing a breach of the peace.

F. THE INCHOATE OFFENCES: ELEMENTS AND DEFENCES

1. Intentionally encouraging or assisting an offence (s 44)

(a) *The offence*

Section 44 of the SCA 2007 provides: 6.58

(1) A person commits an offence if—
    (a) he does an act capable of encouraging or assisting the commission of an offence; and
    (b) he intends to encourage or assist its commission.

---

[37] Law Com 300, para 5.62.
[38] Law Com No 300, para 5.62; Law Com No 305, para 3.34.
[39] *Brown* (1841) Car & M 314, 174 ER 522; see Law Com No 300, para 5.66.

(2) But he is not to be taken to have intended to encourage or assist the commission of an offence merely because such encouragement or assistance was a foreseeable consequence of his act.

Example

D provides D2 with a torch. D knows that D2 is a habitual burglar, and he knows and *intends* that D2 *will* use the torch to commit at least one act of burglary. D does not intend to be present with D2 in the event that the latter steals property as a trespasser on premises. D2 dies before he commits any offence.

6.59   This section must be read together with s 47(2), (5), (7), (8), and s 49(1) and (2). Section 47(2) describes one set of circumstances in which an offence under s 44 may be committed with the requisite state of mind (see s 47(5)). Section 49(1) states, in terms, that a person may commit an offence under s 44 whether or not the anticipated offence is actually committed. Section 49(2) provides that if D's act is capable of encouraging or assisting the commission of a number of offences, then s 44 will apply separately in relation to each offence that he intends to encourage or assist to be committed. Thus, to elaborate:

(1) D must intend to encourage or to assist D2 to commit the anticipated offence (that is to say, it is D's purpose to encourage or to assist D2);

(2) D must have one of the states of mind set out in s 47(5):
   (a) if the offence is one requiring proof of fault, it must be proved that:
      (i) D *believed* that, were the act to be done, it would be done with that fault;
      (ii) D was *reckless* as to whether or not it would be done with that fault; or
      (iii) D's state of mind was such that, were he to do it, it would be done with that fault; and
   (b) if the offence is one requiring proof of particular circumstances or consequences (or both), it must be proved that:
      (i) D *intended or believed*[40] that, were the act to be done, it would be done in those circumstances or with those consequences; or
      (ii) D was *reckless* as to whether or not it would be done in those circumstances or with those consequences.

(3) D can face multiple counts under s 44 flowing from one act of encouragement or assistance (eg where D provides D2 with an official 'stamp' that assists D2 to ostensibly 'authenticate' a number of instruments, which are in fact false).

The mental element that must be proved with respect to the 'helper' is the subject of detailed consideration at paras **6.96** et seq.

---

[40] See s 47(7)(a) of the Serious Crime Act 2007, which modifies the wording of s 47(5)(b)(i) for the purposes of s 44 of the Act.

(b) *Inchoate liability for encouraging or assisting an inchoate offence*

Note that for the purposes of the offence under s 44 (and not for the purposes of   6.60
s 45 or s 46), D may also be convicted under this section if, for example:

(1) D does an act that is capable of encouraging or assisting D2 and D3 to *conspire*
     to commit an offence; or

(2) D does an act that is capable of encouraging or assisting another person (D2) to
     attempt to commit an offence; or

(3) D does an act that is capable of encouraging/assisting D2 to do an act which is
     capable of assisting or encouraging D3 to commit a crime. For example, D (inten-
     tionally) encourages D2 to hire D3 to firebomb V's house, but D3 is arrested
     before he can commit the offence of arson.

The position under s 44 is to be contrasted with that under s 45 and s 46.

(c) *Defences and exceptions*

By s 44(2), a person is not to be taken as having intended to encourage or to assist   6.61
the commission of an offence merely because such encouragement or assistance was
a foreseeable consequence of his act. Section 44(2) is modelled on cl 18 (1) of the
Law Commission's draft Bill. The provision is designed to make clear that the
defendant's 'intention' refers to his purpose (see para A.100, Law Com No 300; and
see the Explanatory Notes). It is a defence for D to prove that he acted reasonably
(s 50, SCA 2007)—see below for an explanation of this defence. D cannot be
convicted if he comes within the 'protected category' of persons for whom the
anticipated offence was intended to protect.

2. Encouraging/assisting; believing an offence will be committed (s 45)

(a) *Elements of the offence*

The accused (D) will be liable under s 45 of the SCA 2007 in the following   6.62
circumstances:

(1) D *does an act* (eg giving a jemmy to D2) which is capable of encouraging or
     assisting the commission of an offence (eg burglary) (s 45(a)); and

(2) D *believes* that the anticipated offence *will* be committed (eg burglary)
     (s 45(b)(i)); and

(3) D *believes* that his act (eg giving the jemmy to D2) *will* encourage or assist the
     commission of the offence, or more accurately that it will assist D2 to commit
     the conduct element of the offence (s 45(b)(ii)); and

(4) D believes that an act will be done (eg D2 uses the jemmy to enter property
     belonging to another) which 'would amount to the commission' of the anti-
     cipated offence (eg burglary) (s 47(3)(a)).

(5) It is sufficient to prove that D believed that 'his act' (ie D's act) would encourage or assist the doing of 'that act' (eg D2's act in using the jemmy to enter property) (s 47(3)(b)); and

(6) at the time that he believed that the act would be done (ie an act done by D2), D had one of the states of mind described in s 47(5), that is to say:
    (a) if the offence is one requiring proof of fault, it must be proved that:
        (i)   D *believed* that, were the act to be done, it would be done with that fault;
        (ii) D was *reckless* as to whether or not it would be done with that fault; or
        (iii) D's state of mind was such that, were he to do it, it would be done with that fault; and
    (b) if the offence is one requiring proof of particular circumstances or consequences (or both), it must be proved that:
        (i)   D *believed* that, were the act to be done, it would be done in those circumstances or with those consequences; or
        (ii) D was *reckless* as to whether or not it would be done in those circumstances or with those consequences.

The mental element that must be proved with respect to the 'helper' is the subject of detailed consideration at paras **6.96** et seq.

(b) *No inchoate liability for encouraging or assisting an inchoate offence*

6.63 A number of offences which, but for s 49(4)(b) of the SCA 2007, would be regarded as 'anticipated'/principal offences for the purposes of Part 2, are to be 'disregarded'. These are the offences listed in Parts 1, 2, and 3 of Sch 3 (England and Wales) and those offences listed in Parts 1, 4, and 5 (Northern Ireland) of that Schedule, as well as those created under Part 2 (ie ss 44–46). The offences are, for the most part, statutory offences of incitement (eg s 19 of the Misuse of Drugs Act 1971; solicitation of murder, promoting or attempting to promote industrial unrest). This aspect of the legislation is considered in detail at paras **6.92** et seq.

6.64 Accordingly, unlike the offence under s 44 of the SCA 2007, D cannot be convicted under s 45 by, for example:

(1) doing an act that is capable of encouraging or assisting D2 and D3 to *conspire* to commit an offence, believing that the offence (conspiracy) will be committed; or

(2) doing an act that is capable of encouraging or assisting another person (D2) to *attempt* to commit an offence, believing that the offence (attempt) will be committed; or

(3) doing an act that is capable of encouraging/assisting D2 to do act which is *capable of assisting* D3 to commit a crime.

(c) *Defences and exemptions*

6.65 It is a defence for D to prove that he acted reasonably (s 50, SCA 2007)—see below for an explanation of this defence.

D cannot be convicted if he comes within the 'protected category' of persons for whom the anticipated offence was intended to protect. 6.66

3. Encouraging or assisting one or more offences (s 46)

(a) *Purpose of the s 46 offence*

Section 46 of the SCA 2007 is intended to deal with a situation that arose in *Director of Public Prosecutions for Northern Ireland v Maxwell*.[41] A useful illustration was provided by the Law Commission:[42] 6.67

D, a taxi driver, is asked by a group of armed men to drive to a public house in the East End of London. D believes that they *will* commit an offence of violence and, from their comments to each other, he concludes that the offence *might* be robbery or it *might* be causing grievous bodily harm with intent.

(b) *Elements of the offence*

The accused (D) will be liable under s 46 of the SCA 2007 in the following circumstances: 6.68

(1) D *does an act* (eg giving a jemmy to D2) which is capable of encouraging or assisting the commission of one or more of a number of offences (eg one or more burglaries) (s 46(1)(a)); and

(2) D *believes* that one or more anticipated offences *will* be committed (but has no belief as to which one will be committed) (s 46(1)(b)(i)); and

(3) D *believes* that his act (eg giving the jemmy to D2) *will* encourage or assist the commission of at least one offence (s 46(1)(b)(ii)).

(4) It is sufficient to prove that:
   (a) D believes that at least one act will be done (eg D2 uses the jemmy to enter property belonging to another) which 'would amount to the commission' of at least one anticipated offence (eg burglary) (s 47(4)(a)); and
   (b) D believed that 'his act' (ie D's act) would encourage or assist the doing of one or more of 'those acts' (eg D2 would use the jemmy to enter property) (s 47(4)(b)); and

(5) at the time that D believed that at least one of those acts would be done (ie by D2), D had one of the states of mind described in s 47(5), that is to say:
   (a) if the offence is one requiring proof of fault, it must be proved that—
      (i) D *believed* that, were the act to be done, it would be done with that fault;
      (ii) D was *reckless* as to whether or not it would be done with that fault; or

---

[41] [1978] 1 WLR 1350.
[42] Law Com No 300, para A.52.

      (iii) D's state of mind was such that, were he to do it, it would be done with that fault; and

    (b) if the offence is one requiring proof of particular circumstances or consequences (or both), it must be proved that:

      (i) D *believed* that, were the act to be done, it would be done in those circumstances or with those consequences; or

      (ii) D was *reckless* as to whether or not it would be done in those circumstances or with those consequences.

6.69   It follows that s 46 must be read together with s 47(4), (5), s 48, and s 49(4). As with ss 44 and 45, the Law Commission used the expression 'criminal act' rather than 'an offence'. Nevertheless, there is value in analysing a given case by focusing on the conduct element of an offence. For example, if D provides D2 with a face mask and gloves in the belief that D2 will use them to appropriate property belonging to another and he believes that D2 will act either with the fault for burglary, or with the fault for robbery—but he has no fixed belief about which offence D2 will commit—then D will still be liable pursuant to s 46.

6.70   The mental element that must be proved with respect to the 'helper' is the subject of detailed consideration at paras **6.96** et seq.

(c) *Procedural/evidential considerations*

6.71   It is not necessary for the prosecution to specify in the indictment every offence that D potentially might have encouraged or assisted, but the indictment must specify all the offences which the Crown alleges D contemplated might be committed (s 46(3)).

Example[43]

D lends a van to P believing that one of robbery or arson will be committed. The indictment must specify robbery and arson. However, this does not mean that every offence that could have been encouraged or assisted must be specified (subs (3)(b)).

6.72   The prosecution need only prove that D believed that at least one of those offences would have been committed (s 46(1)(b)), and it is immaterial that D did not have a settled/fixed belief as to which offence would be encouraged or assisted (s 46(2)).

(d) *No inchoate liability for encouraging or assisting an inchoate offence*

6.73   A number of offences which, but for s 49(4)(b) of the SCA 2007, would be regarded as 'anticipated'/principal offences for the purposes of Part 2 of the SCA 2007, are to be 'disregarded'. These are the offences listed in Parts 1, 2, and 3 of Sch 3 (England and Wales) and those offences listed in Parts 1, 4, and 5 (Northern Ireland) of that Schedule, as well as those created under Part 2 (ie ss 44–46). The offences are, for

---

[43] Based on the example provided in the Explanatory Notes which accompany the SCA 2007, see para 151.

the most part, statutory offences of incitement (eg s 19 of the Misuse of Drugs Act 1971; solicitation of murder; promoting or attempting to promote industrial unrest). For an expanded commentary regarding s 49(4), see paras **6.92** et seq.

Accordingly, unlike the offence under s 44 of the SCA 2007, D cannot be convicted under s 46 by, for example: 6.74

(1) doing an act that is capable of encouraging or assisting D2 and D3 to *conspire* to commit an offence, believing that the offence (conspiracy) will be committed; or

(2) doing an act that is capable of encouraging or assisting another person (D2) to *attempt* to commit an offence, believing that the offence (attempt) will be committed; or

(3) doing an act that is capable of encouraging/assisting D2 to do an act which is *capable of assisting* D3 to commit a crime.

(e) *Defences, exceptions*

It is a defence for D to prove that he acted reasonably (s 50, SCA 2007)—see below for an explanation of this defence.   6.75

D cannot be convicted if he comes within the 'protected category' of persons for whom the anticipated offence was intended to protect—see below for an explanation of this defence.   6.76

G. CATEGORIES OF ANTICIPATED OFFENCES SUSCEPTIBLE TO PART 2 OF THE SCA 2007

1. Encouraging or assisting the commission of a substantive offence

The 'crime' encouraged or assisted will usually be a substantive offence, eg robbery. There might be circumstances in which D cannot be proved to have conspired with D2.   6.77

Example
D sold an imitation *Luger* to D2, knowing that D2 wanted the 'weapon' in order to carry out a bank robbery. D2 was arrested by police before he could commit the offence. D intended to make a profit from the sale of the imitation firearm to D2. D did not wish to commit the robbery himself, and he did not agree with D2 that the latter should carry out a robbery. D would have sold the imitation firearm to D2 regardless of the latter's purpose. However, D knew of D2's purpose with respect to the weapon and therefore, in that context, D intended to assist D2 to commit the substantive offence of robbery.

2. Encouraging or assisting the commission of a conspiracy

(a) *The position under Part 2 of the SCA 2007*

The Law Commission and Parliament were of the view that D should be liable for doing an act that is capable of encouraging or assisting D2, to *conspire to commit*   6.78

an offence (or to *attempt to commit* an offence) if, but only if, it was D's *intention* (purpose) that D2 should conspire/attempt to commit the offence.[44] Section 44 of the SCA 2007 achieves that result. D may be liable if he/she encourages or assists the commission of an inchoate offence, eg a conspiracy to commit an offence, or (rarely) an attempt to do so, but *only if* it was D's *intention* (purpose) to encourage or to assist D2 to commit the inchoate offence.[45]

6.79   Sections 45 and 46 are to be distinguished from s 44 in this regard. By virtue of s 49(4), there is no liability under either s 45 or s 46 if a person merely *believes* that his/her act is capable of encouraging or assisting D2 to conspire/attempt to commit an offence.

Example

> D owned a cottage in a remote part of Cornwall. D, knowing that 'Goldfinger' and 'Scaramanger' were looking for a quiet place to meet in order that the two men could agree a plan to steal gold from a London bank, suggested that G and S should rent out his cottage for that purpose. G and S rented the cottage but the robbery plan was foiled by police. D had no wish to join a conspiracy to rob, he merely wished to rent out his cottage at a premium rate.

Note that, in this illustration, D does not himself seek to join the conspiracy, he merely intends to assist others who do wish to enter into one.

(b) *Shifting reasoning*

6.80   The reasoning behind the approach mentioned above, is as follows. Prior to the enactment of the Criminal Law Act 1977, it was an offence at common law to incite (encourage) the commission of a conspiracy. The offence was abolished by s 5(7) of the Criminal Law Act 1977. It seems that Parliament acted in haste and in 1989 the Law Commission recommended that conspiracy should cease to be excluded from the scope of incitement (see the *Criminal Law: A Criminal Code for England and Wales*, vol 2; 'Commentary on Draft Criminal Code Bill' (1989) Law Com No 177, para 13.15; and see Law Com No 300, para 7.19; and note the effect of the case of *Sirat* [1985] 83 Cr App R 41. The law has been in a muddle for many years as to the circumstances in which a person is criminally liable for encouraging or assisting inchoate offences (see Law Com No 300, para 7.6). There can be many permutations of assisting or encouraging, eg D assists D2 to assist D3, or D encourages D2 to conspire to commit an offence, or D encourages D2 to attempt the commission of an offence.

6.81   In its Consultation Paper, 'Assisting and Encouraging Crime' (1993),[46] the Law Commission took (what might be thought to be) a somewhat inconsistent position.

---

[44] And in this connection, see Law Com No 300, para A.101, footnote 111.

[45] And it must be proved that D had one of the states of mind set out in s 47(5), SCA 2007. See also Law Com No 300, para A.101, footnote 111.

[46] *Assisting and Encouraging Crime* (1993), Law Commission Consultation Paper No 131.

On the one hand, it said that the two proposed inchoate offences, namely, *encouraging crime* and *assisting crime*, should not be capable of being committed in respect of any inchoate offence, including the new offences themselves.[47] Thus, it proposed that it would not be an offence, for example (a) to *encourage* D2 to *conspire* to commit an offence, or (b) to *encourage* D2 to *attempt* to commit an offence, or (c) *encouraging* D2 to *assist* D3 to commit an offence, or (d) *assist* D2 to *assist* D3 to commit an offence. Its reason for taking that position was that D's conduct would be 'too remote from the commission of the principal crime for it to be justified to pursue him'.[48] On the other hand, the Law Commission proposed[49] that if the law of secondary liability was put on an entirely inchoate basis (which is *not* the effect of Part 2 of the SCA 2007), there was no obvious reason of policy to prevent D being liable for (i) *conspiring* to *encourage* crime, or (ii) *conspiring* to *assist* crime, or (iii) *attempting* to *encourage* crime, or (iv) *attempting* to *assist* crime.[50]

In Law Com No 300, the Law Commission modified its position. It said that D **6.82** should be liable for an inchoate offence of doing an act, which is capable of encouraging or assisting D2 to *conspire* to commit an offence, but *only if* it was his or her *intention* that D2 should do so. In order to give effect to this proposal, Parliament (a) enacted s 44 of the SCA 2007, (b) abolished the common law offence of incitement (s 59), and (c) repealed s 5(7) of the Criminal Law Act 1977.[51] The effect of this is that conspiracy is no longer excluded from the scope of encouraging (formerly inciting) or assisting the commission of an offence. Such acts are now punishable, but only if they can be brought within s 44 (acting intentionally).

There is no such liability under ss 45 and 46 of the 2007 Act, by virtue of s 49(4), **6.83** which provides that two groups of offences are to be 'disregarded' for the purposes of ss 45 and 46. These are:

(1) 'offences under this Part', ie the inchoate offences in ss 44–46; and
(2) 'listed offences',[52] set out in s 49(5)(a), which include the offence of conspiracy,[53] and an offence of conspiracy falling within s 5(2) or (3) of the Criminal Law Act 1977 (forms of conspiracy not affected by abolition of offence of conspiracy at common law).[54] For Northern Ireland, see para 46 of Part 4 of Sch 3.

For a fuller discussion of s 49(4), see paras **6.92** et seq.

---

[47] para 4.184.
[48] para 4.183.
[49] Consultation Paper No 131.
[50] para 4.186.
[51] Paragraph 54 of Part 2 of Sch 6, SCA 2007.
[52] That is to say, those offences mentioned in s 49(5) and Parts 1, 2, or 3 in Sch 3 (England and Wales) or Parts 1, 4, or 5 of Sch 3 (Northern Ireland).
[53] Paragraph 32 of Part 2 of Sch 3 (s 1, CLA 1977).
[54] Paragraph 39 of Sch 3.

3. Encouraging or assisting another to attempt to commit a crime

6.84   The approach discussed in the preceding paragraph has been followed in relation to a person (D) who does an act that is capable of encouraging or assisting D2 to attempt to commit an offence.

6.85   The authors of Smith & Hogan, *The Criminal Law*, 11th edn, (at p 356) make the point that 'a charge of incitement to attempt to commit an offence would generally be inept because to incite to attempt is to incite to commit the full offence'. There is clear logic in that statement. Perhaps it is for that reason that the Law Commission said little about acts of encouraging ('inciting') and assisting attempts to commit an offence, other than to say that there is a 'need for consistency of approach'.[55] Accordingly, the Law Commission proposed that D should be liable for the inchoate offence of doing an act which is capable of encouraging or assisting D2 to *attempt* to commit an offence, but *only if* it was his or her *intention* that D2 should do so. Parliament has given effect to this proposal. Thus, a person is criminally liable, in such circumstances, under s 44, but not under ss 45 and 46. The result has been achieved by leaving out of the reckoning the statutory offence of attempt (under the CAA 1981), when deciding (for the purposes ss 45 and 46) whether an act is capable of encouraging or assisting the commission of an offence (see s 49(4), (5); para 33 of Part 2 of Sch 3; and para 40 of Part 3 of that Schedule[56] (England and Wales), and para 45 of Part 4 of Sch 3 (Northern Ireland). Section 49(4) of the SCA 2007 is explained in further detail at paras **6.92** et seq. The Law Commission noted that, at common law, a charge of incitement to commit attempt is very uncommon because D will nearly always be encouraging D2 to commit the full offence.[57] By 'intention' is meant 'purpose'.

(a) *The trap of s 47(8) (Encouraging or assisting 'an attempt to do an act')*

6.86   The preceding paragraph must not be confused with the effect of s 47(8)(c) of the SCA 2007. Section 47 specifies a number of ways in which an inchoate offence under ss 44-46 of the SCA 2007 may be proved. In each case, the focus is on acts done (the 'doing of an act') by the anticipated *perpetrator* of the offence in question (*not* D, who gave assistance or encouragement). Section 47(8) states that references in that section to the 'doing of an act' includes references to '(c) an attempt to do an act (except an act amounting to the commission of the offence of attempting to commit another offence)'.

6.87   It is submitted that s 47(8)(c) must not be read as meaning that it is sufficient to found liability for an offence under ss 44–46 if D attempts to encourage or assist D2 to commit an offence. It must be stressed that the 'attempt to do an act', for the purposes of s 47(8)(c) is referable to the conduct element of the offence *in respect of*

---

[55] Law Com No 300, para 7.23.
[56] 'An attempt under a special statutory provision'. That sub-paragraph is to be read with s 3 of the Criminal Attempts Act 1981.
[57] Law Com No 300, para 7.22.

actions performed by D2 (the intended *perpetrator*), and not the actions of the person who is alleged to have assisted or encouraged D2.

At this stage, it is useful to compare s 47 of the SCA 2007 and cl 17 of the Law   6.88
Commission's draft Bill. Clause 17(3) states that a reference to the 'doing of a criminal act' includes a reference to '(b) an attempt to do an act (except in relation to an
offence of attempting to commit another offence)'. As an example of cl 17(3)(b)—
the wording of which is identical to s 47(8)(c)—the Law Commission said: 'D can
be liable under [s 45, SCA 2007] in relation to the principal offence of burglary if
he sells P a jemmy in the belief that it will be used to attempt burglary, even though
he believes that the attempt will fail'. The Law Commission added: 'If the principal
offence in question is itself the offence of attempt, contrary to s 1 of the Criminal
Attempts Act 1981, then clause 17(3)(b) is inapplicable. This explains the words in
parentheses.' It is submitted that the 'doing of an act' is the attempted burglary by
P with the aid of the jemmy. But if the principal offence alleged is a statutory attempt
under the CAA 1981, then s 47(8)(c) is not applicable.

4. Encouraging/assisting D2 to encourage or assist D3 to commit a crime

(a) D intentionally encourages D2 to encourage D3 to commit a crime (s 44)

Suppose D *intentionally* encourages D2 to encourage D3 to firebomb V's house, but   6.89
D3 is arrested before he can commit the offence of arson. Is D guilty of an inchoate
offence under s 44 of the SCA 2007? To put the question slightly differently, can
D be convicted of the inchoate offence under s 44 if he has acted with respect to an
accessory rather than with respect to the perpetrator? The answer, on the facts of this
example, is 'yes'. Under pre-existing law this would have been 'incitement to commit
incitement'.[58] The common law offence of incitement has been repealed by s 59 of
the SCA 2007 (but statutory offences of incitement have been preserved) and the
word 'encouragement' embraces most acts that fall within the meaning of 'incitement'. Section 44 is therefore wide enough to catch those who encourage another to
commit the s 44 offence, *but only if it was D's intention to encourage or to assist
another to commit the s 44 offence, and* that D acted with the requisite state of mind
set out in s 47(5).

It follows from the above that the person encouraged or assisted (ie D2) will often   6.90
be the perpetrator of the offending conduct but, for the purpose of Part 2 of the
SCA 2007, D2 might be only one person in a chain/group of individuals who are
accomplices to a crime.

Example
    D supplies a torch to D2 knowing or believing that the torch will be passed to D3 to perpetrate
    a burglary.

---

[58] See Law Com No 300, para 3.36; and see *Sirat* [1985] 83 Cr App R 41.

It is obviously important to identify the role of each person, and to establish what their level of knowledge was, with respect to a given act, for example whether D2 was an 'innocent agent' or not.

(b) *D believes (but does not intend) that D2 will encourage D3 to commit a crime (ss 45 and 46)*

6.91   Suppose D sells a can of petrol to D2, *believing* (but not intending) that D2 will encourage D3 to use the petrol in an arson attack. Is D guilty of an offence, contrary to s 45 of the SCA 2007? The answer, in this instance, is 'no'. The reason is that Part 2 of the SCA 2007 gives effect to the recommendations and thinking of the Law Commission that: 'If it is D's intention that P should encourage or assist X, his or her conduct should not be considered too remote from the principal offence merely because, were P to encourage or assist X, P would not intend X to commit the principal offence'.[59] The Law Commission regarded D's state of mind as being critical and decisive of the issue. It pointed out that (what are now) ss 45 and 46 only require D to *believe* that P will commit a criminal act and that D's act will encourage or assist P to commit a criminal act. The Law Commission said, 'we believe that it would be an over-extension of criminal liability if D were to be criminally liable for the [ss 45 and 46 offences] in cases where he or she has encouraged or assisted P to encourage or assist X'.[60] To give effect to the aforementioned recommendations, Parliament enacted s 49(4) which provides that for the purposes of ss 45 and 46 (but not s 44) 'offences under this Part . . . are to be disregarded'. The relevant 'Part' is of course Part 2 of the Act, and therefore the offences in ss 45 and 46 are taken out of the reckoning for this purpose.

5. The reasoning behind s 49(4)

6.92   Section 49(4) of the SCA 2007 provides that 'in reckoning whether (a) for the purposes of section 45, an act is capable of encouraging or assisting the commission of an offence; or (b) for the purposes of section 46, an act is capable of encouraging or assisting the commission of one or more of a number of offences; offences under this Part and listed offences are to be disregarded'.

(a) *Section 49(4) and the Law Commission's analysis*

6.93   Section 49(4) is based on cl 2(5) of the Law Commission's draft Bill appended to Law Com No 300.[61] The section gives effect to the Law Commission's recommendation that D may commit the s 44 offence—*but not a s 45 or s 46 offence*—if D does an act that is capable of encouraging or assisting D2 to do an act, which is

---

[59] Law Com No 300, para 7.15.
[60] Law Com No 300, paras 7.12–7.13.
[61] And see Law Com No 300, para A.55.

capable of encouraging or assisting D3 to do a criminal act, *and* that D *intended* that D2 should do, or be encouraged to do, the act. It is important to note that the backdrop to the enactment of this provision is the uncertainty of whether it is possible for D to incite D2 to commit an offence *as an accessory* (ie where the anticipated offence has been committed). The case of *Whitehouse*[62] might suggest that the answer is in the affirmative, but *Bodin* appears to say otherwise.[63] The Law Commission explained its reasoning, as follows (emphasis added):[64]

If D encourages or assists P to encourage or assist X to commit an offence, D is encouraging or assisting P to do an act which, were P to do it and were X to commit the offence, would render P an accessory to the offence . . . [We] referred to the uncertainty that exists at common law as to whether D can be convicted in such circumstances of not merely incitement to incite but of incitement to commit the principal offence:

Example 7G:

D encourages P to encourage X to rape V. X ignores P's encouragement. Although D is guilty of incitement to incite rape, according to *Bodin* (1979) Crim. LR 176, D is not guilty of inciting rape because had X raped V, P would have been guilty of the offence *but as an accessory* and not as a principal offender.

The Law Commission added that the effect of *Bodin* was to prevent D incurring   6.94 liability for incitement if D encouraged D2 to *assist* D3 to commit an offence but D3 did not commit or attempt to commit the offence. However, had D encouraged D2 to encourage D3, then D would be guilty of incitement-to-incite (*Sirat* [1985] 83 Cr App R 41).[65] In order to improve the law, the Law Commission recommended that a person be criminally liable for inchoate-on-inchoate acts, but only where D *intended* that D2 should do, or be encouraged to do, the criminal act. It removes a gap which existed at common law.

(b) Is 'procuring' not embraced by 'encouraging'?

However, there is a further strand to this issue that needs to be considered. In Law   6.95 Com No 300, the Law Commission acknowledged that there remains a gap 'if D encourages or assists P to *procure* X to commit an offence which X does not commit' and that it would address the point in its report on secondary liability (see now Law Com No 305).[66] Many readers might find that statement puzzling because it is a widely held view that the word 'incitement' is apt to cover acts of 'counselling' and 'procuring' (see s 8 of the Accessories and Abettors Act 1861). However, in Law Com No 300, the Law Commission states that whilst 'counsel' means to 'encourage',

---

[62] [1977] QB 868; and see Law Com No 300, paras 3.39–3.43.
[63] [1979] Crim LR 176.
[64] Law Com No 300, paras 7.16–7.18.
[65] Law Com No 300, para 7.18; and see *R v Evans* [1986] Crim LR 470.
[66] Law Com No 300, para 7.18, footnote 22.

the expression 'procure' is 'an anomalous "niche" form of secondary liability'.[67] When we look to para 2.22 of Law Com No 305, the Law Commission states that '(it) is doubtful if all cases of "procuring" can be described properly as involving the provision of assistance or encouragement'. The Law Commission points out that in *A-G's Reference (No 1 of 1975)*[68] the Court of Appeal said: 'To procure means to produce by endeavour . . . Causation here is important. You cannot procure an offence unless there is a causal link between what you do and the commission of the offence.' The view of the Law Commission seems to be that some cases of 'procuring' cannot be aptly described as involving the provision of 'assistance' or 'encouragement'. If that is so, does that mean that some cases of 'procuring' fall outside (or might fall outside) the language of Part 2 of the SCA 2007? If the answer is in the affirmative, then a potential gap remains in the law that is not filled by the wording of Part 2. How significant that gap is (if it does exist) is debatable.

H. THE MENTAL ELEMENT AND s 47

1. The purpose and construction of s 47

(a) *Introduction*

6.96 A person may do an act blissfully unaware that it has the effect of assisting or encouraging another person to commit an offence. Unless lawmakers decide that a person should be liable for recklessly assisting or encouraging the commission of an offence, one might not expect a person to be held criminally liable in such circumstances. As Professor William Wilson has pointed out, in relation to accomplices where the anticipated offence has been committed:

> [one] of the great infelicities of the current law is lack of doctrinal precision in relation to the degree of fit necessary between the offence committed and the state of knowledge/intention of the secondary party. How precisely must the offence committed match A's knowledge and intentions in giving support? The current position is that although the party must believe the principal will commit an offence he does not need to know the precise details.[69]

6.97 But what must a person intend or know before he/she may be held criminally liable for encouraging or assisting an offence, which was not in fact committed? Parliament's answer, having regard to the Law Commission's proposals in Law Com No 300, appears in s 47 of the SCA 2007, which must be read together with the relevant inchoate offence, enacted in ss 44–46.

6.98 When considering s 47 of the SCA 2007, it is useful to keep in mind that a criminal offence can have one or more of three external elements, namely, (a) conduct, (b) circumstances, and (c) consequences. It will be seen that s 47 opens with the

---

[67] Law Com No 300, para B.7, footnote 6.
[68] [1975] QB 773.
[69] 'A Rational Scheme of Liability for Participating in Crime' (2008) Crim LR.3, at p 16.

words 'sections 44, 45, 46 are to be read in accordance with [s 47]'. It will also be seen that s 47(2), (3), and (4), relate to the three offences in ss 44–46 respectively.

2. 'Would amount to the commission of that offence'

Common to each inchoate offence is s 47(5), which describes, in detail, what D's 6.99 state of mind must be with respect to the anticipated offence:

(1) For the purposes of proving an offence under s 44 (where D intends to encourage or assist the commission of an offence), s 47(2) states that (emphasis added): 'it is sufficient to prove that [D] intended to encourage or assist the *doing of an act* which would *amount to the commission of that offence*'.

(2) For the purpose of proving the offences in ss 45 and 46 (where D believes that an offence will be committed etc), it is sufficient to prove that D believed that: (a) an act would be done which *would amount to the commission of that offence*; and (b) that his act would encourage or assist the doing of that act (see s 47(3) and (4)).[70]

Note that, in each case, it must be proved that D believed that an act would be 6.100 done '*which would amount to the commission of that offence*' (emphasis added). That expression is explained/defined by s 47(5) which (subject to subss (6) and (7)) provides:

(5) (a) if the offence is one requiring proof of fault, it must be proved that—
  (i) D *believed* that, were the act to be done, it would be done with that fault;
  (ii) D was *reckless* as to whether or not it would be done with that fault; or
  (iii) D's state of mind was such that, were he to do it, it would be done with that fault; and
 (b) if the offence is one requiring proof of particular circumstances or consequences (or both), it must be proved that—
  (i) D *believed* that, were the act to be done, it would be done in those circumstances or with those consequences; or
  (ii) D was *reckless* as to whether or not it would be done in those circumstances or with those consequences.

(6) For the purposes of subsection (5)(a)(iii), D is to be assumed to be able to do the act in question.

(7) In the case of an offence under section 44—
 (a) subsection (5)(b)(i) is to be read as if the reference to 'D believed' were a reference to 'D intended or believed'; but
 (b) D is not to be taken to have intended that an act would be done in particular circumstances or with particular consequences merely because its being done in those circumstances or with those consequences was a foreseeable consequence of his act of encouragement or assistance.

---

[70] Subs (4) relates to multiple offences.

(a) *A worked example*

6.101   The interaction between s 47(5) and the inchoate offences enacted in ss 45 and 46 can be illustrated in the following example.

Example

D gives a knife to D2. D intends that D2 should use the knife to wound V unlawfully by stabbing him. D2 is arrested before he can carry out the deed. The anticipated offence is s 20 of the Offences Against the Person Act (OAPA)1861 (malicious wounding).

6.102   Section 44(1)(b) states that D must *intend* to encourage or assist the commission of the offence by D2. That takes us to s 47(2). It must be proved that D intended to encourage or assist the 'doing of an act'. The doing of an act refers to the conduct element of the *actus reus* of the offence performed by the perpetrator. The relevant act is stabbing V.

6.103   But it is necessary to go further. Section 47(2) states that the act must be one 'which would amount to the commission of that offence'. This is a reference to s 47(5). At this point, it becomes necessary to examine with care the ingredients that must be proved in respect of the anticipated offence. Section 47(5)(a) states that if the offence is one which requires proof of fault, then D must be proved to have acted with one of the states of mind set out in s 47(5)(a)(i)–(iii). If the offence requires proof of a particular *circumstance*, or *consequence*, or both, then it must be proved that D had one of the states of mind set out in s 47(5)(b)(i) or (ii). On the facts of the above example, the anticipated offence does require proof of fault because s 20 of the OAPA 1861 includes the word 'maliciously'. Furthermore, a *consequence* of the unlawful act (ie the act of stabbing) is wounding or inflicting grievous bodily harm.

3. The reasoning behind s 47(5)

6.104   The Law Commission accepted that D ought not to be criminally liable merely because he intended or believed (as the case may be) that D2 should commit the *conduct element* of an offence (eg appropriating property). Many acts can lawfully be carried out but it is only in proscribed circumstances that the same acts become 'criminal acts'. An example of this was given by the Law Commission at para 5.100 of Law Com No 300:

D ought not to incur liability merely because D intends or believes that P should or will commit an 'act' that is criminal. The 'act' that is criminal in theft is the appropriation of property. It would be absurd if D could be criminally liable for doing nothing more than encouraging P to do that act.

6.105   It is submitted that care needs to be taken over this example. It would certainly be absurd if D were held criminally liable under s 44 of the SCA 2007 merely because he intended that P should appropriate property without intending that P should do so with the requisite fault element. However, the Law Commission's proposed offences include an element that a person did an act 'capable of encouraging or assisting the doing of a *criminal act*. This is a reference to the 'conduct' element of the *actus reus* of the offence. However, ss 44–46 of the SCA 2007 are differently constructed in that D's liability is rooted in acts that encourage or assist 'the commission of *an offence*'. Nonetheless, in order to avoid the absurd result mentioned above, both the Law Commission and Parliament devised rules to ensure that D is not convicted of an inchoate offence of the kind enacted in Part 2 of the SCA 2007, without proof of fault.

The Law Commission proposed that D should be liable only if: 6.106

(1) D knew, or believed, or was indifferent[71] whether D2 would perform the criminal act with the fault required for the commission of the full offence (eg dishonestly appropriating property; intending to permanently deprive the 'owner' of it); or

(2) were D to perform the *conduct element* of the offence himself, he would do so with the requisite fault element. For these purposes, D is to be assumed to be able to do the act in question (see s 47(6)).[72]

Section 47 of the SCA 2007 builds on the Law Commission's analysis in Law   6.107 Com No 300. It will be seen that s 47 distinguishes between offences that require proof of fault (eg wounding with intent to cause grievous bodily harm or theft), and those offences which require proof of particular circumstances or consequences (eg unlawful possession of a firearm or occasioning actual bodily harm). Some offences have elements that fall within both s 47(5)(a) and (b). For example, murder requires proof of *mens rea*—an intention to kill or to cause serious bodily harm, but the offence also has a consequence element (death of a person) to which the fault element does not relate.

4. Cases where the anticipated offence requires proof of fault (s 47(5)(a))

The state of mind that is relevant here is D's state of mind, not that of the   6.108 perpetrator.

Example

    D is guilty (as an accessory) of an offence contrary to s 18 of the Offences Against the Person Act 1861 if he encourages or assists D2 to wound V (the latter intending to cause V grievous bodily harm) and D2 does wound V with that intent. However, in the event that D2 does not commit the s 18 offence, it is sufficient that D 'believed' that the act (wounding) would be done with the requisite 'fault' for s 18 of the OAPA 1861 (see s 47(7)(a) and s 47(5)(a)(i)).

If D gives a knife to D2, intending or believing that D2 would use it to stab V, D   6.109 may believe that D2 would do so in order to wound V. But suppose D2 can be

---

[71] For the meaning of 'indifference' in the context of recklessness, see 'Section 47(5) and the concept of recklessness' later in this chapter (para **6.115**).

[72] See Law Com No 300, para 5.103; and see cl 1(2)(a) and (b) of the Law Commission's draft Bill.

shown to have intended to stab V with the knife to cause V grievous bodily harm. It would seem that even if D did not intend, or believe, that D2 would go that far, he stands to be convicted under s 44 if he intended to assist D2 to use the knife to harm V, but he was subjectively reckless as to whether D2 would act with the fault necessary for an offence under s 18 of the OAPA 1861.

5. Cases where D *would* have acted with 'that fault' (s 47(5)(a)(iii))

6.110   Section 47(5)(a)(iii) gives effect to a recommendation of the Law Commission at para 5.103 of the Law Com No 300 when it said:

> We do not believe D ought to be exonerated merely because it would not be possible to convict P of the principal offence were he or she to do the criminal act. Instead, the focus should be on D's state of mind. In principle, it ought to be possible to convict D if D's state of mind is such that, were he or she to do the criminal act, he or she would do it with the fault required for conviction of the principal offence.

6.111   However, it will be seen that s 47(6) provides that, for these purposes, D is to be assumed to be able to do the act in question. This gives effect to the reasoning of the Law Commission at para 5.104 of Law Com No 300, in which the following example was given (it was an example as given, with some modification, by Lord Bassam of Brighton, when this measure was considered as part of the Serious Crime Bill[73]):

> In some cases, D will be incapable of doing the criminal act, for example a woman cannot do the criminal act of rape—penetration 'with the penis'.[74] However, D ought not to escape liability merely by virtue of being incapable of doing the criminal act. If D, a woman, encourages P to penetrate V with his penis believing that, were P to do so, it would be without the consent of V,[75] it ought to be possible to convict D of encouraging or assisting rape even if P would not be guilty of rape because of a reasonable belief that V would consent.[76]

6. Offences that require proof of circumstances and/or consequences (s 47(5)(b))

6.112   Section 47(5)(b)(i) builds on the recommendations of the Law Commission in Law Com No 300, para 5.118. If a charge is brought under s 45 or s 46, then s 47(5)(b)(i) is to be read and applied exactly as stated in that subsection. If the offence is charged under s 44 (intentionally encouraging or assisting), then s 47(7)(a) provides that subs (5)(b)(i) is to be read as if it stated 'D *intended or believed* that, were the act to be done, it would be done in those circumstances or with those consequences'.

6.113   Section 47(5)(b) applies in (at least) the two situations mentioned below:

(1) *Strict liability*: that is to say, the anticipated offence is one in respect of which proof of 'fault' is not required.

---

[73] *Hansard*, 21 Mar 2007, col 1251.
[74] Sexual Offences Act 2003, s 1(1)(a).
[75] Ibid, s 1(1)(b).
[76] Ibid, s 1(1)(c).

Example[77]

> D asks P to drive him home from the pub as he has had too much to drink. P is insured to drive D's car but unknown to D and P, P was disqualified from driving the day before. P is committing the principal offence of driving whilst disqualified, despite the fact he is not aware that he is disqualified, as this is an offence of strict liability. However, it would not be fair to hold D liable in such circumstances.

(2) *Constructive liability:* s 47(5) of the SCA 2007 applies where the anticipated offence is one of constructive liability (eg murder or wounding with intent to cause grievous bodily harm) being an offence which has a consequence and/or a circumstance element, but it is unnecessary to prove fault with respect to one or both of those elements (see Law Com No 300, para 8.35).

Example [78]

> D gives P a baseball bat and intends P to use it to inflict minor bodily harm on V. P however uses the bat to attack V and intentionally kills V. It would not be fair to hold D liable for encouraging and assisting murder, unless he also believes that, or is reckless as to whether, V will be killed.

Section 47(5)(b) is not confined to those two situations. In Law Com No 300, the Law Commission gave two examples that demonstrate just how technical these rules might be found to be in practice: 6.114

Example 1[79]

P approaches D and asks if he can borrow D's baseball bat. P says he intends to use the bat to 'sort out V'. D provides P with the bat, unclear as to P's exact intention but hoping that P will use it to cause V serious harm. P does nothing with the bat.

Answer (as analysed by the Law Commission) modified to reflect the provisions of the SCA 2007

In the first version, D is not liable under s 44 for intentionally encouraging or assisting murder, even though he would have acted with the fault for murder if he himself had committed the conduct element of that offence.[80] Although s 47(5)(a)(i) is satisfied, s 47(5)(b) is not because *D does not believe that V will be killed*[81] (and it was not D's purpose that V should be killed).

Example 2[82]

P approaches D and asks if he can borrow D's baseball bat. P says he intends to use the bat to 'sort out V'. D provides P with the bat, unclear as to P's exact intention but hoping that P will use it to kill V. P does nothing with the bat.

---

[77] This example appears in the Explanatory Notes (as at 10 May 2007), para 134.
[78] This example appears in the Explanatory Notes (as at 10 May 2007), para 135.
[79] Law Com No 300, para A.38.
[80] 'D is, however, liable for intentionally encouraging or assisting the offence of causing grievous bodily harm with intent (Offences Against the Person Act 1861, s 18).'
[81] Emphasis has been added.
[82] Law Com No 300, para A.38.

Answer (as analysed by the Law Commission)

D is liable for the offence of intentionally encouraging or assisting murder. By providing P with a baseball bat, D commits the *actus reus*, that is, he does an act capable of assisting another person to commit the conduct element of murder. With regard to the fault requirement: D intended to assist P to commit the conduct element of that offence (indeed he intended that the conduct element should be committed); D's state of mind was such that, if he had killed V himself, he would have been liable for murder as a perpetrator; and it was his purpose that a person (V) should die.

7. s 47(5) and the concept of recklessness

6.115 Section 47(5) of the SCA 2007 provides that D may be convicted if he was reckless with respect to any fault, or circumstance, or consequence, which must be proved for the commission of the full offence (see s 47(5)(a)(ii) and(b)(ii). It is submitted that s 47(5)(a)(ii) and (b)(ii) must be construed and applied in a manner that is consistent with the decision of the House of Lords in *R v G* [2003] 1 Cr App R 21: that is to say, subjective recklessness.

6.116 The Law Commission spoke only of 'indifference' with respect to the *circumstance element* of the offence, whereas it will be seen that neither s 47(5)(a)(ii) nor(b)(ii), is confined to circumstances.

6.117 The reference to 'recklessness' might strike some readers as surprising, particularly as the notion of recklessness is not expressly mentioned in the Law Commission's draft Bill.[83] There are arguably two reasons why the Law Commission did not need to make explicit reference to 'recklessness'. First, the Commission recommended that a defendant ought to be liable if he/she is 'prepared for a criminal act to be done *not caring* whether or not the *circumstances element* of the offence is present'.[84] The Law Commission did not think it necessary to make specific provision in its draft Bill to embrace 'indifference', believing that the wording of cl 1(2)(a) and cl 2(3)(a)—on which s 47(5)(a)(i) and(iii) are modelled—was adequate to capture such cases. Secondly, as the authors of Smith and Hogan point out,[85] 'a person who knowingly takes an unreasonable risk of causing a forbidden result may hope, sincerely and fervently, that it will never happen; but he is, surely, reckless'.

6.118 The justification for extending liability to recklessness with respect to *fault*, or *circumstances* or *consequences*, was neatly explained by Professor Sir John Smith (albeit in the context of murder) in his commentary to the case of *Hyde and others*, in the Criminal Law Review (emphasis added):[86]

The law as so settled is criticised on the ground that it leaves the accessory liable to conviction for murder although he is only reckless whereas, in the case of the principal offender, intention must

---

[83] Note that s 47(5)(a)(i) and (iii) are modelled on cl 1(2)(a) and (b) ((and cl 1(3)(a), (b))), of the Law Commission's draft Bill.
[84] Law Com No 300, para 5.124, emphasis has been added.
[85] *The Criminal Law*, 11th edn (OUP), p 109.
[86] [1991] Crim LR 133.

be proved. But there is a difference between (i) recklessness whether death be caused (which is sufficient for manslaughter but not for murder) and (ii) recklessness whether murder be committed. The accessory's recklessness must extend to the principal's *mens rea* of murder. The person who embarks on a joint enterprise knowing that his confederate may intentionally kill is taking a deliberate risk of assisting or encouraging not merely killing but murder. It is true that the accessory may also be liable for murder although he foresees no more than that his confederate may intentionally cause serious bodily harm; but that is one of the consequences of the anomaly that an intention to cause serious bodily harm is a sufficient *mens rea* for murder and does not arise from any defect in the law of accessory liability. The principle applied in these cases is not confined to murder but extends to accessory liability generally. *It is not unreasonable that one who is reckless whether he assists or encourages the commission of a crime should be held liable for it when it is committed.*

(a) 'Intention' means 'intention': not foresight of a virtual certainty (s 47(7)(b))

Section 47(7)(b) largely mirrors cl 18(2) of the Law Commission's draft Bill. The wording of cl 18(1) of the draft Bill is now enacted in s 44(2) of the SCA 2007. However, the effect is the same, namely, that the word 'intention' in Part 2 of the SCA 2007 excludes the concept of foresight of a virtual certainty so that a reference to D's intention is a reference to his purpose (see para A.100, Law Com No 300). 6.119

I. ALTERNATIVE VERDICTS AND GUILTY PLEAS (s 57)

1. The general rule

The general rule set out in s 57 (1) and (2) of the SCA 2007 is that a person who is acquitted of an offence contrary to ss 44–46 of the Act, may be found guilty of an 'alternative offence' (or 'alternative offences' in respect of s 46). 6.120

The expression 'alternative offence' is defined by s 57(4) and (9). An 'alternative offence' may simply be an offence that appears on the indictment and which is advanced by the prosecution as an alternative offence, for example (count 1) attempted theft, and (count 2) assisting in the commission of an offence contrary to s 44 of the SCA 2007 (see s 57(4)(a)). 6.121

An offence is also an 'alternative offence' if it is *either* an indictable offence (that is to say, indictable only, or triable either way), or it is an offence to which s 40 of the Criminal Justice Act 1988 applies, and the allegations which encompassed the charge, which had been preferred under ss 44–46 of the SCA 2007 would, if proved, constitute the alternative offence (see s 57(4)(b)). For example, an attempt to commit the full/anticipated offence (see s 57(7)) other than murder or treason (s 57(6)). 6.122

The Act provides (although it perhaps need not have done so) that a person who is arraigned on an indictment for an offence under Part 2 of the SCA, may plead guilty to any offence 'of which he could be found guilty' under s 57 of the 2007 Act, on that indictment (s 57(10)). 6.123

2. Liability under ss 44-46: D guilty of either the inchoate offence or the anticipated offence

6.124   Notwithstanding that D assisted or encouraged D2 to commit an offence, which the latter commits, D can still be charged with, and be convicted of, an inchoate offence under Part 2 of the SCA 2007 (s 49(1), SCA 2007). This is in line with the Law Commission's recommendations.[87] This might occur if the prosecutor formed the view that there was insufficient evidence to convict D as a secondary party to the commission of a substantive offence, or if it is perceived that it would be easier to secure a conviction against D for an inchoate offence rather than for a substantive offence on the basis that D was an accessory.

6.125   To prevent D securing an acquittal in respect of an inchoate offence (brought under Part 2 of the Act), on the grounds that D *might have* committed the full offence, s 56 provides:

(1) In proceedings for an offence under this Part ('the inchoate offence') the defendant may be convicted if—
  (a) it is proved that he must have committed the inchoate offence or the anticipated offence; but
  (b) it is not proved which of those offences he committed.
(2) For the purposes of this section, a person is not to be treated as having committed the anticipated offence merely because he aided, abetted, counselled or procured its commission.
(3) In relation to an offence under s.46, a reference in this section to the anticipated offence is to be read as a reference to an offence specified in the indictment.

6.126   Section 56(1) of the SCA 2007 builds on a pre-existing principle that D may be convicted of an offence if the prosecution cannot prove whether he was a perpetrator, or an accessory, but it can be proved that he must have been one or the other.[88] This principle is readily understandable because if two or more persons attack V, intending to stab him, it might be difficult to prove whether D was the person who used the knife or shouted 'stab him', but there is no doubt that D played one of those roles. Thus, D can be convicted of an inchoate offence under Part 2 if the prosecution can prove that D must have committed *either* the inchoate offence *or* the 'anticipated offence', but it cannot prove which offence he committed, provided that the court was sure that D must have committed one of those two offences.

6.127   The wording of s 56(2) is confusing, but it is submitted that the provision is intended to make clear that the words in s 56(1)(a) 'committed . . . the anticipated offence' mean 'committed the anticipated offence as a *principal offender*, ie not as an accessory pursuant to s 8 of the Accessories and Abettors Act 1861'.

---

[87] Law Com No 300, paras 5.8, A.45; and see footnote 3 (para A.3), footnote 56 (para A.45), footnote 60 (para A.47), footnote 77 (para A.52), footnote 79 (para A.53) and footnote 80 (para A.53).

[88] Law Com No 300, para A.80.

J. DEFENCES, PROTECTIONS, AND LIMITATIONS

1. Defence of acting reasonably (s 50)

(a) *The basic rule*

By s 50 of the SCA 2007, it is a defence for an accused to prove that, at the time that   6.128
he did an act which was capable of encouraging or assisting another person to
commit an offence, he knew, or believed (on reasonable grounds), that 'certain circumstances' existed in respect of which it was reasonable for him to act as he did
(or, if s 50(2) applies, to show that he acted as he did in the circumstances as he
believed them to be).

(b) *Statutory factors that must be considered by the court*

The factors that are to be considered by a court in determining whether the   6.129
defendant's actions were reasonable in the circumstances, include (s 50(3)):

- (a) the seriousness of the anticipated offence (or, in the case of an offence
  under s 46, the offences specified in the indictment);
- (b) any purpose for which he claims to have been acting;
- (c) any authority by which he claims to have been acting.

The above list became part of what was then the Serious Crime Bill on 25 April   6.130
2007.[89] The list is not exhaustive. The defence is broader than that proposed by the
Law Commission in Law Com No 300. The factors were added to the Bill in order
to clarify the ambit of the defence (see below).

(c) *The Law Commission's proposed defence: and the enacted defence under s 50*

The Law Commission also recommended a 'reasonableness' defence, which would   6.131
have been available to a defendant charged with an offence contrary to ss 45 and 46,
but not with an offence contrary to s 44. The Law Commission gave three examples
where the defence would operate:[90]

(1) D, a motorist, changes motorway lanes to allow a following motorist (P) to
    overtake, even though D knows that P is speeding;

(2) D, a reclusive householder, bars his front door to a man trying to get into his
    house to escape from a prospective assailant (P);

(3) D, a member of a DIY shop's checkout staff, believes the man (P) purchasing
    spray paint will use it to cause criminal damage.

---

[89] *Hansard*, House of Lords, 25 Apr, 2007, col 743.
[90] Law Com No 300, para A.63.

6.132   The defence under s 50 of the SCA 2007 is wider than that proposed by the Law Commission to the extent that it applies to all offences created by Part 2 of the Act. Parliament's thinking might have been that it is impossible to foresee all the situations that might arise, in respect of which it would be unjust for D to be convicted of an inchoate offence under Part 2 of the Act, and that the limits of the defence should be set by the courts. The ambit of the defence was only briefly discussed in the House of Lords, on 21 March, 2007, and again on 25 April, 2007. Concern was expressed about whether the defence would be abused. Baroness Scotland of Asthal said:[91]

> I remember that, when this amendment was discussed in Committee, the noble Baroness, Lady Anelay, queried whether the reasonableness defence would cover a whistleblower—a point that has been repeated by the noble Lord, Lord Henley—and gave the example of a civil servant who encourages a journalist. In my letter, I sought to respond to that, following that conversation. As the noble Lord said, I explained that a whistleblower could seek to rely on this defence, but whether the jury accepts that argument is another matter; it is a matter for the jury to judge whether it is reasonable. Both the Home Office and the Law Commission recognised that unmeritorious defendants will seek to rely on this defence. We believe that government Amendment No. 62, which gives examples of factors that can be considered in determining reasonableness, will help to guard against this, and so I hope that noble Lords will support it. We believe that juries will see through unmeritorious arguments. Indeed, in the example given, the fact that a civil servant is bound by the Official Secrets Act would no doubt be borne in mind by the jury when determining whether he had acted reasonably. Nevertheless, it could be that a jury, considering all the facts, would accept this defence.

6.133   There are two powerful disincentives for defendants who might be minded to run an unmeritorious defence under s 50 of the SCA 2007. First, and on the assumption that s 50 is ECHR compliant, the burden of proving an offence rests on the accused. Secondly, in the event of a conviction for an offence under Part 2 of the Act, a defendant is likely to lose the mitigation available to those defendants who plead guilty at the earliest opportunity.

(d) *No 'good purpose' defence under Part 2*

6.134   The Law Commission had recommended a 'good purpose' defence that would have been available in respect of ss 44–46, namely that D's purpose was to prevent (or to limit) the occurrence of harm, and that his conduct was reasonable in the circumstances (see Law Com No 300, para A.57). The 'good purpose' defence does not appear in Part 2 of the SCA 2007. The Serious Crime Bill did include a 'defence of acting to prevent commission of offence' (see cl 45 of the Bill, as at 27 March 2007). However, on 25 April 2007, an amendment moved by the government to leave this provision out of the Bill was agreed in the House of Lords. Their lordships accepted the government's reasoning that it would be better to provide one defence, namely, the 'defence of acting reasonably' under s 50 to all the offences included in

---

[91] *Hansard*, House of Lords, 25 Apr, 2007, col 744.

Part 2 of the 2007 Act. It therefore extended the application of the defence of reasonableness to all the offences under Part 2, and to remove the 'crime prevention' defence (in cl 45).[92]

2. Protective offences: victims not liable (s 51)

For the purposes of any of the offences created by or Part 2 of the SCA 2007, s 51 of the Act preserves the '*Tyrrell*' exemption ([1894] 1 QB 710), that is to say it exempts from liability persons who fall within the category of persons that the principal offence was designed to protect. The example, given by the Law Commission, usefully illustrates the principle: 6.135

D (a 12-year-old girl) and D2 (D's 15-year-old female friend) both encourage a man (P) to have sexual intercourse with D (an act which, if committed by P, would amount to the principal offence of child rape) (see s 5, Sexual Offences Act 2003; para A.64, Law Com No 300).

Section 51 of the Serious Crime Act 2007 is modelled on cl 6 of the Law Commission's draft Bill. The provision exempts D from liability if he/she is, or would have been, the victim of the offence. The provision typically applies to sexual offences (eg s 5, Sexual Offences Act 2003), but it is not confined to such cases.   6.136

K. INSTITUTING PROCEEDINGS

1. General requirements for initiating a prosecution under Part 2

Section 54 makes provision for instituting proceedings under Part 2 of the SCA 2007. This section was added to the Serious Crime Bill on 24 October 2007 when the House of Lords agreed with the House of Commons that the Bill should be amended accordingly.   6.137

The main points concerning s 54 of the SCA 2007 are: 6.138

(1) If the prosecution of a substantive offence requires the consent of a particular office-holder (eg the Attorney General, or the Director Public Prosecutions)—for example, an offence under the Explosive Substances Act 1883, or an offence of bribery, or corruption—the consent of that office-holder must be obtained before proceedings are initiated for encouraging or assisting the commission of that offence (ie an offence charged under Part 2 of the 2007 Act) (s 54(2), SCA 2007).

(2) A prosecuting authority that has power to prosecute a substantive offence (eg an offence under the Customs and Excise Management Act (CEMA) 1979) will also have power to initiate a prosecution for an offence of encouraging or

---

[92] *Hansard*, House of Lords, 25 Apr 2007, col 744.

assisting the commission of that substantive offence (ie an offence charged under Part 2 of the 2007 Act) (s 54(2)(b)).

(3) Powers conferred on investigators and prosecuting authorities, in respect of the seizure, detention, and forfeiture of property relating to the investigation and enforcement of a substantive offence, apply with respect to acts of encouraging or assisting the commission of the substantive offence (ie the inchoate offences enacted under Part 2 of the 2007 Act). There exist a considerable number of statutes which confer on a specified authority a power to 'seize and detain' items relevant to an investigation or the prosecution of an offence (eg s 139, CEMA 1979 or s 22, Police and Criminal Evidence Act (PACE) 1984). However, the powers mentioned in s 54(2)(c) and (d) of the 2007 Act are quite narrow. Section 54 does not, for example, confer a power of search but the 2007 Act did not need to do so because an offence charged under Part 2 of that Act could be investigated and dealt with using general powers of search, enacted under various statutes, eg PACE 1984.

(4) Section 54(2)(d) refers to the power of 'forfeiture'. Many enactments confer such a power (not always exercisable following a conviction for an offence). For example, the CEMA 1979 is peppered with forfeiture provisions. Note that s 54 does not confer a power on a court to make a confiscation order under the Proceeds of Crime Act (POCA) 2002 following a conviction for an offence under ss 44–46 of the SCA 2007. The reason is that such provision is unnecessary. A conviction on indictment will trigger the provisions of Part 2 of the POCA 2002 (England and Wales).

(5) It should be noted that the offence under s 44 of the SCA 2007 (intentionally encouraging or assisting the commission of an offence) has been added to the list of 'lifestyle offences' in Sch 2 to the POCA 2002.[93] This means that a conviction for an offence under s 44 of the SCA 2007 will require the sentencing court to treat the defendant as having a 'criminal lifestyle'[94] and to recover, if it can, the value of property obtained by the defendant in respect of his 'general criminal conduct' (s 76(2))—a value that is arrived at with the assistance of statutory assumptions under s 10 of the POCA 2002. In cases where a defendant is to be treated as having a 'criminal lifestyle', the court is not limited to an examination of the defendant's financial history over a six-year period (a period of six years before the defendant was charged): property obtained by a defendant at any time which represents his general criminal conduct, is recoverable.[95]

---

[93] Sch 6, Part 2, para 62.

[94] s 75, POCA 2002.

[95] It is a myth that, in cases where the defendant has a criminal lifestyle, the prosecution can only trace back six years before proceedings were initiated. The assumption—relating to 'property held' by a defendant at the moment of his conviction or confiscation proceedings—will apply even if the property was held by the defendant for a period exceeding six years before proceedings were initiated.

Where the actions of a defendant were truly inchoate (that is to say, the antici-pated offence was not committed) the question whether the defendant has benefited from the offence itself (and the value of the benefit under that head-ing) could be problematic. A court could not, for example, treat—as a benefit 'obtained' by the defendant—the proceeds of a robbery that D had hoped to receive had the offence been committed. Even if the anticipated offence had been committed, but D was convicted only of an inchoate offence under Part 2 of the SCA 2007, D might well argue that he did not 'benefit' jointly with the perpetrator.

Note that by s 53 of the SCA 2007: 6.139

No proceedings for an offence triable by reason of any provision of Schedule 4 may be instituted—
  (a) in England and Wales, except by, or with the consent of, the Attorney General; or
  (b) in Northern Ireland, except by, or with the consent of, the Advocate General for Northern Ireland.

The Explanatory Notes, which are adequate for present purposes, state: 6.140

. . . where jurisdiction is not governed by section 52 (and therefore comes within the provisions set out in Schedule 4), the Attorney General must give his consent to a prosecution in England and Wales. In Northern Ireland, the Advocate General must give his consent before any prosecu-tion falling under this Schedule.

2. Mode of trial

Section 55 of the SCA 2007 provides: 6.141

(1) An offence under s.44 or 45 is triable in the same way as the anticipated offence.
(2) An offence under s.46 is triable on indictment.

Note that an offence charged under s 46 of the SCA 2007 is triable only on 6.142 indictment (s 55(5), SCA 2007).

L. JURISDICTION

1. Introduction

Section 52 of the SCA 2007, and Sch 4 to that Act, provides rules which govern 6.143 jurisdiction to try offences under Part 2 of the Act. The Explanatory Notes state that the effect of s 52(5) is that:

(the) general jurisdictional rules for Part 2 offences (contained in Section 52 and Schedule 4 of the Bill [sic]) are without prejudice to any specific jurisdictional rules which already exist for certain offences on the statute book. For example, sexual offences have their own jurisdictional rules (provided for in the Sexual Offences Act 2003). As such, jurisdiction for encouraging or assisting an offence under the Sexual Offences Act will be governed by that Act, rather than the rules created in Part 2.

6.144   **2. The Rules relating to jurisdiction for the purposes of Part 2**

(1) A person (D) may be tried in England and Wales if he knew or believed that any part of the anticipated offence might take place there, and it does not matter where D was at the relevant time (s 52(1), SCA 2007). Thus, jurisdiction under s 52(1) is determined by reference to D's state of mind about where acts took place and not the location of D at the moment that he did something which was capable of giving encouragement or assistance to another to commit an offence.

Example (per Explanatory Notes, para 183)
D in Belgium sends a number of emails to P in London, encouraging him to plant a bomb on the tube. D can be prosecuted in England and Wales or Northern Ireland despite the fact he was outside the jurisdiction when he did his act.

(2) If it is not proved that D knew or believed that all or part of the anticipated offence would be performed somewhere in England and Wales, then he/she is 'not guilty' of an offence under Part 2 of the SCA 2007 *unless* paras 1, 2, or 3 apply:

(a) **Sch 4, para 1:** D does something in England and Wales which is capable of encouraging or assisting another person to commit an offence, and:

(i) D knows or believes that the anticipated offence might take place outside England and Wales (Scotland?!);

(ii) the anticipated offence could be tried in England and Wales even if the offending acts occurred outside that jurisdiction.

Example (Explanatory Notes, para 186)
The offence of murder is triable within England, Wales or Northern Ireland regardless of where it is committed if the defendant is 'a subject of Her Majesty' so jurisdiction could fall within para 1 in the following situation (subject to the Attorney General's consent (s 53)): D (a British citizen) in England sends a parcel of poison to P (a British citizen) in France encouraging him to use it to murder V (also in France). It would be possible to try D in England because, as P is a British citizen, the anticipated principal offence (murder) is one which could be tried in England, Wales, or Northern Ireland.

(b) **Sch 4, para 2:** D does something in England and Wales which is capable of encouraging or assisting the commission of an offence, and:

(i) D knows or believes that the anticipated offence might take place outside England and Wales, and

(ii) the anticipated offence is an offence in the place where the offending acts are perpetrated.

Example (Explanatory Notes, para 188)
The offence of theft is an offence in England, Wales, and Northern Ireland and also in Spain so jurisdiction could fall within para 2 in the following situation (subject to the Attorney General's consent (s 53): D in England sends an email

to P in Spain containing details of how to disarm an alarm system used by a bank in Madrid. D intends to assist P to rob the bank.

(c) **Sch 4, para 3:** D does something *outside* England and Wales, and
  (i) D knows or believes that the anticipated offence might also take place outside England and Wales;
  (ii) the anticipated offence is one which could be tried in England and Wales had it been perpetrated in that place.

> *Example* (Explanatory Notes, para 191)
>
> Murder is an offence for which a perpetrator who is a British citizen could be tried in England and Wales or Northern Ireland regardless of where it is committed so jurisdiction could fall within para 3 in the following situation (subject to the Attorney General's consent (s 53)): D (a British citizen) in Canada sends a parcel of poison to P in France encouraging him to use it to murder V (also in France). It would be possible to try D in England because he is a British citizen and the anticipated principal offence (murder) is one which could be tried in England, Wales, or Northern Ireland as it would be committed by a British citizen.

Note that references in s 52 of the SCA 2007, and in Sch 4 to that Act, are to be read as if they were references to Northern Ireland as far as those provisions are applicable there.

M. FURTHER REFORM: ANTICIPATED OFFENCE COMMITTED BY THE PRINCIPAL (LAW COM NO 305)

1. 'Aiding, abetting, counselling and procuring' (s 8, Accessories and Abettors Act 1861)

In cases where D has assisted D2 to commit the anticipated offence, D will incur secondary liability if he/she has 'aided, abetted, counselled or procured' its commission. This is the principle encapsulated in s 8 of the Accessories and Abettors Act 1861 and s 44 of the Magistrates' Courts Act 1980 (see para 1.5, Law Com No 305). The effect of s 8 of the 1861 Act is that the secondary party is liable to be charged, convicted, and sentenced accordingly. 6.145

2. Secondary party need not intend D2 to commit the offence

Where a principal commits an offence, the following three situations need to be carefully distinguished. 6.146

(a) *No joint venture: but perhaps secondary liability*

D assists or encourages D2 to commit the conduct element of an offence (eg hitting V), which the latter goes on to commit, but D does not share the intention of D2 to act with the fault element required for the offence (eg wounding with intent to cause grievous bodily harm contrary to s 18 of the Offences Against the Person Act 1861). Under the Law Commission's recommendations—which have not been enacted under Part 2 of the 2007 Act (but see Law Com No 305; cl 1, draft Bill)—the actions of D might give rise to secondary liability if he has the requisite fault element (liability would be inchoate if (for whatever reason) D2 had not committed the offence he intended to perpetrate). The fault element would be satisfied if D 'intended' that D2 would perform the 'conduct element' (*actus reus*) of the offence (eg when D supplied a bat or a knife to D2, he knew or believed that the latter would use the item to injure V). Intention might be evidenced by showing that D foresaw as a 'virtual certainty' that D2 would perform the 'conduct element' of the offence.[96] A secondary party incurs liability even if he did not share the principal's intention that the offence would be committed.[97]

Example

If D sells a torch to D2, foreseeing or, in some cases, turning a blind eye to the fact that the latter is likely to use it to commit burglary, D will be criminally liable in the event that D2 commits that offence even if D did not intend, desire, or agree that the offence should be committed. D's purpose might be merely to make a profit, or D might be indifferent about whether the principal committed the offence: D might hope that the offence is not committed.

6.147   In its report, 'Participating in Crime' (No 305), the Law Commission recommended changing this state of affairs so that:

(1) the law would prevent D being convicted of a substantive offence committed by a principal, unless D *intended*[98] the principal to commit the offence (Law Com No 305, para 1.9); and

(2) in the absence of the intention mentioned in (1) above, D should be convicted of an inchoate offence of assisting or encouraging the offence. Unfortunately, the recommendations made by the Law Commission (Law Com No 305) have not been given statutory force by Part 2 of the SCA 2007.

For a powerful critique of the Law Commission's Report No 305, see 'Participating in Crime: Law Com No 305—Joint Ventures', by Professor GR Sullivan (2008) Crim LR 19.

(b) *Joint venture*

6.148   'A joint criminal venture is formed when the parties agree to commit an offence or when they share with each other a common intention to commit an offence' ('the agreed offence'): per the Law Commission (Law Com 305, para 1.51).

---

[96] See Law Com No 305, paras 1.49 and 3.84–3.93.
[97] See Law Com No 305, para 1.7.
[98] For the meaning of 'intent', see Law Com No 305, paras 3.84–3.90.

(c) *Joint venture-plus (eg a collateral offence)*

The doctrinal considerations regarding joint ventures and liability for collateral   6.149
offences fall outside the scope of this book, but those considerations were considered
in detail by the Law Commission in three reports, namely, Law Com No 300, Law
Com No 305, and see 'Murder, Manslaughter and Infanticide', Law Com No 304.
For present purposes, it is sufficient to note that whereas Smith & Hogan, *The
Criminal Law* (11th edn) say that joint ventures are governed by the ordinary prin-
ciples of secondary participation, other commentators say that secondary liability
and joint ventures involve separate doctrines (Simester and Sullivan, *Criminal Law
Theory and Doctrine* (2nd edn (2003), pp 224–6); and see the speech of Lord Mustill,
'Powell and Daniels, English';[99] and see paras 1.26 and 3.47–3.58, Law Com
No 300). For three strong commentaries on the Law Commission's proposals in
'Participating in Crime', Law Com No 305, read 'A Rational Scheme of Liability
for Participating in Crime', Professor William Wilson;[100] 'Participating in Crime:
Law Com No 305—Joint Criminal Ventures', Professor GR Sullivan;[101] and
'Procuring, Causation, Innocent Agency and the Law Commission', Professor
Richard Taylor.[102]

It is desirable that a person's liability for a collateral offence should be determined   6.150
in accordance with a single doctrine, but eminent judges have struggled to find an
enduring formula for determining who should be held criminally liable for the commission of a 'collateral offence' committed by another party in pursuance of the
'agreed offence'.

D and D2 share a common intention to commit an offence (the 'agreed offence')   6.151
but D2 goes on to commit a 'collateral offence' (eg during a bank robbery—the
'agreed offence'—D2 kills a security guard).

Consider two other scenarios: 6.152

(1) In order to achieve the result that was *jointly intended* by D and D2, the latter
    commits an offence that was not contemplated by D. For example, D and D2
    agree to steal money from a safe. D believes that D2 is able to 'crack' the combi-
    nation code, but unbeknown to him, D2 burns open the safe and destroys it.
    Is D guilty of criminal damage?

(2) One participant pursues a *result*, which the other parties had not intended.
    For example, D and D2 agree to assault V intending to cause him grievous
    bodily harm, but in the event D2 (who hates V) struck V, intending to kill him,
    and he does kill him. What is the extent of D's criminal liability?

---

[99] [1999] AC 1, p 11.
[100] (2008) Crim LR 3.
[101] (2008) Crim LR 19.
[102] (2008) Crim LR 32.

6.153   The Law Commission summarised the position by way of a general principle, namely (emphasis added):

> . . . D is guilty of any offence committed in the course of a joint criminal venture if he or she foresaw that P might commit the *conduct element* of the offence in the *circumstances* (if any) and with the *fault* required to be convicted of the offence. If the principal offence is not a constructive liability offence, D must also foresee that in committing the conduct element D might also bring about the consequence element (if any) of the offence.[103]

6.154   The problem in relation to 'collateral offences' is most acute with respect to offences of 'constructive liability', for example murder. The courts have struggled to find an enduring answer to the question whether D must know of, or have some awareness of, the *consequence element* of the offence (eg the fact that V might die). The answer, according to the Privy Council in *Chan Wing Siu*,[104] and by the Court of Appeal in *Hyde*,[105] was in the negative. But, in *Powell and Daniels, English*,[106] doubt was cast on this approach when the House of Lords held that it was sufficient to found a conviction for murder if a secondary party realized that, in the course of a joint enterprise, the primary party might kill with intent to do so, or with intent to cause grievous bodily harm. However, in *Neary*,[107] the Court of Appeal held that nothing said in *Powell and Daniels, English* altered the position as decided in *Chan Wing Siu* or in *Hyde*; see also *Rahman*;[108] see also the commentary to that case by Professor David Ormerod,[109] and see *Rook*.[110]

6.155   In *Chan Wing Siu* [1985], the House of Lords held that a secondary party was criminally liable for acts of the principal offender if the crime was foreseen by him/her as a possible incident of the common unlawful enterprise, and that it was proved beyond reasonable doubt that the offender had that foresight. Their lordships referred to *Anderson and Morris*,[111] and remarked that 'in England it appears not to have been found necessary hitherto to analyse more elaborately the test which the jury have to apply'. In *Chan Wing Siu*, the Privy Council stressed that it is what the accused in fact contemplated that matters, and his state of mind can be inferred from his conduct and other evidence. If, during the course of a concerted assault on V by D and D2, the latter pulled out a knife or a gun, D's knowledge of the circumstances in which D2 possessed that weapon might be telling evidence about what D intended, contemplated, or foresaw. No hint was given in *Chan Wing Siu* that D can be convicted of murder only if he foresaw that D2 might in fact *kill* V (ie awareness/foresight of the consequence element of an offence). If such a requirement exists,

---

103 *Chan Wing Siu* [1985] 1 AC 168; and see Law Com No 305, para 2.69.
104 [1985] 1 AC 168.
105 [1991] 1 QB 134.
106 [1998] 1 Cr App R 261.
107 [2002] EWCA Crim 1736.
108 [2007] EWCA Crim 342.
109 (2007) Crim LR 721.
110 [1993] 97 Cr App R 327.
111 [1966] 1 QB 110, 50 Cr App R 216.

then D would not be guilty of murder if he foresaw that D2 might assault V intending to cause grievous bodily harm, but did not contemplate that D2's actions might in fact result in V's death.

In *Powell and Daniels, English*, the House of Lords held, as being correct, the submission of counsel for one appellant[112] that where the primary party kills with a deadly weapon, which the secondary party did not know that he had and, therefore, he did not foresee his use of it, the secondary party should not be guilty of murder. The secondary party must foresee an act of the type which the principal party committed. In *English*, the use of a knife by D2 was 'fundamentally different' from the use of a 'wooden post'. Lord Hutton derived support for that view from the decision of Carswell J in *Gamble*,[113] in which Carswell J commented that persons who inflict harm by shooting a bullet through a person's knee ('kneecapping') do not generally expect that they will endanger life, and 'believe that they are engaged in a lesser offence than murder'. Crucially, Carswell J added: 6.156

Although the rule remains well entrenched that an intention to inflict grievous bodily harm qualifies as the *mens rea* of murder, it is not in my opinion necessary to apply it in such a way as to fix an accessory with liability for a consequence which he did not intend and which stems from an act which he did not have within his contemplation.

If the act which caused V's death (eg cutting the throat) was not foreseen by D, then D is not criminally responsible for V's death because it was a lethal act that was 'fundamentally different' from the act that was foreseen by D (eg knee-capping).   6.157

It is therefore important to focus on the act that caused death. In *Gamble*, the cause of death appears to have been related to injuries other than knee-capping. But if in another case the cause of death, however unlikely, was due to an act of knee-capping by D2, then D is surely liable for V's murder if he foresaw/realized that D2 might carry out the act with the necessary intention for murder.   6.158

In *Rahman*,[114] Lord Justice Hooper said that the proper approach is reflected in the following set of questions:[115]   6.159

1. Are you sure that D intended that one of the attackers would kill V intending to kill him or that D realised that one of the attackers might kill V with intent to kill him? If yes, guilty of murder. If no, go to 2.
2. Are you sure that either:
   (a) D realised that one of the attackers might kill V with intent to cause him really serious bodily harm; or
   (b) D intended that serious really bodily harm would be caused to V; or
   (c) D realised that one of the attackers might cause serious bodily harm to V intending to cause him such harm? If no, not guilty of murder. If yes, go to question 3.

---

[112] Mr Christopher Sallon QC for English.
[113] [1989] NI 268.
[114] [2007] EWCA Crim 342.
[115] And see *Rafferty* [2007] EWCA Crim 1846.

3. What was P's act, which caused the death of V? (e.g. stabbing, shooting, kicking, and beating). Go to question 4.
4. Did D realise that one of the attackers might do this act? If yes, guilty of murder. If no, go to the question 5.
5. What act or acts are you sure D realised that one of the attackers might do to cause V really serious harm? Go to question 6.
6. Are you sure that this act or these acts (which D realised one of the attackers might do) is/are not of a fundamentally different nature to P's act which caused the death of V? If yes, guilty of murder. If no, not guilty of murder.

The weakness of this approach—which is a matter of policy—is that V might be guilty of murder notwithstanding that he/she did not anticipate the use of lethal force.[116]

---

[116] See Law Com No 305, para 2.94.

7

DATA SHARING AND DATA MATCHING: TRENDS AND ISSUES

A. ELECTRONIC DATA PROCESSING

The majority of transactions, as well as the preparation of documents and record keeping, involve the use of computers. The processing of personal data is such a regular occurrence that the legal duties and responsibilities relating to that activity perhaps tend to be overlooked. This might not be due to complacency but to an engrained, albeit outdated perception that, in English law, all actions are permitted unless Parliament, or the judges, say otherwise. This is not an assumption that public authorities can safely make because the legitimacy of their actions often involves examining whether a legal base exists to support their actions. Commercial organizations and public bodies have long employed electronic information technology to store and to process data, and a significant amount of personal data is shared and analysed using elaborate software tools for that purpose. The principal enactment that affects data handling is the Data Protection Act (DPA) 1998, which is not, of course, to minimize the impact of the Freedom of Information Act 2000. 7.01

Chapter 1 to Part 3 of the SCA 2007 ('Chapter 1 SCA') is concerned with two activities in connection with data processing, namely (a) the sharing of information between public and private authorities ('data sharing': s 68, SCA 2007), and (b) 'data matching' (s 73, and Sch 7, SCA 2007). By combining those two exercises, it is possible to create a very powerful analytical process for purposes as diverse as the presentation of statistics relating to patterns and trends, the provision of goods 7.02

and services, the detection of crime, and the profiling of individuals who might have a propensity to commit crimes of a particular kind.

7.03   The government wishes to harness the potential power of such techniques (subject to safeguards) for the purposes of detecting and preventing crime. However, the measures enacted in Chapter 1 SCA are presently confined to disclosures that may be made by 'public authorities' for preventing fraud, but it is likely that these measures will be extended to prevent, and to detect, the commission of other crimes. Some provisions of the SCA 2007 already permit the limited disclosure of information in relation to crimes other than fraud. Thus, s 85, SCA 2007 provides for the disclosure of information by (or with the authority of) the Commissioners of Revenue and Customs, to the Criminal Assets Bureau in Ireland ('CAB'), or to any specified public authority in the United Kingdom or elsewhere, for purposes that include: (a) the identification of 'proceeds of crime'; (b) the bringing of civil proceedings for enforcement purposes in relation to proceeds of crime; and (c) the taking of other action in relation to proceeds of crime (see s 85, SCA 2007). 'Proceeds of crime' is defined by s 85(9), SCA 2007 to mean, 'assets derived, or suspected to be derived, directly or indirectly from criminal conduct (wherever occurring)'. Although the expression 'criminal conduct' is not defined in s 85, it presumably has the meaning given to it by the relevant enactment (principally the Proceeds of Crime Act (POCA) 2002) and therefore 'criminal conduct' refers to just about every offence that could be tried in the United Kingdom if the conduct in question was performed there (see ss 76(1), 326(1), POCA 2002).

1. The build-up to Chapter 1, Part 3, SCA

7.04   The provisions in Chapter 1, Part 3, SCA were enacted following publication of the Performance and Innovation Unit's Report 'Privacy and Data Sharing: The Way Forward for Public Services',[1] and the government's Green Paper 'New Powers Against Organised and Financial Crime'[2] which proposed the use of data sharing to investigate and to prevent fraud. The proposals build on the experience of the Audit Commission's 'National Fraud Initiative' (ACNFI)—an initiative that has run since 1996—and which utilizes 'data matching' techniques to detect and to prevent fraud in the public sector. In its Report for 2004/05, the ACNFI states that the value of detected fraud and overpayments rose from £83 million in 2002/03, to £111 million in 2004/05—an increase of 33 per cent.[3] In 2004/05, the number of participating public sector bodies contributing data was just under 1,300: an increase of 12.7 per cent on 2002/03. It is not entirely clear whether the words 'fraud and overpayments' are to be read conjunctively or disjunctively. Table 7.0 (below) totals some 16,577 cases, and on that basis the mean average is approximately £6,696.

---

[1] April 2002.
[2] Cm 6875.
[3] Page 2.

Table 7.0: NFI 2005/06 results summary

Result summary (NFI 2004/05)	Number of persons
Employees dismissed or resigned	135
Duplicate creditor payments	309
Cautions or administrative penalties	840
HB overpayments involving students	905
HB overpayments involving NHS employees	327
HB overpayments involving failed asylum seekers	163
HB overpayments involving local government employees	2,690
HB overpayments linked to insurance payouts	50
Overpayments to deceased pensioners	2,497
Deceased residents in private care homes	279
Serial insurance claimants under investigation	80
Blue badges: holders confirmed as deceased	5,473
Former tenant arrears cases under investigation	925
Right to buy cases under investigation	83
Payroll and other fraud investigations	1410
Successful prosecutions	396
Social houses recovered	15
£111 million total fraud and overpayments	**16,577 cases**

7.05 Chapter 1 SCA does not give full effect to the proposals set out in the Green Paper. Whereas the Green Paper proposed that there should be appropriate 'data matching' of Suspicious Activity Reports (SARs) in relation to money laundering, and *other forms of serious crime*, the provisions of Chapter 1 SCA relate only to fraud prevention. The Green Paper also proposed that 'data matching' and 'data mining' ought to be permitted to identify 'suspicious profiles'. By 'profiles', the government was referring to 'patterns and trends in criminal activity which might not be spotted when data is looked at individually'. That statement is sufficiently open-ended to embrace patterns that relate to individuals or to geographical areas. However, in the House of Lords, amendments were made to the Serious Crime Bill to prohibit data-matching exercises that suggest nothing more than a person's potential to commit fraud in the future.[4] This aspect of the legislation is considered in detail later in this chapter.

7.06 The Regulatory Impact Assessment to the Serious Crime Bill[5] presented four options for legislative intervention to reduce the harm caused by fraud committed against the private and public sectors. Of these options, the SCA 2007 appears to

---

[4] House of Lords, *Hansard*, 30 April 2007, col 893; new s 32A, ACA 1998, inserted by Sch 7, Part 1, para 2, to the SCA 2007.

[5] June 2007.

give effect to options 2 and 3. Under option 2, the Audit Commission's *National Fraud Initiative* would receive additional statutory powers 'to enable them to expand into new areas, or back into areas which have moved outside the NFI's remit'. Under option 3, public authorities would become members of an anti-fraud organization such as CIFAS (the UK's Fraud Prevention Service). Public sector organizations would be permitted to share information regarding suspected fraud between them and with the private sector. Given the considerable amount of information that could be processed in this way, the government acknowledged that there is a 'particular duty to make sure our use of data is proportionate, and also that law enforcement would be capable of using the information it gathers'.[6]

7.07   The question that arises is whether and to what extent legal restrictions should be imposed on the use of data-analysis techniques and on whom. Chapter 1 of the SCA 2007 provides only a partial answer. Only data sharing and data matching that is carried out by public authorities is put on something of a statutory footing. Chapter 1 of the SCA 2007 adopts the definition of a 'public authority' as it appears in s 6 of the Human Rights Act 1998, and therefore so-called 'functional' public authorities as well as government departments, local authorities, and the police, are embraced by that definition. Chapter 1 of the SCA 2007 says nothing about the storage of data, and it does not seek to prevent data being stored centrally by a public authority. Holding personal data centrally is widely perceived to pose a greater security risk than holding data regionally, or at various 'stations'. It is submitted that the place where data is held is of secondary importance to the measures that ought to be taken to ensure: (a) that data is kept confidential; (b) that data is used only for the purposes that are permitted under the law; (c) that confidential data is retained for a period no longer than is necessary; and (d) that redundant data is destroyed or archived securely. Decentralization would not necessarily prevent the loss of a substantial amount of data (eg by hacking) because many databases that are held on different computers can be networked to share data.

(a) *Voices of concern*

7.08   In the second reading debate in the House of Lords (7 February 2007), Lord Thomas of Gresford described the original clauses in Chapter 1 to Part 3 as 'atrocious':[7]

So what an excellent wheeze Part 3 of this atrocious Bill is. It introduces into our law a high-tech version of the writ of assistance. If the Bill goes through, the Audit Commission, whose job we thought was to concern itself with the efficient and effective delivery of public services, will appear in a new guise as spymaster general.

Although the Audit Commission's NFI has indeed been tasked to data-match personal data for the purposes of detecting and preventing fraud (at least in the public sector) the Audit Commission must be given credit for taking active steps to

---

6   Cm 6875, p 22.
7   7 February 2007, *Hansard*, House of Lords.

install safeguards ahead of legislation. The role of the Commission in this regard is considered in detail later in this chapter.

On 25 April 2007, the Joint Committee on Human Rights expressed its concern 7.09 about Chapter 1 as then drafted.[8] It noted that the Explanatory Notes to the Bill accepted that the data-sharing provisions engaged Article 8, ECHR (respect for a person's private and family life) because the information disclosed is likely to include 'sensitive personal data' (as defined by s 2, DPA 1998), but the Explanatory Notes added that such disclosures would be justified as being necessary for the prevention of crime.[9] The JCHR was not convinced that this view was correct and it highlighted the following features of Chapter 1, which gave cause for concern:

(1) there is no limit on the kind of information which may be disclosed;

(2) the persons or bodies to whom the information can be disclosed are not specified on the face of the Bill but left to the unfettered discretion of the anti-fraud organization: information can be disclosed to 'any other person to whom disclosure is permitted by the arrangements' made by such an organization;

(3) some of the normal safeguards against improper disclosure of personal information, such as the common law of confidence, are expressly disapplied;

(4) the preservation of the restrictions on disclosure contained in the DPA 1998 and the Regulation of Investigatory Powers Act 2000 do not amount to very significant safeguards, since both Acts contain broad exemptions from their protections for the purposes of preventing and detecting crime.

The JCHR recommended that the Bill be amended to limit the width of the s 68 power (to data-share) by, for example: (a) specifying the kind of information which may be disclosed; (b) specifying the categories of people to whom the information may be disclosed; (c) introducing 'additional safeguards' such as 'defining the threshold for reporting information on suspected fraud (the degree of suspicion that should be required)'; (d) limiting disclosure 'so that only information on those suspected of fraud will be shared'; and (e) providing compensation if persons are 'unfairly affected by the information held about them'.[10] Members of the House of Commons who examined the Bill in General Committee were aware of the views of the JCHR.[11]

The four features identified by the JCHR remain features of Chapter 1 of the 7.10 SCA 2007, but some significant amendments were made in the House of Lords to Chapter 1 that included making provision for a code of practice for the disclosure of information to prevent fraud (now s 71, SCA 2007),[12] and a prohibition on using a data-matching exercise 'to identify patterns and trends in an individual's characteristics

---

[8] Legislative Scrutiny: 5th Progress Report; 12th Report of Session 2006–07.

[9] para 320; as at May 2007.

[10] para 1.38; p 13.

[11] See eg *Hansard*, 5 July 2007, col 238/239.

[12] See *Hansard*, General Committee debate, 5 July 2007; the Bill as Ordered, by the House of Commons, to be printed on 10 July 2007; and see *Hansard*, House of Lords, 24 October 2007, col 1101/1102.

or behaviour which suggest nothing more than his potential to commit fraud in the future',[13] (see new s 32A, Audit Commission Act (ACA) 1998).[14] An amendment proposing that the words 'nothing more than' be removed from this provision was withdrawn. Baroness Scotland said:[15]

I understand that the amendment is designed to ensure that data matching cannot be undertaken to profile individuals who are likely to commit fraud in the future . . . However, by removing the words 'nothing more than', we run the serious risk of losing data matches that indicate fraud that is happening right now merely on the basis that they might also be taken as an indication of propensity to commit fraud in the future. We are seeking to preserve not simply ancillary benefits but the integrity of the core exercise itself.

7.11   No sooner had the Serious Crime Act 2007 been enacted than three significant events occurred:

(1) Several serious security lapses were widely reported concerning the loss of a considerable amount of personal data that had been stored on CD-ROMs, or on other portable devices. These included: (a) the reported loss of two computer discs belonging to HMRC, which contained details of child benefit recipients in respect of 25 million individuals and 7.25 million families, including the details of the recipient, their children's names, addresses, and dates of birth, child benefit numbers, national insurance numbers and, where relevant, bank or building society account details;[16] (b) in May 2007, a private contractor to the Driving Standards Agency informed the agency that a hard disc drive, containing the records of just over 3 million candidates for the driving theory test, went missing from the contractor's 'secure facility' in Iowa;[17] and (c) towards the end of December 2007 there were reports that patient data records had been lost by several National Health Service Trusts.[18]

(2) On 12 December 2007, the Information Commissioner and Dr Mark Walport of the Wellcome Trust, published 'A Consultation Paper on the Use and Sharing of Personal Information in the Public and Private Sectors'.[19] The Prime Minister requested the Review on 25 October 2007. One of its tasks is 'to consider whether there should be any changes to the way the DPA 1998 operates and the options for implementing any such changes'. The Review will also make recommendations 'on how data sharing policy should be developed in a way that ensures proper transparency, scrutiny and accountability . . . that ensures appropriate privacy and other safeguards for individuals and society, whilst

---

[13] Inserted by Sch 7, Part 1, para 2 to the SCA 2007.
[14] House of Lords, *Hansard*, 30 April 2007, col 893; new s 32A, ACA 1998, inserted by Sch 7, Part 1, para 2 to the SCA 2007.
[15] *Hansard*, House of Lords, 30 Apr 2007, col 895/6.
[16] *Hansard*, House of Commons, 20 Nov 2007, col 1101; statement by the Chancellor of the Exchequer.
[17] The Secretary of State for Transport (Ruth Kelly), *Hansard*, 17 December 2007, col 624.
[18] BBC News, 23 December 2007.
[19] Produced by the Data Sharing Review.

enabling the sharing of information to protect the public, increasing transparency, enhancing public service delivery and reducing the burden on business'.

(3) On 17 December 2007, the House of Commons Justice Committee printed its First Report 'Protection of Private Data' (First Report of Session 2007/08),[20] in which it said that '. . . [the] very real risks associated with greater sharing of personal data between Government Departments must be acknowledged in order for adequate safeguards to be put in place'.

The aforementioned events serve to reinforce the message that swift action is needed to put the handling of confidential personal information by public authorities on a transparent, legal footing, and that safeguards must be installed.

(b) *Privacy, confidentiality, and chapter 1 of the SCA 2007*

Data protection is frequently discussed in the context of rules relating to privacy but, for the reasons set out below, this approach is, arguably, too restrictive. Data protection engages Article 8.1 of the ECHR, which provides that 'everyone has the right to respect for his private and family life, his home and his correspondence'. But the right is not absolute, because Article 8.2, ECHR provides that 'there shall be no interference by a public authority with the exercise of this right except such as is in accordance with the law and is necessary in a democratic society in the interests of national security, public safety, or the economic well-being of the country, for the prevention of disorder or crime, for the protection of health or morals, or for the protection of the rights and freedoms of others'. Chapter 1 of the SCA 2007 does have something to say about the laws relating to privacy and confidentiality. The orthodox view that in the English law 'there is no separate law of privacy',[21] needs to be revised for the reasons given by Lord Nicholls of Birkenhead in *Campbell v MGN Limited* [2004] UKHL 22:

7.12

[in] this country, unlike the United States of America, there is no over-arching, all-embracing cause of action for 'invasion of privacy': see *Wainwright v Home Office* [2003] 3 WLR 1137. But protection of various aspects of privacy is a fast developing area of the law, here and in some other common law jurisdictions. The recent decision of the Court of Appeal of New Zealand in *Hosking v Runting* (25 March 2004) is an example of this. In this country development of the law has been spurred by enactment of the Human Rights Act 1998.

The law has been further spurred by the enactment of the DPA 1998, and the Freedom of Information Act 2000.

However, the discussion about the handling of sensitive personal data in the context of rules relating to privacy ought not to deflect attention away from the notion of confidentiality as a separate interest. In that regard, it is perhaps useful to have in mind some of the points made by their Lordships in *OBG Ltd, Douglas and*

7.13

---

[20] Published on 3 January 2008.
[21] See the interesting short article by Monica Bhogal (solicitor in the Media Department of Charles Russell, Solicitors) 'United Kingdom Privacy Update 2003', vol 1, issue 1, March 2004.

Others v Hello Ltd, and Others [2007] UKHL 21. Lord Hoffmann said (admittedly in a different context):

> It is first necessary to avoid being distracted by the concepts of privacy and personal information. In recent years, English law has adapted the action for breach of confidence to provide a remedy for the unauthorized disclosure of personal information: see *Campbell v MGN Ltd* [2004] 2 AC 457. This development has been mediated by the analogy of the right to privacy conferred by article 8 of the European Convention on Human Rights and has required a balancing of that right against the right to freedom of expression conferred by article 10.

7.14 Lord Nicholls of Birkenhead reminds us that privacy and confidentiality are two distinct interests:

> As the law has developed, breach of confidence, or misuse of confidential information, now covers two distinct causes of action, protecting two different interests: privacy, and secret ('confidential') information. It is important to keep these two distinct. In some instances, information may qualify for protection both on grounds of privacy and confidentiality. In other instances information may be in the public domain, and not qualify for protection as confidential, and yet qualify for protection on the grounds of privacy. Privacy can be invaded by further publication of information . . . already disclosed to the public. Conversely, and obviously, a trade secret may be protected as confidential information even though no question of personal privacy is involved. This distinction was recognised by the Law Commission in its report on Breach of Confidence (1981) Cmnd 388, [1981] EWLC 110, pages 5–6.

7.15 Although the interests of privacy and confidentiality are distinct, both interests are relevant in the context of the sharing and processing of personal data, having regard to how the information was obtained. Public bodies receive data from a variety of sources—including information that has been obtained by compulsion (eg tax returns) or from third parties (eg letters of complaint). The interests of privacy and confidentiality deserve to be protected equally rigorously.

(c) *Data-processing and UK international/EU obligations*

7.16 The legislative institutions of the three constituent parts of the United Kingdom have a legal obligation to ensure that persons who are subject to the laws applicable there, can live and operate in an area of safety and justice. The obligation has been rooted in Article 29 of the Treaty of the European Union (TEU), which provides that the Union's objective 'shall be to provide citizens with a high level of safety within an area of freedom, security and justice'. That objective is retained by Article 61 of the Reform Treaty (Title IV), to which the United Kingdom became a signatory on 13 December 2007. But the latter treaty also provides that the objective be achieved 'with respect for fundamental rights and the different legal systems and traditions of the Member States'. In order to meet that objective, the legislative institutions of the EU and the United Kingdom are required, among other requirements, (a) to combat crimes affecting the financial interests of the Union and of its citizens, (b) to protect the external borders of the EU, and (c) to provide its citizens with a high level of security. Underpinning these Treaty objectives are the concepts of mutual recognition, judicial cooperation, and police cooperation. Each of these concepts requires a significant degree of data sharing in order to make them efficacious. Thus, Article 69F(2) of the Reform Treaty empowers the European Parliament and the Council to establish measures concerning: (a) 'the collection, storage, processing, analysis and exchange of relevant information'; (b) 'support for the training of staff, and cooperation on the exchange of staff, on equipment and on research into crime-detection'; and (c) 'common investigative techniques in relation to the detection of serious forms of organised crime'. There is nothing in Article 69F that does not reflect all that was taking place under the terms of the TEU.

The sharing of data between members of the EU requires powerful computer technology, for example the 'E-POC system' (European Pool against Organised Crime) that is designed to exchange information,[22] and SIS (the Schengen Information System). The Home Office (UK) is funding a program known as SIRENE, which, according to its website, will deliver access to SIS to UK law enforcement officers. The website describes SIS as 'an established and robust pan-European data system' that 'via a seamless link on the Police National Computer (PNC), law enforcement officers will be able to share and use certain information with other police organisations from all Schengen countries'. 7.17

(d) 'The principle of availability'

On 28 November 2006, the Director General at the European Commission (Mr Faull), gave evidence to the House of Commons Home Affairs Committee, 'Justice and Home Affairs Issues at European Union Level' (Third Report of Session 2006/07) in which he alluded to the 'principle of availability': 7.18

we have agreed at the highest level, at the European Council level in the EU, adopted something called the *principle of availability* which means that information held in one Member State to which the law enforcement authorities in that Member State would have access should be made available to the law enforcement authorities in other Member States on the same terms as the national law enforcement authorities would have to satisfy to have access.

The 'principle of availability' is applicable from January 2008, and it was endorsed by EU Member States as part of the 'Hague programme on Justice and Home Affairs Co-operation 2004–2009' (adopted at the EU Summit in Brussels on 4/5 November 2004: see 'A Coherent Approach to Privacy and Security: Privacy and Security in Sharing of Information: Striking the Right Balance').[23] For further information, read the evidence of Professors Steven Peers, and other experts, given to the House of Commons Home Affairs Committee on 23 January 2007,[24] and note the proposal for a Data Protection Framework Decision.

---

[22] The Annual Report of Eurojust 2004: 9522/05.
[23] <http://ec.europa.eu/justice_home/news/information_dossiers/the_hague_priorities/doc/07_privacy_en.pdf>
[24] HC 76-II; 5 June 2007.

B. DEFINITIONS AND CONCEPTS FOR THE PURPOSES OF CHAPTER 1, PART 3 OF THE SCA 2007

1. The notion of 'fraud prevention'

7.19 Construed literally, s 68 appears not to confer a power on a public authority to disclose information in respect of a fraud that *has been committed*: the stated purpose of s 68 is to *prevent* fraud. However, to construe s 68 in that way is to misunderstand the purpose of the section, and to misunderstand what is meant by the phrase 'preventing fraud' in the context of Chapter 1 of the SCA 2007. The notion of 'fraud-prevention' encompasses both detection and deterrence. The risk of detection, prosecution, conviction, and punishment, is in itself capable of deterring (ie preventing) the commission of crime. Accordingly, disclosures which increase the magnitude of that risk play some part in crime prevention. In its paper 'Good Practice in Tackling External Fraud' (2004), the National Audit Office states that deterrence involves 'convincing potential fraudsters that frauds against a department or agency are not worthwhile':

> Prevention measures aim to stop frauds entering departments' systems. Effective mechanisms for deterring and preventing fraud are essential elements in combating fraud. Realistically however, some fraudsters will never be deterred and not all frauds will be prevented. In these cases, prompt detection and professional investigations are needed.

2. 'Public authorities'

7.20 The expression 'public authority' takes its meaning from the definition of the same expression as appears in s 6 of the Human Rights Act 1998, and therefore Chapter 1 of the SCA 2007 applies to organizations in the public and private sector.

3. 'Anti-fraud Organization'

7.21 An 'anti-fraud organization' (AFO) is any 'unincorporated association, body corporate, or other person which enables or facilitates any sharing of information to prevent fraud, or a particular kind of fraud, or which has any of these functions as its purpose or one of its purposes'.[25] For the purposes of Chapter 1 of the SCA 2007, an anti-fraud organization must be one that is 'specified'[26] by an order made by the Secretary of State (s 68(1)).

7.22 The AFO most likely to be specified by the Secretary of State, is 'CIFAS', a non-profit making association, founded in 1998, and dedicated to the prevention

---

[25] s 68(8), SCA 2007.
[26] See s 68(8), SCA 2007 (definitions).

of financial crime.[27] On its website, CIFAS describes itself, and its work, as follows:

CIFAS provides a range of fraud prevention services to its members, including a fraud avoidance system used by the UK's financial services companies, public authorities and other organisations. This system allows members to exchange details of applications for products or services, which are considered to be fraudulent, because the information provided by the applicant fails verification checks. Members can also exchange information about accounts and services, which are being fraudulently misused or insurance and other claims, which are considered to be fraudulent. CIFAS Members also exchange information about innocent victims of fraud to protect them from further fraud. This exchange of information is referred to in a fair processing notice, or use of personal data clause, on application/proposal/claim forms and agreements.

When a CIFAS member identifies a fraud, a warning is placed against the address or addresses linked to the application/proposal/claim or account/policy/service. The text of the warning says 'CIFAS—Do Not Reject—Refer for Validation'. The warning shows the name used on the application/proposal/claim or account/policy/service but this does not necessarily mean the person named is involved in the fraud, as fraudsters tend to use a variety of names, some false and some genuine. The CIFAS warning will appear on the fraud prevention agency record of any person who has a link with the address. Any CIFAS member subsequently checking that address sees the CIFAS warning. The warning does not mean the address has been blacklisted. It means extra precautions should be taken to ensure the application/proposal/claim or account/policy/service that has prompted the check of the address is genuine and this protects the address from further misuse.

4. 'Fraud'

'Fraud' is not defined in Chapter 1 of the SCA 2007. Presumably, it will be left to the anti-fraud organization to specify the types of conduct or offences that constitute 'fraud' for the purposes of s 68 of the SCA 2007. There is nothing in the 2007 Act to say that 'fraud' is confined to the offences which are specified in the Fraud Act 2006. The expression 'fraud' can be used in two ways: 7.23

(a) to refer to an element of an offence that must be proved before a person can be convicted of it (eg 'conspiracy to defraud', or the 'fraudulent evasion of the payment of duty'); or

(b) to describe an aspect of offending conduct notwithstanding that the offence in question does not require proof of fraud, eg the offences of bribery and corruption (see *Kensington International v Vitol*).[28]

---

[27] see <http://www.cifas.org.uk>. CIFAS is an acronym for Credit Industry Fraud Avoidance System.
[28] [2007] EWCA Civ 1128, CA.

5. 'Information'

7.24   The expression 'information' includes 'documents' (s 68(8)) but, beyond that, the expression is not further defined in the 2007 Act. Section 68(2)(a) states that 'information' can be 'of any kind' (s 68(2)(a)). This arguably refers to *categories* of information that are disclosable under Chapter 1 of the SCA 2007, rather than defining what 'information' is, for the purposes of the Act. It is submitted that information can take the form of proven or admitted facts, and/or suspicions that relate to fraudulent conduct (or which might reveal that fraud is being committed in a particular way). It is further submitted that 'information' includes business documents, emails, photographs, video or audio recordings, faxes, memorandums, and attendance notes. The only limit on the kind of information that may be disclosed under s 68 relates to purpose, namely, to prevent fraud.

7.25   Section 68 provides no statutory 'filters', 'gateways', or criteria with respect to information that may be disclosed for the purposes of Chapter 1 of the SCA 2007. For example, it is not a requirement of s 68 that information may only be disclosed if it is, or might be, suggestive of fraudulent conduct. There is nothing in s 68 to prevent information being disclosed even in the absence of reasonable grounds to suspect the commission of fraud with respect to that information. Section 68 does not stipulate that the information must have significant value to an investigation before it may be disclosed for investigative purposes. It is submitted (a) the information ought not to be disclosed for the purpose of speculative 'fishing expeditions' in the hope that the information might throw up evidence of fraud, and (b) that information ought only to be disclosed under Chapter 1 of the SCA 2007, in accordance with Codes of Practice that have been prepared in consultation with the Information Commissioner and other appropriate persons. The *Code of Practice for Data Matching* (2006, revised November 2007) provides a useful model. Code 2.3.1(j) provides that data disclosed by 'supplying bodies' should be 'the minimum required to undertake [a data-matching exercise] and report the results'. Code 2.3.1(k) states that the data supplied must be 'of a good quality in terms of accuracy and completeness'. The Code makes further provision for the destruction of data 'promptly once no longer required, unless needed by Supplying bodies as working papers for the purposes of audit, or for the purpose of continuing investigations or prosecution (s 2.3.1(l)). Security arrangements are also set out in the Code.

C. DATA SHARING UNDER CHAPTER 1 OF THE SCA 2007

1. An overview of s 68

7.26   Section 68 of the SCA 2007 empowers 'public authorities' to share information between them for a limited purpose, namely, to prevent 'fraud', or fraud of a 'particular kind' (eg benefit fraud or 'phishing'). A public authority may disclose information if it is a member of a specified anti-fraud organization or, even if it is not a member, a public authority may disclose information in accordance with any arrangements made by such an organization (s 68(1)). The information may be disclosed (a) to the specified anti-fraud organization, or (b) to any members of it, or (c) to any other person to whom disclosure is permitted by the arrangements concerned (see s 68(2)(b)).

Disclosures made under s 68 do not breach any obligation of confidence owed by the public authority (s 68(3)(a)), or any other restriction on the disclosure of information (s 68(3)(b)), but any disclosure must not breach the DPA 1998, or Part 1 of the Regulation of Investigatory Powers Act 2000 (s 68(4)). The position in relation to the DPA 1998 is problematic because there are a surprising number of grey areas concerning the level of protection afforded by that Act.   7.27

Section 68 does not authorize the disclosure of information relating to a subject matter that would be within the legislative competence of the Scottish Parliament (s 68(5), (6)).   7.28

Where a person has received information under s 68 of the SCA 2007 (termed 'protected information') but improperly discloses it to another, he/she commits an offence contrary to s 69, subject to the defences set out in s 69(4). No offence is committed under s 69 in circumstances where disclosure is made for the detection, investigation, or prosecution of an offence in the United Kingdom (s 69(2)(b)). The offence is triable either way, and the penalties are set out in s 70. A prosecution cannot be initiated without the consent of the relevant Director, eg the Director of Public Prosecutions (s 70).   7.29

2. No duty to disclose under s 68

Section 68 of the SCA 2007 does not impose an obligation on any person, or organization, to disclose information, or to report a suspicious transaction. Accordingly, comparisons ought not to be made between the disclosure provisions enacted in Chapter 1 of the SCA 2007 and, for example, statutory obligations to report suspicions relating to money laundering.   7.30

3. Making disclosures under s 68

It is important to note that information may not be shared unless (a) the public authority in question is a member of a 'specified antifraud organisation' (s 68(1)), or (b) disclosure is to be made 'in accordance with any arrangements made by such an organisation'. It is not a precondition for disclosure under s 68, that both the 'disclosing authority' and the intended recipient must be members of an 'anti-fraud organization' (AFO). This is because nothing can be disclosed under s 68 unless it is at least done in accordance with arrangements made by the AFO. It is likely that, in practice, every government department would be a member of an AFO.   7.31

A public authority is not restricted to disclosing information to an anti-fraud organization (ie an AFO specified by the Secretary of State). There will be circumstances in which one public authority may disclose information *directly* to another public authority but this may only be done in accordance with arrangements made by the AFO.   7.32

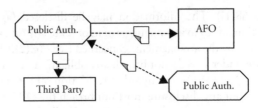

Figure 7.1

Presumably, the AFO will have some responsibility to monitor compliance by public authorities, and to take action if a public authority acts contrary to any of the arrangements, codes, or protocols that bind members of the anti-fraud organization: see Figure 7.1.

4. Practical effect/impact of s 68

7.33 The Regulatory Impact Assessment of the Serious Crime Bill perceives benefits in the following areas with respect to data sharing and data matching:

(1) *Mortgage records*: 'allowing the NFI to match data from mortgage records with housing benefit claims'.

(2) *Public and private sector pension records*. The ACNFI collects about 2.1 million public sector pension records, and 1.1 million private sector records. Data can be matched with housing benefit data.

(3) *Central government: private sector payroll*: 'In the longer term, a move to include employment records from all 3,000 private sector organisations employing 500 or more staff would allow an estimated additional £11m of housing benefit fraud to be detected. However, this is unlikely to be deliverable in the next NFI cycle.'[29]

(4) *NHS foundation trusts*. Benefit fraud; NHS 'tourism' where 'the NFI can detect those who should be denied the services or who should pay for them'

(5) *Housing associations*. Tenancy fraud

(6) *Cross-border data matching*. For example, Newcastle to Scotland.

(7) *Central government*. Duplicate payments to suppliers.

(8) *For tenant arrears*. New contact details obtained to pursue arrears.

(9) *Non-fraud areas*. At first sight, this seems out of place with the scheme of the legislation (ie fraud prevention), but the RIA states that the aim of the Act is to provide 'capacity for the NFI to be used in non fraud areas in the future. Currently, funding does not exist for these options to be pursued, but the [Act] allows the benefits from these areas to be delivered in the future. Having access to the extra data described above would provide potential for the NFI to work with the police in locating absconders from justice.'

---

[29] para 17, Regulatory Impact Assessment: Serious Crime Bill, January 2007.

(10) *Student loan fraud, and immigration fraud.* For example false student loans, or 'over-stayers'.

(11) *Identity fraud.* Negative data matching.[30]

(12) *Deterrent benefits.* Publicity following prosecutions and conviction.

The National Audit Office's publication, 'Good Practice in Tackling External Fraud' (2004), provides useful information about the techniques that might be used by public bodies (and commercial concerns) to analyse personal data.

D. DATA MATCHING

1. Data matching/data mining: the techniques

Provisions relating to data-matching exercises, for the purposes of Chapter 1, are set out in Sch 7 to the SCA 2007 (see s 73).   7.34

(a) *'Data matching' contrasted with 'data mining'*
'Data matching' is sometimes referred to as 'data mining'[31] but there is a significant   7.35
difference between the two concepts, namely, that 'data mining' is a process by which data is analysed to obtain information which can be used for exercises that include 'data matching'. In its Green Paper 'New Powers Against Organised and Financial Crime',[32] the government drew a sharp distinction between data matching and data mining.[33]

The new s 32A of the ACA 1998 (inserted by s 73, Sch 7, SCA 2007) provides   7.36
that a 'data matching-exercise' is 'an exercise involving the comparison of sets of data to determine how far they match (including the identification of any patterns and trends)'.

Redcar and Cleveland Borough Council gives a somewhat fuller description of   7.37
'data matching':

[the process] by which data held for one purpose are taken and compared electronically with data held for other purposes with the aim of establishing any inconsistencies, anomalies or duplications in the data. Depending on the circumstances, this will involve the comparison of data held for different purposes on the same computer; held for the same or different purposes on different computers and, in particular circumstances, against data held by other local authorities or government departments (e.g. during benefit fraud investigation).[34]

---

[30] 'For example, a claimant on income support who is not known to the NHS or a range of other systems may be using a false identity. This type of matching can help identify false identities, preventing fraudulent benefit claims in the public sector and, for example, credit card losses in the private sector. Such negative data matching would require more regular data collection, and the addition of key central applications' (Regulatory Impact Assessments: Serious Crime Bill, January 2007 and June 2007).

[31] See eg the debates in General Committee, *Hansard*, 5 July 2007.

[32] Cm 6875, July 2006.

[33] Cm 6875, p 22.

[34] Redcar and Cleveland <http://www.redcar-cleveland.gov.uk>.

7.38   For a further definition of 'data matching', see para 2.2.1 of the Code of Data Matching Practice 2006 prepared and issued by the Audit Commission.

7.39   A useful definition of 'data mining' appears in the National Audit Office publication 'Good Practice in Tackling External Fraud' (April 2004):

> Data mining is the process of selecting, exploring and modelling large amounts of data to reveal previously unknown patterns, behaviours, trends or relationships which may help to identify cases of fraud. Because of the large amount of data that needs to be analysed, specialist computer software is used which usually contains a range of data mining tools.

(b) *Neural networking*

7.40   The paper by the National Audit Office[35] refers to a technique not mentioned in Chapter 1, namely, 'neural networking'[36]—a computer-based multi-processing system which is designed 'to connect data from multiple sources to identify structures and patterns and exceptions to an identified structure or pattern' and thus 'gives organisations an ability to focus their detective efforts on these exceptions'. The NAO document acknowledges that neural networking is not being used to its full potential (in the public sector) because 'the data may not be held in a way that lends themselves to such analysis. The move towards providing services online may change this and allow real time analysis of transactions through the Department's websites using some of these techniques'.[37] Although the provisions of Chapter 1 permit public authorities to highlight trends and activities with respect to *fraudulent conduct*, it seems likely that information encompassing other areas of the criminal law (eg money laundering, the tracing of assets to enforce court judgments) will be shared and processed by public authorities on a substantial scale, within the EU.

(c) *Sources of data*

7.41   It is important to remember that data may be obtained from a public authority in a variety of ways, for example on demand by way of a VAT or Revenue tax return; by way of a disclosure order (eg s 2, Criminal Justice Act 1987); data collected by an organization; or data that is passed on to an organization/public authority by third parties (eg letters of complaint from members of the public).

2. Data matching and safeguards—the pre-SCA 2007 position

(a) *The response of the United Kingdom, and other countries to concerns about data analysis*

7.42   Data analysis techniques, such as data matching, data mining, neural networking, and data indexing are not new but, by 1997, the UK government recognized that advances made in electronic data processing, and the fact that public bodies were

---

[35] 'Good Practice in Tackling External Fraud'.

[36] This is perhaps a contentious label, it implies something akin to an 'artificial intelligence' model.

[37] paras 3.15, 3.16.

increasingly using and developing computerized databases, required legislative change.[38] Safeguards enacted under the Data Protection Act 1984 became inadequate. The United Kingdom noted that, in Sweden, every data matching-exercise had to be approved by the Data Protection Commissioner; the USA introduced the Computer Matching and Privacy Protection Act (1988), and in Australia, data matching was partially regulated by way of (a) the Privacy Act 1988 (as amended), and (b) the Data-matching Program (Assistance and Tax) Act 1990. The United Kingdom was also required to give legislative effect to Directive 95/46/EC of the European Parliament and of the Council (24 October 1995) on the 'protection of individuals with regard to the processing of personal data and on the free movement of such data'. The House of Commons Research Paper 98/48 (p 15) lists a number of differences between the Directive 95/46/EC, and the Data Protection Act 1984, notably (a) that the Directive included principles relating to 'sensitive data', (b) the conditions that must be satisfied before personal data may be processed (see Article 7 of the Directive), and (c) a requirement that the law must give effect to Article 1.1 of the Directive, namely, to 'protect the fundamental rights and freedoms of natural persons, and in particular their right to privacy with respect to the processing of personal data'. The DPA 1998 was enacted to give effect to Directive 95/46/EC.

(b) *The role of the Audit Commission*
The Audit Commission is a creature of the Local Government Finance Act 1982. 7.43
The National Health Service and Community Care Act 1990 extended its remit. The Commission continues to exist,[39] as an independent body, by virtue of the ACA 1998. Its anti-fraud initiative, known as the 'National Fraud Initiative' (ACNFI), has run since 1996[40] (and not 1998 as the Green Paper states) and was set up 'to study the extent to which the benefits from a successful data-matching exercise, based on local authorities in London, were applicable nationally'. The audit process is run every two years. During the two-year cycle, the ACNFI receives data from participating public sector bodies (of which there were just less than 1,300 in 2004/05) for data-matching exercises.

The ACNFI uses 'advanced data-matching techniques' to assess, and to address, 7.44
fraud risks faced by the public sector. The ACNFI software application for data matching has been distributed to participating bodies on a CD-ROM, but this is 'undergoing further development to respond to requests from users and to integrate the new creditor payment related reports'. The ACNFI contemplate introducing a web-based application to replace the CD-ROM system. The ACNFI recognize that the internet possesses the advantages in 'timeliness and ease of distribution of matches. It will also reduce costs and provide for the first time an audit trail to

---

[38] See the illuminating Note by the Parliamentary Office of Science and Technology (POST), 93, February 1997.
[39] See s 1(1), ACA 1998.
[40] para 1.3.2, Code of Data Matching Practice 2006 (amended November 2007).

monitor access to the matches'. The use of an internet/intranet system *might* also be a safer way of sharing and processing sensitive personal data but it is not clear to what extent data will be encrypted or otherwise protected from illegal interception and use.

(c) Data matching: a legal base, or a code of practice?

7.45 Until relatively recently, it seemed reasonable to subscribe to the notion that, in English law, actions are presumed to be lawful unless Parliament or the Courts provide otherwise. However, over the last 10–20 years, the position appears to have changed: actions performed by public authorities might be judged unlawful in the absence of a legal base that empowers them so to act. The Audit Commission appears to have foreseen that in the absence of a code of practice and statutory regulation relating to data matching, the legitimacy of data-matching exercises might be called into question. It will be noted that the Audit Commission's National Fraud Initiative was up and running for some three years before the DPA 1998 came into force on 1 March 2000 (at which point the Data Protection Act 1984 was repealed).

7.46 As originally drafted, the ACA 1998 only required the Commission to prepare 'a code of audit practice'.[41] It was not under a statutory obligation to prepare a data-matching code. Nevertheless, the Commission, to its credit, published a Code of Data Matching Practice (November 1997) shortly after the NFI was launched, in order to deal with issues that encompass an individual's right to privacy with respect to the processing of personal data. In 2006, the Audit Commission, in consultation with the Information Commissioner, revised the Code of 1997 (and the Code was again revised in November 2007). In the foreword to the 2006 Code, the Information Commissioner welcomes its provisions 'to ensure that National Fraud Initiative data-matching activities take place in accordance with the requirements of the law', and notes that most of the information drawn together is about people who are not engaged in fraudulent activities. A new s 32G(1), ACA 1998 (inserted by s 73 and Sch 7, SCA 2007)[42] now provides that the Commission must prepare, and keep under review, a code of practice with respect to data-matching exercises.

(d) Importance of complying with the Code of Data Matching Practice

7.47 Prior to the enactment of the SCA 2007, public bodies were not under a statutory obligation to have regard to the Codes of Data Matching Practice of 1997 or 2006. Nevertheless, public bodies were expected to comply with the Codes. This was made clear in Parliament on 3 February 1999, when Harry Cohen MP asked the Secretary of State for the Environment, Transport and the Regions, if a local authority is permitted to merge databases containing personal data that had been collected for diverse functions, on the grounds that such a merger would improve the economy,

---

[41] See s 4, ACA 1998.
[42] Corresponding provisions apply in Wales (new s 64G, ACA 1998) and in Northern Ireland (new s 4G, ACA 1998): see Sch 7, SCA 2007.

efficiency, or effectiveness of that authority. The then Secretary of State told Parliament that where arrangements involve the merging of databases which contain personal data, the Data Protection Act 'must be complied with' and that 'the Data Protection Registrar has indicated that she expects them to comply with the [Code of Data Matching 1997]'.[43] Section 32G(2) of the ACA 1998 (inserted by s 73, Sch 7, SCA 2007)[44] provides that regard must be had to the Code in conducting and participating in any such exercise.

3. Data matching under s 73 and Sch 7

(a) *Code of Data Matching Practice*

Paragraph 2 of Sch 7 to the SCA 2007 inserts a new s 32G into the ACA 1998 (audits carried out in England). There are corresponding provisions relating to Wales (s 64G) and Northern Ireland (s 4G).   7.48

The Commission must prepare, and keep under review, a code of practice with respect to data-matching exercises (new s 32G(1), ACA 1998). Before preparing or altering the Code, the Commission must consult (a) 'a body subject to audit', (b) a 'best value authority',[45] (c) the Information Commissioner, and (d) 'such other bodies as the Commission thinks fit'. By s 32G(4), the Commission must send a copy of the Code, or alteration, to the Secretary of State, and a copy must be laid before Parliament. This measure was added to the Serious Crime Bill in the House of Lords on 30 April 2007.[46] By s 32G(2), regard must be had to the Code when conducting and participating in a data-matching exercise.   7.49

(b) *Power of the Audit Commission to data match: purpose(s)*

A new s 32A is inserted into the ACA 1998 by Sch 7 to the SCA 2007. The section applies only to England. Corresponding provisions apply to Wales (s 64A) and to Northern Ireland (s 4A).   7.50

Section 32A of the ACA 1998 empowers the Commission or those acting on its behalf to conduct data-matching exercises for assisting in the 'prevention and detection of fraud' (s 32A(3), ACA 1998). Two points need to be noted: 7.51

(1) Whereas the data-sharing provisions in Part 3 of the SCA 2007 apply with respect to the *prevention* of fraud, the new s 32A of the ACA 1998 makes it clear that data matching encompasses the *detection* of fraud.

(2) The Secretary of State may extend the purposes mentioned in s 32A, namely: (a) crimes other than fraud; (b) to assist in the apprehension and prosecution of

---

[43] *Hansard*, House of Commons, 3 Feb 1999, col 626.

[44] Corresponding provisions apply in Wales (new s 64A) and in Northern Ireland (new s 4A): see s 73, Sch 7, SCA 2007.

[45] Defined in new s 32B(5), ACA 1998; Sch 7, SCA 2007. For Wales, see new s 64B, ACA 1998, and for Northern Ireland, see new s 4B, ACA 1998.

[46] *Hansard*, House of Lords, 30 Apr 2007, cols 899–901.

offenders; and (c) to assist in the recovery of debts owing to public bodies (see new s 32H(1) and (2), ACA 1998).[47] No order shall be made under the new s 32H unless a draft of the order has been laid before Parliament and approved by a resolution of each House of Parliament (s 52(1A), ACA 1998), inserted by para 3 of Sch 7 to the SCA 2007. Section 32H has the potential to considerably widen the power of the Audit Commission, but it is inconceivable that the Commission would be called upon to data match for the purposes of detecting crimes that did not have a substantial financial component (eg firearms offences). Accordingly, the matters, and actions, that might be brought within s 32A of the ACA 1998 by virtue of an order made under s 32H, are offences of money laundering, corruption, and bribery; assisting in the enforcement confiscation orders (eg made under the Proceeds of Crime Act 2002), and the monitoring of Financial Reporting Orders made pursuant to s 76 of the Serious Organised Crime and Police Act 2005.

Note that a data-matching exercise need not form part of a two-yearly audit (s 32A(4), ACA 1998),[48] ie the Audit Commission may carry out a data-matching exercise at any time.

7.52   By s 32A(5) of the ACA 1998, a data-matching exercise may not be used to identify patterns and trends in an individual's characteristics or behaviour which suggest nothing more than his/her potential to commit fraud in the future. This has been discussed earlier in this chapter.

(c) *Data-gathering mechanisms*

7.53   Schedule 7 to the SCA 2007 provides two mechanisms by which data may be submitted to the Audit Commission: (a) mandatory disclosure of information (new s 32B, ACA 1998), and (b) voluntary disclosure (new s 32C, ACA 1998). Corresponding provisions apply in Wales (new ss 64B, 64C) and Northern Ireland (new ss 4B, 4C).

7.54   By s 32B of the ACA 1998, the Commission may require a 'body subject to audit', or a 'best value authority' (defined by s 32B(5), ACA 1998), to provide the Commission, or its agent, with such data as the Commission/agent may reasonably require for conducting data-matching exercises. A failure to comply with a request for information (without reasonable excuse) is a summary-only offence, punishable with a fine.

7.55   By s 32C of the ACA 1998, the Commission may conduct a data-matching exercise using data that is held by a person, or body, *not* subject to the mandatory procedure mentioned above. The Explanatory Notes state that this could include 'central government departments and some private sector bodies such as mortgage providers'.[49] A disclosure made under s 32C does not breach any obligation of

---

[47] See new s 64H (Wales) and s 4H (Northern Ireland).
[48] Inserted by s 73 of and Sch 7, para 2 to the SCA 2007.
[49] para 242.

confidence owed by the person making the disclosure, or any other restriction on disclosure ('however imposed'), save for information that is protected by the provisions of the DPA 1998, or by Part 1 of the Regulation of Investigatory Powers Act 2000, or 'patient data' as defined by s 32C(5) of the ACA 1998.

(d) *Disclosure of results and publication of reports*

A new s 32D and s 32E of the ACA 1998 make provision with respect to the disclosure of results of data matching and the publication of reports by the Commission. Corresponding provisions apply in Wales (new ss 64D and 64E) and in Northern Ireland (new ss 4D and 4E). 7.56

By new s 32D of the ACA 1998, information may be disclosed by or on behalf of the Commission for one of the purposes set out in s 32D(2)(a)–(c), for example in connection with a purpose for which the data-matching exercise was conducted, or in connection with an auditing function of the type mentioned in s 32D(2)(b). 7.57

If the Audit Commission publishes a report on a data-matching exercise, it must not include information relating to a person or body that is the subject of any of the data included in the data-matching exercise, or the person/body can be identified from the information contained in the report, or the information is not otherwise in the public domain. 7.58

E. SAFEGUARDS

1. General protections

There is concern that 'data sharing' and 'data matching' might result in data being shared for purposes other than those for which it was collected,[50] and which, as the authors of Research Paper 07/52 have pointed out, might conflict with the DPA 1998 which provides that:[51] 7.59

Personal data shall be obtained only for one or more specified and lawful purposes, and shall not be further processed in any manner incompatible with that purpose or those purposes.

Section 73 of and Sch 7 to the SCA 2007 amends the ACA 1998 to include the following general protection and requirements (among others) concerning data matching:[52] 7.60

(a) *No disclosure to establish propensity.* A data-matching exercise is not to be used to identify patterns and trends in an individual's characteristics or behaviour, which suggests nothing more than his potential to commit fraud in the future.[53]

---

[50] See Research Paper, 07/52, p 58.
[51] See s 4 of and Sch 1, Part 1, para 2 to the DPA 1998; and see p 58 of Research Paper 07/52.
[52] See the speech of Baroness Scotland, *Hansard*, House of Lords, 21 March 2007, col 1281.
[53] s 32A(5), ACA 1998; Sch 7, SCA 2007.

(b) *Restrictions on 'patient data'.* Insofar as the Audit Commission seeks the voluntary disclosure of information for a data-matching exercise under new s 32C of the ACA 1998, data must not be disclosed if it is comprised of, or includes, 'patient data' (ie it is held for medical purposes from which a person can be identified).[54] 'Patient data' that is disclosed under the new s 32B of the ACA 1998, 'can only be used to combat fraudulent activity in the NHS'.[55]

(c) *Passing on disclosed information.* Information may not be further disclosed except (a) for or in connection with the purposes for which it was disclosed, or (b) for the investigation or prosecution of an offence, or (c) in pursuance of a duty imposed by or under a statue provision (new s 32D(7), ACA 1998; Sch 7, SCA 2007).

2. The DPA 1998 and data sharing

7.61   During the second reading debate in the House of Lords,[56] Baroness Scotland said that data shared under Chapter 1 of the SCA 2007 would be done in accordance with the provisions of the DPA 1998. This was also a point made by the Minister for Security, Counter Terrorism and Police (Mr Tony McNulty MP) in the House of Commons during the Bill's second reading in that House.[57]

7.62   The problem that arises is whether the sharing of data between public authorities, for the purposes of detecting fraud or fraud prevention, would (or might) entail disclosing 'sensitive personal data' that would conflict with the requirements of the DPA 1998. In order to give public authorities added comfort against allegations of violating the 1998 Act, Parliament enacted s 72 of the SCA 2007. The section amends Sch 3 to the DPA 1998 by inserting new para 7A into that Schedule, with the result that when read together with s 29 of the DPA 1998 (crime and taxation exemption), the 'processing' of 'sensitive personal data' which is *necessary* for the purposes of preventing fraud or a particular kind of fraud is exempt from what is called the 'first data protection principle' (fair and lawful processing), s 7 of the DPA 1998 (right of access to personal data), and the DPA non-disclosure provisions[58] insofar as disclosure is made for any of the purposes mentioned in s 29(1). A new para 7A is confined to two actions that may be carried out by a public authority for these purposes: (a) the *disclosure* of 'sensitive personal data' by a person as a member of an anti-fraud organization or otherwise in accordance with any arrangements made by such an organization; or (b) any *processing* by that person, or by another person, of 'sensitive personal data' which has been disclosed. The foregoing requires some elaboration.

---

[54] s 32C(4), (5), ACA 1998; Sch 7, SCA 2007.
[55] s 32B, ACA 1998; Sch 7, SCA 2007.
[56] *Hansard*, 7 Feb 2007, col 731 (HL).
[57] *Hansard*, 12 Jun 2007, col 665.
[58] See ss 27(3), (4) and 29(3), DPA 1998.

For the purposes of the DPA 1998, information must be handled in accordance   7.63
with the eight 'data protection principles' set out in Part 1 of Sch 1 to the DPA
1998,[59] namely, that data must be:

1. Processed fairly and lawfully: *and shall not be processed unless* one of the conditions in schedule 2 ('personal data') or schedule 3 ('sensitive personal data') is met;

2. Obtained only for one or more specified lawful purposes;

3. Adequate, relevant and not excessive in relation to the purpose or purposes for
   which the data is processed;

4. Accurate, and where necessary, kept up to date;

5. Not kept for longer than is necessary for the purpose or purposes mentioned
   above;

6. Processed in accordance with the rights of the individual;

7. Protected against unauthorised or unlawful processing, or against accidental loss
   or destruction, or damaged;

8. Kept within the correct jurisdiction, i.e. not transferred to jurisdictions outside
   the EEA unless that jurisdiction/territory ensures an adequate level of protection
   for the rights and freedoms of data subjects in relation to the processing of
   personal data.[60]

Section 1(1) of the DPA 1998 defines 'data' as information which is dealt with in   7.64
the manner set out in s 1(1)(a)–(e) (eg that it is part of a 'relevant filing system', or
it is held with the intention that it should be form part of a 'relevant filing system'
(s 1(1)(c)), or it 'forms part of an accessible record',[61] or it is 'recorded information'
held by a 'public authority'.[62]

Data includes 'personal data' (s 1(1), DPA 1998), as well as 'sensitive personal   7.65
data' (s 2, DPA 1998). 'Personal data' means data which relate to a living individual
who can be identified from the data and includes any expression of opinion about
the individual. 'Sensitive personal data' is personal data that consists of information
specified in s 2(a)–(h), for example political opinions (s 2(b)), religious beliefs
(s 2(c)), or the commission or alleged commission of any offence (s 2(g)), or information as to 'any proceedings for any offence committed or alleged to have been
committed by him, the disposal of such proceedings or the sentence of any court in
such proceedings' (s 2(h)). For present purposes, s 2(g) and (h) are particularly
important in the context of s 72 of the SCA 2007.

---

[59] Subject to the remaining schedules—particularly, Schs 2, 3, and 4 of the DPA 1998.
[60] Emphasis added.
[61] As defined by s 68, DPA 1998.
[62] And that the information does not fall within s 1(1)(a)–(d), DPA 1998. 'Public authority' means a public
authority as defined by the Freedom of Information Act 2000, or a 'Scottish public authority' as defined by the
Freedom of Information (Scotland) Act 2002. For the meaning of 'held by a public authority' see s 1(5), DPA
1998 (as amended), and see s 3(2) of the Freedom of Information Act 2000, and s 3(2), (4), and (5) of the
Freedom of Information (Scotland) Act 2002.

7.66   The DPA 1998 defines 'processing' (data or information) as (emphasis added): 'obtaining, recording or holding the information or data or carrying out any operation or set of operations on the information or data, including—(a) organisation, adaptation or alteration of the information or data, (b) retrieval, consultation or use of the information or data, (c) *disclosure of the information* or data by transmission, *dissemination or otherwise making available*, or (d) alignment, combination, blocking, erasure or destruction of the information or data' (s 1(1), DPA 1998).

7.67   Section 29(1) of the DPA 1998 exempts from the 'first data protection principle' (and from s 7, DPA) personal data that is processed for (a) the prevention or detection of crime, or (b) the apprehension of or prosecution of offenders, or (c) the assessment or collection of any tax or duty or of any imposition of a similar nature. The exemption is 'to the extent to which the application of those provisions to the data would be likely to prejudice any of the matters mentioned in [s 29(1) of the DPA 1998]'. However, the exemption takes subject to Sch 2 DPA 1998 (with regards to 'personal data') and Sch 3 DPA 1998 (with regards to 'sensitive personal data'). Those two Schedules impose further conditions on the processing of personal data. Information which comes within s 2(h) of the DPA 1998 can be processed under Sch 3 to the DPA 1998, if *necessary* (a) '. . . for the administration of justice',[63] or (b) 'for the exercise of any functions conferred on any person by or under an enactment',[64] or (c) 'for the exercise of any functions of the Crown, a Minister of the Crown or a government department'.[65] If a public authority shares personal data with another authority for the purpose of detecting fraud, or for the purpose of preventing fraud, the question might arise whether the data included 'sensitive personal data' (eg within s 2(h), DPA 1998). Thus, without the amendment made by s 72 of the SCA 2007 to Sch 3 to the DPA 1998, it could be argued, in some cases, that although the disclosure and processing of 'sensitive personal data' for the purpose of preventing fraud satisfies s 29(1)(a) (ie the prevention of crime), those actions do not fall squarely within any of the pre-existing conditions set out in Sch 3 to the DPA 1998 and, if that is the case, then the processing of such data is forbidden by the 'first data protection principle'.

7.68   When s 72 of the SCA 2007 was being debated in General Committee,[66] the Parliamentary Under-Secretary of State for the Home Department (Vernon Coaker, MP) stated that although many public bodies will be able to rely on one of the current conditions specified in Sch 3 of the DPA 1998, 'it is unlikely that the existing conditions would cover all cases of data sharing to prevent fraud'. The government denied that the provision was 'a move to overturn the Data Protection Act or the principles that form its basis'.

---

[63] Sch 3, para 7(1)(a), DPA 1998.
[64] Sch 3, para 7(1)(b), DPA 1998.
[65] Sch 3, para 7(1)(c), DPA 1998.
[66] *Hansard*, House of Commons, 5 July 2007.

The amendment made by s 72 of the SCA 2007 to add para 7 of Sch 3 to the   7.69
DPA 1998 was to provide 'consistency throughout the full range of bodies that will
share the information':

. . . it is also possible that in disclosing information relating to offences or suspected offences, other
sensitive personal data are necessarily disclosed. For example, information that a person was
suspected of claiming sickness benefit for longer than he was entitled has the effect of disclosing
information about his physical health, namely that he was initially entitled to such benefit. Physical
or mental health or condition is also included in the definition of sensitive personal data. Although
many of the disclosures to an anti-fraud organisation will be covered by one or another of the
existing conditions, not all will.

In General Committee, the Parliamentary Under-Secretary highlighted other   7.70
safeguards that are not the subject of specific statutory measures enacted under the
SCA 2007:

. . . individuals will be informed that their data may be shared for the purpose of fraud prevention
at the point that they provide the data. Individuals will be able to require the Information
Commissioner to assess whether their data are being processed in compliance with the Data
Protection Act. The commissioner may also investigate whether the data controller is complying
with the Act on his own initiative. He will also be able to investigate using his normal powers and,
where appropriate, he will be able to use an enforcement notice to require the data controller to
take steps to comply with the Data Protection Act.

The importance of complying with the DPA 1998 is reinforced by a provision in   7.71
the Criminal Justice and Immigration Bill which will increase the penalty for a
breach of s 55 of the 1998 Act, from a financial penalty (see s 60(2), DPA 1998) to
two years' imprisonment following conviction on indictment, and 12 months'
imprisonment on summary conviction.[67] For an interesting paper in which the
rights of data subjects, the role of the National Supervisory Authorities, and the role
of the European Data Protection Supervisor are concisely described, see McGinley
and Parkes: 'Data Protection at the EU Level: A Stocktaking of the Current State of
Affairs'.[68]

It is important to remember that data protection principles are not only relevant   7.72
domestically: they also have an EU/international relevance. The DPA 1998 gives
effect to Directive 95/46/EC of the European Parliament and of the Council of
24 October 1995 on the 'protection of individuals with regard to the processing
of personal data and on the free movement of such data'. Other relevant EU instruments include:

(a) Directive 97/66/EC (15 December 1997) concerning the 'processing of
    personal data and the protection of privacy in the telecommunications sector';

---

[67] cl 75, Criminal Justice and Immigration Bill, as at 26 June 2007.
[68] Marie McGinley and Roderick Parkes, Research Unit EU Integration, Stiftung Wissenschaft und Politik.
German Institute for International and Security Affairs (Working Paper FG1, 2007/03), May 2007, SWP
Berlin.

(b) Regulation (EC) 45/2001 (18 December 2000), on the 'protection of individuals with regard to the processing of personal data by the Community institutions and bodies and on the free movement of such data';

(c) Directive 2002/58/EC (12 July 2002) concerning the 'processing of personal data and the protection of privacy in the electronic communications sector (Directive on privacy and electronic communications)';

(d) Directive 2006/24/EC (15 March 2006) on 'the retention of data generated or processed in connection with the provision of publicly available electronic communications services or of public communications networks and amending Directive 2002/58/EC'.

3. Safeguards: Code of Practice

7.73 Note that s 71 of the SCA 2007 imposes a requirement on the Secretary of State to prepare, and to keep under review, a code of practice with respect to disclosure of information by public authorities for the purposes of preventing fraud, or a particular kind of fraud.[69] Section 71(3) of the SCA 2007 imposes an obligation on public authorities to have regard to the code when considering whether to disclose information pursuant to s 69 of that Act.

F. OFFENCE OF DISCLOSING 'PROTECTED INFORMATION' (s 69, SCA 2007)

1. The *actus reus* of the s 69 offence

7.74 The *actus reus* of the offence (s 69(1)) is:

(1) That a person disclosed 'protected information' to another.[70] 'Protected information' can be one of two types: (a) 'Revenue and Customs information' that reveals the identity[71] of the person to whom it relates, or (b) information that was specified or described in an order made by the Secretary of State ('specified information'),[72] and which was disclosed by a 'specified public authority'.[73]

---

[69] And see the ACA 1998, and see (for England) new s 32G, ACA 1998, inserted into that Act by Sch 7, SCA 2007, which imposes an obligation on the Audit Commission to prepare a code of data-matching practice. The obligation to prepare such a code is imposed on the Auditor General for Wales by virtue of new s 64G, Part 3A of Part 3 of the Public Audit (Wales) Act 2004 (inserted by Sch 7, SCA 2007; and on the Comptroller and Auditor General Audit (Northern Ireland) by new Art 4A inserted into the Accountability (Northern Ireland) Order 2003 (SI 2003/418 (NI 5)) by Sch 7, SCA 2007.

[70] Defined by s 69(6)(a), SCA 2007.

[71] That is to say, (i) it specifies his identity, or (ii) his identity can be deduced from it (see s 69(6)(b), SCA 2007).

[72] See s 69(7), SCA 2007.

[73] Ibid.

(2) The 'protected information' was disclosed by a public authority as a result of (a) that authority being a member of the 'specified anti-fraud organization',[74] or (b) in accordance with any arrangements made by such an organization.

(3) The information was (a) disclosed by the public authority to the alleged offender, or (b) it came into his/her possession as a result (directly or indirectly) of a disclosure being made to another person.

In General Committee, the Parliamentary Under-Secretary of State for the Home Office explained that the purpose of this provision is to ensure that if a person receives information from a public authority, directly or indirectly, that information remains protected by the offence of wrongful disclosure.[75] The offence protects against improper disclosures of 'protected information' that have been made by, for example, a 'mole' within a public authority. Note that not all information that has been disclosed under s 68 is protected by this offence: just 'protected information' (as defined by s 69(5), SCA 2007). The prosecution need only prove that 'protected information' was disclosed by a person other than in accordance with s 68 of the SCA 2007. An offence under s 69(1) may be committed even if disclosure of the information would have been permitted by an enactment but D failed to invoke that power (see s 69(2), SCA 2007). This provision is presumably intended to drive home the message that a person must not lightly disclose 'protected information', and that he/she may only do so conscious of the legal rule (eg a statutory power) that permits such disclosure.

Parliament has enacted two statutory defences to the s 69 offence, namely, that the accused (a) 'reasonably believed' that the disclosure was lawful (s 69(4)(a)), or (b) that the information in question had already been made available (lawfully) to the public (s 69(4)(b)). However, in each case, the burden of proof is on the defendant (s 69(4)). Whether this burden is the evidential or persuasive burden is discussed at para **7.85**.   7.75

2. The *mens rea* of the s 69 offence

The *mens rea* of the s 69 offence is that the accused 'knows or suspects, or has reasonable grounds for suspecting' that the information is of the kind mentioned above (s 69(1)(a), SCA 2007). For the reasons given later in this chapter, it is submitted that the expression 'reasonable grounds for suspecting' has a subjective element as well as an objective element. The *subjective* element is satisfied if it is proved that the accused did in fact suspect that the information was of the kind mentioned above. The *objective* element is satisfied if there are reasonable grounds for a person to suspect the fact in question. It is submitted that this result follows the reasoning of the Court of Appeal in *R v Da Silva*, and the decision of the House of Lords in *R v Saik*.   7.76

---

[74] Ibid.
[75] *Hansard*, 5 July 2007, col 247.

The obvious objection to this construction is that the expression 'reasonable grounds for suspecting' adds nothing to the section if it remains necessary to prove actual suspicion.

3. The meaning of 'suspicion'

7.77 The expressions 'suspects', 'suspicion',[76] 'reasonable grounds to suspect', and 'reasonable grounds for suspecting', appear frequently in UK legislation, but none of those expressions is easy to define. Nevertheless, when considering what is meant by 'suspects', and 'reasonable grounds for suspecting' (ie the two expressions that appear in s 69, SCA 2007), some assistance might be derived from the cases decided in connection with the UK's money laundering legislation.

7.78 In *Da Silva*,[77] the Court of Appeal considered the meaning of the word 'suspecting' in the context of s 93A(1)(a) of the Criminal Justice Act 1988.[78] The Court remarked that using words such as 'inkling' or 'fleeting thought' is liable to mislead (emphasis added):

> . . . the essential element in the word 'suspect' and its affiliates, in this context, is that the defendant must think that there is a possibility, which is more than fanciful, that the relevant facts exist. A vague feeling of unease would not suffice. *But the statute does not require the suspicion to be 'clear' or 'firmly grounded and targeted on specific facts', or based upon 'reasonable grounds'.*

The Court added that in instances where the word 'suspects' appears without words of qualification[79] (such as s 93A(1)(a)), there is no justification for importing them into the statutory provision in question. The Court had referred to the civil law notion of 'blind-eye knowledge', stating that the authorities indicate that the suspicion has to be 'clear' or 'firmly grounded' and that in certain civil cases 'there is a requirement that the suspicion must be of a certain strength'. The Court cited *Manifest Shipping Co Ltd v Uni-Polaris Insurance Co Ltd ('The Star Sea')* [2003] 1 AC 469, as an example of alleged blind-eye knowledge of unseaworthiness. In that case, Lord Scott stated the following at para 116:

> . . . blind-eye knowledge requires, in my opinion, a suspicion that the relevant facts do exist and a deliberate decision to avoid confirming that they exist. But a warning should be sounded. Suspicion is a word that can be used to describe a state-of-mind that may, at one extreme, be no more than a vague feeling of unease and, at the other extreme, reflect a firm belief in the existence of the

---

[76] In its 'Guidance for the UK Financial Sector' (13 November 2007, ch 6.9), the Joint Money Laundering Steering Group of the United Kingdom (JMLSG) describes 'suspicion' as something that is '. . . subjective and falls short of proof based on firm evidence'.

[77] [2006] EWCA Crim 1654.

[78] '. . . if a person enters into or is otherwise concerned in an arrangement whereby—(a) the retention or control by or on behalf of another ('A') of A's proceeds of criminal conduct is facilitated (whether by concealment, removal from the jurisdiction, transfer to nominees or otherwise). . . knowing or suspecting that A is a person who is or has been engaged in criminal conduct or has benefited from criminal conduct, he is guilty of an offence.'

[79] For example 'on reasonable grounds' or 'reasonably suspects'.

relevant facts. In my opinion, in order for there to be blind-eye knowledge, the suspicion must be firmly grounded and targeted on specific facts. The deliberate decision must be a decision to avoid obtaining confirmation of facts in whose existence the individual has good reason to believe. To allow blind-eye knowledge to be constituted by a decision not to enquire into an untargeted or speculative suspicion would be to allow negligence, albeit gross, to be the basis of a finding of privity.

In *Da Silva*, the Court did not equate 'suspicion' with the seemingly contradictory notion of 'blind-eye knowledge'. It is submitted that the Court was right not to do so because the words 'wilful blindness', or 'blind-eye knowledge', have more to say about proving knowledge or belief than they say about the meaning of 'suspicion'.

It is submitted that there is no justification for glossing the word 'suspicion' other than to limit the reach of a criminal provision (ie on policy grounds). In the earlier case of *Schahhou* [2005] EWCA Crim 1258, the Court of Appeal did not rule out the possibility that Parliament was extending the s 93A CJA 1988 offence (now s 328, POCA 2002) to suspicions, which might in a particular case even be unreasonable suspicions. The Court recognized that there might be cases where a jury should be directed that the suspicion must be of a settled nature, for example if a defendant entertained a suspicion but after further reflection 'honestly dismissed it from his or her mind as being unworthy or as contrary to such evidence as existed or as being outweighed by other considerations' (see *Da Silva*). However, the Court added that before such a direction was necessary there would have to be some reason to suppose that the defendant went through some such thought process.

4. The meaning of 'reasonable grounds for suspecting'

The expression 'reasonable grounds for suspecting' appears in a number of enactments (mainly in connection with police powers) and it appears in several places in the POCA 2002: ss 289, 294, 296, 346, 353, 358, 365, 371, 381, 388, 392, 399, and 405.

One might have thought that the condition is entirely objective but the actual position is less straightforward. In *Da Silva*, the Court of Appeal did not need to consider what is meant by 'reasonable grounds for suspecting' or 'having reasonable cause to suspect', but in *Saik* [2006] UKHL18, the House of Lords held that for the purposes of s 93C(2), CJA 1988,[80] proof that the accused had *reasonable grounds to suspect* the origin of the property is treated in the same way as proof of knowledge. Lord Hope said that the subsection assumes that a person who is proved to have had reasonable grounds to suspect that the property had a criminal origin, did in fact suspect that this was so when he proceeded to deal with it: '[in] other words, the first requirement contains both a subjective part—that the person suspects—and an objective part—that there are reasonable grounds for the suspicion'.

7.79

7.80

7.81

---

[80] 'A person is guilty of an offence if, knowing or having reasonable grounds to suspect that any property is, or in whole or in part directly or indirectly represents, another person's proceeds of criminal conduct, he—(a) conceals or disguises that property; or (b) converts or transfers that property or removes it from the jurisdiction, for the purpose of assisting any person to avoid prosecution for an offence to which this Part of this Act applies or the making or enforcement in his case of a confiscation order.'

7.82   Lord Hope added that the 'objective test is introduced in the interests of fairness, to ensure that the suspicion has a reasonable basis for it': and see *O'Hara v Chief Constable of the Royal Ulster Constabulary* [1997] AC 286, where the issue related to the test in s 12(1) of the Prevention of Terrorism (Temporary Provisions) Act 1984 which gave power to a constable to arrest a person without warrant if he had reasonable grounds for suspecting that he was concerned in acts of terrorism.

7.83   It is tempting to take the view that *Saik* is authority for the proposition that, wherever the words 'reasonable grounds to suspect' (or 'reasonable grounds for suspecting') appear in an enactment, it is incumbent on the prosecution to prove both a subjective and an objective element. Unhappily, one cannot be confident that this is so. In his powerful commentary to the case of *Saik*,[81] Professor David Ormerod remarked that the expression 'reasonable grounds to suspect' would seem to be 'a redundant alternative because no prosecutor is likely to take the more onerous route', and that their Lordships' conclusion 'is heavily influenced by the fact that it would be illogical for [s 93C(2), CJA 1988 and s 49(2) DTA 1994] to have an objective element of *mens rea* as to the provenance of the property and yet simultaneously require proof of a purpose to assist a person to avoid prosecution'. That point was made in the context of s 93C(2) of the CJA 1988 and s 42(2) pf the DTA 1994, but s 327 of the POCA 2002 is differently constructed: the ingredients as to purpose that appear in s 93C and s 49(2) do not feature in s 327. One cannot rule out the prospect that a court might construe the expression 'reasonable grounds for suspecting' in different ways, depending on context, but there is a strong case for saying that, as a matter of policy, a person ought not to be criminally culpable for his/her failure to suspect even if, objectively viewed, there were grounds for suspecting the existence of the facts mentioned in s 69(1)(a) and (b) of the SCA 2007.

5. Circumstances in which the offence applies and does not apply

7.84   There are five situations in respect of which the offence created in s 69(1) does not apply:

(1) The accused 'B' acted on behalf of a person 'A' to whom the information was disclosed, and 'B' disclosed the information to 'C' in circumstances where 'C'

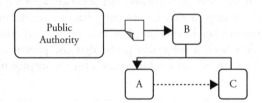

Figure 7.2

81 *R v Saik* [2006] Crim LR 998, HL.

was also acting on behalf of 'A' (s 69(2)(a)): see Figure 7.2. This saving applies where information is passed within an organization.

(2) Disclosure is made by the accused for the purpose of the detection, investigation, or prosecution of an offence *in the United Kingdom* (s 69(2)(a)).

(3) Disclosure is made with the consent of the public authority concerned. This seems to mean that even if a person made an improper disclosure, but he/she acted with the consent of the public authority concerned, then the authority cannot (on that basis) be prosecuted as a secondary party. It is submitted that a public authority (if it exists as a legal entity) can be dealt with under s 69 as a principal offender.

(4) Disclosure is made in pursuance of a community obligation or a duty imposed by an enactment (s 69(2)(a)).

(5) The subject-matter of a disclosure falls within the legislative competence of the Scottish parliament (s 69(3)).

6. Statutory defences under s 69(4)

Two defences are created under s 69(4) of the SCA 2007. The burden of proving each defence is on the accused.   7.85

It is a defence that the accused 'reasonably believed' that the disclosure was lawful (s 69(4)(a)). It is submitted that the expression 'reasonably believed' means a belief based on reasonable grounds and, to quote Baroness Scotland, 'in the circumstances that he was aware of, or in the circumstances he reasonably believed existed, that it was reasonable to act as he did'.[82] Usually, ignorance of the law is no defence, but s 69(4)(a) of the SCA 2007 makes an exception where: (a) the accused mistakenly believed, but reasonably believed, that the law did not prohibit disclosure; or (b) that the accused acted with knowledge of the statutory provisions, but applied those provisions on a construction which he/she reasonably, albeit mistakenly, believed to be correct; or (c) that the accused reasonably believed that, having regard to the circumstances in which the disclosure was made, the law would excuse his/her conduct. An example of (a) might be the case of an employee of a public authority who acted in ignorance of s 68 of the SCA 2007. If a defence is available at all on such facts, it is unlikely to succeed very often in cases where it can be shown that an employee had been adequately trained to make disclosures in accordance with the legislation. As for (c), an indication was sought in Parliament whether s 69(4) of the SCA 2007 afforded a defence in relation to 'whistle-blowing'.[83] The government's answer was in the negative, '[otherwise], we are saying that people can disclose information on the basis that they believe that it is good journalism and that in their opinion sensitive personal information could be disclosed and put in the public arena in an inappropriate way'.[84]   7.86

---

[82] See the speech of Baroness Anelay of St Johns, *Hansard*, House of Lords, 21 Mar 2007.
[83] General Committee, *Hansard*, 5 July 2007, James Brokenshire MP, col 247.
[84] Mr Vernon Coaker, Parliamentary Under-Secretary of State for the Home Office.

7.87   The second defence is that the accused 'reasonably believed' that the information in question had already been lawfully made available to the public (s 69(4)(b)). It would seem not to be sufficient for these purposes that the information had lawfully been made available to the person to whom the accused made the disclosure— the defence applies only if the information is in the *public* domain, and was lawfully disclosed into that domain. Thus, if the information appeared on the internet, and it was accessible by anyone, the defence would not be available if the information had been unlawfully placed there.

7.88   It is an open question whether the courts will hold that s 69(4) imposes a persuasive burden of proof on the accused, or merely an evidential burden (see eg: *R v Lambert* [2002] 2 AC 545; *R v Carass* [2002] 1 WLR 1714, CA; *R v Daniel* [2003] 1 Cr App R 6, CA; *Sheldrake v DPP, A-G's Reference (No 4 of 2002)* [2005] 1 AC 264, HL; *R v Keogh* [2007] 1 WLR 1500, but see *R v Edwards, Denton, and Others* [2004] 2 Cr App R 27, and contrast with *SL (A Juvenile) v DPP* [2002] 1 Cr App R 32, DC; *R v Matthews* [2003] 3 WLR 693; *R v Drummond* [2002] 2 Cr App R 25; *R v Navabi, The Times*, 5 December 5; *R v Makuwa* [2006] 2 Cr App R 11.

7. Sanctions

7.89   The penalty for committing an offence under s 69, on summary conviction, is imprisonment not exceeding 12 months, and/or a fine not exceeding the statutory maximum. The penalty on indictment is two years' imprisonment, and/or an unlimited fine (s 70).

8. Initiating a prosecution for an offence under s 69

7.90   In cases that involve the disclosure of 'Revenue and Customs information'[85] a prosecution for an offence under s 69 may be initiated in England and Wales, with the consent of the Director of Public Prosecutions, or by the Director of Revenue and Customs Prosecutions. In any other case, a prosecution may be initiated only with the consent of the Director of Public Prosecutions. For Northern Ireland, see s 70(3) of the SCA 2007. In the event that an offence under s 69 of the SCA 2007 is committed by a 'body corporate',[86] or by a partnership, any officer, partner, or 'senior officer of a partnership'[87] who connives in, or who consents to, the commission of the offence, is guilty of it, and he/she may be punished accordingly (s 70(4), SCA 2007).

---

[85] Defined by s 69(6)(a), SCA 2007.
[86] See s 70(6), SCA 2007.
[87] Defined by s 70(6), SCA 2007.

8

THE DEMISE OF THE ASSETS RECOVERY AGENCY

A. INTRODUCTION

Section 74 of the SCA 2007 abolishes (from 1 April 2008) the Assets Recovery Agency   8.01
(ARA) and redistributes its functions to other agencies—chiefly to the Serious
Organised Crime Agency (SOCA). Section 74 must be read together with Schs 8
and 9 to the 2007 Act. Schedule 8 to the SCA 2007 amends various enactments
(particularly POCA 2002) to transfer ARA's functions to other agencies. The plan to
transfer the functions of ARA to SOCA was announced in the House of Lords by
way of a written statement by Baroness Scotland of Asthal on 11 January 2007.[1]

B. TRANSFER OF ARA'S FUNCTIONS TO OTHER AGENCIES

The functions of ARA with respect to (a) the making of confiscation orders, and   8.02
(b) restraint orders[2] are repealed (Sch 8, Part 1, SCA 2007). ARA's powers to bring
civil recovery proceedings in the High Court (England and Wales, and Northern
Ireland) are transferred to: (a) SOCA; (b) the Director of Public Prosecutions (England
and Wales); (c) the Director of Revenue and Customs Prosecutions; (d) the Director

---

[1] *Hansard*,11 Jan 2007, HL, col WS19 and see now SI 2008/574; SI 2008/575.

[2] Part 2, POCA 2002, with respect to confiscation proceedings in England and Wales; Part 4, POCA 2002,
for Northern Ireland.

of the Serious Fraud Office; and (e) the Director of Public Prosecutions for Northern Ireland (see chapter 2 of Part 3, SCA 2007). Concern has been expressed about whether SOCA is the most appropriate body to exercise civil recovery powers because, although that agency is intelligence led, it is not an enforcement authority and it is not 'equipped to manage large-scale criminal or civil litigation'.[3]

8.03   The revenue functions which vested in ARA by virtue of Part 6 of the POCA 2002 are transferred to SOCA. As Jonathan Fisher QC has pointed out,[4] ARA had used the power with increasing frequency, and to good effect (see *Khan v the Director of ARA*),[5] and it would seem more logical to transfer revenue functions to HMRC. This may happen because para 102 of Part 3 of Sch 8 to the SCA 2007 empowers the Secretary of State for the Home Office to repeal Part 6 of the POCA 2002, and to make such provision as appears to him to be appropriate in consequence of the repeal of Part 6. Mr Fisher QC states that the enactment of a power to repeal Part 6 is 'surprising' given that HMRC has power to raise individual tax assessments against 'criminal businesses generating substantial income from untaxed assets'. It is submitted that it is unlikely that the Secretary of State would repeal Part 6 without substituting for it a modified/new scheme under which one or more prosecuting agencies would be empowered to raise assessments, and/or to initiate appropriate criminal proceedings.

8.04   ARA's investigative powers with respect to (a) the making of confiscation orders following conviction, and (b) civil recovery orders (Part 8, POCA 2002), are transferred to SOCA by virtue of Sch 8, Part 4, SCA 2007.

C. CONSEQUENTIAL AMENDMENTS

8.05   Following the abolition of ARA, a number of consequential amendments, which are made to existing legislation by virtue of Part 4 of Sch 8 to the SCA 2007, will take effect, and include:

(a)   inserting s 449A into POCA 2002, to permit staff to operate under POCA 2002 using 'pseudonyms' (para 118);

(b)   in connection with a 'confiscation investigation', a prosecutor may only apply for a 'disclosure order' (requiring a person to furnish information) on the request of an 'appropriate officer' (see s 357, POCA 2002, amended by para 108 of Sch 8, SCA 2007);

(c)   in connection with 'civil recovery investigations', it will be open to SOCA, or to any one of the aforementioned Directors, to apply for a 'disclosure order' (requiring a person to furnish information) pursuant to s 357 of the POCA 2002 (see s 357, amended by para 108(7) of Sch 8, SCA 2007).

---

[3] Jonathan Fisher QC, 'The Serious Crime Bill', *The Tax Journal*, 19 February 2007, p 9.
[4] *The Tax Journal*, 19 February 2007, p 9.
[5] [2006] UKSPC SPC00523.

Note that, by virtue of Part 5 of Sch 8, SCA 2007, ARA's powers to train, accredit, 8.06 and to monitor 'financial investigators' under s 3, POCA 2002, are transferred to the National Policing Improvement Agency (see Part 1 of the Police and Justice Act 2006) (see Sch 8, Part 5, SCA 2007).

Part 6 of Sch 8 to the SCA 2007 makes a number of amendments to POCA 2002: 8.07

(a) A new s 2A of the POCA 2002 requires the Directors (SOCA, DPP, HMRC, SFO, DPP(NI)) to exercise their functions under POCA 2002 in the manner best calculated to contribute to the reduction of crime, having regard to guidance that has been issued under s 2A of the POCA 2002 and which is 'best secured by means of criminal investigations and criminal proceedings' (see new s 2A(4), POCA 2002; Sch 8, para 124, SCA 2007). It is submitted that this represents a shift in policy because, for a time, it seemed that the government's thinking was that civil enforcement measures might be as effective as, or preferable to, criminal proceedings. There has been concern that the use of civil enforcement measures to tackle serious organised crime, rather than bringing criminal proceedings, risks bringing the law into disrepute on the grounds that the 'big fish' might escape criminal sanctions while lesser players (whose cases might be easier and cheaper to prosecute) do not.

(b) Sections 435–438 of the POCA 2002 are amended by paras 131–134 of Sch 8 to the SCA 2007 to empower the aforementioned Directors to use information disclosed to them for the purposes set out in those sections. Concern was expressed in the House of Commons by Mr James Brokenshire MP, about the breadth of the revised wording of s 435 of the POCA 2002 and the inclusion of the words 'or otherwise' as they appear in that section, on the grounds that they could be construed as embracing all the relevant duties of the Directors 'in all their contexts' and that there appears to be no limit on the use to which information gained under the 2002 Act can be put.[6] The Under-Secretary of State replied that it was not the government's purpose to give any of the enforcement authorities a completely free hand to disclose information. Section 435 is one of a number of 'supporting provisions to ensure that the new agencies can effectively pursue civil recovery'. He stressed that the effect of the section (and other amendments made to the POCA 2002 by Part 6 of Sch 8, SCA 2007) is that the enforcement authorities will receive only the information that they need to carry out their civil recovery functions, and that the provisions 'are not intended to circumvent restrictions on disclosure between other bodies'.[7]

Part 7 of Sch 8 to the SCA 2007 amends s 33 of the Serious Organised Crime and 8.08 Police Act 2005 (see Sch 8, para 172, SCA 2007), and s 40 of the Commissioners for Revenue and Customs Act 2005 (see Sch 8, para 167, SCA 2007). The amendments relate to the statutory exceptions to the 'confidentiality requirements' that are

---

[6] *Hansard*, 22 Oct 2007, col 61.
[7] *Hansard*, 22 Oct 2007, col 64.

specified in each Act in order to provide 'information gateways' in SOCPA 2005 and CRCA 2005, so that SOCA and HMRC may carry out its functions under the POCA 2002,[8] with respect to:

(a) the exercise of any functions of the prosecutor under Parts 2, 3, and 4 of the POCA 2002 (the making of confiscation orders following conviction);

(b) the exercise of any functions of the Serious Organised Crime Agency under the POCA 2002;

(c) the exercise of any functions of the Director of Public Prosecutions, the Director of the Serious Fraud Office, the Director of Public Prosecutions for Northern Ireland, or the Scottish Ministers under, or in relation to, Part 5 or Part 8 of the POCA 2002;

(d) the exercise of any functions of an officer of Revenue and Customs or a constable under Chapter 3 of Part 5 of the POCA 2002; or

(e) investigations or proceedings outside the United Kingdom, which have led or may lead to the making of an external order within the meaning of s 447 of the POCA 2002

D. WHAT WENT WRONG?

8.09   The reasons for the collapse of the ARA are less material to practitioners than the transference of its functions to other agencies, and the enhanced/modified powers of the Serious Organised Crime Agency. Suffice to say that the ARA was set up in February 2003 under the POCA 2002, with statutory powers to recover the proceeds of 'criminal conduct' by way of: (a) confiscation proceedings following a person's conviction for a criminal offence; or (b) by taxation; or (c) by way of the civil recovery regime enacted under Part 5 of the POCA 2002 (regardless of whether the person holding 'criminal property' had been convicted of a criminal offence or not). Part of the government's case for the enactment of Part 5 of the POCA 2002 (Chapters 1 and 2) was that 'successful criminals acquire significant fortunes and act as bad role models for others, by demonstrating that crime can pay'.[9] The Home Office estimated that some £440 million of criminal assets could be targeted by civil forfeiture across 400 individual cases.

8.10   The PIU Report did little to mask the government's disappointment that the confiscation legislation, as it then existed, was not more effective at taking the proceeds of crime out of the hands of criminals. It reported that in the preceding five years confiscation orders had been raised in an average of only 20 per cent of drugs cases in which such orders were available, and in a mere 0.3 per cent of other

---

[8] See new s 33(2)(ca)–(ce), SOCPA 2005, and s 40(2)(ca)(i)–(v), CRCA 2005.
[9] Para 3.5, 'Recovering the Proceeds of Crime', Performance and Innovation Unit (PIU), Cabinet Office, June 2000.

crime cases. The 'collection rate' was running at an average of 40 per cent, or less, of the amounts ordered by the courts to be seized, and 'law enforcement officers struggle to investigate the financial aspects of crime to support this effort, but their effectiveness is limited by their numbers and modest training'.[10] It said that the 'pursuit and recovery of criminal assets in the UK is failing to deliver the intended attack on the proceeds of crime'. The paper proposed setting up the 'National Confiscation Agency' (later called the 'Assets Recovery Agency'), which would have responsibility 'for a new Centre of Excellence in financial investigation to recruit, train and accredit financial investigators, both for its own requirements and for those of law enforcement agencies'.[11]

The ARA was set up amid well-publicized claims that it would hit the biggest 8.11 criminals in their pockets. The ARA hoped to recover some £10 million in the year 2004/05. During the second reading of the Proceeds of Crime Bill, the Minister for Police, Courts and Drugs (Mr John Denham MP) said the government had set a target of doubling receipts from the proceeds of crime by 2004, which in 'real money . . . is a target of just under £60 million'.[12] However, during that debate, the Parliamentary Under-Secretary of State for the Home Office (Mr Bob Ainsworth MP) sought to clear up any confusion, by pointing out that the target of £60 million related to 'the asset recovery strategy' but it was not a target for the agency, and that '[it] will not be tied to the £60 million target in any way'.[13]

Although the ARA did reach a number of its targets for the year 2004/05, it did 8.12 not meet its target for collecting the value of recoverable property, or becoming self-financing by 2005/06. A Report by the Comptroller and Auditor General indicates that the ARA had revised its target and that it was aiming to be self-financing by 2009/10.[14] The Report identified a number of weaknesses in the processes of the ARA including: (a) poor 'quality referrals', noting that despite efforts made by the ARA to encourage bodies to refer cases to it, 'four police forces and most local authorities and Trading Standards Offices have yet to refer cases to the Agency'; (b) the case management information was poor; (c) it lacked a central database; (d) it experienced a high turnover of staff; (e) high receivership costs; and (f) the 'revised expectation that it will break even by 2009/10 cannot be supported by financial modelling given the relatively short period of operation and the irregular flow of receipts, which preclude the modelling of a reliable trend'.[15] The Report noted that the ARA had expended £15.7 million on receivers' fees, up to 31 December 2006, including over £5 million (31 per cent of expenditure) in 2006/07, in 79 cases. The ARA expected the cost to rise to £16.4 million by the end of 2006/07, giving an average cost per case, where receivers are involved, of some £208,000.

[10] para 1.6.
[11] para 5.44.
[12] *Hansard*, 30 Oct 2001, HC, col 757.
[13] *Hansard*, 30 Oct 2001, HC, col 805.
[14] HC 253, Session 2006/07, 21 February 2007.
[15] Executive summary, para 4.

8.13   On 9 July 2007, the House of Commons Committee of Public Accounts, 'Assets Recovery Agency',[16] found that 'asset recovery has been slow because in most cases the Agency pursued the full value of the assets through the courts rather than negotiate a settlement for a proportion of the assets. It did not prioritise the higher value cases and those that were more likely to realise receipts. In setting its targets the Agency also under-estimated the time it would take to pursue cases through the courts.'

8.14   Despite the criticisms made of the ARA, it is respectfully submitted that there is a truth which is all too often minimized, and which was neatly put by Lord Lloyd of Berwick, in the House of Lords, when the POCA 2002 was then being debated as a Bill:[17]

> ... there is a danger that Part 5 will, all too soon, become a dead letter. There may be one or two high-profile cases, but, as soon as the director begins to discover some of the pitfalls connected with Part 5—there are many—and has been taken to Strasbourg once or twice, he may take the view that his time and money would be better spent pursuing convicted offenders under Part 2 [POCA]. That is where his efforts should be concentrated. It is fanciful to suppose that the 400 major criminals will stand around waiting for an interim receiving order to be served on them ... If they are sophisticated enough to have become untouchable by the criminal law, will they not also be sufficiently sophisticated to get round the provisions of the civil law? They might take all their possessions to Ireland; I do not wish to suggest to them what they might do. There must be many ways in which those 400 criminals could avoid the effect of the civil procedure that is proposed. We will then have yet another piece of criminal legislation that looks good on paper but is useless in practice.[18]

8.15   In none of the aforementioned reports was it suggested that defence lawyers had contributed to the demise of the ARA, or improperly frustrated the ARA's work but, for what the point is worth, during the second reading of the Serious Crime Bill in the House of Commons on 12 June 2007, the Minister for Security, Counter Terrorism and Police (Tony McNulty MP) asserted that:

> the current situation owes more to the shenanigans—that is probably the technical term—of assorted defence lawyers who are seeking to defend their clients and prevent the recovery of their assets and ill-gotten gains. I honestly do not think that that charge could be levelled unduly at the ARA, or that the issue would lead to a lack of success on the part of the ARA. Those are matters that the ARA, SOCA and, more generally, the Home Office are looking to take forward with colleagues in the criminal justice system. Although there might be abuses around the edges, people are perfectly entitled to pursue objections to their ill-gotten gains being recovered, and we do not want to throw the proverbial baby out with the bath water.

Time will tell whether restructuring under the SCA 2007 produces better results.

8.16   During the passage of the Serious Crime Bill in the House of Lords, concern was expressed about the cost of restructuring, and that there ought not to be change for

---

[16] 50th Report of Session 2006/07.

[17] *Hansard*, 13 May 2002, HL, cols 65–69.

[18] And see Fortson 'Civil Recovery Claims', available at <http://www.rudifortson4law.co.uk/legaltexts/Civil_Recovery_Fortson_Lecture_handout_Red_Lion_Court.pdf>

change's sake (Viscount Bridgeman, 30 April 2007: *Hansard*, col 914). In an earlier debate, Baroness Scotland said that she was 'hopeful that the amalgamation of the two agencies will greatly accelerate our ability to asset-manage'.[19]

E. THE ASSET RECOVERY ACTION PLAN

The government believes that by extending civil recovery powers to SOCA and to the Directors of the main prosecuting authorities,[20] those powers will be used in a wider range of cases. The 'Asset Recovery Action Plan' (Home Office, May 2007) reveals that SOCA has increased the number of employees 'working on criminal finances and profits' including 58 additional Financial Investigators. From 1 January 2007, the Revenue and Customs Prosecutions Office created a Division 'dedicated entirely to asset forfeiture work' with responsibility 'for conducting all of RCPO's restraint and receivership casework and, once a confiscation order has been obtained, its enforcement casework'.[21]   8.17

The government also appears to believe that existing powers relating to asset recovery are not enough. In its consultation document, 'Asset Recovery Action Plan' (May 2007) the Home Office states that the plan is about 'embedding the use of asset recovery tools across the Justice system' with the following options and objectives in view: 8.18

(1) To reach a recovery of assets to the value of £250 million by 2009/10. This is having regard to the estimate which is stated in the Action Plan that 'organised criminals alone are probably generating around £2b of recoverable assets in the UK every year, with possibly another £3b of revenue sent overseas'.

(2) To improve co-operation between all agencies involved in asset recovery and particularly in confiscation, which involves investigation, prosecution, and court enforcement.

(3) Possible additional powers:
   (a) new powers to seize the high value goods of those charged with acquisitive crimes and enable them to be sold if necessary to meet confiscation claims;
   (b) a new administrative procedure for cash forfeitures—cash is forfeited automatically unless the owner exercises his right to a court hearing;
   (c) possible extension of cash seizure powers to cover other high value goods, enabling forfeiture to civil standard of goods that might have served as tools in crime, for example vehicles;
   (d) removing loopholes in the civil recovery powers in the POCA 2002.

---

[19] *Hansard*, 7 Feb 2007, col 76.
[20] The Director of Public Prosecutions, the Director Public Prosecutions for Northern Ireland, the Director of Revenue and Customs Prosecutions, the Director of the Serious Fraud Office.
[21] Asset Recovery Action Plan, p 13.

(4) To clarify, 'as a fundamental principle of sentencing that nobody should leave the system still profiting from the crime they committed'.

(5) To review the use of compensation orders 'with a view to multiplying our current performance several times over'.

(6) A fundamental review of the use of tax against criminals.

(7) The possible introduction in England and Wales 'of US style *"qui tam"* provisions,[22] which enable private citizen whistleblowers to sue organisations defrauding the government, securing a share of the damages in return'.

---

[22] See the False Claims Act, 31 USC §3729.

9

'CASH FORFEITURE' IN CIVIL PROCEEDINGS

A. INTRODUCTION

The Criminal Justice (International Co-operation) Act 1990 (CJ(IC)A) introduced   9.01
a new power to enable Customs officers and constables to seize cash (but only cash)
of an amount exceeding £10,000 that was entering or leaving the United Kingdom
if there were reasonable grounds to suspect that the cash directly or indirectly represented any person's proceeds of drug trafficking, or it was intended by any person for
use in drug trafficking (s 25(1), CJ(IC)A). The power was re-enacted in s 42 of the
Drug Trafficking Act (DTA) 1994. Chapter 3 of Part 5 of the POCA 2002 is much
wider and it only has shades of the former scheme. Chapter 3 of Part 5 applies across
the United Kingdom (see Home Office Circular HOC71/2002).

It has been said that the original power was introduced in response to criminals   9.02
moving drug cash to countries less well regulated than the United Kingdom in connection with its tougher anti-money-laundering laws (Home Office Working Group
on Confiscation; 3rd Report: 'Criminal Assets', November 1997, p 27, para 4.7).
At one time, the United Kingdom had strict exchange-control regulations in place
which were strictly enforced. It is no longer an offence to move money in and out of
the United Kingdom. It was partly because of representations made by American and

British law enforcement officers to the Home Affairs Select Committee in 1989 that the power in s 25 of the 1990 Act came to be introduced (see the 7th Report, vol 1, para 87).

9.03   Powers of cash forfeiture enacted under s 25 of the CJ(IC)A 1990 (and later s 42, DTA 1994) proved to be inadequate, and a new regime was enacted under chapter 3 of Part 5 of the POCA 2002.

9.04   The following legislative instruments are currently relevant:

- Proceeds of Crime Act 2002;
- Crown Court (Amendment) (No 2) Rules 2002 (SI 2002/2997);
- Magistrates' Courts (Detention and Forfeiture of Cash) Rules 2002 (SI 2002/2998);
- Proceeds of Crime Act 2002 (Commencement No 1 and Savings) Order 2002 (SI 2002/3015);
- Proceeds of Crime Act 2002 (Cash Searches: Code of Practice) Order 2002 (SI 2002/3115); to be replaced by a 2008 Order on 1 April 2008;
- Magistrates Courts (Detention and Forfeiture of Cash) (Amendment) Rules 2003 (SI 2003/638);
- Proceeds of Crime Act 2002 (Recovery of Cash in Summary Proceedings: Minimum Amount) Order 2006 (SI 2006/1699);
- Serious Organised Crime and Police Act 2005;
- Serious Crime Act 2007, ss 75–77 and Sch10; and ss 79–80 and Sch 11.

9.05

Sections 75–77 of and Sch 10 to, and ss 79–80 of and Sch11 to the SCA 2007, amend the 'cash forfeiture' provisions in Chapter 3 of Part 5 of the POCA 2002 in two main ways. First, the powers of a customs officer or a constable to seize and to detain 'cash' under Chapter 3 of Part 5 of the POCA 2002 are extended to certain 'accredited financial investigators' (ss 79–80). Secondly, amendments are made by ss 75–77 to create a new type of investigation, described in the SCA 2007 as a 'detained cash investigation', for investigating the provenance or intended destination of cash seized under Chapter 3 of Part 5 of the POCA 2002.[1] The Explanatory Notes tell us that '[these] new investigation powers will assist in the preparation of a case for forfeiting the cash before the magistrates' court in England and Wales and Northern Ireland or the Sheriff in Scotland'.[2] The SCA 2007 extends the use of production orders and search and seizure warrants (under Part 8, POCA 2002) for detained cash investigations. Amendments made by the SCA 2007 to various provisions of the POCA 2002 that have been reproduced in this chapter, appear as words in square brackets.

---

[1] See the Explanatory Notes to the Act which deal briefly with these amendments (paras 265-274).
[2] para 265.

B. DEFECTS IN THE CASH FORFEITURE REGIME
UNDER PART II OF THE DTA 1994

The following list identifies the defects in the cash forfeiture regime under Part II of   9.06
the DTA 1994:

(1) *Cash too narrowly defined.* Part II of the DTA 1994 was confined to cash and did
    not include cheques or other money orders.

(2) *Forfeiture limited to cash imported/exported.* Cash forfeiture powers were confined
    to cash imported into, or exported out of, the United Kingdom. 'Exported'
    included cash being brought to any place in the United Kingdom for the pur-
    pose of being exported (s 48, DTA 1994): the chances of the Crown being able
    to prove that matter was slender.

(3) *No power of search for cash.* There was no express power to search for cash.
    Accordingly, although a cash seizure under the DTA 1994 might have been
    intelligence-led, the use of the power under s 42 amounted to little more than a
    power to intercept and to seize cash.

(4) *Little scope in practice for police to seize cash.* Although the power under Part II
    of the 1994 Act was exercisable by a constable, as well as by a customs officer,
    the reality was that the police had little scope for seizing and detaining cash
    under s 42.

(5) *Cash had to be linked to drug trafficking.* The cash had to be linked to drug
    trafficking.

C. THE CHANGES MADE BY THE POCA 2002 TO
THE CASH FORFEITURE REGIME

1. Definition of cash widened

The definition of 'cash' is widely drawn (ss 289(6) and (7), 316(1), POCA 2002).   9.07
'Cash' when found at any place in the United Kingdom, means:

(a) notes and coins in any currency;
(b) personal orders;
(c) cheques of any kind including travellers' cheques;
(d) banker's drafts;
(e) bearer bonds and bearer shares.

Cash also includes 'any kind of monetary instrument which is found at any place in
the United Kingdom, if the instrument is specified by the Secretary of State by an
order made after consultation with the Scottish ministers'. The powers under the
POCA 2002 may be exercised anywhere in the United Kingdom.

2. Not all of the cash need be recoverable, or intended for an illicit purpose

9.08 There is power to seize cash even if only *part* of it is suspected by the officer (on reasonable grounds) to be either 'recoverable property', or intended for use in 'unlawful conduct' (see s 294(1) and (2), POCA 2002). It would appear that 'part' is intended to relate to an 'indivisible part', for example a cheque for £50,000, where only £20,000 is expected to be 'recoverable property' (see Home Office Circular 71/2002).

3. Cash treated as 'recoverable property'

9.09 The definition of 'recoverable property' is wider than cash that 'directly or indirectly represents' unlawful conduct. This is because on each occasion that the proceeds of unlawful conduct are transferred, or converted, a new thread of 'recoverable property' is created, and therefore each thread can create new ones, as property changes hands. However, in practice, the courts look for cogent evidence that cash is the proceeds of unlawful conduct, or that it is intended for use in unlawful conduct.

4. Concept of 'unlawful conduct'

9.10 The definition of 'unlawful conduct' (s 241, POCA 2002) is narrower than 'criminal conduct' because dual criminality is an ingredient of 'unlawful conduct' in s 241, whereas there is no dual criminality requirement in respect of Parts 2–4, and Part 7 of POCA 2002 (except to the extent provided for by amendments made to Part 7 by SOCPA 2005 in relation to money laundering offences). As to what must be proved in order to establish that cash is derived from 'unlawful conduct' see *ARA v Szepietowski* [2006] EWHC 2406 (Admin); *ARA v Green* [2005] EWHC 3168 (Admin); *R v NW and Others* [2008] EWCA Crim 2.

5. Power of search extended

9.11 Under Chapter 3 of Part 5 of the POCA 2002, there is power for an officer of Customs and Excise, or for a constable, to search persons or property for 'cash' (s 289). It is a power that must be approved before it may be exercised (unless it is not practicable to do so). 'Approval' means approved by a magistrate (or in Scotland, by a sheriff), or by a 'senior officer' (defined by s 290(4), (5) POCA 2002). These powers are described more fully below.

(a) *Premises*

9.12 Section 289 of the POCA 2002 provides (as amended by Sch 11, para 2(2), SCA 2007: the amended wording appears in square brackets):

(1) If a customs officer or, [a constable or an accredited financial investigator] is lawfully on any premises [and] has reasonable grounds for suspecting that there is on the premises cash—

    (a) which is recoverable property or is intended by any person for use in unlawful conduct, and

(b) the amount of which is not less than the minimum amount, he may search for the cash there.

The officer must be lawfully on premises, for example pursuant to a search warrant. The officer must have reasonable grounds to suspect that the cash is 'on the premises' and that it is either 'recoverable property' as defined by ss 304 to 310 (ie that it is or represents property obtained through unlawful conduct), or that the cash is *intended for use* in unlawful conduct by any person. The amount of cash must be for the 'minimum amount' (s 303), a figure specified by the Secretary of State, currently £1,000 (see the Proceeds of Crime Act 2002 (Recovery of Cash in Summary Proceedings: Minimum Amount) Order 2006 (SI 2006/1699)).

(b) *Persons*

Section 289 of the POCA 2002 provides (as amended by Sch 11, para 2, SCA 2007,   9.13 the amended wording appears in square brackets):

(2) If a customs officer [a constable or an accredited financial investigator] has reasonable grounds for suspecting that a person (the suspect) is carrying cash—
    (a) which is recoverable property or is intended by any person for use in unlawful conduct, and
    (b) the amount of which is not less than the minimum amount,

he may exercise the following powers.

(3) The officer [a constable or an accredited financial investigator] may, so far as he thinks it necessary or expedient, require the suspect—
    (a) to permit a search of any article he has with him,
    (b) to permit a search of his person.

(4) An officer [a constable or an accredited financial investigator] exercising powers by virtue of subsection (3)(b) may detain the suspect for so long as is necessary for their exercise.

(5) The powers conferred by this section—
    (a) are exercisable only so far as reasonably required for the purpose of finding cash,
    (b) are exercisable by a customs officer only if he has reasonable grounds for suspecting that the unlawful conduct in question relates to an assigned matter (within the meaning of the Customs and Excise Management Act 1979 (c.2)).
    [(c) are exercisable by an accredited financial investigator only in relation to premises or (as the case may be) suspects in England, Wales or Northern Ireland].
. . .

(8) This section does not require a person to submit to an intimate search or strip search (within the meaning of section 164 of the Customs and Excise Management Act 1979 (c.2)).

These provisions need to be read in conjunction with ss 290 to 293 of the POCA 2002, as amended by Sch 11 to the SCA 2007. Powers are exercisable under s 289(2) of the POCA 2002 if the officer/investigator suspects that a person is carrying cash, and his suspicion is on reasonable grounds. An officer/investigator may require the suspect to permit a search of his person (other than an intimate or strip search (see s 289(8)), or to permit a search of any article he has with him eg a suitcase or a car (s 289(3)(a)). If the suspect declines to cooperate voluntarily, the officer/investigator may detain the suspect for so long as is necessary for that purpose (s 289(4)). What is not clear is whether an officer/investigator has power to search a person who is concealing a high value monetary instrument in an intimate place. The answer, by virtue of s 289(8), seems to be 'no', and Chapter 3 makes no provision for a power of arrest to carry out an intimate search.

(c) *Approval*

9.14   In cases where an officer/investigator performs a search on his/her own initiative (or with the prior authority of a senior officer[3]), and the searching officer *either* fails to seize cash that is recoverable property, *or* he is duty-bound to return the cash within 48 hours after seizing it, that officer must submit a written report to a person approved by the Secretary of State (s 290(6)). The period of 48 hours is to be calculated in accordance with s 295(1B) of the POCA 2002, inserted by s 100(2) of the Serious Organised Crime and Police Act 2005.

9.15   The report must include particulars as to why it was not practicable to obtain the approval of a Justice of the Peace (s 290(7)(b), POCA 2002). It follows that no report need be completed if the searching officer obtains prior approval from a Justice of the Peace. The thinking of the legislature appears to be that it can be assumed that a court is impartial and will only give prior approval for a search after carefully examining the merits of the application. The role of the 'appointed person' is to monitor the circumstances and manner in which the powers conferred by s 289 of the POCA 2002 have been exercised, and to make recommendations to the government (see s 291, POCA 2002).

6. 'Minimum amount' threshold reduced

9.16   The 'minimum amount' that may be seized under s 294 of the POCA 2002 was lowered on 16 March 2004, from £10,000 to £5,000 by the Proceeds of Crime Act 2002 (Recovery of Cash in Summary Proceedings: Minimum Amount) Order 2004 (SI 2004/420); and lowered again to £1,000 by the Proceeds of Crime Act 2002 (Recovery of Cash in Summary Proceedings: Minimum Amount) Order 2006 (SI 2006/1699) and which came into force on 31 July 2006.

9.17   Note that it is permissible for an officer to detain, and for the court to forfeit, cash with an aggregate value that equates to at least the 'minimum amount' of £1,000 that had been seized from more than one person. This may not apply if individuals, who are apparently unconnected, hold cash. It is therefore permissible to aggregate sums if it can be shown that the money came from a common source, or had a

---

[3] Defined by s 290(4), SCA 2007.

common destination, or purpose (see *Commissioners of Customs and Excise v Duffy* [2002] EWCA (Admin) 425), and see the commentary to this case by Professor David Ormerod [2002] Crim LR 583. The 'minimum amount' requirement features in s 289 of the POCA 2002 (search) and s 294 (seizure), but the amount is not mentioned in s 295 (detention of cash) or s 298 (forfeiture of cash). It is submitted that this leaves unanswered a question raised by Professor Ormerod [2002] Crim Law 583, namely, whether a magistrates' court is entitled to forfeit a sum of cash, if the amount falls below the 'minimum amount' (eg because the remainder of the money seized is shown not to be 'recoverable property'). It is tentatively submitted that the court does not lose jurisdiction because, by then, either there will be evidence to prove (to the civil standard) that the money is 'recoverable property' or there is no such evidence. A contrary construction would result in the money (that could be shown to be 'recoverable property') being unrecoverable under this provision.

Note that the officer must suspect that the amount he/she intends to seize is worth £1,000 or more. The officer might be wrong, but if there is a dispute about the precise amount of money involved, the officer must count it as soon as practicable (see Home Office Circular 71/2002, para 20). 9.18

7. Persons who may act in forfeiture proceedings

Note that s 84 of the SCA 2007 amends the POCA 2002 and the Commissioners for Revenue and Customs Act (CRCA) (2005), to enable the following persons to act in cash forfeiture proceedings: 9.19

(a) the Director of Public Prosecutions, and the DPP for Northern Ireland, to act on behalf of constables if the Director is asked by, or on behalf of, a constable to do so, and he/she considers it appropriate to do so;

(b) the Director of Revenue and Customs Prosecutions to act on behalf of officers of HMRC, and the Director is asked by, or on behalf of, the Commissioners for HMRC or (as the case may be) an officer of Revenue and Customs, to do so, and the Director considers it appropriate to do so.

In the case of the Director of Revenue and Customs Prosecutions, the CRCA 2005 is amended by the SCA 2007 to allow the additional persons to appear in summary 'cash forfeiture' proceedings, namely: 9.20

(a) A designated member of staff: s 39(1A) of the CRCA 2005 (subs 1A is inserted by s 84(4), SCA 2007).

(b) Persons who are not members of HMRC: s 38(1A) of the CRCA 2005 (subs 1A is inserted by s 84(3), SCA 2007).

Accredited Financial Investigators may also appear in such proceedings where their functions are extended in relation to civil forfeiture proceedings (see s 79, Sch 11, para 12, SCA 2007).

D. WEAKNESSES IN THE POCA 2002,
RE CASH FORFEITURE

9.21 It will be seen from the above that although the POCA 2002 confers on a customs officer/constable, powers to search for and to seize cash that he has reasonable grounds for suspecting to be 'recoverable property', or intended by any person for use in unlawful conduct, those powers do not enable an officer/constable to investigate the provenance of that cash in order to prove (to the civil standard of proof) that the property is either 'recoverable property', or intended for use in unlawful conduct. Prior to the enactment of the SCA 2007, it was not open to a law enforcement agency to apply to a court for a 'production order', or a 'search and seizure warrant', to investigate the provenance of the cash that had been seized. It is not clear to what extent the lack of such powers have proved to be a handicap as substantial amounts of 'cash' have been recovered under Chapter 3 of Part 5 of the POCA 2002. It seems likely that the most problematic cases are those where officers make an unanticipated discovery of a large quantity of cash (eg during the course of a lawful search for items other than cash). Chapter 2 of Part 2 of the SCA 2007 amends Part 8 of the POCA 2002 ('investigations') by enacting and adding to that Part of the POCA 2002 a new investigation styled a 'detained cash investigation' that is intended 'to assist in the preparation of a case for forfeiting the cash before the magistrates' court in England and Wales, and Northern Ireland, or the sheriff in Scotland' (para 265, Explanatory Notes). Furthermore, and prior to the enactment of the SCA 2007, 'Accredited Financial Investigators' did not have the power to seize and release cash. Amendments that have been made by the SCA 2007 to Chapter 3 of Part 5 of the POCA 2002, are scattered across the 2007 Act, and some attempt has been made in these pages to put the most significant amendments into context.

E. SEIZURE AND FORFEITURE OF CASH—SUMMARY
PROCEEDINGS

1. Powers for the seizure of cash

9.22 Section 294 of the POCA 2002 provides (as amended by s 79, Sch 11, para 6):

(1) A customs officer [a constable or an accredited financial investigator] may seize any cash if he has reasonable grounds for suspecting that it is—
(a) recoverable property, or
(b) intended by any person for use in unlawful conduct.

(2) A customs officer [a constable or an accredited financial investigator] may also seize cash part of which he has reasonable grounds for suspecting to be—
(a) recoverable property, or
(b) intended by any person for use in unlawful conduct,
if it is not reasonably practicable to seize only that part.

(3) This section does not authorise the seizure of an amount of cash if it or, as the case may be, the part to which his suspicion relates, is less than the minimum amount.

[(4) This section does not authorise the seizure by an accredited financial investigator of cash found in Scotland.]

The officer/investigator may seize cash if he has reasonable grounds for suspect-   9.23
ing that it is either 'recoverable property' or 'intended . . . for use in unlawful conduct' (s 294(1), POCA 2002), and he may seize cash even if his suspicion relates to 'part' of it (s 294(2), POCA 2002)—but *that* part must be worth at least the 'minimum amount' (see s 294(3), POCA 2002). The latter provision may only be exercised if it is not reasonably practicable to seize the relevant 'part', for example the officer finds a wealth of monetary instruments of which 'part' is suspected to be used in unlawful conduct, but only by careful and time-consuming examination of the remainder, would it be practicable to seize the relevant portion. Note that s 294(4) of the POCA 2002 (inserted by Sch 11, para 6(3), SCA 2007) does not authorize the seizure by an accredited financial investigator of cash found in Scotland.

The officer/investigator must have reasonable grounds for this suspicion. Matters   9.24
that might give rise to suspicion include: whether the cash was concealed; explanations offered by persons who have an interest in the cash; the circumstances in which the cash was being handled (see *Bassick and Osbourne*, 22 March 1993, unreported, DC); the amount of cash that was being transported; whether traces of a controlled drug were detected on part or all of the cash (see *Thomas*, 20 January 1995, unreported, DC). It is not necessary for the officer to suspect that the person carrying the cash has himself been engaged in unlawful conduct, or that he intended to use the cash for that purpose (see *Thomas*). An officer/investigator can seize cash that is already in the possession of the police (eg by exercising a power of seizure under another enactment) and no time limit is fixed by s 294 or s 295 by which 'cash' must be seized (*Chief Constable of Merseyside v Hickman* [2006] EWHC 451 (Admin)).

2. Detention of seized cash

Section 295 of the POCA 2002 is derived from s 42(2) and (3) of the Drug Trafficking   9.25
Act (DTA) 1994. An order for the detention of cash cannot endure for a period longer than three months (s 295(2), POCA 2002). Further orders can be made by the court if the total period of detention does not exceed two years from the date of the first order (s 295(2), POCA 2002, formerly s 42(3) of the DTA 1994).

It should be noted that these powers might be exercised even if no criminal   9.26
proceedings have been instituted (or even contemplated) against any person for an offence in connection with cash seized. Where criminal proceedings are instituted, or where application is made to forfeit the money on the basis that it represents the proceeds of unlawful conduct, or that it is intended to be used for that purpose, the cash is not to be released until the relevant proceedings have been concluded (see s 295(5)(b) and s 296(6)(b), POCA 2002).

9.27   The fact that there as been a defect in the process by which the application was made, for example an inappropriate form was used, will probably not render the detention of cash unlawful (see *Luton JJ ex p Abecasis* (2000) 164 JP 265; and see *Halford v Colchester Magistrates' Court* (25 October 2000); and *Chief Constable of Merseyside v Reynolds* [2004] EWHC 2862 (Admin); and consider *Soneji* [2005] UKHL 49 and *Knights* [2005] UKHL 50. Note that s 100 of the SOCPA 2005 allows for the calculation of the 48-hour period to exclude Saturday, Sunday, Christmas Day, Good Friday, and any bank holiday in any part of the United Kingdom where cash was seized (see Home Office Circular 32/2005).

3. Release of detained cash

9.28   Section 297 of the POCA 2002 provides (as amended by Sch 11, SCA 2007):

(1) This section applies while any cash is detained under section 295.

(2) A magistrates' court or (in Scotland) the sheriff may direct the release of the whole or any part of the cash if the following condition is met.

(3) The condition is that the court or sheriff is satisfied, on an application by the person from whom the cash was seized, that the conditions in section 295 for the detention of the cash are no longer met in relation to the cash to be released.

(4) A customs officer, [a constable or an accredited financial investigator] or (in Scotland) procurator fiscal may, after notifying the magistrates' court, sheriff or justice under whose order cash is being detained, release the whole or any part of it if satisfied that the detention of the cash to be released is no longer justified.

9.29   A party who seeks the release of cash, seized under s 294 of the POCA 2002, has two possible routes. First, he may attempt to negotiate the return of the cash with the agency that seized it. The relevant agency can only do so if it is satisfied that the detention of the cash is no longer justified. The agency must inform the court that it proposes to release the money. The usual route for the release of cash will be by way of an application to the magistrates' court (or to the sheriff in Scotland) under s 297 of the POCA 2002. The applicant must be the person from whom the cash was seized (s 297(3), POCA 2002): this restriction exists to prevent the court from becoming immersed in a dispute between the person from whom the cash was seized, and the person claiming to be the rightful owner of the cash. There is separate statutory provision under s 301 of the Act for victims and those beneficially entitled to the cash, or any part of it, to make an application to the court for the release of the cash, or part of it.

9.30   The applicant must establish that the conditions justifying the detention of the cash no longer exist. In this regard, consider *Customs and Excise Commissioners v Shah* (1999) 163 JP 759 (a DTA case). It is arguable that the wording of ss 295 and 297 of the POCA 2002 might lead to a different result.

4. Forfeiture

Section 298 of the POCA 2002 provides (as amended by Sch 11, SCA 2007):   9.31

(1) While cash is detained under section 295, an application for the forfeiture of the whole or any part of it may be made—
   (a) to a magistrates' court by the Commissioners of Customs and Excise [an accredited financial investigator] or a constable,
   (b) (in Scotland) to the sheriff by the Scottish Ministers.

(2) The court or sheriff may order the forfeiture of the cash or any part of it if satisfied that the cash or part—
   (a) is recoverable property, or
   (b) is intended by any person for use in unlawful conduct.

(3) But in the case of recoverable property which belongs to joint tenants, one of whom is an excepted joint owner, the order may not apply to so much of it as the court thinks is attributable to the excepted joint owner's share.

(4) Where an application for the forfeiture of any cash is made under this section, the cash is to be detained (and may not be released under any power conferred by this Chapter) until any proceedings in pursuance of the application (including any proceedings on appeal) are concluded.

It is not necessary to establish that the person from whom the cash was seized 9.32
obtained the cash through unlawful conduct or that he/she intended that the cash should be used in unlawful conduct (consider *Thomas* (20 January 1995, unreported, DC); and see *Pruijsen v HMCE* (18 October 1999).

The court is entitled to look at all the surrounding circumstances including 9.33
explanations given by those who, for example, intended to use the cash, or why it was being transported in a particular way; the circumstances in which the cash was packaged/concealed; the presence (or absence) of traces of a controlled drug on the cash (see *Thomas, and Bassick*, 22 March 1993, unreported, DC).

The fact that the person from whom the cash was seized has been acquitted of 9.34
criminal charges in respect of the unlawful conduct alleged, does not necessarily prevent the Crown adducing the same facts in evidence in forfeiture proceedings (*HMCE v Thorp*, unreported 28 November 1996, DC).

Section 298(3) of the POCA 2002 is necessary because of the nature of a joint 9.35
ownership/tenancy. Such tenancies create potential legal difficulties under the Act because joint tenants are treated as a single owner of property. For example, H and W might be joint tenants of property that was acquired by each drawing from their own resources. The respondent's contribution is intended to be recoverable under Part 5. If 'cash' is held jointly, similar problems might arise without express statutory provision. Subsection (3) is intended to ensure that in such a case the third party is an 'excepted joint owner' against whom his share of the cash is not recoverable under Chapter 3.

5. Appeals

9.36 Section 299 of the POCA 2002, as originally enacted, broadly corresponded to s 44 of the DTA 1994. The original wording of s 299 was substituted with the current wording by s 101 of the SOCPA 2005, which provides:

299 Appeal against decision under section 298

(1) Any party to proceedings for an order for the forfeiture of cash under section 298 who is aggrieved by an order under that section or by the decision of the court not to make such an order may appeal—

    (a) in relation to England and Wales, to the Crown Court;

    (b) in relation to Scotland, to the Sheriff Principal;

    (c) in relation to Northern Ireland, to a county court.

(2) An appeal under subsection (1) must be made before the end of the period of 30 days starting with the day on which the court makes the order or decision.

(3) The court hearing the appeal may make any order it thinks appropriate.

(4) If the court upholds an appeal against an order forfeiting the cash, it may order the release of the cash.

9.37 Note that the time limit is 30 days, beginning on the day the forfeiture order is made. Appeal is to the Crown Court and it is an appeal by way of a rehearing. There is no power to extend the period for an appeal: *West London JJ ex parte Lamai* (6 July 2000). Unlike s 44(4) of the DTA 1994, there is no provision for the release of forfeited cash to meet reasonable legal expenses (see *Commissioners of C & E v Harris* (29 January 1999)). One effect of the substituted wording in s 299 of the POCA 2002, is that the prosecution may appeal a decision of the court of first instance not to make an order for the forfeiture of cash.

F. THE CIVIL NATURE OF FORFEITURE PROCEEDINGS

9.38 It is beyond argument that powers of forfeiture under chapter 3 of Part 5 of the POCA 2002 are civil in nature. This was also the position under Part II of the DTA 1994 (and see *Mudie v Kent Magistrates* [2003] EWCA Civ 237; and see *Best* (unreported, 23 May 1995, DC). As a result, the forfeiture of cash does not constitute a criminal sanction, or give rise to a 'criminal charge' for the purposes of the ECHR. In *Butler v the United Kingdom* (20 June 2002), the European Court of Human Rights said that, in its opinion (and in the context of Part II of the DTA 1994):

... the forfeiture order was a preventative measure and cannot be compared to a criminal sanction, since it was designed to take out of circulation money which was presumed to be bound up with the international trade in illicit drugs.

The European Court of Human Rights stressed that the legal burden of proving   9.39
the link between the cash seized, and the unlawful conduct, 'rests on the relevant
authority seeking a detention or forfeiture order', but the court's reference to 'money
which was presumed to be bound up with the international trade in illicit drugs' is
puzzling. This must be a slip, because there are no presumptions that operate under
Part II of the DTA 1994, or that operate under Chapter 3 of Part 5 of the POCA
2002. In *Butler v the United Kingdom*, the applicant's submission appears to have
been that a 'criminal charge' arose because he was 'compelled to bear the burden of
proving beyond reasonable doubt (the criminal standard) that the money at issue
was unconnected with drug trafficking'. If that was the submission, it was hopelessly
misconceived. There is no such burden of proof on the person from whom the
money was seized, or on any person to whom the money belongs.

G. STANDARD OF PROOF

The standard proof is the civil standard. This is now well established. In *Butt v*   9.40
HMCE [2001] EWHC (Admin) 1066, the Divisional Court held that the appropriate standard was the civil standard of proof, or (to adopt the phase used by the judge
at first instance, Her Honour Judge Adele Williams), 'the civil standard, but with
great care'. The Divisional Court said:

> . . . it is obviously important to note . . . that Parliament specifically provided that the civil stand-
> ard of proof should apply to proceedings under section 43. It would, in my view, defeat Parliament's
> clearly expressed and enacted intention if the courts were to find that every case of forfeiture under
> section 43 involves a finding of criminal activity and, therefore, the standard to be applied is the
> criminal standard of proof.

> 26. . . .

> 27. I have obtained considerable guidance from *B v Chief Constable of Avon and Somerset*
> *Constabulary* referred to us by counsel, but also from the speech of Lord Nicholls in *In Re H*
> *(minors)*, House of Lords 1996 at page 586, referred to counsel by my Lord, Kennedy LJ, during
> the course of argument. Lord Nicholls said this:

> > The balance of probability standard means that a court is satisfied an event has occurred if the
> > court considers that, on the evidence, the occurrence of the event was more likely than not.
> > When assessing the probabilities the court will have in mind as a factor, to whatever extent is
> > appropriate in the particular case, that the more serious the allegation the less likely it is that the
> > event occurred and, hence, the stronger should be the evidence before the court concludes that
> > the allegation is established on the balance of probability.

In *R (Director of ARA) v He and Chen* [2004] EWHC 3021, the court said: 9.41

> As a general rule, no doubt, criminal conduct may be regarded as less probable than non criminal
> conduct. But where there is evidence from which a court can be satisfied that it is more probable
> than not that criminal conduct has been involved, it does not seem to me that that is something

that is so improbable as to require a gloss on the standard of proof. However, I recognise, and it is no doubt right, that since it is necessary to establish that there has been criminal conduct in the obtaining of the property, the court should look for cogent evidence before deciding that the balance of probabilities has been met. But I have no doubt that Parliament deliberately referred to the balance of probabilities, and that the court should not place a gloss upon it, so as to require that the standard approaches that appropriate in a criminal case.

The standard of proof under Part 5 of the POCA 2002 was considered *In The Matter Of Warnock* [2005] NIQB 16, and the court reached a similar conclusion to that reached in *R (Director of ARA) v He and Chen*; and see *Daura v HMCE* (unreported, 2002) Admin.

H. DETAINED CASH INVESTIGATIONS

1. Creation of the 'detained cash investigation'

9.42   For the purposes of Part 8 of the POCA 2002, s 75(1) of the SCA 2007 inserts a new subs (3A) to s 341 of the POCA 2002 which creates and adds to that section a new investigation, namely, the 'detained cash investigation'. It becomes the fourth type of investigation in respect of which powers enacted under Part 8 of the POCA 2002 are provided. The other three are: (a) a confiscation proceedings (s 341(1)); (b) a civil recovery investigation (s 342(2)); and (c) a money laundering investigation (s 342(4)).

9.43   For the purpose of carrying out a 'detained cash investigation' an application for (a) a 'production order' under s 345 of the POCA 2002, or (b) an 'order to grant entry to premises' (s 347), or (c) a 'search and seizure warrant' (s 352) may be made to the High Court (s 344(b)).[4] Any of those applications are heard by a judge of that Court (s 343(3)).[5]

2. Production orders

9.44   A 'production order' is an order of the High Court which either (a) requires a person specified in the order to produce it to 'an appropriate officer', or (b) requires that person to give the officer access to the material (s 345(4), POCA 2002).

9.45   A judge of the High Court may make a 'production order' if he is satisfied that the property specified in the application is subject to a 'detained cash investigation' (s 345(2)(b), POCA 2002). The application must also state that the order is sought for the purpose of that investigation (s 345(3)(a)) in relation to material, or material of a description, specified in the application (s 345(3)(b)), and a person specified in the application appears to be in possession or control of the material (s 345(3)(c)).

---

4 Amended by s 77, Sch 10, para 4, SCA 2007.
5 Amended by s 77, Sch 10, para 3, SCA 2007.

A production order must not be made unless there are reasonable grounds for suspect-   9.46
ing that 'in the case of a detained cash investigation into the derivation of cash' either:

(a) the property (ie the cash with the subject of the investigation, or a 'part of it') is
'recoverable property';[6] or
(b) that the property was 'intended by any person to be used in unlawful conduct'.[7]

There must be reasonable grounds for believing that (a) the person specified in the
order appears to be in possession or control of the material sought to be obtained
(s 346(3), POCA 2002), and (b) the material is likely to be of substantial value
(whether or not by itself) to the investigation (s 346(4)), and (c) that it is in the
public interest for the material to be produced or that access be given to it having
regard to the benefit likely to accrue to the investigation, and the circumstances
under which the person holds that material (s 346(5)). Material protected by 'legal
professional privilege', or 'excluded material', need not be produced (s 348).

An application for a production order may be made *ex parte* (s 351(1)). Note that   9.47
s 351(2)–(7) do not apply to production orders made in England and Wales for the
purpose of a detained cash investigation (see s 351(8) as amended by s 77, Sch 10,
para 6, SCA 2007).

3. Search and seizure warrants

A 'search and seizure warrant' is a warrant that authorizes an 'appropriate person' (a) to   9.48
enter and to search premises specified in the application, and (b) to seize and retain
any material found there which is likely to be of substantial value to the investigation
(s 352(4), POCA 2002). An 'appropriate person' is a constable, or customs officer, or
(now) an 'accredited financial investigator',[8] or an 'officer of Revenue and Customs, if
the warrant is sought for the purposes of a detained cash investigation'.[9] The 'relevant
Director' means, in relation to England and Wales, the Director of Public Prosecutions,
the Director of Revenue and Customs Prosecutions, or the Director of the Serious
Fraud Office; and, in relation to Northern Ireland, the Director of the Serious Fraud
Office or the Director of Public Prosecutions for Northern Ireland.[10]

A 'search and seizure warrant' may be sought and made if a 'production order' is   9.49
not available. Such a warrant may be made unless:

(a) in the case of a 'detained cash investigation' into the derivation of cash, the property specified in the application for the warrant, or a part of it, is recoverable
property;[11] or

---

[6] See new s 346(2)(ba) inserted by s 75(3), SCA 2007.

[7] New s 346(2)(bb), POCA 2002 inserted by s 75(3), SCA 2007.

[8] See s 80(1)(b), SCA 2007, which amends new s 352(5)(c), POCA 2002, inserted by s 77, Sch10,
para 7(3), SCA 2007.

[9] See new s 352(5)(c), POCA 2002, inserted by s 77, Sch 10, para 7(3), SCA 2007.

[10] See new s 353(5A), POCA 2002, inserted by Sch 8, Part 4, para 105(3), SCA 2007.

[11] See new s 353(2)(ba), POCA 2002, inserted by s 76(2), SCA 2007.

(b) in the case of a 'detained cash investigation into the intended use of cash, the property specified in the application for the warrant, or a part of it, is intended by any person to be used in unlawful conduct';[12] and

(c) either:

    (i) that there are reasonable grounds for believing that any material on premises is likely to be of substantial value to the investigation, and it would be in the public interest to obtain the material, but it is not possible to obtain a production order for one of the reasons set out in s 353(4) of the POCA 2002 (see s 353(3)); or

    (ii) that there are reasonable grounds for believing that there is material on premises which (emphasis added):[13]

> (7A) In the case of a detained cash investigation *into the derivation of cash*, material falls within this subsection if it cannot be identified at the time of the application but it—
> (a) relates to the property specified in the application, the question whether the property, or a part of it, is recoverable property or any other question as to its derivation, and
> (b) is likely to be of substantial value (whether or not by itself) to the investigation for the purposes of which the warrant is sought.

> (7B) In the case of a detained cash investigation *into the intended use of cash*, material falls within this subsection if it cannot be identified at the time of the application but it—
> (a) relates to the property specified in the application or the question whether the property, or a part of it, is intended by any person to be used in unlawful conduct, and
> (b) is likely to be of substantial value (whether or not by itself) to the investigation for the purposes of which the warrant is sought.

Note that a 'search and seizure warrant' may be made *ex parte* (see s 356(1), POCA 2002, as amended by s 77, Sch 10, para 9(3), SCA 2007).

4. Other amendments relating to cash investigations

9.50 Note that the following may not be made in relation to a 'detained cash investigation':

(a) 'Disclosure orders' under s 357 of the POCA 2002 (see s 357(2) as amended by s 77, Sch 10, para 10, SCA 2007);

(b) 'Customer Information orders' under s 363 of the POCA 2002 (see new s 363(1A) inserted by s 77, Sch 10, para 11, SCA 2007);

(c) 'Account Monitoring orders' under s 370 of the POCA 2002 (see s 370(1A) inserted by s 77, Sch 10, para 12, SCA 2007).

---

[12] See new s 353(2)(bb), POCA 2002, inserted by s 76(2), SCA 2007.
[13] New s 353(7A) and (7B), POCA 2002, inserted by s 76(3), SCA 2007.

Note that s 342(1) of the POCA 2002—offence of prejudicing an investigation— 9.51
is amended by s 77, Sch 10, para 2 of the SCA 2007, so that the section applies
if 'a person knows or suspects that an appropriate officer or (in Scotland) a proper
person is acting (or proposing to act) in connection with a confiscation investigation, a civil recovery investigation, [a detained cash investigation] or a money laundering investigation which is being or is about to be conducted'

10

ACCREDITED FINANCIAL
INVESTIGATORS

A. WHAT IS AN 'ACCREDITED FINANCIAL INVESTIGATOR'?

'Accredited Financial Investigators' (AFIs) are specialist investigators who exercise the powers conferred upon them under the POCA 2002. Those powers include the power to seize 'realisable property',[1] to apply for restraint orders with respect to property that is specified in the relevant part of the 2002 Act,[2] and to exercise powers in connection with a 'confiscation investigation'.[3] Such investigators are accredited under s 3 of the POCA 2002, and they need not be constables or officers of HMRC. Note that constables and officers of HMRC need not be accredited under s 3 of the POCA 2002 in order to exercise powers that are available to AFIs.   10.01

B. ACCREDITATION AND FUNCTIONS OF AN AFI

In order to be accredited as an AFI, a person may have to attain a particular grade (see s 453(2), POCA 2002). An AFI may be accredited to exercise only some of the powers under the POCA 2002 that *could* be conferred on a financial investigator. This is because s 453(1) of the POCA 2002 empowers the Secretary of State to specify (by order) AFIs who fall within a 'specified description'. Section 453(2) of the POCA 2002 is amended by s 81(1) of the SCA 2007, with the result that a   10.02

---

[1] For example, s 45, POCA 2002.

[2] See s 42, POCA 2002.

[3] Note s 378, POCA 2002, and note the definition of an 'appropriate officer', not to be confused with the definition of an 'appropriate person'.

description may be referable to 'particular types of training undertaken'. A new s 303A of the POCA 2002 (inserted by s 79, Sch 11, para 13, SCA 2007) provides that an accredited financial investigator (who falls within a description specified in an order made by the Secretary of State under s 453, POCA 2002) may exercise powers enacted under Chapter 3 of Part 5 of the POCA 2002, with respect to the forfeiture of cash.

C. EXTENDING THE POWERS OF AN AFI UNDER THE SCA 2007

10.03 The range of powers that may be exercised by an AFI under the POCA 2002 has been extended by the SCA 2007. Thus, an AFI may:

(a) seize any property that is subject to a restraint order made to prevent that property being removed from England, Wales, and Northern Ireland (s 78, SCA 2007, amending ss 45 and 194 POCA 2002). This power was previously limited to constables and officers of HMRC;

(b) search for cash on a person, or on premises, in accordance with the provisions of Chapter 3 of Part 5 of the POCA 2002 (s 79, Sch 11, SCA 2007);

(c) seize cash found on a person or on premises, following a search for cash (pursuant to Chapter 3, Part 5, POCA 2002) if the AFI suspects (i) that the cash is the proceeds of unlawful conduct, or (ii) that the cash is intended for unlawful use (s 79, Sch 11, SCA 2007);

(d) apply for the detention of cash pursuant to Chapter 3 of Part 5 of the POCA 2002 (see s 79, Sch 11, SCA 2007);

(e) apply for the forfeiture of cash in civil proceedings before a magistrates' court, pursuant to Chapter 3 of Part 5 of the POCA 2002 (see s 79, Sch 11, SCA 2007).

The Codes of Practice that must be prepared under s 292 of the POCA 2002, in connection with the power of officers of HMRC (in England, Wales, and Northern Ireland) and to constables, to search persons or premises for cash that is liable to forfeiture in summary proceedings (Chapter 3, Part 5, POCA 2002), are extended to AFIs (see Sch 11, para 5(1), SCA 2007).

D. NEW OFFENCES RELATING TO AN AFI

10.04 It is an offence to assault (new s 453A(1), POCA 2002), or to resist (new s 453A(2)), or to wilfully obstruct an AFI (new s 453A(2)), who is acting in the exercise of a relevant power (see s 81(2), SCA 2007) that inserts new s 453A into the POCA 2002. A person who commits an offence under s 453A(1) of the POCA 2002 is liable on summary conviction: (a) to imprisonment for a term not exceeding 51 weeks; or (b) to a fine not exceeding level 5 on the standard scale; or (c) to both. A person who commits an offence under s 453A(2) is liable on summary conviction: (a) to imprisonment for a term not exceeding 51 weeks; or (b) to a fine not exceeding level 3 on the standard scale; or (c) to both. The maximum penalty in Northern Ireland is six months' imprisonment (and the maximum in England and Wales is six months' imprisonment pending the commencement of s 281(5) of the Criminal Justice Act 2003).

11

POWERS RELATING TO RECEIVERS APPOINTED UNDER THE POCA 2002

A. MANAGEMENT RECEIVERS AND ENFORCEMENT RECEIVERS

Where criminal proceedings are underway in England and Wales, ss 49 and 51 of the POCA 2002 empower a Crown Court to appoint a 'management receiver' (s 44, POCA 2002), or an Enforcement Receiver (s 51 POCA 2002) in relation to assets that are the subject-matter of a restraint order made by that Court. The difference between the two types of receiver is that a 'management receiver' preserves assets, in respect of which a defendant has an interest, pending the outcome of criminal proceedings. The aim of the management receiver is to ensure that the assets will be realized for their best value in the event that a confiscation order is made against the defendant in criminal proceedings. An 'enforcement receiver' may be appointed by the Crown Court, following the conviction of a defendant, in order to realize the value of his interest in the receivership estate and satisfy the payment of a confiscation order that has been made against the defendant. The appointment of a receiver of either kind is a drastic step and one that is often expensive to take. 11.01

1. Perishable goods and goods of diminishing value

A problem which prosecuting authorities often encounter is that an asset may be perishable or have diminishing value (for whatever reason). The value of boats and motor vehicles depreciate year on year. 11.02

Section 49(2)(b) of the POCA 2002 confers a power on *management receivers* to 'manage or otherwise deal with the property'. Section 49(2)(d) confers a further power on management receivers to realize so much of the property as is necessary to meet the receiver's remuneration and expenses. An *enforcement receiver* may also manage 11.03

or otherwise deal with the property and realize it (s 51(2)(b) and (c), POCA 2002). Similar provisions exist in Part 4 of the POCA 2002 so far as Northern Ireland is concerned (see s 197(2)(b) and (d), POCA 2002 in relation to *management receivers*, and see s 199(2)(b) and (c) for powers conferred on *enforcement receivers*). None of these powers may be exercised by a receiver unless the Court gives persons holding interests in the property 'a reasonable opportunity to make representations to it' (ss 49(8), 51(8), 197(8), and 199(8), POCA 2002).

11.04   Even before s 82 of the SCA 2007 was enacted, it had been open to a receiver to sell perishable goods, or to sell assets that were diminishing in value, but only if the Court made an order to that effect having given interested parties the opportunity to make representations pursuant to subs (8) of the relevant section (ss 49, 51, 197, 199). Section 82 of the SCA 2007 inserts a new subs (8A) into ss 49, 51, 197, and 199 of the POCA 2002 which disapplies subs (8) in each case of the aforementioned sections in respect of perishable property, or in respect of property that ought to be disposed of before its value diminishes.

11.05   Section 82 was added to the Bill in General Committee on 10 July 2007. The reasoning of the legislature appears to be that there might be cases where the value of the asset in question will diminish significantly during any period that a person with an interest in the property seeks to be heard by a court with respect to a receiver's application to dispose of the property in question. This is reasoning that has to be inferred because little was actually said in Parliament when a new subs (8A) was included as part of the Serious Crime Bill. In the House of Lords, Lord Bassam of Brighton said that subs (8A) was part of a larger group of technical amendments which 'support the changes that the Bill had already made to the Proceeds of Crime Act before leaving this House on the first occasion in what my noble and learned friend Lady Scotland described as "good order"'.[1]

11.06   The merits or otherwise of the new subs (8A) can be debated from several points of view. On the one hand, there ought to be, as a general rule, no interference by the State with property that belongs to another, without the persons who hold an interest in that property being heard. On the other hand, where property of diminishing value is restrained by an order of a court, its conversion into property that has a stable value (or an appreciating value) might be financially beneficial to the persons whose property it is, and a receiver could even be criticised for not taking steps to maintain (or to improve) the value of assets which he/she is required to manage.

B. MANAGEMENT RECEIVERS IN CIVIL RECOVERY PROCEEDINGS

11.07   In civil proceedings, for the recovery of 'criminal property' without conviction (pursuant to Part 5, POCA 2002) the High Court may appoint an 'interim receiver'

---

[1] *Hansard*, 24 Oct 2007, HL, col 1107.

under s 246 of the POCA 2002. Such a receiver not only has power to manage the property in question, but he/she may also exercise investigative functions under the POCA 2002 with respect to it.

Section 83 of the SCA 2007 amends the POCA 2002 by creating yet another 11.08 type of receiver in civil recovery proceedings (to be known as a 'civil recovery management receiver'), whose function is to manage property that has been made subject to a 'freezing order' under the POCA 2002 (see new s 245E, POCA 2002). The High Court orders the appointment of a receiver in respect of any property to which the property freezing order applies (new s 245E(2), POCA 2002). It was made clear in Parliament that a receiver of this type will not be entitled to exercise investigative functions (per the Parliamentary Under-Secretary of State for the Home Office, Mr Vernon Coaker MP).[2] This is supported by the Explanatory Notes to the SCA 2007 (para 276):

The new management receiver will have no investigation function and so will have no influence on the progress or final outcome of the case, accordingly the role does not need to be independent and therefore can be performed by a member of staff of the enforcement authority that is pursuing the civil recovery case.

An 'enforcement authority' that is applying to the High Court for an order under 11.09 the new s 245E of the POCA 2002 must nominate a suitably qualified person for appointment as a receiver (s 245E(4)). Such a person 'may be a member of staff of the enforcement authority' (s 245E(5)). There might be some concern about a member of staff of the enforcement authority performing such a task. When this provision was considered in Parliament, Lord Bassam of Brighton stated the government's view that '[as] this role will not be decisive on the outcome of the case, as it is strictly management, such a role does not need to be independent and could be taken by a member of the enforcement authority, such as the Serious Organised Crime Agency'.[3] Time will tell whether the use of a member of staff in this way proves satisfactory or not. It is tentatively submitted that the lack of independence of such a member of staff might prove to be a handicap, and that the role is more complex and more expensive than Parliament appears to have anticipated. The Parliamentary Under-Secretary of State for the Home Office, Mr Vernon Coaker, made no secret of the fact that the move was intended to result in significant savings because 'the primary expense in civil recovery cases is meeting the remuneration and expenses of an interim receiver' and that 'in-house management receivers would be much more cost-effective'. The Assets Recovery Agency had a number of cases where the sums spent on the interim receivership already exceed the value of the assets it was pursuing.[4]

---

[2] *Hansard*, 22 Oct 2007, col 57.
[3] *Hansard*, 24 Oct 2007, col 1107.
[4] *Hansard*, 22 Oct 2007, col 57.

11.10   The powers of receivers appointed under the new s 245E of the POCA 2002 are set out in a new s 245F (see s 83, SCA 2007). Provision is made in a new s 245G of the POCA 2002 for the persons specified in that section to have a right to be heard by a judge of the High Court in connection with directions that the Court might make as to the exercise of the functions of a receiver appointed under s 245E.

12

EXTENSION OF INVESTIGATORY POWERS OF HM REVENUE & CUSTOMS

A. AMENDMENTS TO VARIOUS ENACTMENTS AND THEIR EFFECTS

Section 88 of and Sch 12 to the SCA 2007 make a large number of amendments to   12.01
various enactments, the main effect of which is to make powers that are available to
HMRC exercisable with respect to Revenue functions as well as ex-Customs functions. It is a classic example of predictable incremental reform because many (if not
all) of the amendments made by s 88 could have been made (one might have
thought) at the time that the functions of HMCE and the Inland Revenue were
combined to form the HMRC. As the Explanatory Notes to the SCA 2007 point
out (para 285), the CRCA 2005 'ring-fenced' the statutory powers of HMCE and
the Inland Revenue, 'to constrain the use of the powers to their original purposes'.
The 'ring-fence' is now breached in several places by the provisions of the SCA
2007, which make the following amendments (among others):

(a) s 93 of the Police Act 1997 is amended so that references to an 'officer of HMCE'
    become references to an 'officer of Revenue and Customs' (Sch 12, para 1, SCA
    2007);

(b) regardless of whether the matter in question relates to a Revenue function or a
    Customs function, an 'authorising officer' may authorize action to 'interfere
    with property', eg to place a listening device in property, or in a car, or elsewhere;
    or to take action with respect to wireless telegraphy if the 'authorising officer'
    believes such action to be necessary for the purpose of preventing or detecting
    serious crime, and it is proportionate to take that action (s 93(2), Police Act (PA)
    1997). This result has been achieved as follows:

    (i) Section 92 of the Police Act 1997 states that '[no] entry on or interference
        with property or with wireless telegraphy shall be unlawful if it is authorised
        by an authorisation having effect under [the Act]'.

(ii) Authorisation is the subject of s 93 of the 1997 Act which states that interference with property can only be authorized by an 'authorising officer' (an expression defined by s 93(5), PA 1997), and that the action is necessary and proportionate (s 93(2), PA 1997).

(iii) Section 93(5(h) of the PA 1997, as originally drafted, included a 'customs officer designated by the Commissioners of Customs and Excise' as an 'authorising officer'. Paragraph 1(c) of Sch 12 to the SCA 2007 substitutes a new s 93(5)(h), PA 1997, which reads: 'an officer of Revenue and Customs who is a senior official within the meaning of the Regulation of Investigatory Powers Act 2000 and who is designated for the purposes of this paragraph by the Commissioners for Her Majesty's Revenue and Customs'.

(iv) Section 81(1) of the Regulation of Investigatory Powers Act 2000 defines 'a senior official' to mean a 'member of the Senior Civil Service' who is designated for the purpose of s 93(5)(h), PA 1997.

(v) 'Serious crime', for the purpose of the Police Act 1997 involves (a) the use of violence, or results in substantial financial gain, or it is conduct by a large number of persons in pursuit of a common purpose, or (b) the offence or one of the offences is an offence for which a person who has attained the age of 21 and has no previous convictions could reasonably be expected to be sentenced to imprisonment for a term of three years or more (s 93(4), PA 1997).

(c) Persons who can apply for an interception warrant pursuant to s 6(2) of the Regulation of Investigatory Powers Act (RIPA) 2000 include the Commissioners for HMRC, rather than the Commissioners for HMCE (the pre-existing position) (see Sch 12, para 6, SCA 2007).

(d) Paragraph 7 of Sch 12 to the SCA 2007 amends s 21(5) of the RIPA 2000 by substituting the words 'officers of Revenue and Customs' for 'customs officers', and para 8 of that Schedule amends s 21(1) of the RIPA 2000 by defining a 'relevant public authority' to include 'Her Majesty's Revenue and Customs'. If HMRC seek 'traffic data' (see s 21(4)(a), RIPA 2000) to prevent or to detect crime relating to a Revenue function, only data relating to a postal service can be obtained but not data relating to a telecommunications system. This is the effect of Article 10 of the Regulation of Investigatory Powers (Communications Data) Order 2003 (SI 2003/3172). According to the Explanatory Notes which accompany the SCA 2007 (see para 297) 'when SI 2003/3172 (The Regulation of Investigatory Powers (Communications Data) Order 2003) is amended the intention is to remove this restriction in article 10 relating to ex-Inland Revenue matters. Once that is done HMRC will be able to obtain traffic data relating to both postal services and telecommunications systems where that is believed necessary, and proportionate, for tackling crime or preventing disorder'.

(e) HMRC will be able to use intrusive surveillance techniques for both Revenue matters and Customs matters. This is the effect of para 9 of Sch 12 to the SCA

2007, which amends s 27(4)(c) of the RIPA 2000. The conditions that must be satisfied before intrusive surveillance can take place remain unchanged.

(f) Schedule 12 to the SCA 2007 makes a number of amendments to Part III of the RIPA 2000 (investigation of electronic data protected by encryption) so that Part III of the Act encompasses both Revenue functions and Customs functions undertaken by HMRC.

(g) Paragraph 21 of Sch 12 to the SCA 2007 amends s 54 of the RIPA 2000 by substituting 'Her Majesty's Revenue and Customs' for 'the customs and excise'. The effect of the amendment is that regardless of whether HMRC is performing a Revenue function or a Customs function, a notice issued under s 49 of the RIPA 2000 may include a requirement that (a) the person to whom the notice is given, and (b) every other person who becomes aware of it, or of its contents, keeps secret (i) the giving of the notice, (ii) its contents, and (iii) the things done in pursuance of it.

(h) Paragraph 22 of Sch 12 to the SCA 2007 amends s 55 of the RIPA 2000 by substituting 'the Commissioners for Her Majesty's Revenue and Customs' for 'the Commissioners of Customs and Excise'. The effect of the amendment is that regardless of whether HMRC is performing a Revenue function or a Customs function, data encryption keys shall be used and/or disclosed subject to the safeguards set out in the RIPA 2000. 'Keys' is defined by s 56 of the RIPA 2000 to include 'any key, code, password, algorithm or other data the use of which (with or without other keys) (a) allows access to the electronic data, or (b) facilitates the putting of the data into an intelligible form'.

(i) The amendments made by para 29 of Sch 12 to the SCA 2007 apply s 49(2) of the RIPA 2000 in a consistent fashion regardless of whether HMRC is carrying out a Revenue function or a Customs function. By s 49(2) of the RIPA 2000, if a member of HMRC believes (a) that a person is in possession of protected information which has been secured by a 'key' (see s 56, RIPA 2000 for the definition of 'key'), and (b) that disclosure to HMRC in respect of the protected information is 'necessary' and 'proportionate' (ie for the purposes of s 49(3) of the RIPA 2000, or for securing the effective exercise, or proper performance, by any public authority of any statutory power, or statutory duty), and (c) that it is not reasonably practicable to obtain possession of the protected information in an intelligible form without the giving of a notice under s 49 of the RIPA 2000, then HMRC may with 'appropriate permission' serve a notice of disclosure in respect of the protected information. Usually the permission of a judge is required under para 1 of Sch 2 to the RIPA 2000 before an officer can have appropriate permission in relation to a Customs function, except in the two situations described in the Explanatory Notes (para 317):

Under paragraph 2 of Schedule 2 where certain protected information was obtained under a warrant issued by the Secretary of State, or a person holding judicial office, or an authorisation under

Part III of the Police Act 1997 and the warrant or authorisation gave permission for the section 49 notice to be given. Alternatively, written permission could be obtained from the 'relevant authority' (as defined at paragraph 2(6) of Schedule 2) for the issue of the notice after the issue of the warrant or authorisation.

Under paragraph 4 of Schedule 2 where unintelligible information is, or is likely to be, obtained under statutory powers but without a warrant issued by the Secretary of State or a person holding judicial office, or an authorisation under Part III of the Police Act 1997.

12.02   Section 85 of the SCA 2007 provides for the disclosure of information by (or with the authority of) the Commissioners of Revenue and Customs, to the Criminal Assets Bureau in Ireland (CAB), or to any specified public authority in the United Kingdom or elsewhere, for purposes that include: (a) the identification of 'proceeds of crime'; (b) the bringing of civil proceedings for enforcement purposes in relation to proceeds of crime; and (c) the taking of other action in relation to proceeds of crime (see s 85, SCA 2007). 'Proceeds of crime' is defined by s 85(9) to mean, 'assets derived, or suspected to be derived, directly or indirectly from criminal conduct (wherever occurring)'. Although the expression 'criminal conduct' is not defined in s 85 of the SCA 2007, it presumably has the meaning given to it by the relevant enactment (principally POCA 2002) and therefore 'criminal conduct' refers to just about every offence that could be tried in the United Kingdom if the conduct in question was performed there (see ss 76(1) and 326(1), POCA 2002). Information disclosed under s 85(2) of the SCA 2007 must not be further disclosed except in connection with any of the functions set out in s 85(3) (without the consent of the Commissioners of HMRC, or on 'authorised officer', if the function is one undertaken by HMRC) (see s 84(5), SCA 2007). Consent or authorization that is required for the purposes of s 85(4) of the SCA 2007 may be 'general' or 'specific' (s 85(5), SCA 2007).

12.03   It is an offence under s 19 of the CRCA 2005 to make an improper disclosure (ie in contravention of s 85(4), SCA 2007) (see s 85(6), SCA 2007). No information may be disclosed under s 85 of the SCA 2007 in contravention of the Data Protection Act 1998, or Part 1 of the Regulation of Investigatory Powers Act 2000 (s 85(8), SCA 2007).

13

STOP AND SEARCH AMENDMENT
(s 87, SCA 2007)

Section 60(1) of the Criminal Justice and Public Order Act (CJPOA) 1994 provides   13.01
that if a police officer of or above the rank of inspector reasonably believes that
incidents involving serious violence may take place in any locality in his police area,
and that it is expedient to give an authorization under this section to prevent their
occurrence, or that persons are carrying dangerous instruments or offensive weapons
in any locality in his police area without good reason, he may give an authorization
that the powers conferred by that section are to be exercisable at any place within
that locality for a specified period not exceeding 24 hours. The powers which are
conferred on an officer in uniform include (under s 60(4), CJPOA 1994) the power
to stop any pedestrian and search him or anything carried by him for offensive
weapons or dangerous instruments; or to stop any vehicle and search the vehicle, its
driver and any passenger for offensive weapons or dangerous instruments. By virtue
of s 60(5) of the CJPOA 1994, a constable may, in the exercise of the powers
conferred by s 60(4), stop any person or vehicle and make any search he thinks
fit whether or not he has any grounds for suspecting that the person or vehicle is
carrying weapons or articles of that kind, and if in the course of a search a constable
discovers a dangerous instrument or an article which he has reasonable grounds for
suspecting to be an offensive weapon, he may seize it.

Section 87 of the SCA 2007 adds a further circumstance in which those powers   13.02
can be used, namely, that an incident involving serious violence has taken place in
England and Wales in the relevant police area; and a dangerous instrument or offensive weapon used in the incident, is being carried in any locality in that area by a
person; and it is expedient to give an authorization under s 60 of the CJPOA 1994
to find the instrument or weapon. The Explanatory Notes state that the purpose
of this is to 'assist the police in locating the weapon used in the incident, and in
apprehending the offender' (para 282) and that 'the police would be able to make
an authorisation orally in the first instance, to be followed in writing as soon as is
practicable. In the existing two circumstances they will continue to need to make
any authorisation in writing' (para 283). This provision was added to the Serious
Crime Bill on 22 October 2007 in the House of Commons, and it was extensively
debated there.

APPENDIX 1

Serious Crime Act 2007

CHAPTER 27

CONTENTS

PART 1
SERIOUS CRIME PREVENTION ORDERS

General

General safeguards in relation to orders

Information safeguards

Duration, variation and discharge of orders

PART 2

ENCOURAGING OR ASSISTING CRIME

PART 3
OTHER MEASURES TO PREVENT OR DISRUPT
SERIOUS AND OTHER CRIME

CHAPTER 1
PREVENTION OF FRAUD

Sharing information with anti-fraud organisations

Data matching

CHAPTER 2
PROCEEDS OF CRIME

Assets Recovery Agency

Detained cash investigations: use of production orders and warrants

Extension of powers of accredited financial investigators

Miscellaneous

CHAPTER 3
OTHER MEASURES

PART 4
GENERAL AND FINAL PROVISIONS

General

Final

SERIOUS CRIME ACT 2007

2007 Chapter 27

An Act to make provision about serious crime prevention orders; to create offences in respect of the encouragement or assistance of crime; to enable information to be shared or processed to prevent fraud or for purposes relating to proceeds of crime; to enable data matching to be conducted both in relation to fraud and for other purposes; to transfer functions of the Director of the Assets Recovery Agency to the Serious Organised Crime Agency and other persons and to make further provision in connection with the abolition of the Agency and the office of Director; to amend the Proceeds of Crime Act 2002 in relation to certain investigations and in relation to accredited financial investigators, management receivers and enforcement receivers, cash recovery proceedings and search warrants; to extend stop and search powers in connection with incidents involving serious violence; to make amendments relating to Her Majesty's Revenue and Customs in connection with the regulation of investigatory powers; and for connected purposes.

[30th October 2007]

BE IT ENACTED by the Queen's most Excellent Majesty, by and with the advice and consent of the Lords Spiritual and Temporal, and Commons, in this present Parliament assembled, and by the authority of the same, as follows:—

PART 1
SERIOUS CRIME PREVENTION ORDERS

General

1 Serious crime prevention orders

(1) The High Court in England and Wales may make an order if—

  (a) it is satisfied that a person has been involved in serious crime (whether in England and Wales or elsewhere); and

  (b) it has reasonable grounds to believe that the order would protect the public by preventing, restricting or disrupting involvement by the person in serious crime in England and Wales.

192

(2) The High Court in Northern Ireland may make an order if—
  (a) it is satisfied that a person has been involved in serious crime (whether in Northern Ireland or elsewhere); and
  (b) it has reasonable grounds to believe that the order would protect the public by preventing, restricting or disrupting involvement by the person in serious crime in Northern Ireland.
(3) An order under this section may contain—
  (a) such prohibitions, restrictions or requirements; and
  (b) such other terms;
  as the court considers appropriate for the purpose of protecting the public by preventing, restricting or disrupting involvement by the person concerned in serious crime in England and Wales or (as the case may be) Northern Ireland.
(4) The powers of the court in respect of an order under this section are subject to sections 6 to 15 (safeguards).
(5) In this Part 'serious crime prevention order' means—
  (a) an order under this section; or
  (b) an order under section 19 (corresponding order of the Crown Court on conviction).
(6) For the purposes of this Part references to the person who is the subject of a serious crime prevention order are references to the person against whom the public are to be protected.

2 Involvement in serious crime: England and Wales orders

(1) For the purposes of this Part, a person has been involved in serious crime in England and Wales if he—
  (a) has committed a serious offence in England and Wales;
  (b) has facilitated the commission by another person of a serious offence in England and Wales; or
  (c) has conducted himself in a way that was likely to facilitate the commission by himself or another person of a serious offence in England and Wales (whether or not such an offence was committed).
(2) In this Part 'a serious offence in England and Wales' means an offence under the law of England and Wales which, at the time when the court is considering the application or matter in question—
  (a) is specified, or falls within a description specified, in Part 1 of Schedule 1; or
  (b) is one which, in the particular circumstances of the case, the court considers to be sufficiently serious to be treated for the purposes of the application or matter as if it were so specified.
(3) For the purposes of this Part, involvement in serious crime in England and Wales is any one or more of the following—
  (a) the commission of a serious offence in England and Wales;
  (b) conduct which facilitates the commission by another person of a serious offence in England and Wales;
  (c) conduct which is likely to facilitate the commission, by the person whose conduct it is or another person, of a serious offence in England and Wales (whether or not such an offence is committed).

(4) For the purposes of section 1(1)(a), a person has been involved in serious crime elsewhere than in England and Wales if he—

    (a) has committed a serious offence in a country outside England and Wales;

    (b) has facilitated the commission by another person of a serious offence in a country outside England and Wales; or

    (c) has conducted himself in a way that was likely to facilitate the commission by himself or another person of a serious offence in a country outside England and Wales (whether or not such an offence was committed).

(5) In subsection (4) 'a serious offence in a country outside England and Wales' means an offence under the law of a country outside England and Wales which, at the time when the court is considering the application or matter in question—

    (a) would be an offence under the law of England and Wales if committed in or as regards England and Wales; and

    (b) either—

        (i) would be an offence which is specified, or falls within a description specified, in Part 1 of Schedule 1 if committed in or as regards England and Wales; or

        (ii) is conduct which, in the particular circumstances of the case, the court considers to be sufficiently serious to be treated for the purposes of the application or matter as if it meets the test in sub-paragraph (i).

(6) The test in subsection (4) is to be used instead of the test in section 3(1) in deciding for the purposes of section 1(1)(a) whether a person has been involved in serious crime in Northern Ireland.

(7) An act punishable under the law of a country outside the United Kingdom constitutes an offence under that law for the purposes of subsection (5), however it is described in that law.

3 Involvement in serious crime: Northern Ireland orders

(1) For the purposes of this Part, a person has been involved in serious crime in Northern Ireland if he—

    (a) has committed a serious offence in Northern Ireland;

    (b) has facilitated the commission by another person of a serious offence in Northern Ireland; or

    (c) has conducted himself in a way that was likely to facilitate the commission by himself or another person of a serious offence in Northern Ireland (whether or not such an offence was committed).

(2) In this Part 'a serious offence in Northern Ireland' means an offence under the law of Northern Ireland which, at the time when the court is considering the application or matter in question—

    (a) is specified, or falls within a description specified, in Part 2 of Schedule 1; or

    (b) is one which, in the particular circumstances of the case, the court considers to be sufficiently serious to be treated for the purposes of the application or matter as if it were so specified.

(3) For the purposes of this Part, involvement in serious crime in Northern Ireland is any one or more of the following—

    (a) the commission of a serious offence in Northern Ireland;

    (b) conduct which facilitates the commission by another person of a serious offence in Northern Ireland;

(c) conduct which is likely to facilitate the commission, by the person whose conduct it is or another person, of a serious offence in Northern Ireland (whether or not such an offence is committed).

(4) For the purposes of section 1(2)(a), a person has been involved in serious crime elsewhere than in Northern Ireland if he—

(a) has committed a serious offence in a country outside Northern Ireland;

(b) has facilitated the commission by another person of a serious offence in a country outside Northern Ireland; or

(c) has conducted himself in a way that was likely to facilitate the commission by himself or another person of a serious offence in a country outside Northern Ireland (whether or not such an offence was committed).

(5) In subsection (4) 'a serious offence in a country outside Northern Ireland' means an offence under the law of a country outside Northern Ireland which, at the time when the court is considering the application or matter in question—

(a) would be an offence under the law of Northern Ireland if committed in or as regards Northern Ireland; and

(b) either—

(i) would be an offence which is specified, or falls within a description specified, in Part 2 of Schedule 1 if committed in or as regards Northern Ireland; or

(ii) is conduct which, in the particular circumstances of the case, the court considers to be sufficiently serious to be treated for the purposes of the application or matter as if it meets the test in sub-paragraph (i).

(6) The test in subsection (4) is to be used instead of the test in section 2(1) in deciding for the purposes of section 1(2)(a) whether a person has been involved in serious crime in England and Wales.

(7) An act punishable under the law of a country outside the United Kingdom constitutes an offence under that law for the purposes of subsection (5), however it is described in that law.

4 Involvement in serious crime: supplementary

(1) In considering for the purposes of this Part whether a person has committed a serious offence—

(a) the court must decide that the person has committed the offence if—

(i) he has been convicted of the offence; and

(ii) the conviction has not been quashed on appeal nor has the person been pardoned of the offence; but

(b) the court must not otherwise decide that the person has committed the offence.

(2) In deciding for the purposes of this Part whether a person ('the respondent') facilitates the commission by another person of a serious offence, the court must ignore—

(a) any act that the respondent can show to be reasonable in the circumstances; and

(b) subject to this, his intentions, or any other aspect of his mental state, at the time.

(3) In deciding for the purposes of this Part whether a person ('the respondent') conducts himself in a way that is likely to facilitate the commission by himself or another person of a serious offence (whether or not such an offence is committed), the court must ignore—

(a) any act that the respondent can show to be reasonable in the circumstances; and

(b) subject to this, his intentions, or any other aspect of his mental state, at the time.

(4) The Secretary of State may by order amend Schedule 1.

5 Type of provision that may be made by orders

(1) This section contains examples of the type of provision that may be made by a serious crime prevention order but it does not limit the type of provision that may be made by such an order.

(2) Examples of prohibitions, restrictions or requirements that may be imposed by serious crime prevention orders in England and Wales or Northern Ireland include prohibitions, restrictions or requirements in relation to places other than England and Wales or (as the case may be) Northern Ireland.

(3) Examples of prohibitions, restrictions or requirements that may be imposed on individuals (including partners in a partnership) by serious crime prevention orders include prohibitions or restrictions on, or requirements in relation to—

(a) an individual's financial, property or business dealings or holdings;

(b) an individual's working arrangements;

(c) the means by which an individual communicates or associates with others, or the persons with whom he communicates or associates;

(d) the premises to which an individual has access;

(e) the use of any premises or item by an individual;

(f) an individual's travel (whether within the United Kingdom, between the United Kingdom and other places or otherwise).

(4) Examples of prohibitions, restrictions or requirements that may be imposed on bodies corporate, partnerships and unincorporated associations by serious crime prevention orders include prohibitions or restrictions on, or requirements in relation to—

(a) financial, property or business dealings or holdings of such persons;

(b) the types of agreements to which such persons may be a party;

(c) the provision of goods or services by such persons;

(d) the premises to which such persons have access;

(e) the use of any premises or item by such persons;

(f) the employment of staff by such persons.

(5) Examples of requirements that may be imposed on any persons by serious crime prevention orders include—

(a) a requirement on a person to answer questions, or provide information, specified or described in an order—

(i) at a time, within a period or at a frequency;

(ii) at a place;

(iii) in a form and manner; and

(iv) to a law enforcement officer or description of law enforcement officer;

notified to the person by a law enforcement officer specified or described in the order;

(b) a requirement on a person to produce documents specified or described in an order—

(i) at a time, within a period or at a frequency;

(ii) at a place;

(iii) in a manner; and

(iv) to a law enforcement officer or description of law enforcement officer;

notified to the person by a law enforcement officer specified or described in the order.

(6) The prohibitions, restrictions or requirements that may be imposed on individuals by serious crime prevention orders include prohibitions, restrictions or requirements in relation to an individual's private dwelling (including, for example, prohibitions or restrictions on, or requirements in relation to, where an individual may reside).

(7) In this Part—

'document' means anything in which information of any description is recorded (whether or not in legible form);

'a law enforcement officer' means—

   (a) a constable;
   (b) a member of the staff of the Serious Organised Crime Agency who is for the time being designated under section 43 of the Serious Organised Crime and Police Act 2005 (c. 15);
   (c) an officer of Revenue and Customs; or
   (d) a member of the Serious Fraud Office; and

'premises' includes any land, vehicle, vessel, aircraft or hovercraft.

(8) Any reference in this Part to the production of documents is, in the case of a document which contains information recorded otherwise than in legible form, a reference to the production of a copy of the information in legible form.

General safeguards in relation to orders

6 Any individual must be 18 or over

An individual under the age of 18 may not be the subject of a serious crime prevention order.

7 Other exceptions

A person may not be the subject of a serious crime prevention order if the person falls within a description specified by order of the Secretary of State.

8 Limited class of applicants for making of orders

A serious crime prevention order may be made only on an application by—

(a) in the case of an order in England and Wales—
   (i) the Director of Public Prosecutions;
   (ii) the Director of Revenue and Customs Prosecutions; or
   (iii) the Director of the Serious Fraud Office; and
(b) in the case of an order in Northern Ireland, the Director of Public Prosecutions for Northern Ireland.

9 Right of third parties to make representations

(1) The High Court must, on an application by a person, give the person an opportunity to make representations in proceedings before it about the making of a serious crime prevention order if it considers that the making of the order would be likely to have a significant adverse effect on that person.

(2) The High Court must, on an application by a person, give the person an opportunity to make representations in proceedings before it about the variation of a serious crime prevention order if it considers that—

(a) the variation of the order; or
(b) a decision not to vary it;

would be likely to have a significant adverse effect on that person.

(3) The High Court must, on an application by a person, give the person an opportunity to make representations in proceedings before it about the discharge of a serious crime prevention order if it considers that—
   (a) the discharge of the order; or
   (b) a decision not to discharge it;
   would be likely to have a significant adverse effect on that person.

(4) The Crown Court must, on an application by a person, give the person an opportunity to make representations in proceedings before it arising by virtue of section 19, 20 or 21 if it considers that the making or variation of the serious crime prevention order concerned (or a decision not to vary it) would be likely to have a significant adverse effect on that person.

(5) A court which is considering an appeal in relation to a serious crime prevention order must, on an application by a person, give the person an opportunity to make representations in the proceedings if that person was given an opportunity to make representations in the proceedings which are the subject of the appeal.

10 Notice requirements in relation to orders

(1) The subject of a serious crime prevention order is bound by it or a variation of it only if—
   (a) he is represented (whether in person or otherwise) at the proceedings at which the order or (as the case may be) variation is made; or
   (b) a notice setting out the terms of the order or (as the case may be) variation has been served on him.

(2) The notice may be served on him by—
   (a) delivering it to him in person; or
   (b) sending it by recorded delivery to him at his last-known address (whether residential or otherwise).

(3) For the purposes of delivering such a notice to him in person, a constable or a person authorised for the purpose by the relevant applicant authority may (if necessary by force)—
   (a) enter any premises where he has reasonable grounds for believing the person to be; and
   (b) search those premises for him.

(4) In this Part 'the relevant applicant authority' means—
   (a) in relation to a serious crime prevention order in England and Wales—
      (i) where the order was applied for by the Director of Public Prosecutions, the Director of Public Prosecutions;
      (ii) where the order was applied for by the Director of Revenue and Customs Prosecutions, the Director of Revenue and Customs Prosecutions; and
      (iii) where the order was applied for by the Director of the Serious Fraud Office, the Director of the Serious Fraud Office; and
   (b) in relation to a serious crime prevention order in Northern Ireland, the Director of Public Prosecutions for Northern Ireland.

Information safeguards

11 Restrictions on oral answers

A serious crime prevention order may not require a person to answer questions, or provide information, orally.

Serious Crime Act 2007, s 14

12 Restrictions for legal professional privilege

(1) A serious crime prevention order may not require a person—
  (a) to answer any privileged question;
  (b) to provide any privileged information; or
  (c) to produce any privileged document.

(2) A 'privileged question' is a question which the person would be entitled to refuse to answer on grounds of legal professional privilege in proceedings in the High Court.

(3) 'Privileged information' is information which the person would be entitled to refuse to provide on grounds of legal professional privilege in such proceedings.

(4) A 'privileged document' is a document which the person would be entitled to refuse to produce on grounds of legal professional privilege in such proceedings.

(5) But subsection (1) does not prevent an order from requiring a lawyer to provide the name and address of a client of his.

13 Restrictions on excluded material and banking information

(1) A serious crime prevention order may not require a person to produce—
  (a) in the case of an order in England and Wales, any excluded material as defined by section 11 of the Police and Criminal Evidence Act 1984 (c. 60); and
  (b) in the case of an order in Northern Ireland, any excluded material as defined by Article 13 of the Police and Criminal Evidence (Northern Ireland) Order 1989 (S.I. 1989/1341 (N.I.12)).

(2) A serious crime prevention order may not require a person to disclose any information or produce any document in respect of which he owes an obligation of confidence by virtue of carrying on a banking business unless condition A or B is met.

(3) Condition A is that the person to whom the obligation of confidence is owed consents to the disclosure or production.

(4) Condition B is that the order contains a requirement—
  (a) to disclose information, or produce documents, of this kind; or
  (b) to disclose specified information which is of this kind or to produce specified documents which are of this kind.

14 Restrictions relating to other enactments

(1) A serious crime prevention order may not require a person—
  (a) to answer any question;
  (b) to provide any information; or
  (c) to produce any document;
  if the disclosure concerned is prohibited under any other enactment.

(2) In this section—
  'enactment' includes an Act of the Scottish Parliament, Northern Ireland legislation and an enactment comprised in subordinate legislation, and includes an enactment whenever passed or made; and
  'subordinate legislation' has the same meaning as in the Interpretation Act 1978 (c. 30) and also includes an instrument made under—
  (a) an Act of the Scottish Parliament; or
  (b) Northern Ireland legislation.

15 Restrictions on use of information obtained

(1) A statement made by a person in response to a requirement imposed by a serious crime prevention order may not be used in evidence against him in any criminal proceedings unless condition A or B is met.

(2) Condition A is that the criminal proceedings relate to an offence under section 25.

(3) Condition B is that—
  (a) the criminal proceedings relate to another offence;
  (b) the person who made the statement gives evidence in the criminal proceedings;
  (c) in the course of that evidence, the person makes a statement which is inconsistent with the statement made in response to the requirement imposed by the order; and
  (d) in the criminal proceedings evidence relating to the statement made in response to the requirement imposed by the order is adduced, or a question about it is asked, by the person or on his behalf.

Duration, variation and discharge of orders

16 Duration of orders

(1) A serious crime prevention order must specify when it is to come into force and when it is to cease to be in force.

(2) An order is not to be in force for more than 5 years beginning with the coming into force of the order.

(3) An order can specify different times for the coming into force, or ceasing to be in force, of different provisions of the order.

(4) Where it specifies different times in accordance with subsection (3), the order—
  (a) must specify when each provision is to come into force and cease to be in force; and
  (b) is not to be in force for more than 5 years beginning with the coming into force of the first provision of the order to come into force.

(5) The fact that an order, or any provision of an order, ceases to be in force does not prevent the court from making a new order to the same or similar effect.

(6) A new order may be made in anticipation of an earlier order or provision ceasing to be in force.

17 Variation of orders

(1) The High Court in England and Wales may, on an application under this section, vary a serious crime prevention order in England and Wales if it has reasonable grounds to believe that the terms of the order as varied would protect the public by preventing, restricting or disrupting involvement, by the person who is the subject of the order, in serious crime in England and Wales.

(2) The High Court in Northern Ireland may, on an application under this section, vary a serious crime prevention order in Northern Ireland if it has reasonable grounds to believe that the terms of the order as varied would protect the public by preventing, restricting or disrupting involvement, by the person who is the subject of the order, in serious crime in Northern Ireland.

(3) An application for the variation of an order under this section may be made by—
  (a) the relevant applicant authority; or

(b) subject as follows—
(i) the person who is the subject of the order; or
(ii) any other person.

(4) The court must not entertain an application by the person who is the subject of the order unless it considers that there has been a change of circumstances affecting the order.

(5) The court must not entertain an application by any person falling within sub-section (3)(b)(ii) unless it considers that—
(a) the person is significantly adversely affected by the order;
(b) condition A or B is met; and
(c) the application is not for the purpose of making the order more onerous on the person who is the subject of it.

(6) Condition A is that—
(a) the person falling within subsection (3)(b)(ii)—
(i) has, on an application under section 9, been given an opportunity to make representations; or
(ii) has made an application otherwise than under that section;
in earlier proceedings in relation to the order (whether before the High Court or the Crown Court); and
(b) there has been a change of circumstances affecting the order.

(7) Condition B is that—
(a) the person falling within subsection (3)(b)(ii) has not made an application of any kind in earlier proceedings in relation to the order (whether before the High Court or the Crown Court); and
(b) it was reasonable in all the circumstances for the person not to have done so.

(8) A variation on an application under subsection (3)(a) may include an extension of the period during which the order, or any provision of it, is in force (subject to the original limits imposed on the order by section 16(2) and (4)(b)).

18 Discharge of orders

(1) On an application under this section—
(a) the High Court in England and Wales may discharge a serious crime prevention order in England and Wales; and
(b) the High Court in Northern Ireland may discharge a serious crime prevention order in Northern Ireland.

(2) An application for the discharge of an order may be made by—
(a) the relevant applicant authority; or
(b) subject as follows—
(i) the person who is the subject of the order; or
(ii) any other person.

(3) The court must not entertain an application by the person who is the subject of the order unless it considers that there has been a change of circumstances affecting the order.

(4) The court must not entertain an application by any person falling within sub-section (2)(b)(ii) unless it considers that—
(a) the person is significantly adversely affected by the order; and
(b) condition A or B is met.

(5) Condition A is that—
(a) the person—

   (i) has, on an application under section 9, been given an opportunity to make representations; or

   (ii) has made an application otherwise than under that section;
         in earlier proceedings in relation to the order (whether before the High Court or the Crown Court); and

   (b) there has been a change of circumstances affecting the order.

(6) Condition B is that—

   (a) the person has not made an application of any kind in earlier proceedings in relation to the order (whether before the High Court or the Crown Court); and

   (b) it was reasonable in all the circumstances for the person not to have done so.

Extension of jurisdiction to Crown Court

19 Orders by Crown Court on conviction

(1) Subsection (2) applies where the Crown Court in England and Wales is dealing with a person who—

   (a) has been convicted by or before a magistrates' court of having committed a serious offence in England and Wales and has been committed to the Crown Court to be dealt with; or

   (b) has been convicted by or before the Crown Court of having committed a serious offence in England and Wales.

(2) The Crown Court may, in addition to dealing with the person in relation to the offence, make an order if it has reasonable grounds to believe that the order would protect the public by preventing, restricting or disrupting involvement by the person in serious crime in England and Wales.

(3) Subsection (4) applies where the Crown Court in Northern Ireland is dealing with a person who has been convicted by or before the Crown Court of having committed a serious offence in Northern Ireland.

(4) The Crown Court may, in addition to dealing with the person in relation to the offence, make an order if it has reasonable grounds to believe that the order would protect the public by preventing, restricting or disrupting involvement by the person in serious crime in Northern Ireland.

(5) An order under this section may contain—

   (a) such prohibitions, restrictions or requirements; and

   (b) such other terms;

as the court considers appropriate for the purpose of protecting the public by preventing, restricting or disrupting involvement by the person concerned in serious crime in England and Wales or (as the case may be) Northern Ireland.

(6) The powers of the court in respect of an order under this section are subject to sections 6 to 15 (safeguards).

(7) An order must not be made under this section except—

   (a) in addition to a sentence imposed in respect of the offence concerned; or

   (b) in addition to an order discharging the person conditionally.

(8) An order under this section is also called a serious crime prevention order.

20 Powers of Crown Court to vary orders on conviction

(1) Subsection (2) applies where the Crown Court in England and Wales is dealing with a person who—

(a) has been convicted by or before a magistrates' court of having committed a serious offence in England and Wales and has been committed to the Crown Court to be dealt with; or

(b) has been convicted by or before the Crown Court of having committed a serious offence in England and Wales.

(2) The Crown Court may—

(a) in the case of a person who is the subject of a serious crime prevention order in England and Wales; and

(b) in addition to dealing with the person in relation to the offence;

vary the order if the court has reasonable grounds to believe that the terms of the order as varied would protect the public by preventing, restricting or disrupting involvement by the person in serious crime in England and Wales.

(3) Subsection (4) applies where the Crown Court in Northern Ireland is dealing with a person who has been convicted by or before the Crown Court of having committed a serious offence in Northern Ireland.

(4) The Crown Court may—

(a) in the case of a person who is the subject of a serious crime prevention order in Northern Ireland; and

(b) in addition to dealing with the person in relation to the offence;

vary the order if the court has reasonable grounds to believe that the terms of the order as varied would protect the public by preventing, restricting or disrupting involvement by the person in serious crime in Northern Ireland.

(5) A variation under this section may be made only on an application by the relevant applicant authority.

(6) A variation must not be made except—

(a) in addition to a sentence imposed in respect of the offence concerned; or

(b) in addition to an order discharging the person conditionally.

(7) A variation may include an extension of the period during which the order, or any provision of it, is in force (subject to the original limits imposed on the order by section 16(2) and (4)(b)).

21 Powers of Crown Court to vary orders on breach

(1) Subsection (2) applies where the Crown Court in England and Wales is dealing with a person who—

(a) has been convicted by or before a magistrates' court of having committed an offence under section 25 in relation to a serious crime prevention order and has been committed to the Crown Court to be dealt with; or

(b) has been convicted by or before the Crown Court of having committed an offence under section 25 in relation to a serious crime prevention order.

(2) The Crown Court may—

(a) in the case of an order in England and Wales; and

(b) in addition to dealing with the person in relation to the offence;

vary the order if it has reasonable grounds to believe that the terms of the order as varied would protect the public by preventing, restricting or disrupting involvement by the person in serious crime in England and Wales.

(3) Subsection (4) applies where the Crown Court in Northern Ireland is dealing with a person who has been convicted by or before the Crown Court of an offence under section 25 in relation to a serious crime prevention order.

(4) The Crown Court may—

(a) in the case of an order in Northern Ireland; and

(b) in addition to dealing with the person in relation to the offence;

vary the order if it has reasonable grounds to believe that the terms of the order as varied would protect the public by preventing, restricting or disrupting involvement by the person in serious crime in Northern Ireland.

(5) A variation under this section may be made only on an application by the relevant applicant authority.

(6) A variation must not be made except—

(a) in addition to a sentence imposed in respect of the offence concerned; or

(b) in addition to an order discharging the person conditionally.

(7) A variation may include an extension of the period during which the order, or any provision of it, is in force (subject to the original limits imposed on the order by section 16(2) and (4)(b)).

22 Inter-relationship between different types of orders

(1) The fact that a serious crime prevention order has been made or varied by the High Court does not prevent it from being varied by the Crown Court in accordance with this Part.

(2) The fact that a serious crime prevention order has been made or varied by the Crown Court does not prevent it from being varied or discharged by the High Court in accordance with this Part.

(3) A decision by the Crown Court not to make an order under section 19 does not prevent a subsequent application to the High Court for an order under section 1 in consequence of the same offence.

(4) A decision by the Crown Court not to vary a serious crime prevention order under section 20 or 21 does not prevent a subsequent application to the High Court for a variation of the order in consequence of the same offence.

Appeals

23 Additional right of appeal from High Court

(1) An appeal may be made to the Court of Appeal in relation to a decision of the High Court—

(a) to make a serious crime prevention order;

(b) to vary, or not to vary, such an order; or

(c) to discharge or not to discharge such an order;

by any person who was given an opportunity to make representations in the proceedings concerned by virtue of section 9(1), (2) or (as the case may be) (3).

(2) Subsection (1) is without prejudice to the rights of other persons to make appeals, by virtue of section 16 of the Senior Courts Act 1981 (c. 54) or section 35 of the Judicature

(Northern Ireland) Act 1978 (c. 23), in relation to any judgments or orders of the High Court about serious crime prevention orders.

24 Appeals from Crown Court

(1) An appeal against a decision of the Crown Court in relation to a serious crime prevention order may be made to the Court of Appeal by—
  (a) the person who is the subject of the order; or
  (b) the relevant applicant authority.
(2) In addition, an appeal may be made to the Court of Appeal in relation to a decision of the Crown Court—
  (a) to make a serious crime prevention order; or
  (b) to vary, or not to vary, such an order;
  by any person who was given an opportunity to make representations in the proceedings concerned by virtue of section 9(4).
(3) Subject to subsection (4), an appeal under subsection (1) or (2) lies only with the leave of the Court of Appeal.
(4) An appeal under subsection (1) or (2) lies without the leave of the Court of Appeal if the judge who made the decision grants a certificate that the decision is fit for appeal under this section.
(5) Subject to any rules of court made under section 53(1) of the Senior Courts Act 1981 (c. 54) (distribution of business between civil and criminal divisions), the criminal division of the Court of Appeal is the division which is to exercise jurisdiction in relation to an appeal under subsection (1) or (2) from a decision of the Crown Court in the exercise of its jurisdiction in England and Wales under this Part.
(6) An appeal against a decision of the Court of Appeal on an appeal to that court under subsection (1) or (2) may be made to the Supreme Court by any person who was a party to the proceedings before the Court of Appeal.
(7) An appeal under subsection (6) lies only with the leave of the Court of Appeal or the Supreme Court.
(8) Such leave must not be granted unless—
  (a) it is certified by the Court of Appeal that a point of law of general public importance is involved in the decision; and
  (b) it appears to the Court of Appeal or (as the case may be) the Supreme Court that the point is one which ought to be considered by the Supreme Court.
(9) The Secretary of State may for the purposes of this section by order make provision corresponding (subject to any specified modifications) to that made by or under an enactment and relating to—
  (a) appeals to the Court of Appeal under Part 1 of—
    (i) the Criminal Appeal Act 1968 (c. 19); or
    (ii) the Criminal Appeal (Northern Ireland) Act 1980 (c. 47);
  (b) appeals from any decision of the Court of Appeal on appeals falling within paragraph (a); or
  (c) any matter connected with or arising out of appeals falling within paragraph (a) or (b).
(10) An order under subsection (9) may, in particular, make provision about the payment of costs.

(11) The power to make an appeal to the Court of Appeal under subsection (1)(a) operates instead of any power for the person who is the subject of the order to make an appeal against a decision of the Crown Court in relation to a serious crime prevention order by virtue of—

(a) section 9 or 10 of the Criminal Appeal Act 1968; or

(b) section 8 of the Criminal Appeal (Northern Ireland) Act 1980.

(12) Section 33(3) of the Criminal Appeal Act 1968 (limitation on appeal from criminal division of the Court of Appeal: England and Wales) does not prevent an appeal to the Supreme Court under subsection (6) above.

Enforcement

25 Offence of failing to comply with order

(1) A person who, without reasonable excuse, fails to comply with a serious crime prevention order commits an offence.

(2) A person who commits an offence under this section is liable—

(a) on summary conviction, to imprisonment for a term not exceeding 12 months or to a fine not exceeding the statutory maximum or to both;

(b) on conviction on indictment, to imprisonment for a term not exceeding 5 years or to a fine or to both.

(3) In the application of subsection (2)(a) in Northern Ireland, the reference to 12 months is to be read as a reference to 6 months.

(4) In proceedings for an offence under this section, a copy of the original order or any variation of it, certified as such by the proper officer of the court which made it, is admissible as evidence of its having been made and of its contents to the same extent that oral evidence of those things is admissible in those proceedings.

26 Powers of forfeiture in respect of offence

(1) The court before which a person is convicted of an offence under section 25 may order the forfeiture of anything in his possession at the time of the offence which the court considers to have been involved in the offence.

(2) Before making an order under subsection (1) in relation to anything the court must give an opportunity to make representations to any person (in addition to the convicted person) who claims to be the owner of that thing or otherwise to have an interest in it.

(3) An order under subsection (1) may not be made so as to come into force at any time before there is no further possibility (ignoring any power to appeal out of time) of the order being varied or set aside on appeal.

(4) Where the court makes an order under subsection (1), it may also make such other provision as it considers to be necessary for giving effect to the forfeiture.

(5) That provision may, in particular, include provision relating to the retention, handling, destruction or other disposal of what is forfeited.

(6) Provision made by virtue of this section may be varied at any time by the court that made it.

27 Powers to wind up companies etc: England and Wales and Scotland

(1) The Director of Public Prosecutions, the Director of Revenue and Customs Prosecutions or the Director of the Serious Fraud Office may present a petition to the court for the winding up of a company, partnership or relevant body if—

(a) the company, partnership or relevant body has been convicted of an offence under section 25 in relation to a serious crime prevention order; and

(b) the Director concerned considers that it would be in the public interest for the company, partnership or (as the case may be) relevant body to be wound up.

(2) The Insolvency Act 1986 (c. 45) applies in relation to—

(a) a petition under this section for the winding up of a company; and

(b) the company's winding up;

as it applies in relation to a petition under section 124A of the Act of 1986 for the winding up of a company and the company's winding up (winding up on grounds of public interest) but subject to the modifications in subsections (3) and (4).

(3) Section 124(4)(b) of the Act of 1986 (application for winding up) applies in relation to a petition under this section as if it permits the petition to be presented by the Director of Public Prosecutions, the Director of Revenue and Customs Prosecutions or the Director of the Serious Fraud Office.

(4) The court may make an order under section 125 of the Act of 1986 (powers of court on hearing of petition) to wind up the company only if—

(a) the company has been convicted of an offence under section 25 in relation to a serious crime prevention order; and

(b) the court considers that it is just and equitable for the company to be wound up.

(5) Section 420 of the Act of 1986 (power to make provision about insolvent partnerships) applies for the purposes of this section as if the reference to an insolvent partnership were a reference to a partnership to which this section applies.

(6) The appropriate Minister may by order provide for the Act of 1986 to apply, with such modifications as that person considers appropriate, in relation to a petition under this section for the winding up of a relevant body and the relevant body's winding up.

(7) An order made by virtue of subsection (5) or (6) must ensure that the court may make an order to wind up the partnership or relevant body only if—

(a) the partnership or relevant body has been convicted of an offence under section 25 in relation to a serious crime prevention order; and

(b) the court considers that it is just and equitable for the partnership or relevant body to be wound up.

(8) No petition may be presented to, or order to wind up made by, a court in Scotland by virtue of this section in respect of a company, partnership or relevant body whose estate may be sequestrated under the Bankruptcy (Scotland) Act 1985 (c. 66).

(9) No petition may be presented, or order to wind up made, by virtue of this section if—

(a) an appeal against conviction for the offence concerned has been made and not finally determined; or

(b) the period during which such an appeal may be made has not expired.

(10) No petition may be presented, or order to wind up made, by virtue of this section if the company, partnership or relevant body is already being wound up by the court.

(11) In deciding for the purposes of subsection (9) whether an appeal is finally determined or whether the period during which an appeal may be made has expired, any power to appeal out of time is to be ignored.

(12) In this section—
'appropriate Minister' means—
- (a) in relation to a relevant body falling within paragraphs (a) to (c) of the definition of 'relevant body' below, the Treasury; and
- (b) in relation to any other relevant body, the Secretary of State;

'company' has the same meaning as in Parts 1 to 7 of the Insolvency Act 1986 (c. 45) (see section 251 of that Act) but—
- (a) does not include a relevant body; and
- (b) subject to this, does include an unregistered company within the meaning of Part 5 of that Act (see section 220 of that Act);

'the court' has the same meaning as in Parts 1 to 7 of the Insolvency Act 1986 but does not include a court in Northern Ireland;

'an industrial and provident society' means a society registered under the Industrial and Provident Societies Act 1965 (c. 12) or a society deemed by virtue of section 4 of that Act to be so registered;

'partnership' does not include a relevant body; and

'relevant body' means—
- (a) a building society (within the meaning of the Building Societies Act 1986 (c. 53));
- (b) an incorporated friendly society (within the meaning of the Friendly Societies Act 1992 (c. 40));
- (c) an industrial and provident society;
- (d) a limited liability partnership; or
- (e) such other description of person as may be specified by order made by the Secretary of State;

and the references to sections 124 to 125 of the Insolvency Act 1986 (c. 45) include references to those sections as applied by section 221(1) of that Act (unregistered companies).

28 Powers to wind up companies etc: Northern Ireland

(1) The Director of Public Prosecutions for Northern Ireland may present a petition to the court for the winding up of a company, partnership or relevant body if—
- (a) the company, partnership or relevant body has been convicted of an offence under section 25 in relation to a serious crime prevention order; and
- (b) the Director of Public Prosecutions for Northern Ireland considers that it would be in the public interest for the company, partnership or (as the case may be) relevant body to be wound up.

(2) The Insolvency (Northern Ireland) Order 1989 (S.I. 1989/2405 (N.I.19)) applies in relation to—
- (a) a petition under this section for the winding up of a company; and
- (b) the company's winding up;

as it applies in relation to a petition under Article 104A of the Order of 1989 for the winding up of a company and the company's winding up (winding up on grounds of public interest) but subject to the modifications in subsections (3) and (4).

(3) Article 104(5)(b) of the Order of 1989 (application for winding up) applies in relation to a petition under this section as if it permits the petition to be presented by the Director of Public Prosecutions for Northern Ireland.

(4) The court may make an order under Article 105 of the Order of 1989 (powers of court on hearing of petition) to wind up the company only if—

    (a) the company has been convicted of an offence under section 25 in relation to a serious crime prevention order; and

    (b) the court considers that it is just and equitable for the company to be wound up.

(5) Article 364 of the Order of 1989 (power to make provision about insolvent partnerships) applies for the purposes of this section as if the reference to an insolvent partnership were a reference to a partnership to which this section applies.

(6) The appropriate Minister may by order provide for the Order of 1989 to apply, with such modifications as that person considers appropriate, in relation to a petition under this section for the winding up of a relevant body and the relevant body's winding up.

(7) An order made by virtue of subsection (5) or (6) must ensure that the court may make an order to wind up the partnership or relevant body only if—

    (a) the partnership or relevant body has been convicted of an offence under section 25 in relation to a serious crime prevention order; and

    (b) the court considers that it is just and equitable for the partnership or relevant body to be wound up.

(8) No petition may be presented, or order to wind up made, by virtue of this section if—

    (a) an appeal against conviction for the offence concerned has been made and not finally determined; or

    (b) the period during which such an appeal may be made has not expired.

(9) No petition may be presented, or order to wind up made, by virtue of this section if the company, partnership or relevant body is already being wound up by the court.

(10) In deciding for the purposes of subsection (8) whether an appeal is finally determined or whether the period during which an appeal may be made has expired, any power to appeal out of time is to be ignored.

(11) In this section—

    'appropriate Minister' means—

        (a) in relation to a relevant body falling within paragraph (a) or (b) of the definition of 'relevant body' below, the Treasury; and

        (b) in relation to any other relevant body, the Secretary of State;

    'company' has the same meaning as in Parts 2 to 7 of the Insolvency (Northern Ireland) Order 1989 (S.I. 1989/2405 (N.I.19)) (see Article 5 of that Order) but—

        (a) does not include a relevant body; and

        (b) subject to this, does include an unregistered company within the meaning of Part 6 of that Order (see Article 184 of that Order);

    'the court' means the High Court in Northern Ireland;

    'an industrial and provident society' means a society registered under the Industrial and Provident Societies Act (Northern Ireland) 1969 (c. 24) or a society deemed by virtue of section 4 of that Act to be so registered;

    'partnership' does not include a relevant body; and

    'relevant body' means—

        (a) a building society (within the meaning of the Building Societies Act 1986 (c. 53));

        (b) an incorporated friendly society (within the meaning of the Friendly Societies Act 1992 (c. 40));

        (c) an industrial and provident society;

        (d) a limited liability partnership; or

(e) such other description of person as may be specified by order made by the Secretary of State;

and the references to Articles 104 to 105 of the Insolvency (Northern Ireland) Order 1989 (S.I. 1989/2405 (N.I.19)) include references to those Articles as applied by Article 185(1) of that Order (unregistered companies).

29 Powers to wind up: supplementary

(1) The Secretary of State may by order make such modifications as he considers appropriate to the application of—

(a) the Insolvency Act 1986 (c. 45) by virtue of section 27(2); or

(b) the Insolvency (Northern Ireland) Order 1989 (S.I. 1989/2405 (N.I.19)) by virtue of section 28(2).

(2) Any modifications made by virtue of subsection (1) are in addition to the modifications made by section 27(3) and (4) or (as the case may be) section 28(3) and (4).

(3) The Secretary of State may by order make such consequential or supplementary provision, applying with or without modifications any provision made by or under an enactment, as he considers appropriate in connection with section 27(2) to (4) or 28(2) to (4).

(4) An order made by virtue of section 27(5) or (6), section 28(5) or (6) or subsection (1) above may, in particular, contain consequential or supplementary provision applying, with or without modifications, any provision made by or under an enactment.

Particular types of persons

30 Bodies corporate including limited liability partnerships

(1) For the purposes of section 10 in its application to a serious crime prevention order against a body corporate or to the variation of such an order—

(a) a notice setting out the terms of the order or variation—

(i) is delivered to the body corporate in person if it is delivered to an officer of the body corporate in person; and

(ii) is sent by recorded delivery to the body corporate at its last known address if it is so sent to an officer of the body corporate at the address of the registered office of that body or at the address of its principal office in the United Kingdom; and

(b) the power conferred by subsection (3) of that section is a power to enter any premises where the person exercising the power has reasonable grounds for believing an officer of the body corporate to be and to search those premises for the officer.

(2) If an offence under section 25 committed by a body corporate is proved to have been committed with the consent or connivance of—

(a) an officer of the body corporate; or

(b) a person who was purporting to act in any such capacity;

he (as well as the body corporate) is guilty of the offence and liable to be proceeded against and punished accordingly.

(3) Nothing in this section prevents a serious crime prevention order from being made against an officer or employee of a body corporate or against any other person associated with a body corporate.

(4) In this section—

'body corporate' includes a limited liability partnership;

'director', in relation to a body corporate whose affairs are managed by its members, means a member of the body corporate; and 'officer of a body corporate' means any director, manager, secretary or other similar officer of the body corporate.

31 Other partnerships

(1) A serious crime prevention order against a partnership must be made in the name of the partnership (and not in that of any of the partners).

(2) An order made in the name of the partnership continues to have effect despite a change of partners provided that at least one of the persons who was a partner before the change remains a partner after it.

(3) For the purposes of this Part, a partnership is involved in serious crime in England and Wales, Northern Ireland or elsewhere if the partnership, or any of the partners, is so involved; and involvement in serious crime in England and Wales or Northern Ireland is to be read accordingly.

(4) For the purposes of section 10 in its application to a serious crime prevention order against a partnership or to the variation of such an order—

    (a) a notice setting out the terms of the order or variation—

        (i) is delivered to the partnership in person if it is delivered to any of the partners in person or to a senior officer of the partnership in person; and

        (ii) is sent by recorded delivery to the partnership at its last-known address if it is so sent to any of the partners or to a senior officer of the partnership at the address of the principal office of the partnership in the United Kingdom; and

    (b) the power conferred by subsection (3) of that section is a power to enter any premises where the person exercising the power has reasonable grounds for believing a partner or senior officer of the partnership to be and to search those premises for the partner or senior officer.

(5) Proceedings for an offence under section 25 alleged to have been committed by a partnership must be brought in the name of the partnership (and not in that of any of the partners).

(6) For the purposes of such proceedings—

    (a) rules of court relating to the service of documents have effect as if the partnership were a body corporate; and

    (b) the following provisions apply as they apply in relation to a body corporate—

        (i) section 33 of the Criminal Justice Act 1925 (c. 86) and Schedule 3 to the Magistrates' Courts Act 1980 (c. 43);

        (ii) sections 70 and 143 of the Criminal Procedure (Scotland) Act 1995 (c. 46); and

        (iii) section 18 of the Criminal Justice Act (Northern Ireland) 1945 (c. 15 (N.I.)) and Schedule 4 to the Magistrates' Courts (Northern Ireland) Order 1981 (S.I. 1981/1675 (N.I.26)).

(7) A fine imposed on the partnership on its conviction for an offence under section 25 is to be paid out of the partnership assets.

(8) If an offence under section 25 committed by a partnership is proved to have been committed with the consent or connivance of a partner or a senior officer of the partnership, he (as well as the partnership) is guilty of the offence and liable to be proceeded against and punished accordingly.

(9) For the purposes of subsection (8)—

    (a) references to a partner or to a senior officer of a partnership include references to any person purporting to act in such a capacity; and

(b) subsection (5) is not to be read as prejudicing any liability of a partner under subsection (8).

(10) Nothing in this section prevents a serious crime prevention order from being made against—
  (a) a particular partner; or
  (b) a senior officer or employee of a partnership or any other person associated with a partnership.

(11) In this section—
  'senior officer of a partnership' means any person who has the control or management of the business carried on by the partnership at the principal place where it is carried on; and
  'partnership' does not include a limited liability partnership.

32 Unincorporated associations

(1) A serious crime prevention order against an unincorporated association must be made in the name of the association (and not in that of any of its members).

(2) An order made in the name of the association continues to have effect despite a change in the membership of the association provided that at least one of the persons who was a member of the association before the change remains a member after it.

(3) For the purposes of section 10 in its application to a serious crime prevention order against an unincorporated association or to the variation of such an order—
  (a) a notice setting out the terms of the order or variation—
    (i) is delivered to the association in person if it is delivered to an officer of the association in person; and
    (ii) is sent by recorded delivery to the association at its last-known address if it is so sent to an officer of the association at the address of the principal office of the association in the United Kingdom; and
  (b) the power conferred by subsection (3) of that section is a power to enter any premises where the person exercising the power has reasonable grounds for believing an officer of the association to be and to search those premises for the officer.

(4) Proceedings for an offence under section 25 alleged to have been committed by an unincorporated association must be brought in the name of the association (and not in that of any of its members).

(5) For the purposes of such proceedings—
  (a) rules of court relating to the service of documents have effect as if the association were a body corporate; and
  (b) the following provisions apply as they apply in relation to a body corporate—
    (i) section 33 of the Criminal Justice Act 1925 (c. 86) and Schedule 3 to the Magistrates' Courts Act 1980 (c. 43);
    (ii) sections 70 and 143 of the Criminal Procedure (Scotland) Act 1995 (c. 46); and
    (iii) section 18 of the Criminal Justice Act (Northern Ireland) 1945 (c. 15 (N.I.)) and Schedule 4 to the Magistrates' Courts (Northern Ireland) Order 1981 (S.I. 1981/1675 (N.I.26)).

(6) A fine imposed on the association on its conviction for an offence under section 25 is to be paid out of the funds of the association.

(7) If an offence under section 25 committed by an unincorporated association is proved to have been committed with the consent or connivance of an officer of the association, he (as well as the association) is guilty of the offence and liable to be proceeded against and punished accordingly.

(8) For the purposes of subsection (7)—

    (a) references to an officer of an unincorporated association include references to any person purporting to act in such a capacity; and

    (b) subsection (4) is not to be read as prejudicing any liability of an officer of an unincorporated association under subsection (7).

(9) Nothing in this section prevents a serious crime prevention order from being made against—

    (a) a member, officer or employee of an unincorporated association; or

    (b) any other person associated with an unincorporated association.

(10) In this section—

    'officer of an unincorporated association' means any officer of an unincorporated association or any member of its governing body; and

    'unincorporated association' means any body of persons unincorporated but does not include a partnership.

33 Overseas bodies

The Secretary of State may by order modify section 30, 31 or 32 in its application to a body of persons formed under law having effect outside the United Kingdom.

34 Providers of information society services

(1) A serious crime prevention order may not include terms which restrict the freedom of a service provider who is established in an EEA state other than the United Kingdom to provide information society services in relation to an EEA state unless the conditions in subsections (2) and (3) are met.

(2) The condition in this subsection is that the court concerned considers that the terms—

    (a) are necessary for the objective of protecting the public by preventing, restricting or disrupting involvement in—

        (i) in the case of an order in England and Wales, serious crime in England and Wales; and

        (ii) in the case of an order in Northern Ireland, serious crime in Northern Ireland;

    (b) relate to an information society service which prejudices that objective or presents a serious and grave risk of prejudice to it; and

    (c) are proportionate to that objective.

(3) The conditions in this subsection are that—

    (a) a law enforcement officer has requested the EEA state in which the service provider is established to take measures which the law enforcement officer considers to be of equivalent effect under the law of the EEA state to the terms and the EEA state has failed to take the measures; and

    (b) a law enforcement officer has notified the Commission of the European Communities and the EEA state of—

        (i) the intention to seek an order containing the terms; and

        (ii) the terms.

(4) It does not matter for the purposes of subsection (3) whether the request or notification is made before or after the making of the application for the order.

(5) A serious crime prevention order may not include terms which impose liabilities on service providers of intermediary services so far as the imposition of those liabilities would result in a contravention of Article 12, 13 or 14 of the E-Commerce Directive (various protections for service providers of intermediary services).

(6) A serious crime prevention order may not include terms which impose a general obligation on service providers of intermediary services covered by Articles 12, 13 and 14 of the E-Commerce Directive—

(a) to monitor the information which they transmit or store when providing those services; or

(b) actively to seek facts or circumstances indicating illegal activity when providing those services.

(7) For the purposes of this section—

(a) a service provider is established in a particular EEA state if he effectively pursues an economic activity using a fixed establishment in that EEA state for an indefinite period and he is a national of an EEA state or a company or firm mentioned in Article 48 of the EEC Treaty;

(b) the presence or use in a particular place of equipment or other technical means of providing an information society service does not, of itself, constitute the establishment of a service provider;

(c) where it cannot be determined from which of a number of establishments a given information society service is provided, that service is to be regarded as provided from the establishment where the service provider has the centre of his activities relating to the service; and references to a person being established in an EEA state are to be read accordingly.

(8) In this section—

'the E-Commerce Directive' means Directive 2000/31/EC of the European Parliament and of the Council of 8 June 2000 on certain legal aspects of information society services, in particular electronic commerce, in the Internal Market (Directive on electronic commerce);

'information society services'—

(a) has the meaning given in Article 2(a) of the E-Commerce Directive (which refers to Article 1(2) of Directive 98/34/EC of the European Parliament and of the Council of 22 June 1998 laying down a procedure for the provision of information in the field of technical standards and regulations); and

(b) is summarised in recital 17 of the E-Commerce Directive as covering 'any service normally provided for remuneration, at a distance, by means of electronic equipment for the processing (including digital compression) and storage of data, and at the individual request of a recipient of a service';

'intermediary services' means an information society service which—

(a) consists in the provision of access to a communication network or the transmission in a communication network of information provided by a recipient of the service;

(b) consists in the transmission in a communication network of information which—

(i) is provided by a recipient of the service; and

(ii) is the subject of automatic, intermediate and temporary storage which is solely for the purpose of making the onward transmission of the information to other recipients of the service at their request more efficient; or

(c) consists in the storage of information provided by a recipient of the service;

'recipient', in relation to a service, means any person who, for professional ends or otherwise, uses an information society service, in particular for the purposes of seeking information or making it accessible; and

'service provider' means a person providing an information society service.

(9) For the purposes of paragraph (a) of the definition of 'intermediary services', the provision of access to a communication network and the transmission of information in a communication network includes the automatic, intermediate and transient storage of the information transmitted so far as the storage is for the sole purpose of carrying out the transmission in the network.

(10) Subsection (9) does not apply if the information is stored for longer than is reasonably necessary for the transmission.

Supplementary

35 Proceedings in the High Court

(1) Proceedings before the High Court in relation to serious crime prevention orders are civil proceedings.

(2) One consequence of this is that the standard of proof to be applied by the court in such proceedings is the civil standard of proof.

36 Proceedings in the Crown Court

(1) Proceedings before the Crown Court arising by virtue of section 19, 20 or 21 are civil proceedings.

(2) One consequence of this is that the standard of proof to be applied by the court in such proceedings is the civil standard of proof.

(3) Two other consequences of this are that the court—
    (a) is not restricted to considering evidence that would have been admissible in the criminal proceedings in which the person concerned was convicted; and
    (b) may adjourn any proceedings in relation to a serious crime prevention order even after sentencing the person concerned.

(4) The Crown Court, when exercising its jurisdiction in England and Wales under this Part, is a criminal court for the purposes of Part 7 of the Courts Act 2003 (c. 39) (procedure rules and practice directions).

(5) A serious crime prevention order may be made as mentioned in section 19(7)(b) in spite of anything in sections 12 and 14 of the Powers of Criminal Courts (Sentencing) Act 2000 (c. 6) or (as the case may be) Articles 4 and 6 of the Criminal Justice (Northern Ireland) Order 1996 (S.I. 1996/3160 (N.I.24)) (which relate to orders discharging a person absolutely or conditionally and their effect).

(6) A variation of a serious crime prevention order may be made as mentioned in section 20(6)(b) or 21(6)(b) in spite of anything in sections 12 and 14 of the Act of 2000 or (as the case may be) Articles 4 and 6 of the Order of 1996.

37 Functions of applicant authorities

Schedule 2 (functions of applicant authorities under this Part) has effect.

38 Disclosure of information in accordance with orders

(1) A person who complies with a requirement imposed by a serious crime prevention order to answer questions, provide information or produce documents does not breach—
    (a) any obligation of confidence; or
    (b) any other restriction on making the disclosure concerned (however imposed).

(2) But see sections 11 to 14 (which limit the requirements that may be imposed by serious crime prevention orders in connection with answering questions, providing information or producing documents).

39 Compliance with orders: authorised monitors

(1) A serious crime prevention order against a body corporate, partnership or unincorporated association may authorise a law enforcement agency to enter into arrangements with—
(a) a specified person; or
(b) any person who falls within a specified description of persons;
to perform specified monitoring services or monitoring services of a specified description.

(2) A person with whom the agency has entered into arrangements in accordance with such an authorisation is known for the purposes of this section as an authorised monitor.

(3) A serious crime prevention order which provides for an authorised monitor may, for the purpose of enabling the performance of monitoring services, impose requirements of the type mentioned in section 5(5) as if the references in paragraph (a)(iv) and (b)(iv) of that provision to a law enforcement officer included references to an authorised monitor.

(4) A serious crime prevention order which provides for an authorised monitor may require any body corporate, partnership or unincorporated association which is the subject of the order to pay to the law enforcement agency concerned some or all of the costs incurred by the agency under the arrangements with the authorised monitor.

(5) Any such order—
(a) must specify the period, or periods, within which payments are to be made;
(b) may require the making of payments on account;
(c) may include other terms about the calculation or payment of costs.

(6) The tests for making or varying a serious crime prevention order in sections 1(1)(b), (2)(b) and (3), 17(1) and (2), 19(2), (4) and (5), 20(2) and (4) and 21(2) and (4) do not operate in relation to an order so far as the order contains terms of the kind envisaged by subsections (4) and (5) above (or by subsection (1) above for the purposes of those subsections).

(7) But a court must not include in a serious crime prevention order (whether initially or on a variation) terms of the kind envisaged by subsection (4) or (5) unless it considers that it is appropriate to do so having regard to all the circumstances including, in particular—
(a) the means of the body corporate, partnership or unincorporated association concerned;
(b) the expected size of the costs; and
(c) the effect of the terms on the ability of any body corporate, partnership or unincorporated association which is carrying on business to continue to do so.

(8) A law enforcement agency must inform the subject of a serious crime prevention order which provides for an authorised monitor of the name of, and an address for, any person with whom the agency has entered into arrangements in accordance with the authorisation in the order.

(9) Nothing in this section affects the ability of law enforcement agencies to enter into arrangements otherwise than in accordance with an authorisation under this section.

(10) In this section—
'law enforcement agency' means—
(a) a police authority or the Northern Ireland Policing Board;
(b) the Serious Organised Crime Agency;

(c) the Commissioners for Her Majesty's Revenue and Customs; or

(d) the Director of the Serious Fraud Office;

'monitoring services' means—

(a) analysing some or all information received in accordance with a serious crime prevention order;

(b) reporting to a law enforcement officer as to whether, on the basis of the information and any other information analysed for this purpose, the subject of the order appears to be complying with the order or any part of it; and

(c) any related services; and

'specified', in relation to a serious crime prevention order, means specified in the order.

40 Costs in relation to authorised monitors

(1) The Secretary of State may by order make provision about the practice and procedure for determining the amount of—

(a) any costs payable by virtue of section 39(4) and (5); and

(b) any interest payable in respect of those costs.

(2) Such provision may, in particular, include provision about appeals.

(3) Where any amounts required to be paid by virtue of section 39(4) and (5) have not been paid within a required period, the law enforcement agency concerned must take reasonable steps to recover them and any interest payable in respect of them.

(4) The Secretary of State must by order provide for what are reasonable steps for the purposes of subsection (3).

(5) Any amounts which have not been recovered despite the taking of the reasonable steps are recoverable as if due to the law enforcement agency concerned by virtue of a civil order or judgment.

(6) Where any amounts required to be paid by virtue of section 39(4) and (5) are, in the case of an order of the Crown Court, not paid within a required period, the unpaid balance from time to time carries interest at the rate for the time being specified in section 17 of the Judgments Act 1838 (c. 110) (interest on civil judgment debts).

(7) For the purposes of section 25, a failure to comply with a requirement imposed by virtue of section 39(4) and (5) to make payments occurs when the amounts become recoverable as mentioned in subsection (5) above (and not before).

(8) In this section 'law enforcement agency' has the same meaning as in section 39.

41 Powers of law enforcement officers to retain documents

(1) A law enforcement officer—

(a) may take and retain copies of, or extracts from, any document produced to a law enforcement officer in pursuance of a serious crime prevention order; and

(b) may retain any document so produced for as long as he considers that it is necessary to retain it (rather than any copy of it) for the purposes for which the document was obtained.

(2) A law enforcement officer may retain any document produced to a law enforcement officer in pursuance of a serious crime prevention order until the conclusion of any legal proceedings if he has reasonable grounds for believing that the document—

(a) may have to be produced for the purposes of those proceedings; and

(b) might be unavailable unless retained.

Interpretation: Part 1

42 Interpretation: Part 1

In this Part—
'act' and 'conduct' include omissions and statements;
'country' includes territory;
'modifications' includes additions and omissions (and 'modify' is to be read accordingly);
'the public' includes a section of the public or a particular member of the public.

43 Index of defined expressions: Part 1

In this Part, the expressions listed in the left-hand column have the meaning given by, or are to be interpreted in accordance with, the provisions listed in the right-hand column.

Expression	*Provision*
act	section 42
committed a serious offence	section 4(1)
conduct	section 42
conducts oneself in a way likely to facilitate the commission by oneself or another person of a serious offence	section 4(3)
country	section 42
Director of Public Prosecutions, Director of Revenue and Customs Prosecutions, Director of the Serious Fraud Office and Director of Public Prosecutions for Northern Ireland	Paragraphs 2(2), 7(2), 13(2) and 17 of Schedule 2
document	section 5(7)
facilitates the commission by another person of a serious offence	section 4(2)
involvement in serious crime: England and Wales orders	sections 2, 4 and 31(3)
involvement in serious crime: Northern Ireland orders	sections 3, 4 and 31(3)
law enforcement officer	section 5(7)
modifications (and modify)	section 42
person who is the subject of a serious crime prevention order	section 1(6)
Premises	section 5(7)
production of documents	section 5(8)
the public	section 42
relevant applicant authority	section 10(4)
serious crime prevention order	section 1(5)
serious offence in England and Wales	section 2(2)
serious offence in Northern Ireland	section 3(2)

PART 2

ENCOURAGING OR ASSISTING CRIME

Inchoate offences

44 Intentionally encouraging or assisting an offence

(1) A person commits an offence if—
   (a) he does an act capable of encouraging or assisting the commission of an offence; and
   (b) he intends to encourage or assist its commission.
(2) But he is not to be taken to have intended to encourage or assist the commission of an offence merely because such encouragement or assistance was a foreseeable consequence of his act.

45 Encouraging or assisting an offence believing it will be committed

A person commits an offence if—
(a) he does an act capable of encouraging or assisting the commission of an offence; and
(b) he believes—
   (i) that the offence will be committed; and
   (ii) that his act will encourage or assist its commission.

46 Encouraging or assisting offences believing one or more will be committed

(1) A person commits an offence if—
   (a) he does an act capable of encouraging or assisting the commission of one or more of a number of offences; and
   (b) he believes—
       (i) that one or more of those offences will be committed (but has no belief as to which); and
       (ii) that his act will encourage or assist the commission of one or more of them.
(2) It is immaterial for the purposes of subsection (1)(b)(ii) whether the person has any belief as to which offence will be encouraged or assisted.
(3) If a person is charged with an offence under subsection (1)—
   (a) the indictment must specify the offences alleged to be the 'number of offences' mentioned in paragraph (a) of that subsection; but
   (b) nothing in paragraph (a) requires all the offences potentially comprised in that number to be specified.
(4) In relation to an offence under this section, reference in this Part to the offences specified in the indictment is to the offences specified by virtue of subsection (3)(a).

47 Proving an offence under this Part

(1) Sections 44, 45 and 46 are to be read in accordance with this section.
(2) If it is alleged under section 44(1)(b) that a person (D) intended to encourage or assist the commission of an offence, it is sufficient to prove that he intended to encourage or assist the doing of an act which would amount to the commission of that offence.

(3) If it is alleged under section 45(b) that a person (D) believed that an offence would be committed and that his act would encourage or assist its commission, it is sufficient to prove that he believed—

    (a) that an act would be done which would amount to the commission of that offence; and

    (b) that his act would encourage or assist the doing of that act.

(4) If it is alleged under section 46(1)(b) that a person (D) believed that one or more of a number of offences would be committed and that his act would encourage or assist the commission of one or more of them, it is sufficient to prove that he believed—

    (a) that one or more of a number of acts would be done which would amount to the commission of one or more of those offences; and

    (b) that his act would encourage or assist the doing of one or more of those acts.

(5) In proving for the purposes of this section whether an act is one which, if done, would amount to the commission of an offence—

    (a) if the offence is one requiring proof of fault, it must be proved that—

        (i) D believed that, were the act to be done, it would be done with that fault;

        (ii) D was reckless as to whether or not it would be done with that fault; or

        (iii) D's state of mind was such that, were he to do it, it would be done with that fault; and

    (b) if the offence is one requiring proof of particular circumstances or consequences (or both), it must be proved that—

        (i) D believed that, were the act to be done, it would be done in those circumstances or with those consequences; or

        (ii) D was reckless as to whether or not it would be done in those circumstances or with those consequences.

(6) For the purposes of subsection (5)(a)(iii), D is to be assumed to be able to do the act in question.

(7) In the case of an offence under section 44—

    (a) subsection (5)(b)(i) is to be read as if the reference to 'D believed' were a reference to 'D intended or believed'; but

    (b) D is not to be taken to have intended that an act would be done in particular circumstances or with particular consequences merely because its being done in those circumstances or with those consequences was a foreseeable consequence of his act of encouragement or assistance.

(8) Reference in this section to the doing of an act includes reference to—

    (a) a failure to act;

    (b) the continuation of an act that has already begun;

    (c) an attempt to do an act (except an act amounting to the commission of the offence of attempting to commit another offence).

(9) In the remaining provisions of this Part (unless otherwise provided) a reference to the anticipated offence is—

    (a) in relation to an offence under section 44, a reference to the offence mentioned in subsection (2); and

    (b) in relation to an offence under section 45, a reference to the offence mentioned in subsection (3).

48 Proving an offence under section 46

(1) This section makes further provision about the application of section 47 to an offence under section 46.

(2) It is sufficient to prove the matters mentioned in section 47(5) by reference to one offence only.

(3) The offence or offences by reference to which those matters are proved must be one of the offences specified in the indictment.

(4) Subsection (3) does not affect any enactment or rule of law under which a person charged with one offence may be convicted of another and is subject to section 57.

49 Supplemental provisions

(1) A person may commit an offence under this Part whether or not any offence capable of being encouraged or assisted by his act is committed.

(2) If a person's act is capable of encouraging or assisting the commission of a number of offences—

   (a) section 44 applies separately in relation to each offence that he intends to encourage or assist to be committed; and

   (b) section 45 applies separately in relation to each offence that he believes will be encouraged or assisted to be committed.

(3) A person may, in relation to the same act, commit an offence under more than one provision of this Part.

(4) In reckoning whether—

   (a) for the purposes of section 45, an act is capable of encouraging or assisting the commission of an offence; or

   (b) for the purposes of section 46, an act is capable of encouraging or assisting the commission of one or more of a number of offences;

offences under this Part and listed offences are to be disregarded.

(5) 'Listed offence' means—

   (a) in England and Wales, an offence listed in Part 1, 2 or 3 of Schedule 3; and

   (b) in Northern Ireland, an offence listed in Part 1, 4 or 5 of that Schedule.

(6) The Secretary of State may by order amend Schedule 3.

(7) For the purposes of sections 45(b)(i) and 46(1)(b)(i) it is sufficient for the person concerned to believe that the offence (or one or more of the offences) will be committed if certain conditions are met.

Reasonableness defence

50 Defence of acting reasonably

(1) A person is not guilty of an offence under this Part if he proves—

   (a) that he knew certain circumstances existed; and

   (b) that it was reasonable for him to act as he did in those circumstances.

(2) A person is not guilty of an offence under this Part if he proves—

   (a) that he believed certain circumstances to exist;

   (b) that his belief was reasonable; and

   (c) that it was reasonable for him to act as he did in the circumstances as he believed them to be.

(3) Factors to be considered in determining whether it was reasonable for a person to act as he did include—
    (a) the seriousness of the anticipated offence (or, in the case of an offence under section 46, the offences specified in the indictment);
    (b) any purpose for which he claims to have been acting;
    (c) any authority by which he claims to have been acting.

Limitation on liability

51 Protective offences: victims not liable

(1) In the case of protective offences, a person does not commit an offence under this Part by reference to such an offence if—
    (a) he falls within the protected category; and
    (b) he is the person in respect of whom the protective offence was committed or would have been if it had been committed.
(2) 'Protective offence' means an offence that exists (wholly or in part) for the protection of a particular category of persons ('the protected category').

Jurisdiction and procedure

52 Jurisdiction

(1) If a person (D) knows or believes that what he anticipates might take place wholly or partly in England or Wales, he may be guilty of an offence under section 44, 45 or 46 no matter where he was at any relevant time.
(2) If it is not proved that D knows or believes that what he anticipates might take place wholly or partly in England or Wales, he is not guilty of an offence under section 44, 45 or 46 unless paragraph 1, 2 or 3 of Schedule 4 applies.
(3) A reference in this section (and in any of those paragraphs) to what D anticipates is to be read as follows—
    (a) in relation to an offence under section 44 or 45, it refers to the act which would amount to the commission of the anticipated offence;
    (b) in relation to an offence under section 46, it refers to an act which would amount to the commission of any of the offences specified in the indictment.
(4) In their application to Northern Ireland, this section and Schedule 4 have effect as if references to—
    (a) England or Wales; and
    (b) England and Wales;
    were references to Northern Ireland.
(5) Nothing in this section or Schedule 4 restricts the operation of any enactment by virtue of which an act constituting an offence under this Part is triable under the law of England and Wales or Northern Ireland.

53 Prosecution of offences triable by reason of Schedule 4

No proceedings for an offence triable by reason of any provision of Schedule 4 may be instituted—
(a) in England and Wales, except by, or with the consent of, the Attorney General; or

(b) in Northern Ireland, except by, or with the consent of, the Advocate General for Northern Ireland.

54 Institution of proceedings etc. for an offence under this Part

(1) Any provision to which this section applies has effect with respect to an offence under this Part as it has effect with respect to the anticipated offence.

(2) This section applies to provisions made by or under an enactment (whenever passed or made) that—

    (a) provide that proceedings may not be instituted or carried on otherwise than by, or on behalf or with the consent of, any person (including any provision which also makes exceptions to the prohibition);

    (b) confer power to institute proceedings;

    (c) confer power to seize and detain property;

    (d) confer a power of forfeiture, including any power to deal with anything liable to be forfeited.

(3) In relation to an offence under section 46—

    (a) the reference in subsection (1) to the anticipated offence is to be read as a reference to any offence specified in the indictment; and

    (b) each of the offences specified in the indictment must be an offence in respect of which the prosecutor has power to institute proceedings.

(4) Any consent to proceedings required as a result of this section is in addition to any consent required by section 53.

(5) No proceedings for an offence under this Part are to be instituted against a person providing information society services who is established in an EEA State other than the United Kingdom unless the derogation condition is satisfied.

(6) The derogation condition is satisfied where the institution of proceedings—

    (a) is necessary to pursue the public interest objective;

    (b) relates to an information society service that prejudices that objective or presents a serious and grave risk of prejudice to it; and

    (c) is proportionate to that objective.

(7) The public interest objective is public policy.

(8) In this section 'information society services' has the same meaning as in section 34, and subsection (7) of that section applies for the purposes of this section as it applies for the purposes of that section.

55 Mode of trial

(1) An offence under section 44 or 45 is triable in the same way as the anticipated offence.

(2) An offence under section 46 is triable on indictment.

56 Persons who may be perpetrators or encouragers etc.

(1) In proceedings for an offence under this Part ('the inchoate offence') the defendant may be convicted if—

    (a) it is proved that he must have committed the inchoate offence or the anticipated offence; but

    (b) it is not proved which of those offences he committed.

(2) For the purposes of this section, a person is not to be treated as having committed the anticipated offence merely because he aided, abetted, counselled or procured its commission.

(3) In relation to an offence under section 46, a reference in this section to the anticipated offence is to be read as a reference to an offence specified in the indictment.

57 Alternative verdicts and guilty pleas

(1) If in proceedings on indictment for an offence under section 44 or 45 a person is not found guilty of that offence by reference to the specified offence, he may be found guilty of that offence by reference to an alternative offence.

(2) If in proceedings for an offence under section 46 a person is not found guilty of that offence by reference to any specified offence, he may be found guilty of that offence by reference to one or more alternative offences.

(3) If in proceedings for an offence under section 46 a person is found guilty of the offence by reference to one or more specified offences, he may also be found guilty of it by reference to one or more other alternative offences.

(4) For the purposes of this section, an offence is an alternative offence if—
   (a) it is an offence of which, on a trial on indictment for the specified offence, an accused may be found guilty; or
   (b) it is an indictable offence, or one to which section 40 of the Criminal Justice Act 1988 (c. 33) applies (power to include count for common assault etc. in indictment), and the condition in subsection (5) is satisfied.

(5) The condition is that the allegations in the indictment charging the person with the offence under this Part amount to or include (expressly or by implication) an allegation of that offence by reference to it.

(6) Subsection (4)(b) does not apply if the specified offence, or any of the specified offences, is murder or treason.

(7) In the application of subsection (5) to proceedings for an offence under section 44, the allegations in the indictment are to be taken to include an allegation of that offence by reference to the offence of attempting to commit the specified offence.

(8) Section 49(4) applies to an offence which is an alternative offence in relation to a specified offence as it applies to that specified offence.

(9) In this section—
   (a) in relation to a person charged with an offence under section 44 or 45, 'the specified offence' means the offence specified in the indictment as the one alleged to be the anticipated offence;
   (b) in relation to a person charged with an offence under section 46, 'specified offence' means an offence specified in the indictment (within the meaning of subsection (4) of that section), and related expressions are to be read accordingly.

(10) A person arraigned on an indictment for an offence under this Part may plead guilty to an offence of which he could be found guilty under this section on that indictment.

(11) This section applies to an indictment containing more than one count as if each count were a separate indictment.

(12) This section is without prejudice to—
   (a) section 6(1)(b) and (3) of the Criminal Law Act 1967 (c. 58);
   (b) section 6(1)(b) and (2) of the Criminal Law Act (Northern Ireland) 1967 (c. 18).

58 Penalties

(1) Subsections (2) and (3) apply if—
    (a) a person is convicted of an offence under section 44 or 45; or
    (b) a person is convicted of an offence under section 46 by reference to only one offence ('the reference offence').
(2) If the anticipated or reference offence is murder, he is liable to imprisonment for life.
(3) In any other case he is liable to any penalty for which he would be liable on conviction of the anticipated or reference offence.
(4) Subsections (5) to (7) apply if a person is convicted of an offence under section 46 by reference to more than one offence ('the reference offences').
(5) If one of the reference offences is murder, he is liable to imprisonment for life.
(6) If none of the reference offences is murder but one or more of them is punishable with imprisonment, he is liable—
    (a) to imprisonment for a term not exceeding the maximum term provided for any one of those offences (taking the longer or the longest term as the limit for the purposes of this paragraph where the terms provided differ); or
    (b) to a fine.
(7) In any other case he is liable to a fine.
(8) Subsections (3), (6) and (7) are subject to any contrary provision made by or under—
    (a) an Act; or
    (b) Northern Ireland legislation.
(9) In the case of an offence triable either way, the reference in subsection (6) to the maximum term provided for that offence is a reference to the maximum term so provided on conviction on indictment.

Consequential alterations of the law

59 Abolition of common law replaced by this Part

The common law offence of inciting the commission of another offence is abolished.

60 Amendments relating to service law

Schedule 5 (which amends enactments relating to service law) has effect.

61 Repeal of offence of enabling unauthorised access to computer material

(1) The Police and Justice Act 2006 (c. 48) is amended as follows.
(2) In section 35 (unauthorised access to computer material), omit subsection (2).
(3) In section 36 (unauthorised acts with intent to impair operation of computer, etc.), in the section to be substituted for section 3 of the Computer Misuse Act 1990 (c. 18)—
    (a) in subsection (2)—
        (i) at the end of paragraph (b), insert 'or'; and
        (ii) omit paragraph (d) and the word 'or' preceding it;
    (b) in subsection (3) for 'to (d)' substitute 'to (c)'.
(4) In section 38 (transitional and saving provision), omit subsection (1).
(5) In Schedule 14 (minor and consequential amendments), omit paragraphs 19(2) and 29(2).

62 No individual liability in respect of corporate manslaughter

In section 18 of the Corporate Manslaughter and Corporate Homicide Act 2007 (c. 19) (no individual liability for offences under that Act) after subsection (1) insert—

'(1A) An individual cannot be guilty of an offence under Part 2 of the Serious Crime Act 2007 (encouraging or assisting crime) by reference to an offence of corporate manslaughter.'

63 Consequential amendments: Part 2

(1) In the provisions listed in Part 1 of Schedule 6, any reference however expressed to (or to conduct amounting to) the offence abolished by section 59 has effect as a reference to (or to conduct amounting to) the offences under this Part.

(2) Part 2 of Schedule 6 contains other minor and consequential amendments.

(3) The Secretary of State may by order amend Part 1 of Schedule 6 by adding or removing a provision.

Interpretation: Part 2

64 Encouraging or assisting the commission of an offence

A reference in this Part to encouraging or assisting the commission of an offence is to be read in accordance with section 47.

65 Being capable of encouraging or assisting

(1) A reference in this Part to a person's doing an act that is capable of encouraging the commission of an offence includes a reference to his doing so by threatening another person or otherwise putting pressure on another person to commit the offence.

(2) A reference in this Part to a person's doing an act that is capable of encouraging or assisting the commission of an offence includes a reference to his doing so by—
   (a) taking steps to reduce the possibility of criminal proceedings being brought in respect of that offence;
   (b) failing to take reasonable steps to discharge a duty.

(3) But a person is not to be regarded as doing an act that is capable of encouraging or assisting the commission of an offence merely because he fails to respond to a constable's request for assistance in preventing a breach of the peace.

66 Indirectly encouraging or assisting

If a person (D1) arranges for a person (D2) to do an act that is capable of encouraging or assisting the commission of an offence, and D2 does the act, D1 is also to be treated for the purposes of this Part as having done it.

67 Course of conduct

A reference in this Part to an act includes a reference to a course of conduct, and a reference to doing an act is to be read accordingly.

PART 3
OTHER MEASURES TO PREVENT OR DISRUPT SERIOUS
AND OTHER CRIME

CHAPTER 1
PREVENTION OF FRAUD

Sharing information with anti-fraud organisations

68 Disclosure of information to prevent fraud

(1) A public authority may, for the purposes of preventing fraud or a particular kind of fraud, disclose information as a member of a specified anti-fraud organisation or otherwise in accordance with any arrangements made by such an organisation.

(2) The information—
(a) may be information of any kind; and
(b) may be disclosed to the specified anti-fraud organisation, any members of it or any other person to whom disclosure is permitted by the arrangements concerned.

(3) Disclosure under this section does not breach—
(a) any obligation of confidence owed by the public authority disclosing them information; or
(b) any other restriction on the disclosure of information (however imposed).

(4) But nothing in this section authorises any disclosure of information which—
(a) contravenes the Data Protection Act 1998 (c. 29); or
(b) is prohibited by Part 1 of the Regulation of Investigatory Powers Act 2000 (c. 23).

(5) Nothing in this section authorises any disclosure by a relevant public authority of information whose subject-matter is a matter about which provision would be within the legislative competence of the Scottish Parliament if it were included in an Act of that Parliament.

(6) In subsection (5) 'relevant public authority' means a public authority which has (whether alone or in addition to other functions) functions which are exercisable within devolved competence (within the meaning given by section 54 of the Scotland Act 1998 (c. 46)).

(7) This section does not limit the circumstances in which information may be disclosed apart from this section.

(8) In this section—
'an anti-fraud organisation' means any unincorporated association, body corporate or other person which enables or facilitates any sharing of information to prevent fraud or a particular kind of fraud or which has any of these functions as its purpose or one of its purposes;
'information' includes documents;
'public authority' means any public authority within the meaning of section 6 of the Human Rights Act 1998 (c. 42) (acts of public authorities); and
'specified' means specified by an order made by the Secretary of State.

69 Offence for certain further disclosures of information

(1) A person ('B') commits an offence, subject as follows, if—
(a) B discloses protected information which has been disclosed by a public authority—
(i) as a result of the public authority being a member of a specified anti-fraud organisation; or

(ii) otherwise in accordance with any arrangements made by such an organisation;
(b) the information—
  (i) has been so disclosed by the public authority to B; or
  (ii) has come into B's possession as a result (whether directly or indirectly) of such a disclosure by the public authority to another person; and
(c) B knows or suspects, or has reasonable grounds for suspecting, that the information is information of the kind mentioned in paragraphs (a) and (b).

(2) Subsection (1) does not apply to a disclosure made by B—
(a) where B is acting (whether as an employee or otherwise) on behalf of the person to whom the information was disclosed by the public authority concerned and the disclosure by B is to another person acting (whether as an employee or otherwise) on behalf of that person;
(b) for the purposes of the detection, investigation or prosecution of an offence in the United Kingdom;
(c) with the consent of the public authority concerned; or
(d) in pursuance of a Community obligation or a duty imposed by an enactment;

but it does apply to a disclosure made by B which does not fall within paragraphs (a) to (d) above but which (but for the offence) would have been permitted by a power conferred by an enactment.

(3) Subsection (1) does not apply to a disclosure made by B of information—
(a) which has been disclosed by a relevant public authority; and
(b) whose subject-matter is a matter about which provision would be within the legislative competence of the Scottish Parliament if it were included in an Act of that Parliament;

and subsection (6) of section 68 applies for the purposes of this subsection as it applies for the purposes of subsection (5) of that section.

(4) It is a defence for a person charged with an offence under this section to prove that the person reasonably believed—
(a) that the disclosure was lawful; or
(b) that the information had already and lawfully been made available to the public.

(5) In this section 'protected information' means—
(a) any revenue and customs information disclosed by Revenue and Customs and revealing the identity of the person to whom it relates; or
(b) any specified information disclosed by a specified public authority.

(6) For the purposes of this section—
(a) 'revenue and customs information' means information about, acquired as a result of or held in connection with the exercise of a function of the Commissioners of Revenue and Customs or an officer of Revenue and Customs in respect of a person;
(b) revenue and customs information reveals a person's identity if—
  (i) it specifies his identity; or
  (ii) his identity can be deduced from it; and
(c) revenue and customs information relates to a person if he is the person in respect of whom the function mentioned in paragraph (a) is exercised.

(7) In this section—
'Commissioners of Revenue and Customs' means Commissioners for Her Majesty's Revenue and Customs;
'enactment' has the same meaning as in section 14;
'public authority' has the same meaning as in section 68;

'Revenue and Customs' means—
- (a) the Commissioners of Revenue and Customs;
- (b) an officer of Revenue and Customs; or
- (c) a person acting on behalf of the Commissioners or an officer of Revenue and Customs;

'specified anti-fraud organisation' means any person which is a specified anti-fraud organisation for the purposes of section 68;

'specified information' means information specified or described in an order made by the Secretary of State; and

'specified public authority' means a public authority specified or described in an order made by the Secretary of State.

70 Penalty and prosecution for offence under section 69

(1) A person who commits an offence under section 69 is liable—
- (a) on summary conviction, to imprisonment for a term not exceeding 12 months or to a fine not exceeding the statutory maximum or to both;
- (b) on conviction on indictment, to imprisonment for a term not exceeding two years or to a fine or to both.

(2) A prosecution for an offence under section 69 may be begun in England and Wales only—
- (a) in the case of revenue and customs information disclosed by Revenue and Customs—
  - (i) by the Director of Revenue and Customs Prosecutions; or
  - (ii) with the consent of the Director of Public Prosecutions; and
- (b) in any other case, with the consent of the Director of Public Prosecutions.

(3) A prosecution for an offence under section 69 may be begun in Northern Ireland only—
- (a) in the case of revenue and customs information disclosed by Revenue and Customs—
  - (i) by the Commissioners of Revenue and Customs; or
  - (ii) with the consent of the Director of Public Prosecutions for Northern Ireland; and
- (b) in any other case, with the consent of the Director of Public Prosecutions for Northern Ireland.

(4) If an offence under section 69 committed by a body corporate or a partnership is proved to have been committed with the consent or connivance of—
- (a) an officer of the body corporate or (as the case may be) a partner or a senior officer of the partnership; or
- (b) a person who was purporting to act in any such capacity;

he (as well as the body corporate or partnership) is guilty of the offence and liable to be proceeded against and punished accordingly.

(5) In the application of subsection (1)(a) in Northern Ireland, the reference to 12 months is to be read as a reference to 6 months.

(6) In this section—
'body corporate' includes a limited liability partnership;
'Commissioners of Revenue and Customs', 'Revenue and Customs' and
'revenue and customs information' have the same meaning as in section 69;
'director', in relation to a body corporate whose affairs are managed by its members, means a member of the body corporate;
'officer of a body corporate' means any director, manager, secretary or other similar officer of the body corporate; and

'senior officer of a partnership' means any person who has the control or management of the business carried on by the partnership at the principal place where it is carried on.

71 Code of practice for disclosure of information to prevent fraud

(1) The Secretary of State must prepare, and keep under review, a code of practice with respect to the disclosure, for the purposes of preventing fraud or a particular kind of fraud, of information by public authorities as members of specified anti-fraud organisations or otherwise in accordance with any arrangements made by such organisations.

(2) Before preparing or altering the code, the Secretary of State must consult—

(a) any specified anti-fraud organisation;

(b) the Information Commissioner; and

(c) such other persons as the Secretary of State considers appropriate.

(3) A public authority must have regard to the code in (or in connection with) disclosing information, for the purposes of preventing fraud or a particular kind of fraud, as a member of a specified anti-fraud organisation or otherwise in accordance with any arrangements made by such an organisation.

(4) Nothing in this section applies in relation to any disclosure by a relevant public authority of information whose subject-matter is a matter about which provision would be within the legislative competence of the Scottish Parliament if it were included in an Act of the Scottish Parliament.

(5) The Secretary of State must—

(a) lay a copy of the code, and of any alterations to it, before Parliament; and

(b) from time to time publish the code as for the time being in force.

(6) In this section—

'information' and 'public authority' have the same meaning as in section 68;

'relevant public authority' has the meaning given by section 68(6); and

'specified anti-fraud organisation' means any person which is a specified anti-fraud organisation for the purposes of section 68.

72 Data protection rules

In Schedule 3 to the Data Protection Act 1998 (c. 29) (conditions for processing sensitive personal data), after paragraph 7, insert—

'7A (1) The processing—

(a) is either—

(i) the disclosure of sensitive personal data by a person as a member of an anti-fraud organisation or otherwise in accordance with any arrangements made by such an organisation; or

(ii) any other processing by that person or another person of sensitive personal data so disclosed; and

(b) is necessary for the purposes of preventing fraud or a particular kind of fraud.

(2) In this paragraph "an anti-fraud organisation" means any unincorporated association, body corporate or other person which enables or facilitates any sharing of information to prevent fraud or a particular kind of fraud or which has any of these functions as its purpose or one of its purposes.'

Data matching

73 Data matching

Schedule 7 (which makes provision about data matching) has effect.

CHAPTER 2

PROCEEDS OF CRIME

Assets Recovery Agency

74 Abolition of Assets Recovery Agency and redistribution of functions etc.

(1) The Assets Recovery Agency and the corporation sole that is its Director shall cease to exist on such day as the Secretary of State may by order appoint.

(2) The following Parts of Schedule 8 (abolition of Assets Recovery Agency and its Director) have effect—

    (a) Part 1 (abolition of confiscation functions);

    (b) Part 2 (transfer to SOCA and prosecution authorities of civil recovery functions);

    (c) Part 3 (transfer to SOCA of Revenue functions and power to abolish those functions);

    (d) Part 4 (transfer of investigation functions);

    (e) Part 5 (transfer of accreditation and training functions to National Policing Improvement Agency);

    (f) Part 6 (other amendments to the Proceeds of Crime Act 2002 (c. 29)); and

    (g) Part 7 (amendments to other enactments).

(3) Schedule 9 (which makes provision about the transfer of the Director and staff of the Agency, and property, rights and liabilities of the Director and the Agency, to SOCA and the National Policing Improvement Agency) has effect.

(4) In this section and Schedules 8 and 9 'SOCA' means the Serious Organised Crime Agency.

Detained cash investigations: use of production orders and warrants

75 Use of production orders for detained cash investigations

(1) After section 341(3) of the Proceeds of Crime Act 2002 (types of investigation to which Part 8 applies) insert—

    '(3A) For the purposes of this Part a detained cash investigation is—

        (a) an investigation for the purposes of Chapter 3 of Part 5 into the derivation of cash detained under section 295 or a part of such cash, or

        (b) an investigation for the purposes of Chapter 3 of Part 5 into whether cash detained under section 295, or a part of such cash, is intended by any person to be used in unlawful conduct.'

(2) In section 345(2) of that Act (investigations in respect of which production orders may be made), in paragraph (b), after 'a civil recovery investigation' insert 'or a detained cash investigation'.

(3) In section 346(2) of that Act (reasonable suspicion requirement for making a production order), after paragraph (b), insert—

'(ba) in the case of a detained cash investigation into the derivation of cash, the property the application for the order specifies as being subject to the investigation, or a part of it, is recoverable property;

(bb) in the case of a detained cash investigation into the intended use of cash, the property the application for the order specifies as being subject to the investigation, or a part of it, is intended by any person to be used in unlawful conduct;'.

(4) In section 380(3) of that Act (investigations in respect of which production orders may be made in Scotland), in paragraph (b), after 'a civil recovery investigation' insert 'or a detained cash investigation'.

(5) In section 381(2) of that Act (reasonable suspicion requirement for making a production order in Scotland), after paragraph (b), insert—

'(ba) in the case of a detained cash investigation into the derivation of cash, the property the application for the order specifies as being subject to the investigation, or a part of it, is recoverable property;

(bb) in the case of a detained cash investigation into the intended use of cash, the property the application for the order specifies as being subject to the investigation, or a part of it, is intended by any person to be used in unlawful conduct;'.

76 Use of search warrants etc. for detained cash investigations

(1) In section 352(2) of the Proceeds of Crime Act 2002 (c. 29) (investigations in respect of which a search and seizure warrant may be issued), in paragraph (b), after 'a civil recovery investigation' insert 'or a detained cash investigation'.

(2) In section 353(2) of that Act (reasonable suspicion grounds for warrant where no production order), after paragraph (b), insert—

'(ba) in the case of a detained cash investigation into the derivation of cash, the property specified in the application for the warrant, or a part of it, is recoverable property;

(bb) in the case of a detained cash investigation into the intended use of cash, the property specified in the application for the warrant, or a part of it, is intended by any person to be used in unlawful conduct;'.

(3) After section 353(7) of that Act (types of material in respect of which warrant may be issued where no production order) insert—

'(7A) In the case of a detained cash investigation into the derivation of cash, material falls within this subsection if it cannot be identified at the time of the application but it—

(a) relates to the property specified in the application, the question whether the property, or a part of it, is recoverable property or any other question as to its derivation, and

(b) is likely to be of substantial value (whether or not by itself) to the investigation for the purposes of which the warrant is sought.

(7B) In the case of a detained cash investigation into the intended use of cash, material falls within this subsection if it cannot be identified at the time of the application but it—

(a) relates to the property specified in the application or the question whether the property, or a part of it, is intended by any person to be used in unlawful conduct, and

(b) is likely to be of substantial value (whether or not by itself) to the investigation for the purposes of which the warrant is sought.'

(4) In section 387(3) of that Act (investigations in respect of which a search warrant may be issued in Scotland), in paragraph (b), after 'a civil recovery investigation' insert 'or a detained cash investigation'.

(5) In section 388(2) of that Act (reasonable suspicion grounds for issue of warrant in Scotland where no production order), after paragraph (b), insert—

'(ba) in the case of a detained cash investigation into the derivation of cash, the property specified in the application for the warrant, or a part of it, is recoverable property;

(bb) in the case of a detained cash investigation into the intended use of cash, the property specified in the application for the warrant, or a part of it, is intended by any person to be used in unlawful conduct;'.

(6) After section 388(7) of that Act (types of material in respect of which warrant may be issued in Scotland where no production order) insert—

'(7A) In the case of a detained cash investigation into the derivation of cash, material falls within this subsection if it cannot be identified at the time of the application but it—

(a) relates to the property specified in the application, the question whether the property, or a part of it, is recoverable property or any other question as to its derivation, and

(b) is likely to be of substantial value (whether or not by itself) to the investigation for the purposes of which the warrant is sought.

(7B) In the case of a detained cash investigation into the intended use of cash, material falls within this subsection if it cannot be identified at the time of the application but it—

(a) relates to the property specified in the application or the question whether the property, or a part of it, is intended by any person to be used in unlawful conduct, and

(b) is likely to be of substantial value (whether or not by itself) to the investigation for the purposes of which the warrant is sought.'

77 Further provision about detained cash investigations

Schedule 10 (which makes further provision about detained cash investigations) has effect.

Extension of powers of accredited financial investigators

78 Powers to seize property to which restraint orders apply

(1) In section 45(1) of the Proceeds of Crime Act 2002 (c. 29) (seizure of property to which restraint order applies: England and Wales) after 'constable' insert, 'an accredited financial investigator'.

(2) After section 45(2) of that Act insert—

'(3) The reference in subsection (1) to an accredited financial investigator is a reference to an accredited financial investigator who falls within a description specified in an order made for the purposes of that subsection by the Secretary of State under section 453.'

(3) In section 194(1) of that Act (seizure of property to which restraint order applies: Northern Ireland) after 'constable' insert, 'an accredited financial investigator'.

(4) After section 194(2) of that Act insert—

'(3) The reference in subsection (1) to an accredited financial investigator is a reference to an accredited financial investigator who falls within a description specified in an order made for the purposes of that subsection by the Secretary of State under section 453.'

79 Powers to recover cash

Schedule 11 (which gives accredited financial investigators powers to recover cash under Chapter 3 of Part 5 of the Proceeds of Crime Act 2002 (c. 29) and makes related amendments) has effect.

80 Powers in relation to certain investigations

(1) In section 352(5) of the Proceeds of Crime Act 2002 (search and seizure warrants in connection with confiscation, money laundering and detained cash investigations etc.)—
 (a) in paragraph (a), after 'constable' insert, 'an accredited financial investigator'; and
 (b) in paragraph (c) (as inserted by Schedule 10 to this Act), after 'constable' insert, 'an accredited financial investigator'.

(2) After section 352(6) of that Act insert—

'(7) The reference in paragraph (a) or (c) of subsection (5) to an accredited financial investigator is a reference to an accredited financial investigator who falls within a description specified in an order made for the purposes of that paragraph by the Secretary of State under section 453.'

(3) In section 353(10) of that Act (requirements in relation to search and seizure warrants)—
 (a) in paragraph (a), after 'constable' insert, 'an accredited financial investigator'; and
 (b) in paragraph (c) (as inserted by Schedule 10 to this Act), after 'constable' insert, 'an accredited financial investigator'.

(4) After section 353(10) of that Act insert—

'(11) The reference in paragraph (a) or (c) of subsection (10) to an accredited financial investigator is a reference to an accredited financial investigator who falls within a description specified in an order made for the purposes of that paragraph by the Secretary of State under section 453.'

(5) In section 356(11)(b) of that Act (as inserted by Schedule 10 to this Act) (further provisions in relation to search and seizure warrants: detained cash investigations) after 'constable' insert, 'an accredited financial investigator'.

(6) After section 356(11) of that Act (as inserted by Schedule 10 to this Act) insert—

'(12) The reference in paragraph (b) of subsection (11) to an accredited financial investigator is a reference to an accredited financial investigator who falls within a description specified in an order made for the purposes of that paragraph by the Secretary of State under section 453.'

(7) In section 378(3A) of that Act (as inserted by Schedule 10 to this Act) (meaning of 'officers' for purposes of Part 8 in relation to detained cash investigations) after paragraph (a) insert—

'(ab) an accredited financial investigator;'.

(8) After section 378(3A) of that Act (as inserted by Schedule 10 to this Act) insert—

'(3B) The reference in paragraph (ab) of subsection (3A) to an accredited financial investigator is a reference to an accredited financial investigator who falls within a description specified in an order made for the purposes of that paragraph by the Secretary of State under section 453.'

81 Supplementary provision in relation to new powers

(1) In section 453(2) of the Proceeds of Crime Act 2002 (c. 29) (power to modify references to accredited financial investigators)—

(a) after 'may' insert, 'in particular,'; and

(b) after 'person' insert 'or by reference to particular types of training undertaken'.

(2) After section 453 of that Act insert—

'**453A Certain offences in relation to financial investigators**

(1) A person commits an offence if he assaults an accredited financial investigator who is acting in the exercise of a relevant power.

(2) A person commits an offence if he resists or wilfully obstructs an accredited financial investigator who is acting in the exercise of a relevant power.

(3) A person guilty of an offence under subsection (1) is liable on summary conviction—

(a) to imprisonment for a term not exceeding 51 weeks; or

(b) to a fine not exceeding level 5 on the standard scale;

  or to both.

(4) A person guilty of an offence under subsection (2) is liable on summary conviction—

(a) to imprisonment for a term not exceeding 51 weeks; or

(b) to a fine not exceeding level 3 on the standard scale;

  or to both.

(5) In this section "relevant power" means a power exercisable under—

(a) section 45 or 194 (powers to seize property to which restraint orders apply);

(b) section 289 (powers to search for cash);

(c) section 294 (powers to seize cash);

(d) section 295(1) (power to detain seized cash); or

(e) a search and seizure warrant issued under section 352.

(6) In the application of this section to England and Wales in relation to an offence committed before the commencement of section 281(5) of the Criminal Justice Act 2003 (c. 44) (alteration of penalties for summary offences), and in the application of this section to Northern Ireland—

(a) the reference to 51 weeks in subsection (3)(a) is to be read as a reference to 6 months; and

(b) the reference to 51 weeks in subsection (4)(a) is to be read as a reference to 1 month.'

Miscellaneous

82 Powers of management receivers and enforcement receivers

(1) After section 49(8) of the Proceeds of Crime Act 2002 (c. 29) (opportunity for persons to make representations before powers conferred on management receivers to manage or otherwise deal with property: England and Wales) insert—

'(8A) Subsection (8), so far as relating to the power mentioned in subsection (2)(b), does not apply to property which—

(a) is perishable; or

(b) ought to be disposed of before its value diminishes.'

(2) After section 51(8) of that Act (opportunity for persons to make representations before powers conferred on enforcement receivers to manage or otherwise deal with property: England and Wales) insert—

'(8A) Subsection (8), so far as relating to the power mentioned in subsection (2)(b), does not apply to property which—
   (a) is perishable; or
   (b) ought to be disposed of before its value diminishes.'

(3) After section 197(8) of that Act (opportunity for persons to make representations before powers conferred on management receivers to manage or otherwise deal with property: Northern Ireland) insert—

'(8A) Subsection (8), so far as relating to the power mentioned in subsection (2)(b), does not apply to property which—
   (a) is perishable; or
   (b) ought to be disposed of before its value diminishes.'

(4) After section 199(8) of that Act (opportunity for persons to make representations before powers conferred on enforcement receivers to manage or otherwise deal with property: Northern Ireland) insert—

'(8A) Subsection (8), so far as relating to the power mentioned in subsection (2)(b), does not apply to property which—
   (a) is perishable; or
   (b) ought to be disposed of before its value diminishes.'

83 Civil recovery management receivers

(1) After section 245D of the Proceeds of Crime Act 2002 (property freezing orders) insert—

'**245E Receivers in connection with property freezing orders**
(1) Subsection (2) applies if—
   (a) the High Court makes a property freezing order on an application by an enforcement authority, and
   (b) the authority applies to the court to proceed under subsection (2) (whether as part of the application for the property freezing order or at any time afterwards).
(2) The High Court may by order appoint a receiver in respect of any property to which the property freezing order applies.
(3) An application for an order under this section may be made without notice if the circumstances are such that notice of the application would prejudice any right of the enforcement authority to obtain a recovery order in respect of any property.
(4) In its application for an order under this section, the enforcement authority must nominate a suitably qualified person for appointment as a receiver.
(5) Such a person may be a member of staff of the enforcement authority.
(6) The enforcement authority may apply a sum received by it under section 280(2) in making payment of the remuneration and expenses of a receiver appointed under this section.
(7) Subsection (6) does not apply in relation to the remuneration of the receiver if he is a member of the staff of the enforcement authority (but it does apply in relation to such remuneration if the receiver is a person providing services under arrangements made by the enforcement authority).

245F Powers of receivers appointed under section 245E

(1) If the High Court appoints a receiver under section 245E on an application by an enforcement authority, the court may act under this section on the application of the authority.

(2) The court may by order authorise or require the receiver—

    (a) to exercise any of the powers mentioned in paragraph 5 of Schedule 6 (management powers) in relation to any property in respect of which the receiver is appointed,

    (b) to take any other steps the court thinks appropriate in connection with the management of any such property (including securing the detention, custody or preservation of the property in order to manage it).

(3) The court may by order require any person in respect of whose property the receiver is appointed—

    (a) to bring the property to a place (in England and Wales or, as the case may be, Northern Ireland) specified by the receiver or to place it in the custody of the receiver (if, in either case, he is able to do so),

    (b) to do anything he is reasonably required to do by the receiver for the preservation of the property.

(4) The court may by order require any person in respect of whose property the receiver is appointed to bring any documents relating to the property which are in his possession or control to a place (in England and Wales or, as the case may be, Northern Ireland) specified by the receiver or to place them in the custody of the receiver.

(5) In subsection (4) 'document' means anything in which information of any description is recorded.

(6) Any prohibition on dealing with property imposed by a property freezing order does not prevent a person from complying with any requirements imposed by virtue of this section.

(7) If—

    (a) the receiver deals with any property which is not property in respect of which he is appointed under section 245E, and

    (b) at the time he deals with the property he believes on reasonable grounds that he is entitled to do so by virtue of his appointment,

the receiver is not liable to any person in respect of any loss or damage resulting from his dealing with the property except so far as the loss or damage is caused by his negligence.

245G Supervision of section 245E receiver and variations

(1) Any of the following persons may at any time apply to the High Court for directions as to the exercise of the functions of a receiver appointed under section 245E—

    (a) the receiver,

    (b) any party to the proceedings for the appointment of the receiver or the property freezing order concerned,

    (c) any person affected by any action taken by the receiver,

    (d) any person who may be affected by any action proposed to be taken by the receiver.

(2) Before giving any directions under subsection (1), the court must give an opportunity to be heard to—

    (a) the receiver,

    (b) the parties to the proceedings for the appointment of the receiver and for the property freezing order concerned,

(c) any person who may be interested in the application under subsection (1).

(3) The court may at any time vary or set aside the appointment of a receiver under section 245E, any order under section 245F or any directions under this section.

(4) Before exercising any power under subsection (3), the court must give an opportunity to be heard to—

    (a) the receiver,

    (b) the parties to the proceedings for the appointment of the receiver, for the order under section 245F or, as the case may be, for the directions under this section;

    (c) the parties to the proceedings for the property freezing order concerned,

    (d) any person who may be affected by the court's decision.'

(2) In sections 273(4)(b) and 277(7)(b) of that Act (recovery orders and consent orders: recovery of costs of pension scheme trustees or managers) after 'enforcement authority,' insert 'receiver appointed under section 245E,'.

(3) In paragraph 1 of Schedule 10 to that Act (disapplication of special income tax and capital gains tax rules for receivers), after paragraph (c), insert—

    '(ca) a receiver appointed under section 245E;'.

84 Powers for prosecutors to appear in cash recovery proceedings

(1) After section 302 of the Proceeds of Crime Act 2002 (c. 29) (recovery of cash in summary proceedings: compensation) insert—

'302A Powers for prosecutors to appear in proceedings

(1) The Director of Public Prosecutions or the Director of Public Prosecutions for Northern Ireland may appear for a constable in proceedings under this Chapter if the Director—

    (a) is asked by, or on behalf of, a constable to do so, and

    (b) considers it appropriate to do so.

(2) The Director of Revenue and Customs Prosecutions may appear for the Commissioners for Her Majesty's Revenue and Customs or an officer of Revenue and Customs in proceedings under this Chapter if the Director—

    (a) is asked by, or on behalf of, the Commissioners for Her Majesty's Revenue and Customs or (as the case may be) an officer of Revenue and Customs to do so, and

    (b) considers it appropriate to do so.

(3) The Directors may charge fees for the provision of services under this section.'

(2) After section 2C(3) of that Act (prosecuting authorities) (as inserted by Schedule 8 to this Act) insert—

    '(3A) Subsection (3) does not apply to the functions of the Director of Public Prosecutions for Northern Ireland and the Director of Revenue and Customs Prosecutions under section 302A.'

(3) After section 38(1) of the Commissioners for Revenue and Customs Act 2005 (c. 11) (conduct of prosecutions on behalf of the Office) insert—

    '(1A) An individual who is not a member of the Office may be appointed by the Director to appear in—

    (a) specified proceedings, or

    (b) a specified class or description of proceedings,

    in which the Director or a Prosecutor would otherwise appear by virtue of section 302A of the Proceeds of Crime Act 2002 (cash recovery proceedings).'

(4) After section 39(1) of that Act (designation of non-legal staff) insert—

'(1A) he Director may designate a member of the Office to appear in—
   (a) specified proceedings, or
   (b) a specified class or description of proceedings, in which the Director or a Prosecutor would otherwise appear by virtue of section 302A of the Proceeds of Crime Act 2002 (cash recovery proceedings).'

85 Disclosure of information by Revenue and Customs

(1) This section applies to information held as mentioned in section 18(1) of the Commissioners for Revenue and Customs Act 2005 (c. 11) (confidentiality).

(2) Information to which this section applies may be disclosed by or with the authority of the Commissioners of Revenue and Customs—
   (a) to the Criminal Assets Bureau in Ireland ('the CAB') for the purpose of enabling or assisting the CAB to exercise any of its functions in connection with any matter within subsection (3); or
   (b) to any specified public authority (in the United Kingdom or elsewhere)—
      (i) for the purpose of enabling or assisting the public authority to exercise any of its functions in connection with any matter within subsection (3); or
      (ii) (if the specifying order so provides) for the purpose of enabling or assisting the public authority to exercise any of its functions in connection with any matter within that subsection that is specified, or of a description specified, in the order.

(3) The matters within this subsection are—
   (a) the identification of proceeds of crime;
   (b) the bringing of civil proceedings for enforcement purposes in relation to proceeds of crime; and
   (c) the taking of other action in relation to proceeds of crime.

(4) Information disclosed in accordance with subsection (2) must not be further disclosed except—
   (a) in connection with the exercise of any of the functions of the CAB or a specified public authority in connection with any matter within subsection (3) (or, in a subsection (2)(b)(ii) case, any such matter as is mentioned there); and
   (b) with the consent of the Commissioners of Revenue and Customs or an authorised officer of the Commissioners of Revenue and Customs.

(5) For the purposes of this section any consent or authorisation may be general or specific.

(6) If a person in the United Kingdom discloses, in contravention of subsection (4), any revenue and customs information relating to a person whose identity—
   (a) is specified in the disclosure; or
   (b) can be deduced from it;
section 19 of the 2005 Act (wrongful disclosure) applies in relation to that disclosure as it applies in relation to a disclosure of such information in contravention of section 20(9) of that Act.

(7) Any reference in this section to a disclosure to the CAB or a specified public authority is a reference to a disclosure to such person, or to persons of such description, as may be specified in relation to the CAB or the public authority (as the case may be).

(8) Nothing in this section authorises any disclosure of information which—
   (a) contravenes the Data Protection Act 1998 (c. 29); or
   (b) is prohibited by Part 1 of the Regulation of Investigatory Powers Act 2000 (c. 23).

(9) In this section—

'the 2005 Act' means the Commissioners for Revenue and Customs Act 2005 (c. 11);

'assets' means property of any description, wherever situated;

'civil proceedings' means civil proceedings of whatever nature and whether brought in the United Kingdom or elsewhere;

'Commissioners of Revenue and Customs' means the Commissioners for Her Majesty's Revenue and Customs;

'enforcement purposes', in relation to the proceeds of crime, means with a view to—

(a) recovering, forfeiting or freezing assets constituting proceeds of crime; or

(b) otherwise depriving persons (to any extent) of, or of access to, such assets or the benefit of such assets;

'functions' includes powers, duties and objectives, and references to the exercise of functions include the pursuit of objectives;

'proceeds of crime' means assets derived, or suspected to be derived, directly or indirectly from criminal conduct (wherever occurring);

'public authority' means any body or person discharging functions of a public nature;

'revenue and customs information relating to a person' has the meaning given by section 19(2) of the 2005 Act;

'specified' means specified in an order made by the Treasury; and

'the specifying order', in relation to a specified public authority, means the order specifying the authority for the purposes of this section.

86 Use of force in executing search warrants: Scotland

In section 387 of the Proceeds of Crime Act 2002 (c. 29) (issue of search warrants in Scotland in connection with certain investigations), after subsection (4), insert—

'(4A) A proper person may, if necessary, use reasonable force in executing a search warrant.'

CHAPTER 3
OTHER MEASURES

87 Incidents involving serious violence: powers to stop and search

(1) In section 60(1) of the Criminal Justice and Public Order Act 1994 (c. 33) (powers to authorise stop and search if reasonable belief that there may be incidents involving serious violence etc.), before the word 'or' at the end of paragraph (a), insert—

'(aa) that—

(i) an incident involving serious violence has taken place in England and Wales in his police area;

(ii) a dangerous instrument or offensive weapon used in the incident is being carried in any locality in his police area by a person; and

(iii) it is expedient to give an authorisation under this section to find the instrument or weapon;'.

(2) In section 60(9) of that Act (authorisation must be in writing), at the beginning, insert 'Subject to subsection (9ZA),'.

(3) After section 60(9) of that Act insert—

'(9ZA) An authorisation under subsection (1)(aa) need not be given in writing where it is not practicable to do so but any oral authorisation must state the matters which would otherwise have to be specified under subsection (9) and must be recorded in writing as soon as it is practicable to do so.'

(4) In section 60(9A) of that Act (application to British Transport Police)—
  (a) after 'place' insert 'in England and Wales'; and
  (b) after '2003' insert 'and as if the reference in subsection (1)(aa)(i) above to his police area were a reference to any place falling within section 31(1)(a) to (f) of the Act of 2003'.

(5) In section 60(11) of that Act (definitions), in the definition of 'offensive weapon', after '1995' insert; 'but in subsections (1)(aa), (4), (5) and (6) above and subsection (11A) below includes, in the case of an incident of the kind mentioned in subsection (1)(aa)(i) above, any article used in the incident to cause or threaten injury to any person or otherwise to intimidate'.

(6) In the heading to section 60 of that Act after 'of' insert, 'or after,'.

88 Extension of investigatory powers of Revenue and Customs

Schedule 12 (which makes provision about the regulation of investigatory powers of Her Majesty's Revenue and Customs) has effect.

PART 4

GENERAL AND FINAL PROVISIONS

General

89 Orders

(1) Any power of the Secretary of State, the Treasury or the Scottish Ministers to make an order under this Act is exercisable by statutory instrument.

(2) Any power of the Secretary of State or the Treasury to make an order under this Act—
  (a) may be exercised so as to make different provision for different cases or descriptions of case or different purposes;
  (b) includes power to make such supplementary, incidental, consequential, transitional, transitory or saving provision as the Secretary of State or (as the case may be) the Treasury considers appropriate.

(3) No order is to be made under section 4(4), 49(6), 63(3), 69 or 90, or paragraph 102 of Schedule 8, unless a draft of the order has been laid before, and approved by a resolution of, each House of Parliament.

(4) Subsection (3) does not apply to an order under section 90 which does not amend or repeal any provision of an Act.

(5) An order under section 90 which does not amend or repeal any provision of an Act is subject to annulment in pursuance of a resolution of either House of Parliament.

(6) An order under section 7, 24(9), 27(6) or (12), 28(6) or (11), 29, 33, 40, 68 or 85 is subject to annulment in pursuance of a resolution of either House of Parliament.

90 Supplementary, incidental and consequential provision

(1) The Secretary of State may by order make such supplementary, incidental or consequential provision as he considers appropriate for the general purposes, or any particular purpose, of this Act or in consequence of any provision made by or under this Act or for giving full effect to this Act or any such provision.

(2) The power conferred by this section may, in particular, be exercised by amending, repealing, revoking or otherwise modifying any provision made by or under an enactment (including this Act and any Act passed in the same Session as this Act).

(3) The power conferred by this section does not include the power to make provision which would be within the legislative competence of the Scottish Parliament if it were included in an Act of that Parliament.

91 Transitional and transitory provisions and savings

(1) Schedule 13 (transitional and transitory provisions and savings) has effect.

(2) The Secretary of State may by order make such transitional, transitory or saving provision as he considers appropriate in connection with the coming into force of any provision of this Act (other than the provisions specified in section 94(4)).

(3) The Scottish Ministers may by order make such transitional, transitory or saving provision as they consider appropriate in connection with the coming into force of the provisions of this Act specified in section 94(4).

92 Repeals and revocations

Schedule 14 (which contains repeals and revocations) has effect.

Final

93 Extent

(1) The following provisions extend to England and Wales only—
   (a) section 78(1) and (2);
   (b) section 82(1) and (2);
   (c) section 87; and
   (d) Parts 1 and 2 of Schedule 7 and section 73 so far as relating to those Parts.

(2) The following provisions extend to England and Wales and Northern Ireland only—
   (a) Part 1 (including Schedules 1 and 2) but excluding sections 25 to 29 (and any provision of that Part so far as relating to those sections) and paragraphs 10, 11 and 19 of Schedule 2;
   (b) Part 2 (including Schedules 3 and 4 and Part 1 of Schedule 6) but excluding sections 60 and 61, Schedule 5 and Part 2 of Schedule 6;
   (c) section 75(2) and (3);
   (d) section 76(1) to (3);
   (e) section 80;
   (f) section 81(2); and
   (g) section 83(1) and (2).

(3) The following provisions extend to Scotland only—
   (a) section 68(5) and (6);
   (b) section 69(3);

(c) section 71(4);

(d) section 75(4) and (5);

(e) section 76(4) to (6); and

(f) section 86.

(4) The following provisions extend to Northern Ireland only—

(a) section 78(3) and (4);

(b) section 82(3) and (4); and

(c) Part 3 of Schedule 7 and section 73 so far as relating to that Part.

(5) Any provision of section 61 or Part 2 of Schedule 6 (and any corresponding entry in Schedule 14) has the same extent as the enactment amended, repealed or revoked by it except that—

(a) it does not extend to Scotland; and

(b) paragraph 53 of Schedule 6 does not extend to Northern Ireland.

(6) Any amendment, repeal or revocation by Schedule 5, 8, 10 or 14 of an enactment has (subject to subsection (5)) the same extent as the enactment amended, repealed or revoked.

(7) Subject as above, this Act extends to England and Wales, Scotland and Northern Ireland.

94 Commencement

(1) The preceding provisions of this Act (other than sections 89, 90, 91(2) and (3) and 93 and the provisions specified in subsection (4) but, subject to this, including the Schedules) come into force on such day as the Secretary of State may by order appoint; and different days may be appointed for different purposes.

(2) The Secretary of State must consult the Scottish Ministers before making an order under subsection (1) in relation to—

(a) section 75(1);

(b) paragraph 2 of Schedule 10; or

(c) paragraph 24 of that Schedule.

(3) The provisions of this Act specified in subsection (4) come into force on such day as the Scottish Ministers may by order appoint; and different days may be appointed for different purposes.

(4) Those provisions are—

(a) section 75(4) and (5);

(b) section 76(4) to (6);

(c) section 86;

(d) paragraphs 14 to 23 and, so far as extending to Scotland, paragraph 25 of Schedule 10; and

(e) so far as relating to the provisions falling within paragraph (d) above, paragraph 1 of that Schedule and section 77.

95 Short title

This Act may be cited as the Serious Crime Act 2007.

SCHEDULES

SCHEDULE 1   Sections 2 and 3
SERIOUS OFFENCES

PART 1
SERIOUS OFFENCES IN ENGLAND AND WALES

Drug trafficking

1 (1) An offence under any of the following provisions of the Misuse of Drugs Act 1971
(c. 38)—
    (a) section 4(2) or (3) (unlawful production or supply of controlled drugs);
    (b) section 5(3) (possession of controlled drug with intent to supply);
    (c) section 8 (permitting etc. certain activities relating to controlled drugs);
    (d) section 20 (assisting in or inducing the commission outside the United Kingdom
        of an offence punishable under a corresponding law).
  (2) An offence under any of the following provisions of the Customs and Excise
      Management Act 1979 (c. 2) if it is committed in connection with a prohibition or
      restriction on importation or exportation which has effect by virtue of section 3 of the
      Misuse of Drugs Act 1971—
    (a) section 50(2) or (3) (improper importation of goods);
    (b) section 68(2) (exportation of prohibited or restricted goods);
    (c) section 170 (fraudulent evasion of duty etc.).
  (3) An offence under either of the following provisions of the Criminal Justice (International
      Co-operation) Act 1990 (c. 5)—
    (a) section 12 (manufacture or supply of a substance for the time being specified in
        Schedule 2 to that Act);
    (b) section 19 (using a ship for illicit traffic in controlled drugs).

People trafficking

2 (1) An offence under section 25, 25A or 25B of the Immigration Act 1971 (c. 77) (assisting
      unlawful immigration etc.).
  (2) An offence under any of sections 57 to 59 of the Sexual Offences Act 2003 (c. 42)
      (trafficking for sexual exploitation).
  (3) An offence under section 4 of the Asylum and Immigration (Treatment of Claimants,
      etc.) Act 2004 (c. 19) (trafficking people for exploitation).

Arms trafficking

3 (1) An offence under either of the following provisions of the Customs and Excise
      Management Act 1979 (c. 2) if it is committed in connection with a firearm or ammunition—
    (a) section 68(2) (exportation of prohibited or restricted goods);
    (b) section 170 (fraudulent evasion of duty etc.).
  (2) An offence under section 3(1) of the Firearms Act 1968 (c. 27) (dealing etc. in firearms
      or ammunition by way of trade or business without being registered).

(3) In this paragraph 'firearm' and 'ammunition' have the same meanings as in section 57 of the Firearms Act 1968.

Prostitution and child sex

4 (1) An offence under section 33A of the Sexual Offences Act 1956 (c. 69) (keeping a brothel used for prostitution).

(2) An offence under any of the following provisions of the Sexual Offences Act 2003 (c. 42)—
   (a) section 14 (arranging or facilitating commission of a child sex offence);
   (b) section 48 (causing or inciting child prostitution or pornography);
   (c) section 49 (controlling a child prostitute or a child involved in pornography);
   (d) section 50 (arranging or facilitating child prostitution or pornography);
   (e) section 52 (causing or inciting prostitution for gain);
   (f) section 53 (controlling prostitution for gain).

Armed robbery etc.

5 (1) An offence under section 8(1) of the Theft Act 1968 (c. 60) (robbery) where the use or threat of force involves a firearm, an imitation firearm or an offensive weapon.

(2) An offence at common law of an assault with intent to rob where the assault involves a firearm, imitation firearm or an offensive weapon.

(3) In this paragraph—
   'firearm' has the meaning given by section 57(1) of the Firearms Act 1968;
   'imitation firearm' has the meaning given by section 57(4) of that Act;
   'offensive weapon' means any weapon to which section 141 of the Criminal Justice Act 1988 (c. 33) (offensive weapons) applies.

Money laundering

6 An offence under any of the following provisions of the Proceeds of Crime Act 2002 (c. 29)—
   (a) section 327 (concealing etc. criminal property);
   (b) section 328 (facilitating the acquisition etc. of criminal property by or on behalf of another);
   (c) section 329 (acquisition, use and possession of criminal property).

Fraud

7 (1) An offence under section 17 of the Theft Act 1968 (c. 60) (false accounting).

(2) An offence under any of the following provisions of the Fraud Act 2006 (c. 35)—
   (a) section 1 (fraud by false representation, failing to disclose information or abuse of position);
   (b) section 6 (possession etc. of articles for use in frauds);
   (c) section 7 (making or supplying articles for use in frauds);
   (d) section 9 (participating in fraudulent business carried on by sole trader etc.);
   (e) section 11 (obtaining services dishonestly).

(3) An offence at common law of conspiracy to defraud.

Offences in relation to public revenue

8 (1) An offence under section 170 of the Customs and Excise Management Act 1979
　　(c. 2) (fraudulent evasion of duty etc.) so far as not falling within paragraph 1(2)(c)
　　or 3(1)(b) above.

　(2) An offence under section 72 of the Value Added Tax Act 1994 (c. 23) (fraudulent
　　evasion of VAT etc.).

　(3) An offence under section 144 of the Finance Act 2000 (c. 17) (fraudulent evasion of
　　income tax).

　(4) An offence under section 35 of the Tax Credits Act 2002 (c. 21) (tax credit fraud).

　(5) An offence at common law of cheating in relation to the public revenue.

Corruption and bribery

9 (1) An offence under section 1 of the Public Bodies Corrupt Practices Act 1889 (c. 69)
　　(corruption in public office).

　(2) An offence which is the first or second offence under section 1(1) of the Prevention of
　　Corruption Act 1906 (c. 34) (corrupt transactions with agents other than those of
　　giving or using false etc. documents which intended to mislead principal).

　(3) An offence at common law of bribery.

Counterfeiting

10 An offence under any of the following provisions of the Forgery and Counterfeiting Act
　1981 (c. 45)—
　　(a) section 14 (making counterfeit notes or coins);
　　(b) section 15 (passing etc. counterfeit notes or coins);
　　(c) section 16 (having custody or control of counterfeit notes or coins);
　　(d) section 17 (making or having custody or control of counterfeiting materials or
　　　implements).

Blackmail

11 (1) An offence under section 21 of the Theft Act 1968 (c. 60) (blackmail).

　(2) An offence under section 12(1) or (2) of the Gangmasters (Licensing) Act 2004
　　(c. 11) (acting as a gangmaster other than under the authority of a licence, possession
　　of false documents, etc.).

Intellectual property

12 (1) An offence under any of the following provisions of the Copyright, Designs and
　　Patents Act 1988 (c. 48)—
　　(a) section 107(1)(a), (b), (d)(iv) or (e) (making, importing or distributing an article
　　　which infringes copyright);
　　(b) section 198(1)(a), (b) or (d)(iii) (making, importing or distributing an illicit recording);
　　(c) section 297A (making or dealing etc. in unauthorised decoders).

　(2) An offence under section 92(1), (2) or (3) of the Trade Marks Act 1994 (c. 26)
　　(unauthorised use of trade mark etc.).

Environment

13 (1) An offence under section 1 of the Salmon and Freshwater Fisheries Act 1975 (c. 51) (fishing for salmon, trout or freshwater fish with prohibited implements etc.).

   (2) An offence under section 14 of the Wildlife and Countryside Act 1981 (c. 69) (introduction of new species etc.).

   (3) An offence under section 33 of the Environmental Protection Act 1990 (c. 43) (prohibition on unauthorised or harmful deposit, treatment or disposal etc. of waste).

   (4) An offence under regulation 8 of the Control of Trade in Endangered Species (Enforcement) Regulations 1997 (S.I. 1997/1372) (purchase and sale etc. of endangered species and provision of false statements and certificates).

Inchoate offences

14 (1) An offence of attempting or conspiring the commission of an offence specified or described in this Part of this Schedule.

   (2) An offence under Part 2 of this Act (encouraging or assisting) where the offence (or one of the offences) which the person in question intends or believes would be committed is an offence specified or described in this Part of this Schedule.

   (3) An offence of aiding, abetting, counselling or procuring the commission of an offence specified or described in this Part of this Schedule.

   (4) The references in sub-paragraphs (1) to (3) to offences specified or described in this Part of this Schedule do not include the offence at common law of conspiracy to defraud.

Earlier offences

15 (1) This Part of this Schedule (apart from paragraph 14(2)) has effect, in its application to conduct before the passing of this Act, as if the offences specified or described in this Part included any corresponding offences under the law in force at the time of the conduct.

   (2) Paragraph 14(2) has effect, in its application to conduct before the passing of this Act or before the coming into force of section 59 of this Act, as if the offence specified or described in that provision were an offence of inciting the commission of an offence specified or described in this Part of this Schedule.

Scope of offences

16 Where this Part of this Schedule refers to offences which are offences under the law of England and Wales and another country, the reference is to be read as limited to the offences so far as they are offences under the law of England and Wales.

PART 2
SERIOUS OFFENCES IN NORTHERN IRELAND

Drug trafficking

17 (1) An offence under any of the following provisions of the Misuse of Drugs Act 1971 (c. 38)—
(a) section 4(2) or (3) (unlawful production or supply of controlled drugs);
(b) section 5(3) (possession of controlled drug with intent to supply);
(c) section 8 (permitting etc. certain activities relating to controlled drugs);
(d) section 20 (assisting in or inducing the commission outside the United Kingdom of an offence punishable under a corresponding law).
(2) An offence under any of the following provisions of the Customs and Excise Management Act 1979 (c. 2) if it is committed in connection with a prohibition or restriction on importation or exportation which has effect by virtue of section 3 of the Misuse of Drugs Act 1971—
(a) section 50(2) or (3) (improper importation of goods);
(b) section 68(2) (exportation of prohibited or restricted goods);
(c) section 170 (fraudulent evasion of duty etc.).
(3) An offence under either of the following provisions of the Criminal Justice (International Co-operation) Act 1990 (c. 5)—
(a) section 12 (manufacture or supply of a substance for the time being specified in Schedule 2 to that Act);
(b) section 19 (using a ship for illicit traffic in controlled drugs).

People trafficking

18 (1) An offence under section 25, 25A or 25B of the Immigration Act 1971 (c. 77) (assisting unlawful immigration etc.).
(2) An offence under any of sections 57 to 59 of the Sexual Offences Act 2003 (c. 42) (trafficking for sexual exploitation).
(3) An offence under section 4 of the Asylum and Immigration (Treatment of Claimants, etc.) Act 2004 (c. 19) (trafficking people for exploitation).

Arms trafficking

19 (1) An offence under either of the following provisions of the Customs and Excise Management Act 1979 (c. 2) if it is committed in connection with a firearm or ammunition—
(a) section 68(2) (exportation of prohibited or restricted goods);
(b) section 170 (fraudulent evasion of duty etc.).
(2) An offence under Article 24 of the Firearms (Northern Ireland) Order 2004 (S.I. 2004/702 (N.I.3)) (dealing etc. in firearms or ammunition by way of trade or business without being registered).
(3) In this paragraph 'firearm' and 'ammunition' have the same meanings as in Article 2(2) of the Firearms (Northern Ireland) Order 2004.

Prostitution and child sex

20 (1) An offence under section 13(1) of the Criminal Law Amendment Act 1885 (c. 69) (keeping a brothel used for prostitution).

(2) An offence under any of the following provisions of the Sexual Offences Act 2003—
   (a) section 48 (causing or inciting child prostitution or pornography);
   (b) section 49 (controlling a child prostitute or a child involved in pornography);
   (c) section 50 (arranging or facilitating child prostitution or pornography);
   (d) section 52 (causing or inciting prostitution for gain);
   (e) section 53 (controlling prostitution for gain).

Armed robbery etc.

21 (1) An offence under section 8(1) of the Theft Act (Northern Ireland) 1969 (c. 16 (N.I.)) (robbery) where the use or threat of force involves a firearm, an imitation firearm or an offensive weapon.

(2) An offence at common law of an assault with intent to rob where the assault involves a firearm, imitation firearm or an offensive weapon.

(3) In this paragraph—
   'firearm' and 'imitation firearm' have the meaning given by Article 2(2) of the Firearms (Northern Ireland) Order 2004;
   'offensive weapon' means any weapon to which section 141 of the Criminal Justice Act 1988 (c. 33) (offensive weapons) applies.

Money laundering

22 An offence under any of the following provisions of the Proceeds of Crime Act 2002 (c. 29)—
   (a) section 327 (concealing etc. criminal property);
   (b) section 328 (facilitating the acquisition etc. of criminal property by or on behalf of another);
   (c) section 329 (acquisition, use and possession of criminal property).

Fraud

23 (1) An offence under section 17 of the Theft Act (Northern Ireland) 1969 (c. 16 (N.I.)) (false accounting).

(2) An offence under any of the following provisions of the Fraud Act 2006 (c. 35)—
   (a) section 1 (fraud by false representation, failing to disclose information or abuse of position);
   (b) section 6 (possession etc. of articles for use in frauds);
   (c) section 7 (making or supplying articles for use in frauds);
   (d) section 9 (participating in fraudulent business carried on by sole trader etc.);
   (e) section 11 (obtaining services dishonestly).

(3) An offence at common law of conspiracy to defraud.

Offences in relation to public revenue

24 (1) An offence under section 170 of the Customs and Excise Management Act 1979 (c. 2) (fraudulent evasion of duty etc.) so far as not falling within paragraph 17(2)(c) or 19(1)(b) above.

(2) An offence under section 72 of the Value Added Tax Act 1994 (c. 23) (fraudulent evasion of VAT etc.).

(3) An offence under section 144 of the Finance Act 2000 (c. 17) (fraudulent evasion of income tax).

(4) An offence under section 35 of the Tax Credits Act 2002 (c. 21) (tax credit fraud).

(5) An offence at common law of cheating in relation to the public revenue.

Corruption and bribery

25 (1) An offence under section 1 of the Public Bodies Corrupt Practices Act 1889 (c. 69) (corruption in public office).

(2) An offence which is the first or second offence under section 1(1) of the Prevention of Corruption Act 1906 (c. 34) (corrupt transactions with agents other than those of giving or using false etc. documents which intended to mislead principal).

(3) An offence at common law of bribery.

Counterfeiting

26 An offence under any of the following provisions of the Forgery and Counterfeiting Act 1981 (c. 45)—
(a) section 14 (making counterfeit notes or coins);
(b) section 15 (passing etc. counterfeit notes or coins);
(c) section 16 (having custody or control of counterfeit notes or coins);
(d) section 17 (making or having custody or control of counterfeiting materials or implements).

Blackmail

27 (1) An offence under section 20 of the Theft Act (Northern Ireland) 1969 (c. 16) (blackmail).

(2) An offence under section 12(1) or (2) of the Gangmasters (Licensing) Act 2004 (c. 11) (acting as a gangmaster other than under the authority of a licence, possession of false documents, etc.).

Intellectual property

28 (1) An offence under any of the following provisions of the Copyright, Designs and Patents Act 1988 (c. 48)—
(a) section 107(1)(a), (b), (d)(iv) or (e) (making, importing or distributing an article which infringes copyright);
(b) section 198(1)(a), (b) or (d)(iii) (making, importing or distributing an illicit recording);
(c) section 297A (making or dealing etc. in unauthorised decoders).

(2) An offence under section 92(1), (2) or (3) of the Trade Marks Act 1994 (c. 26) (unauthorised use of trade mark etc.).

Environment

29 (1) An offence under section 62 or 63 of the Fisheries Act (Northern Ireland) 1966 (c. 17 (N.I.)) (prohibition of certain methods of fishing).

(2) An offence under Article 15 of the Wildlife (Northern Ireland) Order 1985 (S.I. 1985/171 (N.I.2)) (introduction of new species, etc.).

(3) An offence under Article 4 of the Waste and Contaminated Land (Northern Ireland) Order 1997 (S.I. 1997/2778 (N.I.19)) (prohibition on unauthorised or harmful deposit, treatment or disposal, etc. of waste).

(4) An offence under regulation 8 of the Control of Trade in Endangered Species (Enforcement) Regulations 1997 (S.I. 1997/1372) (purchase and sale etc. of endangered species and provision of false statements and certificates).

Inchoate offences

30 (1) An offence of attempting or conspiring the commission of an offence specified or described in this Part of this Schedule.

(2) An offence under Part 2 of this Act (encouraging or assisting) where the offence (or one of the offences) which the person in question intends or believes would be committed is an offence specified or described in this Part of this Schedule.

(3) An offence of aiding, abetting, counselling or procuring the commission of an offence specified or described in this Part of this Schedule.

(4) The references in sub-paragraphs (1) to (3) to offences specified or described in this Part of this Schedule do not include the offence at common law of conspiracy to defraud.

Earlier offences

31 (1) This Part of this Schedule (apart from paragraph 30(2)) has effect, in its application to conduct before the passing of this Act, as if the offences specified or described in this Part included any corresponding offences under the law in force at the time of the conduct.

(2) Paragraph 30(2) has effect, in its application to conduct before the passing of this Act or before the coming into force of section 59 of this Act, as if the offence specified or described in that provision were an offence of inciting the commission of an offence specified or described in this Part of this Schedule.

Scope of offences

32 Where this Part of this Schedule refers to offences which are offences under the law of Northern Ireland and another country, the reference is to be read as limited to the offences so far as they are offences under the law of Northern Ireland.

SCHEDULE 2   Section 37
FUNCTIONS OF APPLICANT AUTHORITIES UNDER PART 1

Director of Public Prosecutions

1 The functions of the Director of Public Prosecutions under this Part are—
   (a) to have the conduct of applications for serious crime prevention orders in England and Wales or for their variation or discharge;
   (b) to appear on any application made under section 17 or 18 by another person for the variation or discharge of a serious crime prevention order in England and Wales;
   (c) to have the conduct of, or (as the case may be) appear in, any other proceedings in connection with serious crime prevention orders (whether proceedings on appeal, by virtue of section 27 or otherwise);
   (d) to give advice in connection with any proceedings or possible proceedings in connection with serious crime prevention orders; and
   (e) to do anything for the purposes of, or in connection with, the functions in paragraphs (a) to (d).

2 (1) The Director may, to such extent as he may decide, delegate the exercise of his functions under this Part to a Crown Prosecutor.
   (2) References in this Part to the Director are accordingly to be read, so far as necessary for the purposes of sub-paragraph (1), as references to the Director or any Crown Prosecutor.

3 The functions of the Director under this Part are exercisable under the superintendence of the Attorney General.

4 (1) The Code for Crown Prosecutors issued under section 10 of the Prosecution of Offences Act 1985 (c. 23) (guidelines for Crown Prosecutors) may include guidance by the Director on general principles to be applied by Crown Prosecutors in determining in any case—
   (a) whether to make an application for a serious crime prevention order in England and Wales or for the variation or discharge of such an order;
   (b) whether to present a petition by virtue of section 27 of this Act; or
   (c) where such an application has been made or petition presented, whether the proceedings concerned should be discontinued.
   (2) Section 10(2) and (3) of that Act (power to make alterations in the Code and duty to set out alterations in Director's report) are to be read accordingly.

5 Section 14 of that Act (power of Attorney General to make regulations about fees of legal representatives and costs and expenses of witnesses) applies in relation to proceedings in connection with serious crime prevention orders and attendance for the purposes of such cases as it applies in relation to criminal proceedings and attendance for the purposes of such cases.

Director of Revenue and Customs Prosecutions

6 The functions of the Director of Revenue and Customs Prosecutions under this Part are—
   (a) to have the conduct of applications for serious crime prevention orders in England and Wales or for their variation or discharge;
   (b) to appear on any application made under section 17 or 18 by another person for the variation or discharge of a serious crime prevention order in England and Wales;

(c) to have the conduct of, or (as the case may be) appear in, any other proceedings in connection with serious crime prevention orders (whether proceedings on appeal, by virtue of section 27 or otherwise);

(d) to give advice in connection with any proceedings or possible proceedings in connection with serious crime prevention orders; and

(e) to do anything for the purposes of, or in connection with, the functions in paragraphs (a) to (d).

7 (1) The Director may, to such extent as he may decide, delegate the exercise of his functions under this Part to a Revenue and Customs Prosecutor.

(2) References in this Part to the Director are accordingly to be read, so far as necessary for the purposes of sub-paragraph (1), as references to the Director or any Revenue and Customs Prosecutor.

8 The functions of the Director under this Part are exercisable under the superintendence of the Attorney General.

9 The Director must have regard to the Code for Crown Prosecutors issued under section 10 of the Prosecution of Offences Act 1985 (guidelines for Crown Prosecutors) so far as it applies in relation to serious crime prevention orders in England and Wales, and petitions and proceedings by virtue of section 27 of this Act, by virtue of paragraph 4 above.

10 Section 21 of the Commissioners for Revenue and Customs Act 2005 (c. 11) (disclosure to prosecuting authority) has effect as if the purpose mentioned in subsection (1)(b) included the purpose of enabling the Director to exercise his functions under this Part.

11 Section 41(1) of the Act of 2005 (disclosure of information to Director) applies in relation to a purpose connected with a serious crime prevention order or possible serious crime prevention order as it applies in relation to a purpose connected with a specified investigation or prosecution.

Director of Serious Fraud Office

12 The functions of the Director of the Serious Fraud Office under this Part are—

(a) to have the conduct of applications for serious crime prevention orders in England and Wales or for their variation or discharge;

(b) to appear on any application made under section 17 or 18 by another person for the variation or discharge of a serious crime prevention order in England and Wales;

(c) to have the conduct of, or (as the case may be) appear in, any other proceedings in connection with serious crime prevention orders (whether proceedings on appeal, by virtue of section 27 or otherwise);

(d) to give advice in connection with any proceedings or possible proceedings in connection with serious crime prevention orders; and

(e) to do anything for the purposes of, or in connection with, the functions in paragraphs (a) to (d).

13 (1) The Director may, to such extent as he may decide, delegate the exercise of his functions under this Part to a member of the Serious Fraud Office designated under section 1(7) of the Criminal Justice Act 1987 (c. 38).

(2) References in this Part to the Director are accordingly to be read, so far as necessary for the purposes of sub-paragraph (1) above, as references to the Director or any member of the Serious Fraud Office so designated.

14 The functions of the Director under this Part are exercisable under the superintendence of the Attorney General.

15 Paragraph 8 of Schedule 1 to the Criminal Justice Act 1987 (power of Attorney General to make regulations about fees of counsel and costs and expenses of witnesses) applies in relation to proceedings in connection with serious crime prevention orders and attendance for the purposes of such cases as it applies in relation to criminal proceedings and attendance for the purposes of such cases.

Director of Public Prosecutions for Northern Ireland

16 The functions of the Director of Public Prosecutions for Northern Ireland under this Part are—
    (a) to have the conduct of applications for serious crime prevention orders in Northern Ireland or for their variation or discharge;
    (b) to appear on any application made under section 17 or 18 by another person for the variation or discharge of a serious crime prevention order in Northern Ireland;
    (c) to have the conduct of, or (as the case may be) appear in, any other proceedings in connection with serious crime prevention orders (whether proceedings on appeal, by virtue of section 28 or otherwise);
    (d) to give advice in connection with any proceedings or possible proceedings about serious crime prevention orders; and
    (e) to do anything for the purposes of, or in connection with, the functions in paragraphs (a) to (d).

17 References in this Part to the Director are to be read, so far as necessary for the purposes of functions delegated by him to Public Prosecutors, as references to the Director or any Public Prosecutor.

18 (1) The Code for Public Prosecutors issued under section 37 of the Justice (Northern Ireland) Act 2002 (c. 26) (guidelines for Public Prosecutors) may include guidance by the Director on general principles to be applied by Public Prosecutors in determining in any case—
    (a) whether to make an application for a serious crime prevention order in Northern Ireland or for the variation or discharge of such an order;
    (b) whether to present a petition by virtue of section 28 of this Act; or
    (c) where such an application has been made or petition presented, whether the proceedings concerned should be discontinued.
    (2) Sections 37(4) and 39(2) of that Act (power to make alterations in the Code and duty to set out alterations in Director's report) are to be read accordingly.

19 Sections 75(1) and (2) and 76(1) of, and Schedule 9 to, the Northern Ireland Act 1998 (c. 47) (duties of public authorities) do not apply to the functions of the Director of Public Prosecutions for Northern Ireland under this Part.

20 Section 1 of the Costs in Criminal Cases Act (Northern Ireland) 1968 (c. 10 (N.I.)) (expenses of prosecution) applies in relation to proceedings in connection with serious crime prevention orders and attendance for the purposes of such cases as it applies in relation to criminal proceedings and attendance for the purposes of such cases.

Interpretation

21 In this Schedule references to having the conduct of proceedings include references to starting or discontinuing proceedings.

SCHEDULE 3   Section 49(5)
LISTED OFFENCES

PART 1
OFFENCES COMMON TO ENGLAND AND WALES
AND NORTHERN IRELAND

Offences against the Person Act 1861 (c. 100)

1 An offence under section 4 of the Offences against the Person Act 1861 (solicitation etc. of murder).

2 An offence under section 21 of that Act (attempting to choke etc. in order to commit or assist in the committing of any indictable offence) so far as it may be committed with the intention of enabling any other person to commit, or assisting any other person in the commission of, an indictable offence.

3 An offence under section 22 of that Act (using chloroform etc. to commit or assist in the committing of any indictable offence) so far as it may be committed with the intention of enabling any other person to commit, or assisting any other person in the commission of, an indictable offence.

4 But references in paragraphs 2 and 3 to any other person do not include reference to the person whose act is capable of encouraging or assisting the commission of the offence under section 21 or, as the case may be, section 22 of that Act.

Aliens Restriction (Amendment) Act 1919 (c. 92)

5 An offence under section 3(1) of the Aliens Restriction (Amendment) Act 1919 (acts calculated or likely to cause sedition or disaffection amongst HM forces etc.) consisting in attempting an act calculated or likely to cause sedition or disaffection in contravention of that subsection.

6 An offence under section 3(2) of that Act (promoting or attempting to promote industrial unrest) consisting in attempting to promote industrial unrest in contravention of that subsection.

Official Secrets Act 1920 (c. 75)

7 An offence under section 7 of the Official Secrets Act 1920 (soliciting etc. commission of an offence under that Act or the Official Secrets Act 1911 (c. 28)).

Incitement to Disaffection Act 1934 (c. 56)

8 An offence under section 1 of the Incitement to Disaffection Act 1934 (endeavouring to seduce members of HM forces from their duty or allegiance).

Misuse of Drugs Act 1971 (c. 38)

9 An offence under section 19 of the Misuse of Drugs Act 1971 (inciting any other offence under that Act).

10 An offence under section 20 of that Act (assisting or inducing commission outside United Kingdom of offence punishable under corresponding law).

Immigration Act 1971 (c. 77)

11 An offence under section 25 of the Immigration Act 1971 (assisting unlawful immigration to a member State).

12 An offence under section 25B of that Act (assisting entry to the United Kingdom in breach of deportation or exclusion order).

Representation of the People Act 1983 (c. 2)

13 An offence under section 97(1) of the Representation of the People Act 1983 (public meetings) consisting in the incitement of others to act in a disorderly manner for the purpose of preventing at a lawful public meeting to which that section applies the transaction of the business for which the meeting was called.

Computer Misuse Act 1990 (c. 18)

14 An offence under section 3A(1) of the Computer Misuse Act 1990 (making etc. article intending it to be used to commit, or to assist in the commission of, an offence under section 1 or 3 of that Act).

15 An offence under section 3A(2) of that Act (supply or offer to supply article believing it is likely to be used to commit, or to assist in the commission of, an offence under section 1 or 3 of that Act).

16 An offence under section 3A(3) of that Act (obtaining an article with a view to its being supplied for use to commit, or to assist in the commission of, an offence under section 1 or 3 of that Act).

Criminal Justice Act 1993 (c. 36)

17 An offence under section 52(2)(a) of the Criminal Justice Act 1993 (encouraging insider dealing).

Reserve Forces Act 1996 (c. 14)

18 An offence under section 101 of the Reserve Forces Act 1996 (inducing a person to desert or absent himself).

Landmines Act 1998 (c. 33)

19 An offence under section 2(2) of the Landmines Act 1998 (encouraging, assisting or inducing an offence under section 2(1) of that Act).

Terrorism Act 2006 (c. 11)

20 An offence under section 1(2) of the Terrorism Act 2006 (encouraging terrorism).

21 An offence under section 2(1) of that Act (disseminating terrorist publications).

22 An offence under section 5 of that Act (engaging in conduct in preparation for giving effect to intention to commit or assisting another to commit acts of terrorism).

23 An offence under section 6(1) of that Act (provision of instruction or training knowing that a person trained or instructed intends to use the skills obtained for or in connection with the commission of acts of terrorism or for assisting the commission or preparation of such acts by others).

24 An offence under section 6(2) of that Act as a result of paragraph (b)(ii) of that subsection (receipt of instruction or training intending to use the skills obtained for assisting the commission or preparation of acts of terrorism by others).

PART 2

OFFENCES UNDER PARTICULAR ENACTMENTS: ENGLAND AND WALES

Public Meeting Act 1908 (c. 66)

25 An offence under section 1(2) of the Public Meeting Act 1908 (inciting others to commit offences under that section).

Perjury Act 1911 (c. 6)

26 An offence under section 7(2) of the Perjury Act 1911 (inciting a person to commit an offence under that Act).

Prison Act 1952 (c. 52)

27 An offence under section 39(1) of the Prison Act 1952 (assisting a prisoner to escape).

Criminal Law Act 1967 (c. 58)

28 An offence under section 4(1) of the Criminal Law Act 1967 (assisting persons who have committed an offence).

29 An offence under section 5(1) of that Act (accepting or agreeing to accept consideration for not disclosing information about an offence).

Greater London Council (General Powers) Act 1973 (c. xxx)

30 An offence under section 13 of the Greater London Council (General Powers) Act 1973 (assaults etc. on officers) consisting in the aiding or inciting of any person to assault,

resist or obstruct an officer of the Thames Water Authority duly exercising or performing any power or duty under a section or byelaw mentioned in that section.

Greater London Council (General Powers) Act 1974 (c. xxiv)

31 An offence under section 21(6) of the Greater London Council (General Powers) Act 1974 (assaults etc. on officers of a borough council) consisting in the aiding or inciting of any person to assault, resist or obstruct an officer of a borough council duly exercising or performing any power or duty under section 21 of that Act.

Criminal Law Act 1977 (c. 45)

32 An offence under section 1(1) of the Criminal Law Act 1977 (conspiracy).

Criminal Attempts Act 1981 (c. 47)

33 An offence under section 1(1) of the Criminal Attempts Act 1981 (attempting to commit an offence).

Public Order Act 1986 (c. 64)

34 An offence under section 12(6) of the Public Order Act 1986 (inciting commission of offences under section 12(5) of that Act).
35 An offence under section 13(9) of that Act (inciting commission of offences under section 13(8) of that Act).
36 An offence under section 14(6) of that Act (inciting commission of offences under section 14(5) of that Act).
37 An offence under section 14B(3) of that Act (inciting commission of offences under section 14B(2) of that Act).

Terrorism Act 2000 (c. 11)

38 An offence under section 59 of the Terrorism Act 2000 (inciting in England and Wales the commission of acts of terrorism outside the United Kingdom).

PART 3
OTHER OFFENCES: ENGLAND AND WALES

39 An offence of conspiracy falling within section 5(2) or (3) of the Criminal Law Act 1977 (c. 45) (forms of conspiracy not affected by abolition of offence of conspiracy at common law).
40 (1) An attempt under a special statutory provision.
    (2) Sub-paragraph (1) is to be read with section 3 of the Criminal Attempts Act 1981 (c. 47).

PART 4
OFFENCES UNDER PARTICULAR ENACTMENTS: NORTHERN IRELAND

Prison Act (Northern Ireland) 1953 (c. 18)

41 An offence under section 29(a) of the Prison Act (Northern Ireland) 1953 (rescuing or assisting a person sentenced to imprisonment for life, or in lawful custody for an offence carrying that sentence, to escape or attempt to escape) so far as it consists in assisting a person.

42 An offence under section 30(a) of that Act (rescuing or assisting a person sentenced to imprisonment for a term less than life, or in lawful custody for an offence carrying such a sentence, to escape or attempt to escape) so far as it consists in assisting a person.

Criminal Law Act (Northern Ireland) 1967 (c. 18)

43 An offence under section 4(1) of the Criminal Law Act (Northern Ireland) 1967 (assisting persons who have committed an offence).

Perjury (Northern Ireland) Order 1979 (S.I. 1979/1714 (N.I.19))

44 An offence under Article 12(2) of the Perjury (Northern Ireland) Order 1979 (inciting a person to commit an offence under that Order).

Criminal Attempts and Conspiracy (Northern Ireland) Order 1983 (S.I. 1983/1120 (N.I.13))

45 An offence under Article 3(1) of the Criminal Attempts and Conspiracy (Northern Ireland) Order 1983 (attempting to commit an offence).

46 An offence under Article 9(1) of that Order (conspiracy).

Public Processions (Northern Ireland) Act 1998 (c. 2)

47 An offence under section 8(8) of the Public Processions (Northern Ireland) Act 1998 (inciting commission of offences under section 8(7) of that Act).

48 An offence under section 9A(8) of that Act (inciting commission of offences under section 9A of that Act).

Terrorism Act 2000 (c. 11)

49 An offence under section 60 of the Terrorism Act 2000 (inciting in Northern Ireland the commission of acts of terrorism outside the United Kingdom).

PART 5
OTHER OFFENCES: NORTHERN IRELAND

50 An offence of conspiracy falling within Article 13(2) or (3) of the Criminal Attempts and Conspiracy (Northern Ireland) Order 1983 (S.I. 1983/1120 (N.I.13)) (forms of conspiracy not affected by abolition of offence of conspiracy at common law).

SCHEDULE 4   Section 52(2)

EXTRA-TERRITORIALITY

1 (1) This paragraph applies if—

    (a) any relevant behaviour of D's takes place wholly or partly in England or Wales;

    (b) D knows or believes that what he anticipates might take place wholly or partly in a place outside England and Wales; and

    (c) either—

        (i) the anticipated offence is one that would be triable under the law of England and Wales if it were committed in that place; or

        (ii) if there are relevant conditions, it would be so triable if it were committed there by a person who satisfies the conditions.

(2) 'Relevant condition' means a condition that—

    (a) determines (wholly or in part) whether an offence committed outside England and Wales is nonetheless triable under the law of England and Wales; and

    (b) relates to the citizenship, nationality or residence of the person who commits it.

2 (1) This paragraph applies if—

    (a) paragraph 1 does not apply;

    (b) any relevant behaviour of D's takes place wholly or partly in England or Wales;

    (c) D knows or believes that what he anticipates might take place wholly or partly in a place outside England and Wales; and

    (d) what D anticipates would amount to an offence under the law in force in that place.

(2) The condition in sub-paragraph (1)(d) is to be taken to be satisfied unless, not later than rules of court may provide, the defence serve on the prosecution a notice—

    (a) stating that on the facts as alleged the condition is not in their opinion satisfied;

    (b) showing their grounds for that opinion; and

    (c) requiring the prosecution to show that it is satisfied.

(3) The court, if it thinks fit, may permit the defence to require the prosecution to show that the condition is satisfied without prior service of a notice under sub paragraph (2).

(4) In the Crown Court, the question whether the condition is satisfied is to be decided by the judge alone.

(5) An act punishable under the law in force in any place outside England and Wales constitutes an offence under that law for the purposes of this paragraph, however it is described in that law.

3 (1) This paragraph applies if—

    (a) any relevant behaviour of D's takes place wholly outside England and Wales;

    (b) D knows or believes that what he anticipates might take place wholly or partly in a place outside England and Wales; and

    (c) D could be tried under the law of England and Wales if he committed the anticipated offence in that place.

(2) For the purposes of sub-paragraph (1)(c), D is to be assumed to be able to commit the anticipated offence.

4 In relation to an offence under section 46, a reference in this Schedule to the anticipated offence is to be read as a reference to any of the offences specified in the indictment.

SCHEDULE 5   Section 60
AMENDMENTS RELATING TO SERVICE LAW

Criminal Justice Act 1982 (c. 48)

1 In section 32 of the Criminal Justice Act 1982 (early release of prisoners), in subsection (2A) for 'incitement' substitute 'encouragement and assistance'.

Sexual Offences (Amendment) Act 1992 (c. 34)

2 In section 6 of the Sexual Offences (Amendment) Act 1992 (interpretation), in subsection (1A) for 'incitement' substitute 'encouragement and assistance'.

Powers of Criminal Courts (Sentencing) Act 2000 (c. 6)

3 In section 114 of the Powers of Criminal Courts (Sentencing) Act 2000 (offences under service law), in subsection (3) for 'incitement' substitute 'encouragement and assistance'.

Sexual Offences Act 2003 (c. 42)

4 (1) The Sexual Offences Act 2003 is amended as follows.
   (2) In paragraph 93A of Schedule 3 (sexual offences for purposes of Part 2), in sub paragraph (3) for 'incitement' substitute 'encouragement and assistance'.
   (3) In paragraph 172A of Schedule 5 (other offences for purposes of Part 2), in sub paragraph (2) for 'incitement' substitute 'encouragement and assistance'.

Criminal Justice Act 2003 (c. 44)

5 In section 233 of the Criminal Justice Act 2003 (offences under service law), in subsection (2) for 'incitement' substitute 'encouragement and assistance'.

Gambling Act 2005 (c. 19)

6 In Part 1 of Schedule 7 to the Gambling Act 2005 (relevant offences), in paragraph 22A for 'incitement' substitute 'encouragement and assistance'.

Armed Forces Act 2006 (c. 52)

7 The Armed Forces Act 2006 is amended as follows.
8 In section 39 (attempts), in subsection (4)(b) for 'inciting another person to commit' substitute 'encouraging or assisting the commission of'.
9 For section 40 (incitement) substitute—

'40 Encouraging and assisting
   (1) A person subject to service law commits an offence if he encourages or assists the commission of a service offence (other than an offence under section 42).

261

(2) A civilian subject to service discipline commits an offence if he encourages or assists the commission of an offence mentioned in section 39(4).

(3) Reference in this section to encouraging or assisting the commission of an offence is to the doing of an act that would have constituted an offence under Part 2 of the Serious Crime Act 2007 if the offence encouraged or assisted had been an offence under the law of England and Wales.

(4) In determining whether an act would have constituted an offence under that Part, section 49(4) of that Act has effect as if for "offences under this Part and listed offences" it read "offences under sections 39 and 40 of the Armed Forces Act 2006".

(5) Any requirement in that Part to specify matters in an indictment applies for the purposes of this section as it applies for the purposes of that Part, but with references to the indictment being read as references to the charge sheet.

(6) A person guilty of an offence under this section is liable to the same punishment as he would be liable to if guilty of—

(a) the service offence encouraged or assisted; or

(b) if convicted of the offence under this section by reference to more than one such service offence, any one of those service offences.'

10 Accordingly, in the heading immediately before section 39 for 'incitement' substitute 'encouragement and assistance'.

11 For section 46 (inciting criminal conduct) substitute—

'46 Encouraging or assisting criminal conduct

(1) Subsection (2) applies if a person subject to service law, or a civilian subject to service discipline, encourages or assists the doing of an act (or one or more of a number of acts) that, if done in England or Wales, would be punishable by the law of England and Wales.

(2) Regardless of where that act (or those acts) might be done and of his state of mind with respect to that question, his encouragement or assistance shall be treated for the purposes of section 42(1) as an act that is punishable by the law of England and Wales (so far as it is not such an act in any event).

(3) Reference in this section to encouraging or assisting is to an act that would constitute an offence under Part 2 of the Serious Crime Act 2007 disregarding any provision in that Part about the place where the act (or acts) being encouraged or assisted might be done or the accused's state of mind with respect to that question.'

12 In section 48 (provision supplementary to sections 43 to 47), in subsection (1)(a) for 'incitement' substitute 'encouragement or assistance'.

13 In Schedule 2 (list of serious offences)—

(a) in paragraph 11 for 'inciting another person to commit' substitute 'encouraging or assisting the commission of';

(b) in paragraph 13 for 'of incitement to commit' substitute 'under Part 2 of the Serious Crime Act 2007 of encouraging or assisting the commission of'.

SCHEDULE 6   Section 63(1) and (2)
MINOR AND CONSEQUENTIAL AMENDMENTS: PART 2

PART 1
REFERENCES TO COMMON LAW OFFENCE OF INCITEMENT

1 Section 30(4) of the Theft Act 1968 (c. 60) (restriction of proceedings against spouses and civil partners).

2 Section 1B(2) of the Biological Weapons Act 1974 (c. 6) (Revenue and Customs prosecutions).

3 Section 17(1) of the Industry Act 1975 (c. 68) (no criminal proceedings to lie in respect of contravention of a prohibition order).

4 Section 7(2)(ix) of the Sexual Offences (Amendment) Act 1976 (c. 82) (meaning of 'rape offence' in relation to court martial proceedings).

5 In the Magistrates' Courts Act 1980 (c. 43)—
(a) section 22(11)(b) (aggregation of value in relation to charges involving two or more scheduled offences);
(b) section 103(2)(d) (written statement of child admissible in committal proceedings for certain offences);
(c) paragraph 2 of Schedule 2 (offences for which the value involved is relevant to the mode of trial).

6 Article 8(1A) of the Criminal Justice (Northern Ireland) Order 1980 (S.I. 1980/704 (N.I.6)) (driving disqualification where vehicle used for the purposes of crime).

7 In the Betting and Gaming Duties Act 1981 (c. 63)—
(a) section 9(5) (prohibitions for protection of revenue);
(b) section 9A(4) (prohibitions for protection of revenue: overseas brokers).

8 In section 32(1) of the Criminal Justice Act 1982 (c. 48) (early release of prisoners)—
(a) paragraph (b)(iv) (imprisonment for excluded offence etc.);
(b) paragraph (c)(iv) (imprisonment for service offence corresponding to excluded offence etc.), inserted by paragraph 94(2) of Schedule 16 to the Armed Forces Act 2006 (c. 52).

9 Section 80(3)(c) of the Police and Criminal Evidence Act 1984 (c. 60) (compellability of accused's spouse or civil partner).

10 Section 49(4) of the Airports Act 1986 (c. 31) (no criminal proceedings to lie in respect of contravention of compliance order).

11 Section 12(6)(a) of the Outer Space Act 1986 (c. 38) (offences).

12 Section 30(4) of the Gas Act 1986 (c. 44) (no criminal proceedings to lie in respect of contravention of final or provisional order).

13 Section 7(1) of the Public Order Act 1986 (c. 64) (consent of DPP to prosecution).

14 Section 2(3)(ba) of the Ministry of Defence Police Act 1987 (c. 4) (jurisdiction of members of MoD police).

15 In the Road Traffic Offenders Act 1988 (c. 53)—
(a) section 28(2) (penalty points to be attributed to an offence);
(b) section 34(5) (disqualification for certain offences);
(c) section 35(5A) (disqualification for repeated offences).

16 Paragraph 2(a) of Schedule 1 to the Football Spectators Act 1989 (c. 37) (offences).

17 Article 79(3)(c) of the Police and Criminal Evidence (Northern Ireland) Order 1989 (S.I. 1989/1341 (N.I.12)) (compellability of accused's spouse or civil partner).

18 In the Aviation and Maritime Security Act 1990 (c. 31)—
   (a) section 11(3)(b) (destroying ships or fixed platforms or endangering their safety);
   (b) section 15(2)(c) (master's power of delivery).
19 In the Criminal Justice Act 1991 (c. 53)—
   (a) section 53(7) (cases involving children in which notice of transfer may be given);
   (b) section 86A(4) (offences in respect of which prisoner custody officers have powers in relation to persons other than prisoners).
20 In the Sexual Offences (Amendment) Act 1992 (c. 34)—
   (a) subsections (1)(g) and (3)(k) of section 2 (offences to which Act applies);
   (b) section 6(2A) (person who is to be treated as person against whom inchoate offences are committed).
21 In the Criminal Justice Act 1993 (c. 36)—
   (a) section 1(3)(d) (Group B offences);
   (b) section 5(4) (incitement to commit Group A offence).
22 Section 12(7) of the Finance Act 1994 (c. 9) (offences of fraud and dishonesty).
23 Section 27 of the Antarctic Act 1994 (c. 15) (references to offences under the Act).
24 Section 9A(4) of the Criminal Justice and Public Order Act 1994 (c. 33) (offences in respect of which custody officers at contracted out secure training centres have powers in relation to persons other than those detained in the centre).
25 Paragraph (b) of the definition of 'specified offence' in section 60(6) of the Drug Trafficking Act 1994 (c. 37) (Revenue and Customs prosecutions).
26 Article 40(4) of the Airports (Northern Ireland) Order 1994 (S.I. 1994/426 (N.I.1)) (no criminal proceedings to lie in respect of contravention of compliance order).
27 Article 4(1A) and (7) of the Children's Evidence (Northern Ireland) Order 1995 (S.I. 1995/757 (N.I.3)) (cases involving children in which notice of transfer may be given).
28 Section 30A(2) of the Chemical Weapons Act 1996 (c. 6) (Revenue and Customs prosecutions).
29 Section 29(6)(i) of the Criminal Procedure and Investigations Act 1996 (c. 25) (meaning of 'terrorism offence' for purpose of requirement to hold preparatory hearing).
30 In the Sexual Offences (Conspiracy and Incitement) Act 1996 (c. 29)—
   (a) section 2(1) and (2) (incitement to commit certain sexual acts outside the United Kingdom);
   (b) section 3(8) (extended meaning of offence of incitement to commit a listed sexual offence).
31 In the Proceeds of Crime (Northern Ireland) Order 1996 (S.I. 1996/1299 (N.I.9))—
   (a) paragraph (h) of the definition of 'drug trafficking offence' in Article 2(2) (interpretation);
   (b) paragraph (b) of the definition of 'specified offence' in Article 55 (Revenue and Customs prosecutions).
32 In the Road Traffic Offenders (Northern Ireland) Order 1996 (S.I. 1996/1320 (N.I.10))—
   (a) Article 30(2) (penalty points to be attributed to an offence);
   (b) Article 35(6) (disqualification for certain offences);
   (c) Article 40(7) (disqualification for repeated offences).
33 In the Criminal Justice (Northern Ireland) Order 1996 (S.I. 1996/3160 (N.I.24))—
   (a) Article 38(3)(d) (Group B offences);
   (b) Article 42(2) (incitement to commit Group A offence).

34 Paragraph 8 of the Schedule to the Sexual Offences (Protected Material) Act 1997 (c. 39) (sexual offences for the purposes of that Act).

35 Section 14(2)(d) of the Northern Ireland (Sentences) Act 1998 (c. 35) (inadmissibility).

36 Section 51C(3)(e) of the Crime and Disorder Act 1998 (c. 37) (notices in certain cases involving children).

37 Section 62(2) of the Youth Justice and Criminal Evidence Act 1999 (c. 23) (meaning of 'sexual offence' and other references to offences).

38 Article 3(2) of the Criminal Evidence (Northern Ireland) Order 1999 (S.I. 1999/2789 (N.I.8)) (meaning of 'sexual offence' and other references to offences).

39 Section 147(2) of the Powers of Criminal Courts (Sentencing) Act 2000 (c. 6) (driving disqualification where vehicle used for purposes of crime).

40 Paragraph 3(t)(i) of Schedule 4 to the Criminal Justice and Court Services Act 2000 (c. 43) (meaning of 'offence against a child').

41 Section 34(1)(g) of the Criminal Justice and Police Act 2001 (c. 16) (meaning of 'drug trafficking offence').

42 Sections 55(1)(b) and 62(1)(b) of the International Criminal Court Act 2001 (c. 17) (meaning of 'ancillary offence').

43 Section 53(2) of the Anti-terrorism, Crime and Security Act 2001 (c. 24) (Revenue and Customs prosecutions).

44 In the Proceeds of Crime Act 2002 (c. 29)—
    (a) section 340(11)(b) (interpretation of Part 7: money laundering);
    (b) section 415(2)(a) (money laundering offences for purposes of Part 8: investigations);
    (c) section 447(9)(b) (interpretation of Part 11: national and international co-operation);
    (d) section 451(6)(c) (Revenue and Customs prosecutions).

45 Section 4 of the Dealing in Cultural Objects (Offences) Act 2003 (c. 27) (Revenue and Customs prosecutions).

46 Section 142(7)(a) of the Extradition Act 2003 (c. 41) (extradition from category 1 territory to the United Kingdom).

47 Paragraph 3(a) of Schedule 2 to the Sexual Offences Act 2003 (c. 42) (sexual offences to which section 72 of that Act applies).

48 In the Criminal Justice Act 2003 (c. 44)—
    (a) in Schedule 15 (specified violent and sexual offences for the purposes of Chapter 5 of Part 12 of that Act), paragraphs 64(a) and 153(a);
    (b) in Schedule 17 (Northern Ireland violent and sexual offences specified for the purposes of section 229(4) of that Act), paragraphs 61(a) and 110(a).

49 Paragraph 3(i)(i) of the Schedule to the Protection of Children and Vulnerable Adults (Northern Ireland) Order 2003 (S.I. 2003/417 (N.I.4)) (meaning of 'offence against a child').

50 Section 14 of the Gangmasters (Licensing) Act 2004 (c. 11) (enforcement officer's power of arrest).

51 Section 76(3)(p) of the Serious Organised Crime and Police Act 2005 (c. 15) (offences giving rise to financial reporting order).

52 In the Terrorism Act 2006 (c. 11)—
    (a) section 17(2)(f) (commission of offences abroad);
    (b) paragraph 12(b) of Schedule 1 (Convention offences).

PART 2
OTHER MINOR AND CONSEQUENTIAL AMENDMENTS

Misuse of Drugs Act 1971 (c. 38)

53 In section 19 of the Misuse of Drugs Act 1971 for 'such an offence' substitute 'an offence under any other provision of this Act'.

Criminal Law Act 1977 (c. 45)

54 In section 5 of the Criminal Law Act 1977 (effects of creation of statutory offence of conspiracy) omit subsection (7).

Magistrates' Courts Act 1980 (c. 43)

55 (1) The Magistrates' Courts Act 1980 is amended as follows.
    (2) In section 32(1) (penalties for offences triable either way as a result of Schedule 1 to that Act) omit paragraph (b).
    (3) Omit section 45.
    (4) In Schedule 1 (offences triable either way) omit paragraph 35.

Magistrates' Courts (Northern Ireland) Order 1981 (S.I. 1981/1675 (N.I.26))

56 Omit Article 60(1) of the Magistrates' Courts (Northern Ireland) Order 1981.

Criminal Attempts and Conspiracy (Northern Ireland) Order 1983 (S.I. 1983/1120 (N.I.13))

57 In Article 13 of the Criminal Attempts and Conspiracy (Northern Ireland) Order 1983 (effects of creation of statutory offence of conspiracy) omit paragraph (8).

Public Order Act 1986 (c. 64)

58 (1) The Public Order Act 1986 is amended as follows.
    (2) In each of the provisions mentioned in sub-paragraph (3) omit the words from 'notwithstanding' to the end.
    (3) The provisions are—
        (a) section 12(10);
        (b) section 13(13);
        (c) section 14(10);
        (d) section 14B(7).

Computer Misuse Act 1990 (c. 18)

59 (1) The Computer Misuse Act 1990 is amended as follows.
    (2) In section 6 (incitement) omit subsection (3).

(3) In section 7 (territorial scope of inchoate offences related to offences under external law corresponding to offences under the Act) omit subsection (4).

(4) In section 8(3) (relevance of external law) omit 'or by virtue of section 7(4) above'.

(5) In section 9(2) (offences in relation to which British citizenship is immaterial) omit paragraph (d).

(6) In section 16(4) (application to Northern Ireland) omit the words from 'and any reference' to the end.

60   In section 2(3) of the Sexual Offences (Conspiracy and Incitement) Act 1996 for 'of incitement' substitute 'done'.

61   (1) The International Criminal Court Act 2001 is amended as follows.

(2) In section 55 (meaning of ancillary offence: England and Wales) omit subsection (3).

(3) In section 62 (meaning of ancillary offence: Northern Ireland) omit subsection (3).

62   After sub-paragraph (1) in each of paragraph 10 of Schedule 2 to the Proceeds of Crime Act 2002 and paragraph 10 of Schedule 5 to that Act (inchoate offences which are lifestyle offences) insert the following subparagraph—

'(1A) An offence under section 44 of the Serious Crime Act 2007 of doing an act capable of encouraging or assisting the commission of an offence specified in this Schedule.'

63   (1) The Sexual Offences Act 2003 is amended as follows.

(2) In Schedule 3 (sexual offences for the purposes of Part 2 of that Act), after paragraph 94, insert—

'94A A reference in a preceding paragraph to an offence ("offence A") includes a reference to an offence under Part 2 of the Serious Crime Act 2007 in relation to which offence A is the offence (or one of the offences) which the person intended or believed would be committed.'

(3) In Schedule 5 (other offences which are relevant for the purposes of Part 2 of the Act), after paragraph 173, insert—

'173A A reference in a preceding paragraph to an offence ("offence A") includes a reference to an offence under Part 2 of the Serious Crime Act 2007 in relation to which offence A is the offence (or one of the offences) which the person intended or believed would be committed.'

Serious Organised Crime and Police Act 2005 (c. 15)

64 (1) The Serious Organised Crime and Police Act 2005 is amended as follows.

(2) In section 136 (penalties in relation to demonstrations in the vicinity of Parliament) for subsection (4) substitute—

'(4) A person who is guilty of an offence under section 44 or 45 of the Serious Crime Act 2007 in relation to which an offence mentioned in subsection (1), (2) or (3) is the anticipated offence (as defined by section 47(9) of that Act) is liable on summary conviction to imprisonment for a term not exceeding 51 weeks, to a fine not exceeding level 4 on the standard scale or to both.

(4A) If a person is guilty of an offence under section 46 of that Act by reference to an offence mentioned in subsection (1), (2) or (3), the maximum term of imprisonment applicable for the purposes of section 58(6) of that Act to the offence so mentioned is a term not exceeding 51 weeks.'

(3) In section 175(3) (transitional modification of penalties for summary offences in England and Wales) in the table, for the entry relating to section 136(4) substitute—

'section 136(4)	3 months
section 136(4A)	3 months'.

SCHEDULE 7   Section 73
DATA MATCHING

PART 1
DATA MATCHING: ENGLAND

1 The Audit Commission Act 1998 (c. 18) is amended as follows.

2 After Part 2 insert—

'PART 2A
DATA MATCHING

32A Power to conduct data matching exercises

(1) The Commission may conduct data matching exercises or arrange for them to be conducted on its behalf.

(2) A data matching exercise is an exercise involving the comparison of sets of data to determine how far they match (including the identification of any patterns and trends).

(3) The power in subsection (1) is exercisable for the purpose of assisting in the prevention and detection of fraud.

(4) That assistance may, but need not, form part of an audit.

(5) A data matching exercise may not be used to identify patterns and trends in an individual's characteristics or behaviour which suggest nothing more than his potential to commit fraud in the future.

(6) In the following provisions of this Part, reference to a data matching exercise is to an exercise conducted or arranged to be conducted under this section.

32B Mandatory provision of data

(1) The Commission may require—

    (a) any body mentioned in subsection (2), and

    (b) any officer or member of such a body, to provide the Commission or a person acting on its behalf with such data (and in such form) as the Commission or that person may reasonably require for the purpose of conducting data matching exercises.

(2) The bodies are—

    (a) a body subject to audit,

    (b) an English best value authority which is not a body subject to audit.

(3) A person who without reasonable excuse fails to comply with a requirement of the Commission under subsection (1)(b) is guilty of an offence and liable on summary conviction—

    (a) to a fine not exceeding level 3 on the standard scale, and

    (b) to an additional fine not exceeding £20 for each day on which the offence continues after conviction for that offence.

(4) Any expenses incurred by the Commission in connection with proceedings for an offence under subsection (3) alleged to have been committed by an officer or member of a body, so far as not recovered from any other source, are recoverable from that body.

(5) "English best value authority" means a best value authority other than—

    (a) a county council, county borough council or community council in Wales,

    (b) a National Park authority for a National Park in Wales,

    (c) a police authority for a police area in Wales,

    (d) a fire and rescue authority in Wales constituted by a scheme under section 2 of the Fire and Rescue Services Act 2004 (c. 21) or a scheme to which section 4 of that Act applies.

32C Voluntary provision of data

(1) If the Commission thinks it appropriate to conduct a data matching exercise using data held by or on behalf of a body or person not subject to section 32B, the data may be disclosed to the Commission or a person acting on its behalf.

(2) A disclosure under subsection (1) does not breach—

    (a) any obligation of confidence owed by a person making the disclosure, or

    (b) any other restriction on the disclosure of information (however imposed).

(3) But nothing in this section authorises a disclosure which—

    (a) contravenes the Data Protection Act 1998 (c. 29), or

    (b) is prohibited by Part 1 of the Regulation of Investigatory Powers Act 2000 (c. 23).

(4) Data may not be disclosed under subsection (1) if the data comprise or include patient data.

(5) "Patient data" means data relating to an individual which are held for medical purposes (within the meaning of section 251 of the National Health Service Act 2006 (c. 41)) and from which the individual can be identified.

(6) This section does not limit the circumstances in which data may be disclosed apart from this section.

(7) Data matching exercises may include data provided by a body or person outside England and Wales.

32D Disclosure of results of data matching etc

(1) This section applies to the following information—
    (a) information relating to a particular body or person obtained by or on behalf of the Commission for the purpose of conducting a data matching exercise,
    (b) the results of any such exercise.

(2) Information to which this section applies may be disclosed by or on behalf of the Commission if the disclosure is—
    (a) for or in connection with a purpose for which the data matching exercise is conducted,
    (b) to a body mentioned in subsection (3) (or a related party) for or in connection with a function of that body corresponding or similar to the functions of an auditor under Part 2 or the functions of the Commission under this Part, or
    (c) in pursuance of a duty imposed by or under a statutory provision.

(3) The bodies are—
    (a) the Auditor General for Wales,
    (b) the Auditor General for Scotland,
    (c) the Accounts Commission for Scotland,
    (d) Audit Scotland,
    (e) the Comptroller and Auditor General for Northern Ireland,
    (f) a person designated as a local government auditor under Article 4 of the Local Government (Northern Ireland) Order 2005 (S.I. 2005/1968 (N.I.18)).

(4) "Related party", in relation to a body mentioned in subsection (3), means—
    (a) a body or person acting on its behalf,
    (b) a body whose accounts are required to be audited by it or by a person appointed by it,
    (c) a person appointed by it to audit those accounts.

(5) If the data used for a data matching exercise include patient data—
    (a) subsection (2)(a) applies only so far as the purpose for which the disclosure is made relates to a relevant NHS body,
    (b) subsection (2)(b) applies only so far as the function for or in connection with which the disclosure is made relates to such a body.

(6) In subsection (5)—
    (a) "patient data" has the same meaning as in section 32C,
    (b) "relevant NHS body" means—
        (i) a health service body,
        (ii) a Welsh NHS body,
        (iii) an NHS body as defined in section 22(1) of the Community Care and Health (Scotland) Act 2002 (asp 5),
        (iv) a body to which Article 90 of the Health and Personal Social Services (Northern Ireland) Order 1972 (S.I. 1972/1265 (N.I.14)) applies.

(7) Information disclosed under subsection (2) may not be further disclosed except—
    (a) for or in connection with the purpose for which it was disclosed under paragraph (a) or the function for which it was disclosed under paragraph (b) of that subsection,
    (b) for the investigation or prosecution of an offence (so far as the disclosure does not fall within paragraph (a)), or
    (c) in pursuance of a duty imposed by or under a statutory provision.

(8) Except as authorised by subsections (2) and (7), a person who discloses information to which this section applies is guilty of an offence and liable—

    (a) on conviction on indictment, to imprisonment for a term not exceeding two years, to a fine or to both, or

    (b) on summary conviction, to imprisonment for a term not exceeding 12 months, to a fine not exceeding the statutory maximum or to both.

(9) Section 49 does not apply to information to which this section applies.

(10) In this section, "body" includes office.

32E Publication

(1) Nothing in section 32D prevents the Commission from publishing a report on a data matching exercise (including on the results of the exercise).

(2) But the report may not include information relating to a particular body or person if—

    (a) the body or person is the subject of any data included in the data matching exercise,

    (b) the body or person can be identified from the information, and

    (c) the information is not otherwise in the public domain.

(3) A report published under this section may be published in such manner as the Commission considers appropriate for bringing it to the attention of those members of the public who may be interested.

(4) Section 51 does not apply to information to which section 32D applies.

(5) This section does not affect any powers of an auditor where the data matching exercise in question forms part of an audit under Part 2.

32F Fees for data matching

(1) The Commission must prescribe a scale or scales of fees in respect of data matching exercises.

(2) A body required under section 32B(1) to provide data for a data matching exercise must pay to the Commission the fee applicable to that exercise in accordance with the appropriate scale.

(3) But if it appears to the Commission that the work involved in the exercise was substantially more or less than that envisaged by the appropriate scale, the Commission may charge the body a fee which is larger or smaller than that referred to in subsection (2).

(4) Before prescribing a scale of fees under this section, the Commission must consult—

    (a) the bodies mentioned in section 32B(2), and

    (b) such other bodies or persons as the Commission thinks fit.

(5) If the Secretary of State considers it necessary or desirable to do so, he may by regulations prescribe a scale or scales of fees to have effect, for such period as is specified in the regulations, in place of any scale or scales of fees prescribed by the Commission and, if he does so, references in this section to the appropriate scale are to be read as respects that period as references to the appropriate scale prescribed by the Secretary of State.

(6) Before making any regulations under subsection (5), the Secretary of State must consult—

    (a) the Commission, and

    (b) such other bodies or persons as he thinks fit.

(7) In addition to the power under subsection (2), the Commission may charge a fee to any other body or person providing data for or receiving the results of a data matching exercise, such fee to be payable in accordance with terms agreed between the Commission and that body or person.

32G Code of data matching practice
(1) The Commission must prepare, and keep under review, a code of practice with respect to data matching exercises.
(2) Regard must be had to the code in conducting and participating in any such exercise.
(3) Before preparing or altering the code, the Commission must consult the bodies mentioned in section 32B(2), the Information Commissioner and such other bodies or persons as the Commission thinks fit.
(4) The Commission must—
   (a) send a copy of the code, and of any alterations made to the code, to the Secretary of State, who must lay the copy before Parliament, and
   (b) from time to time publish the code as for the time being in force.

32H Powers of Secretary of State
(1) The Secretary of State may by order amend this Part—
   (a) to add any purpose mentioned in subsection (2) to the purposes for which data matching exercises may be conducted,
   (b) to modify the application of this Part in relation to a purpose so added.
(2) The purposes which may be added are—
   (a) to assist in the prevention and detection of crime (other than fraud),
   (b) to assist in the apprehension and prosecution of offenders,
   (c) to assist in the recovery of debt owing to public bodies.
(3) The Secretary of State may by order amend this Part—
   (a) to add a public body to the list of bodies in section 32B(2),
   (b) to modify the application of this Part in relation to a body so added,
   (c) to remove a body from that list.
(4) An order under this section may include such incidental, consequential, supplemental or transitional provision as the Secretary of State thinks fit.
(5) In this section, "public body" means a body or person whose functions—
   (a) are functions of a public nature, or
   (b) include functions of that nature,
   but, in the latter case, the body or person is a public body to the extent only of those functions.'

3 In section 52 (orders and regulations), after subsection (1) insert—

   '(1A) No order shall be made under section 32H unless a draft of the order has been laid before and approved by a resolution of each House of Parliament.'

PART 2
DATA MATCHING: WALES

4 After Part 3 of the Public Audit (Wales) Act 2004 (c. 23) insert—

'PART 3A
DATA MATCHING

64A Power to conduct data matching exercises

(1) The Auditor General for Wales may conduct data matching exercises or arrange for them to be conducted on his behalf.

(2) A data matching exercise is an exercise involving the comparison of sets of data to determine how far they match (including the identification of any patterns and trends).

(3) The power in subsection (1) is exercisable for the purpose of assisting in the prevention and detection of fraud in or with respect to Wales.

(4) That assistance may, but need not, form part of an audit.

(5) A data matching exercise may not be used to identify patterns and trends in an individual's characteristics or behaviour which suggest nothing more than his potential to commit fraud in the future.

(6) In the following provisions of this Part, reference to a data matching exercise is to an exercise conducted or arranged to be conducted under this section.

64B Mandatory provision of data

(1) The Auditor General for Wales may require—
   (a) any body mentioned in subsection (2), and
   (b) any officer or member of such a body,
   to provide the Auditor General or a person acting on his behalf with such data (and in such form) as the Auditor General or that person may reasonably require for the purpose of conducting data matching exercises.

(2) The bodies are—
   (a) a local government body in Wales (as defined in section 12(1));
   (b) a Welsh NHS body (as defined in section 60).

(3) A person who without reasonable excuse fails to comply with a requirement of the Auditor General under subsection (1)(b) is guilty of an offence and liable on summary conviction—
   (a) to a fine not exceeding level 3 on the standard scale, and
   (b) to an additional fine not exceeding £20 for each day on which the offence continues after conviction for that offence.

(4) If an officer or member of a body is convicted of an offence under subsection (3), any expenses incurred by the Auditor General in connection with proceedings for the offence, so far as not recovered from any other source, are recoverable from that body.

64C Voluntary provision of data

(1) If the Auditor General for Wales thinks it appropriate to conduct a data matching exercise using data held by or on behalf of a body or person not subject to section 64B, the data may be disclosed to the Auditor General or a person acting on his behalf.

(2) A disclosure under subsection (1) does not breach—
   (a) any obligation of confidence owed by a person making the disclosure, or
   (b) any other restriction on the disclosure of information (however imposed).

(3) But nothing in this section authorises a disclosure which—
   (a) contravenes the Data Protection Act 1998 (c. 29), or
   (b) is prohibited by Part 1 of the Regulation of Investigatory Powers Act 2000 (c. 23).

(4) Data may not be disclosed under subsection (1) if the data comprise or include patient data.

(5) "Patient data" means data relating to an individual which are held for medical purposes (within the meaning of section 251 of the National Health Service Act 2006 (c. 41)) and from which the individual can be identified.

(6) This section does not limit the circumstances in which data may be disclosed apart from this section.

(7) Data matching exercises may include data provided by a body or person outside England and Wales.

64D Disclosure of results of data matching etc

(1) This section applies to the following information—

    (a) information relating to a particular body or person obtained by or on behalf of the Auditor General for Wales for the purpose of conducting a data matching exercise,

    (b) the results of any such exercise.

(2) Information to which this section applies may be disclosed by or on behalf of the Auditor General for Wales if the disclosure is—

    (a) for or in connection with a purpose for which the data matching exercise is conducted,

    (b) to a body mentioned in subsection (3) (or a related party) for or in connection with a function of that body corresponding or similar to the functions of an auditor under Chapter 1 of Part 2 or the functions of the Auditor General under Part 3 or this Part, or

    (c) in pursuance of a duty imposed by or under a statutory provision.

(3) The bodies are—

    (a) the Audit Commission,

    (b) the Auditor General for Scotland,

    (c) the Accounts Commission for Scotland,

    (d) Audit Scotland,

    (e) the Comptroller and Auditor General for Northern Ireland,

    (f) a person designated as a local government auditor under Article 4 of the Local Government (Northern Ireland) Order 2005 (S.I. 2005/1968 (N.I.18)).

(4) "Related party", in relation to a body mentioned in subsection (3), means—

    (a) a body or person acting on its behalf,

    (b) a body whose accounts are required to be audited by it or by a person appointed by it,

    (c) a person appointed by it to audit those accounts.

(5) If the data used for a data matching exercise include patient data—

    (a) subsection (2)(a) applies only so far as the purpose for which the disclosure is made relates to a relevant NHS body,

    (b) subsection (2)(b) applies only so far as the function for or in connection with which the disclosure is made relates to such a body.

(6) In subsection (5)—

    (a) "patient data" has the same meaning as in section 64C,

    (b) "relevant NHS body" means—

        (i) a Welsh NHS body as defined in section 60,

        (ii) a health service body as defined in section 53(1) of the Audit Commission Act 1998 (c. 18),

       (iii) an NHS body as defined in section 22(1) of the Community Care and Health (Scotland) Act 2002 (asp 5),

       (iv) a body to which Article 90 of the Health and Personal Social Services (Northern Ireland) Order 1972 (S.I. 1972/1265 (N.I.14)) applies.

(7) Information disclosed under subsection (2) may not be further disclosed except—

  (a) for or in connection with the purpose for which it was disclosed under paragraph (a) or the function for which it was disclosed under paragraph (b) of that subsection,

  (b) for the investigation or prosecution of an offence (so far as the disclosure does not fall within paragraph (a)), or

  (c) in pursuance of a duty imposed by or under a statutory provision.

(8) Except as authorised by subsections (2) and (7), a person who discloses information to which this section applies is guilty of an offence and liable—

  (a) on conviction on indictment, to imprisonment for a term not exceeding two years, to a fine or to both, or

  (b) on summary conviction, to imprisonment for a term not exceeding 12 months, to a fine not exceeding the statutory maximum or to both.

(9) Section 54 does not apply to information to which this section applies.

(10) In this section "statutory provision" has the meaning given in section 59(8).

64E Publication

(1) Nothing in section 64D prevents the Auditor General for Wales from publishing a report on a data matching exercise (including on the results of the exercise).

(2) But the report may not include information relating to a particular body or person if—

  (a) the body or person is the subject of any data included in the data matching exercise,

  (b) the body or person can be identified from the information, and

  (c) the information is not otherwise in the public domain.

(3) A report published under this section may be published in any manner which the Auditor General considers appropriate for bringing it to the attention of those members of the public who may be interested.

(4) This section does not affect any powers of an auditor or the Auditor General where the data matching exercise in question forms part of an audit under Part 2 or 3.

64F Fees for data matching

(1) The Auditor General for Wales must prescribe a scale or scales of fees in respect of data matching exercises.

(2) A body required under section 64B(1) to provide data for a data matching exercise must pay to the Auditor General the fee applicable to that exercise in accordance with the appropriate scale.

(3) But if it appears to the Auditor General that the work involved in the exercise was substantially more or less than that envisaged by the appropriate scale, the Auditor General may charge the body a fee which is larger or smaller than that referred to in subsection (2).

(4) Before prescribing a scale of fees under this section, the Auditor General must consult—

  (a) the bodies mentioned in section 64B(2), and

  (b) such other bodies or persons as the Auditor General thinks fit.

(5) If the Welsh Ministers consider it necessary or desirable to do so, they may by regulations prescribe a scale or scales of fees to have effect, for such period as is specified in the regulations, in place of any scale or scales of fees prescribed by the Auditor General and, if they do so, references in this section to the appropriate scale are to be read as respects that period as references to the appropriate scale prescribed by the Welsh Ministers.

(6) Before making any regulations under subsection (5), the Welsh Ministers must consult—
(a) the Auditor General for Wales, and
(b) such other bodies or persons as they think fit.

(7) The power under subsection (5) is exercisable by statutory instrument subject to annulment in pursuance of a resolution of the Assembly.

(8) In addition to the power under subsection (2), the Auditor General may charge a fee to any other body or person providing data for or receiving the results of a data matching exercise, such fee to be payable in accordance with terms agreed between the Auditor General and that body or person.

64G Code of data matching practice

(1) The Auditor General for Wales must prepare, and keep under review, a code of practice with respect to data matching exercises.

(2) Regard must be had to the code in conducting and participating in any such exercise.

(3) Before preparing or altering the code, the Auditor General must consult the bodies mentioned in section 64B(2), the Information Commissioner and such other bodies or persons as the Auditor General thinks fit.

(4) The Auditor General must—
(a) lay a copy of the code, and of any alterations made to the code, before the Assembly, and
(b) from time to time publish the code as for the time being in force.

64H Powers of Secretary of State

(1) The Secretary of State may by order amend this Part—
(a) to add any purpose mentioned in subsection (2) to the purposes for which data matching exercises may be conducted,
(b) to modify the application of this Part in relation to a purpose so added.

(2) The purposes which may be added are—
(a) to assist in the prevention and detection of crime (other than fraud) in or with respect to Wales,
(b) to assist in the apprehension and prosecution of offenders in or with respect to Wales,
(c) to assist in the recovery of debt owing to Welsh public bodies.

(3) The Secretary of State may by order amend this Part—
(a) to add a Welsh public body to the list of bodies in section 64B(2),
(b) to modify the application of this Part in relation to a body so added,
(c) to remove a body from that list.

(4) Before making an order under this section, the Secretary of State must consult the Auditor General for Wales.

(5) An order under this section—
(a) is to be made by statutory instrument, and
(b) may include such incidental, consequential, supplemental or transitional provision as the Secretary of State thinks fit.

(6) No order under this section may be made unless a draft of the statutory instrument has been laid before, and approved by a resolution of, each House of Parliament.

(7) In this section "Welsh public body" means a public body (as defined in section 12(3)) whose functions relate exclusively to Wales or an area of Wales.'

5 (1) Paragraph 9 of Schedule 8 to the Government of Wales Act 2006 (c. 32) (special finance provisions) is amended as follows.

(2) In sub-paragraph (3)(b) after 'government audit)' insert 'or, so far as the functions relate to local government bodies in Wales, Part 3A of that Act (data matching)'.

(3) In sub-paragraph (4)(c) for the words from 'Part 2' to the end substitute 'the following provisions of the Public Audit (Wales) Act 2004 (c. 23)—

  (i) Part 2 (including those charged as a result of paragraph 11(3)(c)),

  (ii) Part 3A (but only those charged to a local government body in Wales).'

(4) After sub-paragraph (4) insert—

  '(5) "Local government body in Wales" has the meaning given in section 12(1) of the Public Audit (Wales) Act 2004.'

PART 3

DATA MATCHING: NORTHERN IRELAND

6 After Article 4 of the Audit and Accountability (Northern Ireland) Order 2003 (S.I. 2003/418 (N.I.5)) insert—

'Data matching

4A Power to conduct data matching exercises

(1) The Comptroller and Auditor General may conduct data matching exercises or arrange for them to be conducted on his behalf.

(2) A data matching exercise is an exercise involving the comparison of sets of data to determine how far they match (including the identification of any patterns and trends).

(3) The power in paragraph (1) is exercisable for the purpose of assisting in the prevention and detection of fraud.

(4) That assistance may, but need not, form part of an audit.

(5) A data matching exercise may not be used to identify patterns and trends in an individual's characteristics or behaviour which suggest nothing more than his potential to commit fraud in the future.

(6) In Articles 4B to 4H, reference to a data matching exercise is to an exercise conducted or arranged to be conducted under this Article.

4B Mandatory provision of data

(1) The Comptroller and Auditor General may require—

  (a) any body mentioned in paragraph (2); and

  (b) any officer or member of such a body,

  to provide the Comptroller and Auditor General or a person acting on his behalf with such data (and in such form) as the Comptroller and Auditor General or that person may reasonably require for the purpose of conducting data matching exercises.

(2) The bodies are—

    (a) any body (including a holder of a statutory office) whose accounts are required to be audited by the Comptroller and Auditor General, other than a body whose accounts are required to be so audited by virtue of section 55 of the Northern Ireland Act 1998 (c. 47);

    (b) any body whose accounts are required to be audited by a local government auditor.

(3) A person who without reasonable excuse fails to comply with a requirement of the Comptroller and Auditor General under paragraph (1)(b) is guilty of an offence and liable on summary conviction—

    (a) to a fine not exceeding level 3 on the standard scale; and

    (b) to an additional fine not exceeding £20 for each day on which the offence continues after conviction for that offence.

(4) If an officer or member of a body is convicted of an offence under paragraph (3), any expenses incurred by the Comptroller and Auditor General in connection with proceedings for the offence, so far as not recovered from any other source, are recoverable from that body.

4C Voluntary provision of data

(1) If the Comptroller and Auditor General thinks it appropriate to conduct a data matching exercise using data held by or on behalf of a body or person not subject to Article 4B, the data may be disclosed to the Comptroller and Auditor General or a person acting on his behalf.

(2) A disclosure under paragraph (1) does not breach—

    (a) any obligation of confidence owed by a person making the disclosure; or

    (b) any other restriction on the disclosure of information (however imposed).

(3) But nothing in this Article authorises a disclosure which—

    (a) contravenes the Data Protection Act 1998 (c. 29); or

    (b) is prohibited by Part 1 of the Regulation of Investigatory Powers Act 2000 (c. 23).

(4) Data may not be disclosed under paragraph (1) if the data comprise or include patient data.

(5) "Patient data" means data relating to an individual which are held for any of the following purposes and from which the individual can be identified—

    (a) preventative medicine, medical diagnosis, medical research, the provision of care and treatment and the management of health and social care services;

    (b) informing individuals about their physical or mental health or condition, the diagnosis of their condition or their care and treatment.

(6) This Article does not limit the circumstances in which data may be disclosed apart from this Article.

(7) Data matching exercises may include data provided by a body or person outside Northern Ireland.

4D Disclosure of results of data matching etc

(1) This Article applies to the following information—

    (a) information relating to a particular body or person obtained by or on behalf of the Comptroller and Auditor General for the purpose of conducting a data matching exercise;

    (b) the results of any such exercise.

(2) Information to which this Article applies may be disclosed by or on behalf of the Comptroller and Auditor General if the disclosure is—

  (a) for or in connection with a purpose for which the data matching exercise is conducted;

  (b) to a body mentioned in paragraph (3) (or a related party) for or in connection with a function of that body corresponding or similar to the audit functions of the Comptroller and Auditor General or a local government auditor under any statutory provision or the data matching functions of the Comptroller and Auditor General under Article 4A; or

  (c) in pursuance of a duty imposed by or under a statutory provision.

(3) The bodies are—

  (a) the Audit Commission for Local Authorities and the National Health Service in England;

  (b) the Auditor General for Wales;

  (c) the Auditor General for Scotland;

  (d) the Accounts Commission for Scotland;

  (e) Audit Scotland.

(4) "Related party", in relation to a body mentioned in paragraph (3), means—

  (a) a body or person acting on its behalf;

  (b) a body whose accounts are required to be audited by it or by a person appointed by it;

  (c) a person appointed by it to audit those accounts.

(5) If the data used for a data matching exercise include patient data—

  (a) paragraph (2)(a) applies only so far as the purpose for which the disclosure is made relates to a relevant NHS body;

  (b) paragraph (2)(b) applies only so far as the function for or in connection with which the disclosure is made relates to such a body.

(6) In paragraph (5)—

  (a) "patient data" has the same meaning as in Article 4C;

  (b) "relevant NHS body" means—

    (i) a body to which Article 90 of the Health and Personal Social Services (Northern Ireland) Order 1972 (NI 14) applies;

    (ii) a health service body as defined in section 53(1) of the Audit Commission Act 1998 (c. 18);

    (iii) a Welsh NHS body as defined in section 60 of the Public Audit (Wales) Act 2004 (c. 23);

    (iv) an NHS body as defined in section 22(1) of the Community Care and Health (Scotland) Act 2002 (asp 5).

(7) Information disclosed under paragraph (2) may not be further disclosed except—

  (a) for or in connection with the purpose for which it was disclosed under sub paragraph (a) or the function for which it was disclosed under sub-paragraph (b) of that paragraph;

  (b) for the investigation or prosecution of an offence (so far as the disclosure does not fall within sub-paragraph (a)); or

  (c) in pursuance of a duty imposed by or under a statutory provision.

(8) Except as authorised by paragraphs (2) and (7), a person who discloses information to which this Article applies is guilty of an offence and liable—

    (a) on conviction on indictment, to imprisonment for a term not exceeding two years, to a fine or to both; or

    (b) on summary conviction, to imprisonment for a term not exceeding 6 months, to a fine not exceeding the statutory maximum or to both.

(9) Article 27 of the Local Government (Northern Ireland) Order 2005 (NI 18) does not apply to information to which this Article applies.

(10) In this Article "body" includes office.

4E Publication

(1) Nothing in Article 4D prevents the Comptroller and Auditor General from publishing a report on a data matching exercise (including on the results of the exercise).

(2) But the report may not include information relating to a particular body or person if—

    (a) the body or person is the subject of any data included in the data matching exercise;

    (b) the body or person can be identified from the information; and

    (c) the information is not otherwise in the public domain.

(3) A report published under this Article may be published in such manner as the Comptroller and Auditor General considers appropriate for bringing it to the attention of those members of the public who may be interested.

(4) This Article does not affect any powers of the Comptroller and Auditor General or a local government auditor where the data matching exercise in question forms part of an audit carried out by either of them.

4F Fees for data matching

(1) The Comptroller and Auditor General may charge a fee to any body required under Article 4B(1) to provide data for a data matching exercise.

(2) But a body whose functions are discharged on behalf of the Crown may not be charged a fee under paragraph (1) except with the consent of the Department.

(3) In addition to the power under paragraph (1), the Comptroller and Auditor General may charge a fee to any other body or person providing data for or receiving the results of a data matching exercise, such fee to be payable in accordance with terms agreed between the Comptroller and Auditor General and that body or person.

(4) Any fee received by the Comptroller and Auditor General by virtue of this Article is to be paid by him into the Consolidated Fund.

4G Code of data matching practice

(1) The Comptroller and Auditor General must prepare, and keep under review, a code of practice with respect to data matching exercises.

(2) Regard must be had to the code in conducting and participating in any such exercise.

(3) Before preparing or altering the code, the Comptroller and Auditor General must consult the bodies mentioned in Article 4B(2), the Information Commissioner and such other bodies or persons as he thinks fit.

(4) The Comptroller and Auditor General must—

    (a) send a copy of the code, and of any alterations made to the code, to the Department and the Department must lay the copy before the Assembly; and

    (b) from time to time publish the code as for the time being in force.

4H Powers of the Department

(1) The Department may by order amend Articles 4A to 4G—

    (a) to add any purpose mentioned in paragraph (2) to the purposes for which data matching exercises may be conducted;

    (b) to modify the application of those Articles in relation to a purpose so added.

(2) The purposes which may be added are—

    (a) to assist in the prevention and detection of crime (other than fraud);

    (b) to assist in the apprehension and prosecution of offenders;

    (c) to assist in the recovery of debt owing to public bodies.

(3) The Department may by order amend Articles 4A to 4G—

    (a) to add a public body to the list of bodies in Article 4B(2);

    (b) to modify the application of those Articles in relation to a body so added;

    (c) to remove a body from that list.

(4) An order under this Article may include such incidental, consequential, supplemental or transitional provision as the Department thinks fit.

(5) An order under this Article is subject to affirmative resolution.

(6) In this Article "public body" means a body or person whose functions—

    (a) are functions of a public nature; or

    (b) include functions of that nature,

but, in the latter case, the body or person is a public body to the extent only of those functions.'

7 In Article 6 of the Audit (Northern Ireland) Order 1987 (S.I. 1987/460 (N.I.5)) (expenses and accounts of Northern Ireland Audit Office), in paragraph (5) after 'examination' insert 'or in respect of data matching'.

SCHEDULE 8   Section 74(2)
ABOLITION OF ASSETS RECOVERY AGENCY AND ITS DIRECTOR

PART 1
ABOLITION OF CONFISCATION FUNCTIONS

1 The Proceeds of Crime Act 2002 (c. 29) is amended as follows.

2 In section 6(3)(a) (making of confiscation orders in England and Wales) omit 'or the Director'.

3 In section 11(7) (time for payment of order) omit paragraph (b) and the word 'or' before it.

4 In section 14(7)(b) (postponement of proceedings) omit 'or the Director (as the case may be)'.

5 (1) Section 16 (statement of information) is amended as follows.

  (2) In subsection (1) omit 'or the Director (as the case may be)'.

  (3) In subsection (3) omit—

    (a) 'or the Director (as the case may be)'; and

    (b) 'or the Director'.

   (4) In subsection (4) omit 'or Director'.

   (5) In subsection (5) omit—

      (a) 'or the Director (as the case may be)'; and

      (b) 'or the Director'.

   (6) In subsection (6) omit 'or the Director'.

6 In section 17(1) (defendant's response to statement of information) omit 'or the Director'.

7 In section 18(6) (provision of information by defendant) omit 'or the Director (as the case may be)'.

8 In section 19(1)(c) (no order made: reconsideration of case) omit 'or the Director'.

9 (1) Section 20 (no order made: reconsideration of benefit) is amended as follows.

   (2) Omit subsection (3).

   (3) In subsection (4)—

      (a) omit the words from 'If the court' to 'to do so,'; and

      (b) in paragraph (b) omit 'or the Director'.

10 In section 21(1) (order made: reconsideration of benefit), in paragraphs (b), (c) and (d), omit 'or the Director'.

11 In section 22(2) (order made: reconsideration of available amount)—

   (a) omit paragraph (b); and

   (b) in paragraph (c) omit 'or 52'.

12 In section 23(1)(b) (inadequacy of available amount: variation of order) omit 'or 52'.

13 (1) Section 26 (information) is amended as follows.

   (2) In subsection (1)(b) omit 'or the Director'.

   (3) In subsection (2)—

      (a) in paragraph (a) omit 'or the Director (as the case may be)'; and

      (b) in paragraph (b) omit 'or the Director'.

14 (1) Section 27 (defendant convicted or committed) is amended as follows.

   (2) In subsection (3)(a) omit 'or the Director'.

   (3) In subsection (5)(b) omit 'or the Director (as the case may be)'.

   (4) In subsection (7) omit 'or the Director'.

15 (1) Section 28 (defendant neither convicted nor acquitted) is amended as follows.

   (2) In subsection (3)(a) omit 'or the Director'.

   (3) In subsection (5)(b) omit 'or the Director (as the case may be)'.

16 (1) Section 31 (appeal by prosecutor or Director) is amended as follows.

   (2) In the heading omit 'or Director'.

   (3) In subsection (1) omit 'or the Director'.

   (4) In subsection (2) omit 'or the Director'.

17 In section 33(2) (appeal to the House of Lords)—

   (a) in paragraph (a) omit '(if the prosecutor appealed under section 31)'; and

   (b) omit paragraph (b).

18 Omit section 34 (Director as enforcement authority).

19 (1) Section 35 (Director not appointed as enforcement authority) is amended as follows.

   (2) For the heading substitute 'Enforcement as fines'.

   (3) In subsection (1) omit paragraph (b) and the word 'and' before it.

20 Omit sections 36 and 37 (Director appointed as enforcement authority and Director's application for enforcement).

21 (1) Section 39 (reconsideration etc: variation of prison term) is amended as follows.

   (2) In subsection (5) for 'appropriate person' substitute 'prosecutor'.

(3) Omit subsection (6).

22 (1) Section 40 (conditions for exercise of powers) is amended as follows.
   (2) In subsection (4)(a) omit 'or the Director'.
   (3) In subsection (5)(a) omit 'or the Director'.
   (4) In subsection (6)(a) omit 'or the Director'.
   (5) In subsection (8)(b) omit 'or the Director (as the case may be)'.

23 In section 42(2) (application, discharge and variation) omit paragraph (b).

24 Omit sections 52 and 53 (Director's receivers).

25 Omit sections 56 and 57 (Director's receivers and sums received by Director).

26 In section 58(6)(b) (restraint orders: restrictions) for, '50 or 52' substitute 'or 50'.

27 Omit section 60 (Director's receivers).

28 In section 61 (protection) for, '50 or 52' substitute 'or 50'.

29 In section 62(1) (further applications) for, '50 or 52' substitute 'or 50'.

30 In section 63(1) (discharge and variation)—
   (a) for 'to 53' substitute 'to 51'; and
   (b) in paragraph (b) omit the words from 'or', where it first appears, to 'Director'.

31 (1) Section 64 (management receivers: discharge) is amended as follows.
   (2) In subsection (1)(b) omit the words from 'or' to 'section 52'.
   (3) Omit subsection (3).

32 (1) Section 65 (appeal to Court of Appeal) is amended as follows.
   (2) In subsection (1) omit 'or section 53'.
   (3) In subsection (2) omit 'or section 53'.
   (4) In subsection (5)(a) omit the words from 'or', where it first appears, to 'Director'.

33 In section 67(4) (seized money) omit paragraph (c).

34 In section 69(1) (powers of court and receiver)—
   (a) in paragraph (a) for '60' substitute '59'; and
   (b) in paragraph (b) for, '50 or 52' substitute 'or 50'.

35 In section 74(1) (enforcement abroad)—
   (a) in paragraph (b) omit 'or the Director'; and
   (b) in paragraph (c) omit 'or the Director (as the case may be)'.

36 In section 156(3)(a) (making of confiscation orders in Northern Ireland) omit 'or the Director'.

37 In section 161(7) (time for payment of order) omit paragraph (b) and the word 'or' before it.

38 In section 164(7)(b) (postponement of proceedings) omit 'or the Director (as the case may be)'.

39 (1) Section 166 (statement of information) is amended as follows.
   (2) In subsection (1) omit 'or the Director (as the case may be)'.
   (3) In subsection (3) omit—
      (a) 'or the Director (as the case may be)'; and
      (b) 'or the Director'.
   (4) In subsection (4) omit 'or Director'.
   (5) In subsection (5) omit—
      (a) 'or the Director (as the case may be)'; and
      (b) 'or the Director'.
   (6) In subsection (6) omit 'or the Director'.

40 In section 167(1) (defendant's response to statement of information) omit 'or the Director'.

41   In section 168(6) (provision of information by defendant) omit 'or the Director (as the case may be)'.

42   In section 169(1)(c) (no order made: reconsideration of case) omit 'or the Director'.

43   (1) Section 170 (no order made: reconsideration of benefit) is amended as follows.

   (2) Omit subsection (3).

   (3) In subsection (4)—

      (a) omit the words from 'If the court' to 'to do so,'; and

      (b) in paragraph (b) omit 'or the Director'.

44   In section 171(1) (order made: reconsideration of benefit), in paragraphs (b), (c) and (d), omit 'or the Director'.

45   In section 172(2) (order made: reconsideration of available amount)—

   (a) omit paragraph (b); and

   (b) in paragraph (c) omit 'or 200'.

46   In section 173(1)(b) (inadequacy of available amount: variation of order) omit 'or 200'.

47   (1) Section 176 (information) is amended as follows.

   (2) In subsection (1)(b) omit 'or the Director'.

   (3) In subsection (2)—

      (a) in paragraph (a) omit 'or the Director (as the case may be)'; and

      (b) in paragraph (b) omit 'or the Director'.

48   (1) Section 177 (defendant convicted or committed) is amended as follows.

   (2) In subsection (3)(a) omit 'or the Director'.

   (3) In subsection (5)(b) omit 'or the Director (as the case may be)'.

   (4) In subsection (7) omit 'or the Director'.

49   (1) Section 178 (defendant neither convicted nor acquitted) is amended as follows.

   (2) In subsection (3)(a) omit 'or the Director'.

   (3) In subsection (5)(b) omit 'or the Director (as the case may be)'.

50   (1) Section 181 (appeal by prosecutor or Director) is amended as follows.

   (2) In the heading omit 'or Director'.

   (3) In subsection (1) omit 'or the Director'.

   (4) In subsection (2) omit 'or the Director'.

51   In section 183(2) (appeal to the House of Lords)—

   (a) in paragraph (a) omit '(if the prosecutor appealed under section 181)'; and

   (b) omit paragraph (b).

52   Omit section 184 (Director as enforcement authority).

53   Omit section 186 (Director's application for enforcement).

54   (1) Section 188 (reconsideration etc: variation of prison term) is amended as follows.

   (2) In subsection (5) for 'appropriate person' substitute 'prosecutor'.

   (3) Omit subsection (6).

55   (1) Section 189 (conditions for exercise of powers) is amended as follows.

   (2) In subsection (4)(a) omit 'or the Director'.

   (3) In subsection (5)(a) omit 'or the Director'.

   (4) In subsection (6)(a) omit 'or the Director'.

   (5) In subsection (8)(b) omit 'or the Director (as the case may be)'.

56   In section 191(2) (application, discharge and variation) omit paragraph (b).

57   Omit sections 200 and 201 (Director's receivers).

58   Omit sections 204 and 205 (Director's receivers and sums received by Director).

59   In section 206(5)(b) (restraint orders) for, '198 or 200' substitute 'or 198'.

60   Omit section 208 (Director's receivers).

61 In section 209 (protection) for, '198 or 200' substitute 'or 198'.

62 (1) Section 210 (further applications) is amended as follows.

   (2) In subsection (1) for, '198 or 200' substitute 'or 198'.

   (3) In subsection (2)(b) omit 'or 200'.

   (4) In subsection (3) omit 'or 200'.

63 In section 211(1) (discharge and variation)—

   (a) for 'any of sections 198 to 201' substitute 'section 198 or 199'; and

   (b) in paragraph (b) omit the words from 'or', where it first appears, to 'Director'.

64 (1) Section 212 (management receivers: discharge) is amended as follows.

   (2) In subsection (1)(b) omit the words from 'or' to 'section 200'.

   (3) Omit subsection (3).

65 (1) Section 213 (appeal to Court of Appeal) is amended as follows.

   (2) In subsection (1) omit 'or section 201'.

   (3) In subsection (2) omit 'or section 201'.

   (4) In subsection (5)(a) omit the words from 'or', where it first appears, to 'Director'.

66 In section 215(4) (seized money) omit paragraph (d).

67 In section 217(1) (powers of court and receiver)—

   (a) in paragraph (a) for '208' substitute '207'; and

   (b) in paragraph (b) for, '198 or 200' substitute 'or 198'.

68 In section 222(1) (enforcement abroad)—

   (a) in paragraph (b) omit 'or the Director'; and

   (b) in paragraph (c) omit 'or the Director (as the case may be)'.

69 In section 417(2) (insolvency etc: modifications of the 1986 Act)—

   (a) in paragraph (b) omit 'or 52'; and

   (b) in paragraph (d) omit 'or 200'.

70 (1) Section 418 (restriction of powers) is amended as follows.

   (2) In subsection (2)—

      (a) in paragraph (a) for, '50 or 52' substitute 'or 50'; and

      (b) in paragraph (c) for, '198 or 200' substitute 'or 198'.

   (3) In subsection (3)(d) for, '52, 198 or 200' substitute 'or 198'.

71 In section 419(2)(b) (tainted gifts)—

   (a) omit '52,'; and

   (b) for, '198 or 200' substitute 'or 198'.

72 In section 420(2) (modifications of the 1985 Act)—

   (a) in paragraph (b) omit 'or 52'; and

   (b) in paragraph (d) omit 'or 200'.

73 (1) Section 421 (restriction of powers) is amended as follows.

   (2) In subsection (2)—

      (a) in paragraph (a) for, '50 or 52' substitute 'or 50'; and

      (b) in paragraph (c) for, '198 or 200' substitute 'or 198'.

   (3) In subsection (3)(d) for, '52, 198 or 200' substitute 'or 198'.

74 In section 422(2)(b) (tainted gifts)—

   (a) omit '52,'; and

   (b) for, '198 or 200' substitute 'or 198'.

75 In section 423(2) (modifications of the 1989 Order)—

   (a) in paragraph (b) omit 'or 52'; and

   (b) in paragraph (d) omit 'or 200'.

76 (1) Section 424 (restriction of powers) is amended as follows.

(2) In subsection (2)—
    (a) in paragraph (a) for, '50 or 52' substitute 'or 50'; and
    (b) in paragraph (c) for, '198 or 200' substitute 'or 198'.
(3) In subsection (3)(d) for, '52, 198 or 200' substitute 'or 198'.
77 In section 425(2)(b) (tainted gifts)—
    (a) omit '52,'; and
    (b) for, '198 or 200' substitute 'or 198'.
78 (1) Section 426 (winding up under the 1986 Act) is amended as follows.
    (2) In subsection (2)—
        (a) in paragraph (b) omit 'or 52'; and
        (b) in paragraph (d) omit 'or 200'.
    (3) In subsection (5)—
        (a) in paragraph (a) for, '50 or 52' substitute 'or 50'; and
        (b) in paragraph (c) for, '198 or 200' substitute 'or 198'.
79 In section 427(3)(b) (tainted gifts)—
    (a) omit '52,'; and
    (b) for, '198 or 200' substitute 'or 198'.
80 (1) Section 428 (winding up under the 1989 Order) is amended as follows.
    (2) In subsection (2)—
        (a) in paragraph (b) omit 'or 52'; and
        (b) in paragraph (d) omit 'or 200'.
    (3) In subsection (5)—
        (a) in paragraph (a) for, '50 or 52' substitute 'or 50'; and
        (b) in paragraph (c) for, '198 or 200' substitute 'or 198'.
81 In section 429(3)(b) (tainted gifts)—
    (a) omit '52,'; and
    (b) for, '198 or 200' substitute 'or 198'.
82 (1) Section 430 (floating charges) is amended as follows.
    (2) In subsection (2)—
        (a) in paragraph (b) omit 'or 52'; and
        (b) in paragraph (d) omit 'or 200'.
    (3) In subsection (5)—
        (a) in paragraph (a) for, '50 or 52' substitute 'or 50'; and
        (b) in paragraph (c) for, '198 or 200' substitute 'or 198'.
83 In section 432(7) (insolvency practitioners)—
    (a) in paragraph (a) for, '55(3), 56(2) or 57(3)' substitute 'or 55(3)'; and
    (b) in paragraph (c) for, '203(3), 204(2) or 205(3)' substitute 'or 203(3)'.
84 In Schedule 10 (tax), in paragraph 1—
    (a) in paragraph (a) for, '50 or 52' substitute 'or 50'; and
    (b) in paragraph (c) for, '198 or 200' substitute 'or 198'.

PART 2
TRANSFER OF CIVIL RECOVERY FUNCTIONS

85 The Proceeds of Crime Act 2002 (c. 29) is amended as follows.
86 In section 246(7) (application for interim receiving order) for 'Agency' substitute 'enforcement authority'.

87 After section 272(6) (compensation for loss in relation to associated and joint property) insert—

 '(7) In subsection (5) the reference to the enforcement authority is, in the case of an enforcement authority in relation to England and Wales or Northern Ireland, a reference to the enforcement authority which obtained the property freezing order or interim receiving order concerned.'

88 (1) Section 280 (applying realised proceeds) is amended as follows.

 (2) In subsection (3)—

  (a) for 'Director' substitute 'enforcement authority (unless it is the Scottish Ministers)'; and

  (b) for 'him' substitute 'it'.

 (3) In subsection (4) for 'Agency' substitute 'enforcement authority concerned'.

89 After section 283(9) (compensation) insert—

 '(10) In the case of an enforcement authority in relation to England and Wales or Northern Ireland—

  (a) the reference in subsection (5) to the enforcement authority is a reference to the enforcement authority which obtained the property freezing order or interim receiving order concerned, and

  (b) the reference in subsection (8) to the enforcement authority is a reference to the enforcement authority which obtained the recovery order concerned.'

90 Omit section 313 (restriction on performance of Director's functions by police).

91 (1) Section 316 (general interpretation: Part 5) is amended as follows.

 (2) In subsection (1), in the definition of 'enforcement authority'—

  (a) for paragraph (a) substitute—

   '(a) in relation to England and Wales, means SOCA, the Director of Public Prosecutions, the Director of Revenue and Customs Prosecutions or the Director of the Serious Fraud Office,'; and

  (b) after paragraph (b) insert—

   '(c) in relation to Northern Ireland, means SOCA, the Director of the Serious Fraud Office or the Director of Public Prosecutions for Northern Ireland,'.

 (3) After subsection (8) insert—

  '(8A) In relation to an order in England and Wales or Northern Ireland which is a recovery order, a property freezing order, an interim receiving order or an order under section 276, references to the enforcement authority are, unless the context otherwise requires, references to the enforcement authority which is seeking, or (as the case may be) has obtained, the order.'

PART 3
TRANSFER OR ABOLITION OF REVENUE FUNCTIONS

92 The Proceeds of Crime Act 2002 (c. 29) is amended in accordance with paragraphs 93 to 101.

93 (1) Section 317 (Director's general Revenue functions) is amended as follows.

 (2) In the heading for 'Director's' substitute 'SOCA's'.

 (3) In subsection (1) for 'the Director' substitute 'SOCA'.

(4) In subsection (2) for 'the Director', in both places where it appears, substitute 'SOCA'.

(5) In subsection (3) for 'the Director' substitute 'SOCA'.

(6) In subsection (4) for 'The Director' substitute 'SOCA'.

(7) In subsection (6) for 'the Director' substitute 'SOCA'.

(8) In subsection (7) for 'the Director' substitute 'SOCA'.

(9) In subsection (8)(b) for 'the Director' substitute 'SOCA'.

94 (1) Section 318 (Revenue functions regarding employment) is amended as follows.

(2) In subsection (1)(a) for 'the Director' substitute 'SOCA'.

(3) In subsection (2) for 'the Director' substitute 'SOCA'.

(4) In subsection (3)(a) for 'the Director' substitute 'SOCA'.

(5) In subsection (4) for 'the Director' substitute 'SOCA'.

95 (1) Section 319 (source of income) is amended as follows.

(2) In subsection (1)—

   (a) for 'the Director' substitute 'SOCA';

   (b) for 'him' substitute 'it'; and

   (c) for 'he' substitute 'SOCA'.

(3) In subsection (2) for 'the Director' substitute 'SOCA'.

(4) In subsection (3)—

   (a) for 'the Director' substitute 'SOCA'; and

   (b) for 'him' substitute 'SOCA'.

96 (1) Section 320 (appeals) is amended as follows.

(2) In subsection (1) for 'the Director' substitute 'SOCA'.

(3) In subsection (2)—

   (a) for 'the Director' substitute 'SOCA'; and

   (b) for 'his' substitute 'its'.

97 (1) Section 321 (Director's functions: transfers of value) is amended as follows.

(2) In the heading for 'Director's' substitute 'SOCA's'.

(3) In subsection (1)—

   (a) for 'the Director' substitute 'SOCA'; and

   (b) in paragraph (b) for 'it' substitute 'the transfer of value'.

(4) In subsection (2) for 'the Director', in both places where it appears, substitute 'SOCA'.

(5) In subsection (3) for 'the Director' substitute 'SOCA'.

(6) In subsection (4) for 'The Director' substitute 'SOCA'.

(7) In subsection (5) for 'the Director' substitute 'SOCA'.

(8) In subsection (6) for 'the Director' substitute 'SOCA'.

98 (1) Section 322 (Director's functions: certain settlements) is amended as follows.

(2) In the heading for 'Director's' substitute 'SOCA's'.

(3) In subsection (1) for 'the Director' substitute 'SOCA'.

(4) In subsection (2)—

   (a) for 'the Director', in both places where it appears, substitute 'SOCA'; and

   (b) in paragraph (c) for 'he' substitute 'SOCA'.

(5) In subsection (3) for 'the Director' substitute 'SOCA'.

(6) In subsection (4) for 'The Director' substitute 'SOCA'.

(7) In subsection (5) for 'the Director' substitute 'SOCA'.

(8) In subsection (6) for 'the Director' substitute 'SOCA'.

99 (1) Section 324 (exercise of Revenue functions) is amended as follows.

(2) In subsection (1) for 'the Director' substitute 'SOCA'.

(3) In subsection (2) for 'Paragraph (b) of section 1(6)' substitute 'Section 2B(2)'.

(4) In subsection (3) for 'The Director' substitute 'SOCA'.

(5) In subsection (4) for 'The Director' substitute 'SOCA'.

(6) In subsection (5)—

    (a) for 'The Director' substitute 'SOCA'; and

    (b) for 'they' substitute 'the Board'.

100 (1) Section 325 (declarations) is amended as follows.

    (2) Omit subsection (1).

    (3) For subsection (2) substitute—

        '(2) Every member of SOCA's staff who is assigned to carry out any of SOCA's functions under this Part must, as soon as practicable after being so assigned, make a declaration in the form set out in Schedule 8 before a person nominated by the Director General of SOCA for the purpose.'

101 (1) Schedule 8 (forms of declarations) is amended as follows.

    (2) Omit the words from 'The Director', where it first appears, to 'by law.', where it first appears.

    (3) For 'The Staff Of The Agency' substitute 'SOCA's Staff'.

    (4) For 'authorised by the Director of the Assets Recovery Agency' substitute 'assigned by SOCA'.

    (5) For 'to the Director' substitute 'to SOCA'.

    (6) For 'his' substitute 'its'.

102 The Secretary of State may by order—

    (a) repeal Part 6 of the Proceeds of Crime Act 2002 (c. 29); and

    (b) make such amendment, repeal or revocation of any provision made by or under any enactment (including this Schedule to this Act) as appears to the Secretary of State to be appropriate in consequence of the repeal of Part 6 of the Act of 2002.

PART 4

TRANSFER OF INVESTIGATION FUNCTIONS

103 The Proceeds of Crime Act 2002 (c. 29) is amended as follows.

104 In section 351(5) (supplementary)—

    (a) after 'investigator,' where it first appears, insert 'a member of SOCA's staff,'; and

    (b) after 'investigator,' where it appears for the second time, insert 'member of SOCA's staff,'.

105 (1) ection 352 (search and seizure warrants) is amended as follows.

    (2) In subsection (5)(b) for 'named member of the staff of the Agency' substitute 'member of SOCA's staff or of the staff of the relevant Director'.

    (3) After subsection (5) insert—

        '(5A) In this Part "relevant Director"—

            (a) in relation to England and Wales, means the Director of Public Prosecutions, the Director of Revenue and Customs Prosecutions or the Director of the Serious Fraud Office; and

            (b) in relation to Northern Ireland, means the Director of the Serious Fraud Office or the Director of Public Prosecutions for Northern Ireland.'

106 In section 353(10)(b) (requirements where production order not available) for 'the staff of the Agency' substitute 'SOCA's staff or of the staff of the relevant Director'.

107 (1) Section 356 (further provisions: civil recovery) is amended as follows.

(2) Omit subsection (6).

(3) In subsection (11)(a) (as inserted by Schedule 10) for 'the Director' substitute 'an appropriate officer'.

108 (1) Section 357 (disclosure orders) is amended as follows.

(2) In subsection (1) for 'the Director' substitute 'the relevant authority'.

(3) After subsection (2) insert—

'(2A) The relevant authority may only make an application for a disclosure order in relation to a confiscation investigation if the relevant authority is in receipt of a request to do so from an appropriate officer.'

(4) In subsection (3)(a) for 'the Director' substitute 'an appropriate officer'.

(5) In subsection (4)—

(a) for 'the Director', where it first appears, substitute 'an appropriate officer'; and

(b) for 'the Director', where it appears for the second time, substitute 'the appropriate officer'.

(6) In subsection (5) for 'the Director' substitute 'the appropriate officer concerned'.

(7) After subsection (6) insert—

'(7) In this Part "relevant authority" means—

(a) in relation to a confiscation investigation, a prosecutor; and

(b) in relation to a civil recovery investigation, a member of SOCA's staff or the relevant Director.

(8) For the purposes of subsection (7)(a) a prosecutor is—

(a) in relation to a confiscation investigation carried out by a member of SOCA's staff, the relevant Director or any specified person;

(b) in relation to a confiscation investigation carried out by an accredited financial investigator, the Director of Public Prosecutions, the Director of Public Prosecutions for Northern Ireland or any specified person;

(c) in relation to a confiscation investigation carried out by a constable, the Director of Public Prosecutions, the Director of Public Prosecutions for Northern Ireland, the Director of the Serious Fraud Office or any specified person; and

(d) in relation to a confiscation investigation carried out by an officer of Revenue and Customs, the Director of Revenue and Customs Prosecutions, the Director of Public Prosecutions for Northern Ireland or any specified person.

(9) In subsection (8) "specified person" means any person specified, or falling within a description specified, by an order of the Secretary of State.'

109 (1) Section 361 (further provisions) is amended as follows.

(2) In subsection (7) for 'The Director' substitute 'An appropriate officer'.

(3) In subsection (9) for 'the Director' substitute 'an appropriate officer'.

110 (1) Section 362 (supplementary) is amended as follows.

(2) In subsection (3)(a) for 'Director' substitute 'person who applied for the order'.

(3) After subsection (4) insert—

'(4A) If a member of SOCA's staff or a person falling within a description of persons specified by virtue of section 357(9) applies for a disclosure order, an application to discharge or vary the order need not be by the same member of SOCA's staff or (as the case may be) the same person falling within that description.

(4B) References to a person who applied for a disclosure order must be construed accordingly.'

(4) In subsection (5) for '(4)' substitute '(4B)'.

111 (1) Section 369 (supplementary) is amended as follows.

(2) In subsection (5)—

    (a) after 'investigator,' where it first appears, insert 'a member of SOCA's staff,'; and

    (b) after 'investigator,' where it appears for the second time, insert 'member of SOCA's staff,'.

(3) In subsection (7) after 'investigator,' insert 'a member of SOCA's staff,'.

112 In section 375(4) (supplementary)—

    (a) after 'investigator,' where it first appears, insert 'a member of SOCA's staff,'; and

    (b) after 'investigator,' where it appears for the second time, insert 'member of SOCA's staff,'.

113 Omit section 376 (evidence overseas).

114 (1) Section 377 (code of practice) is amended as follows.

(2) In the heading after 'practice' insert 'of Secretary of State etc.'

(3) In subsection (1)—

    (a) in paragraph (a) for 'the Director' substitute 'the Director General of SOCA'; and

    (b) in paragraph (b) for 'members of the staff of the Agency' substitute 'other members of SOCA's staff'.

(4) In subsection (9)—

    (a) after 'officer' insert 'or the relevant authority'; and

    (b) for 'he' substitute 'either'.

115 After section 377 (code of practice of Secretary of State etc.) insert—

'377A Code of practice of Attorney General or Advocate General for Northern Ireland

(1) The Attorney General must prepare a code of practice as to—

    (a) the exercise by the Director of Public Prosecutions, the Director of Revenue and Customs Prosecutions and the Director of the Serious Fraud Office of functions they have under this Chapter; and

    (b) the exercise by any other person, who is the relevant authority by virtue of section 357(9) in relation to a confiscation investigation, of functions he has under this Chapter in relation to England and Wales as the relevant authority.

(2) The Advocate General for Northern Ireland must prepare a code of practice as to—

    (a) the exercise by the Director of Public Prosecutions for Northern Ireland of functions he has under this Chapter; and

    (b) the exercise by any other person, who is the relevant authority by virtue of section 357(9) in relation to a confiscation investigation, of functions he has under this Chapter in relation to Northern Ireland as the relevant authority.

(3) After preparing a draft of the code the Attorney General or (as the case may be) the Advocate General for Northern Ireland—

    (a) must publish the draft;

    (b) must consider any representations made to him about the draft;

    (c) may amend the draft accordingly.

(4) After the Attorney General or the Advocate General for Northern Ireland has proceeded under subsection (3) he must lay the code before Parliament.

(5) When the code has been so laid the Attorney General or (as the case may be) the Advocate General for Northern Ireland may bring the code into operation on such day as he may appoint by order.

(6) A person specified in subsection (1)(a) or (b) or (2)(a) or (b) must comply with a code of practice which is in operation under this section in the exercise of any function he has under this Chapter to which the code relates.

(7) If such a person fails to comply with any provision of such a code of practice the person is not by reason only of that failure liable in any criminal or civil proceedings.

(8) But the code of practice is admissible in evidence in such proceedings and a court may take account of any failure to comply with its provisions in determining any question in the proceedings.

(9) The Attorney General or (as the case may be) the Advocate General for Northern Ireland may from time to time revise a code previously brought into operation under this section; and the preceding provisions of this section apply to a revised code as they apply to the code as first prepared.

(10) In this section references to the Advocate General for Northern Ireland are to be read, before the coming into force of section 27(1) of the Justice (Northern Ireland) Act 2002 (c. 26), as references to the Attorney General for Northern Ireland.'

116 (1) Section 378 (officers) is amended as follows.

(2) In subsection (1)(a) for 'the Director' substitute 'a member of SOCA's staff'.

(3) In subsection (2)(a) for 'the Director' substitute 'a senior member of SOCA's staff'.

(4) In subsection (3) for the words from 'the Director', where it first appears, to the end of the subsection substitute '—

  (a) a member of SOCA's staff or the relevant Director is an appropriate officer;

  (b) a senior member of SOCA's staff is a senior appropriate officer.'

(5) In subsection (5) for 'the Serious Organised Crime Agency' substitute 'SOCA'.

(6) Omit subsection (7).

(7) After subsection (7) insert—

  '(8) For the purposes of this Part a senior member of SOCA's staff is—

    (a) the Director General of SOCA; or

    (b) any member of SOCA's staff authorised by the Director General (whether generally or specifically) for this purpose.'

117 In section 416(2) (other interpretative provisions)—

  (a) after the entry for production order insert—

    'relevant authority: section 357(7) to (9)
    relevant Director: section 352(5A)'; and

  (b) at the end insert—

    'senior member of SOCA's staff: section 378(8).'

118 After section 449 (pseudonyms) insert—

'449A Staff of relevant Directors: pseudonyms

(1) This section applies to a member of the staff of the relevant Director if—

  (a) the member is to exercise a function as a member of that staff under, or in relation to, Part 5 or 8; and

  (b) it is necessary or expedient for the purpose of exercising that function for the member of staff to identify himself by name.

(2) The relevant Director may direct that such a member of staff may for that purpose identify himself by means of a pseudonym.

   (3) For the purposes of any proceedings or application under this Act, a certificate signed by the relevant Director which sufficiently identifies the member of staff by reference to the pseudonym is conclusive evidence that that member of staff is authorised to use the pseudonym.

   (4) In any proceedings or application under this Act a member of the staff of the relevant Director in respect of whom a direction under this section is in force must not be asked (and if asked is not required to answer) any question which is likely to reveal his true identity.

   (5) The relevant Director may not delegate the exercise of his functions under this section or otherwise authorise another person to exercise those functions on his behalf.

   (6) In this section "relevant Director" has the meaning given by section 352(5A).'

119 (1) Section 459 (orders and regulations) is amended as follows.

   (2) In subsection (3) after 'instrument' insert '(other than the power of the Advocate General for Northern Ireland to make an order under section 377A(5) which is exercisable by statutory rule for the purposes of the Statutory Rules (Northern Ireland) Order 1979 (S.I. 1979/1573 (N.I.12)))'.

   (3) In subsection (4)(a) after '377(4)' insert, '377A(5)'.

   (4) After subsection (6)(a) insert—

      '(aa) by the Attorney General or the Advocate General for Northern Ireland under section 377A(5) unless a draft of the order has been laid before Parliament and approved by a resolution of each House;'.

   (5) After subsection (7) insert—

      '(8) In this section references to the Advocate General for Northern Ireland are to be read, before the coming into force of section 27(1) of the Justice (Northern Ireland) Act 2002 (c. 26), as references to the Attorney General for Northern Ireland.'

PART 5
TRANSFER OF ACCREDITATION AND TRAINING FUNCTIONS

120 (1) Section 3 of the Proceeds of Crime Act 2002 (c. 29) (accreditation and training) is amended as follows.

   (2) In subsection (1)—

     (a) for 'Director' substitute 'National Policing Improvement Agency'; and

     (b) for 'establish' substitute 'provide'.

   (3) Omit subsection (6).

   (4) In subsection (7) for 'Director' substitute 'National Policing Improvement Agency'.

   (5) Omit subsection (8).

PART 6
OTHER AMENDMENTS TO 2002 ACT

121 The Proceeds of Crime Act 2002 is amended as follows.

122 In the heading for Part 1 for 'Assets Recovery Agency' substitute 'Introductory'.

123 Omit sections 1 and 2 (the Assets Recovery Agency, its Director and the Director's general functions).

124 After section 2 insert—

'2A Contribution to the reduction of crime

(1) A relevant authority must exercise its functions under this Act in the way which it considers is best calculated to contribute to the reduction of crime.

(2) In this section "a relevant authority" means—

    (a) SOCA,

    (b) the Director of Public Prosecutions,

    (c) the Director of Public Prosecutions for Northern Ireland,

    (d) the Director of Revenue and Customs Prosecutions, or

    (e) the Director of the Serious Fraud Office.

(3) In considering under subsection (1) the way which is best calculated to contribute to the reduction of crime a relevant authority must have regard to any guidance given to it by—

    (a) in the case of SOCA, the Secretary of State,

    (b) in the case of the Director of Public Prosecutions, the Director of Revenue and Customs Prosecutions or the Director of the Serious Fraud Office, the Attorney General, and

    (c) in the case of the Director of Public Prosecutions for Northern Ireland, the Advocate General for Northern Ireland.

(4) The guidance must indicate that the reduction of crime is in general best secured by means of criminal investigations and criminal proceedings.

(5) The reference in this section to the Advocate General for Northern Ireland is to be read, before the coming into force of section 27(1) of the Justice (Northern Ireland) Act 2002 (c. 26), as a reference to the Attorney General for Northern Ireland.

2B SOCA and members of SOCA's staff

(1) For the purposes of this Act SOCA is the Serious Organised Crime Agency.

(2) Anything which SOCA is authorised or required to do under this Act (whether directly or through its staff) may be done by a person providing services under arrangements made by SOCA if the person is authorised by SOCA (whether generally or specifically) for that purpose.

(3) References in this Act to members of SOCA's staff are to be read in accordance with paragraph 8(4) of Schedule 1 to the Serious Organised Crime and Police Act 2005 (c. 15) (employees of SOCA or persons seconded to SOCA to serve as members of its staff).

2C Prosecuting authorities

(1) Anything which the Director of Public Prosecutions is authorised or required to do under, or in relation to, Part 5 or 8 of this Act may be done by a member of his staff if the member of staff is authorised by the Director (generally or specifically) for that purpose.

(2) Anything which the Director of Revenue and Customs Prosecutions or the Director of the Serious Fraud Office is authorised or required to do under, or in relation to, Part 5 or 8 of this Act may be done by a member of his staff if the member of staff is authorised by the Director concerned (generally or specifically) for that purpose.

(3) Anything which a relevant Director or a member of his staff is authorised or required to do under, or in relation to, Part 5 or 8 of this Act may be done by a person providing services under arrangements made by the relevant Director if the person is authorised by the relevant Director (whether generally or specifically) for that purpose.

(4) In this section "relevant Director" means—

(a) the Director of Public Prosecutions,

(b) the Director of Public Prosecutions for Northern Ireland,

(c) the Director of Revenue and Customs Prosecutions, or

(d) the Director of the Serious Fraud Office.'

125 Omit sections 4 and 5 (co-operation and advice and assistance for Secretary of State).

126 In section 330(4)(b) (failure to disclose: regulated sector) for 'the Serious Organised Crime Agency' substitute 'SOCA'.

127 In section 331(4) (failure to disclose: nominated officers in the regulated sector) for 'the Serious Organised Crime Agency' substitute 'SOCA'.

128 In section 332(4) (failure to disclose: other nominated officers) for 'the Serious Organised Crime Agency' substitute 'SOCA'.

129 In section 336(2)(a), (3)(a) and (4)(a) (nominated officer: consent) for 'the Serious Organised Crime Agency' substitute 'SOCA'.

130 In section 340(13) (interpretation: Part 7) for 'the Serious Organised Crime Agency' substitute 'SOCA'.

131 For section 435 (use of information by Director) substitute—

'435 Use of information by certain Directors

(1) Information obtained by or on behalf of the Director in connection with the exercise of any of his functions under, or in relation to, Part 5 or 8 may be used by him in connection with his exercise of any of his other functions (whether under, or in relation to, either Part, another Part of this Act or otherwise).

(2) Information obtained by or on behalf of the Director in connection with the exercise of any of his functions (whether under, or in relation to, this Act or otherwise) which are not functions under, or in relation to, Part 5 or 8 may be used by him in connection with his exercise of any of his functions under, or in relation to, Part 5 or 8.

(3) This section applies to information obtained before the coming into force of the section as well as to information obtained after the coming into force of the section.

(4) In this section "the Director" means—

(a) the Director of Public Prosecutions;

(b) the Director of the Serious Fraud Office; or

(c) the Director of Public Prosecutions for Northern Ireland.'

132 (1) Section 436 (disclosure of information to Director) is amended as follows.

(2) In the heading for 'Director' substitute 'certain Directors'.

(3) In subsection (1)—

(a) for 'this section' substitute 'subsection (10)'; and

(b) after 'functions' insert 'under, or in relation to, Part 5 or 8'.

(4) In subsection (5), omit paragraph (b) and (ga).

(5) After subsection (9) insert—

'(10) In this section "the Director" has the same meaning as in section 435.'

133 (1) Section 437 (further disclosure) is amended as follows.

(2) In subsection (2)(a) after 'functions' insert 'under, or in relation to, Part 5 or 8'.

(3) After subsection (6) insert—

'(7) In this section "the Director" has the same meaning as in section 435.'

134 (1) Section 438 (disclosure of information by Director) is amended as follows.

(2) In the heading for "Director' substitute "certain Directors'.

(3) In subsection (1)—

(a) after 'functions', where it first appears, insert 'under, or in relation to, Part 5 or 8';

(b) in paragraph (c) after 'functions' insert 'under, or in relation to, Part 5 or 8'; and

(c) after paragraph (f) insert—

'(fa) the exercise of any functions of SOCA, another Director or the Director of Revenue and Customs Prosecutions under, or in relation to, Part 5 or 8;'.

(4) Omit subsections (2) to (4).

(5) After subsection (8) insert—

'(8A) This section does not affect a power to disclose which exists apart from this section.

(8B) This section applies to information obtained before the coming into force of subsection (10) as well as to information obtained after the coming into force of that subsection.'

(6) After subsection (9) insert—

'(10) In this section "the Director" has the same meaning as in section 435.'

135 In section 439(5) (disclosure of information to Lord Advocate and to Scottish Ministers)—

(a) in paragraph (b) for 'the Director General of the Serious Organised Crime Agency' substitute 'SOCA but only so far as the information is held by it or on its behalf otherwise than in connection with its functions under this Act'; and

(b) after paragraph (f) insert—

'(fa) the Director of Revenue and Customs Prosecutions;'.

136 In section 441(2) (disclosure of information by Lord Advocate and by Scottish Ministers) for paragraph (f) substitute—

'(fa) the exercise of the functions of the Director of Public Prosecutions, the Director of Revenue and Customs Prosecutions, the Director of the Serious Fraud Office or the Director of Public Prosecutions for Northern Ireland under, or in relation to, Part 5 or 8;'.

137 (1) Section 443 (enforcement in different parts of the United Kingdom) is amended as follows.

(2) In subsection (3)(a) for 'and the Director' substitute, 'SOCA and the relevant Director'.

(3) After subsection (4) insert—

'(5) In this section "relevant Director" has the meaning given by section 352(5A).'

138 In section 444(4)(d) (external requests and orders) for 'the Director' substitute 'SOCA'.

139 In section 445(2)(b) (external investigations) for the words from 'the Director', where it first appears, to 'Agency' substitute 'SOCA, the Director of Public Prosecutions, the Director of Public Prosecutions for Northern Ireland, the Director of Revenue and Customs Prosecutions'.

140 (1) Section 449 (agency staff: pseudonyms) is amended as follows.

(2) In the heading for 'Agency' substitute 'SOCA's'.

(3) In subsection (1)—
   (a) for 'the staff of the Agency', in both places where it appears, substitute 'SOCA's staff'; and
   (b) for 'authorised (generally or specifically) by the Director' substitute 'assigned by SOCA'.

(4) In subsection (2)—
   (a) for 'The Director' substitute 'An authorised person'; and
   (b) for 'the staff of the Agency' substitute 'SOCA's staff'.

(5) In subsection (3)—
   (a) for 'the Director' substitute 'an authorised person'; and
   (b) for 'the staff of the Agency', in both places where it appears, substitute 'SOCA's staff'.

(6) In subsection (4) for 'the staff of the Agency' substitute 'SOCA's staff'.

(7) Omit subsection (5).

(8) After subsection (5) insert—

'(6) In this section "authorised person" means a member of SOCA's staff authorised by SOCA for the purposes of this section.'

141 After section 460(2) (finance) insert—

'(3) Subject to anything in this Act—
   (a) any sums received by the Director of Public Prosecutions, the Director of Revenue and Customs Prosecutions or the Director of the Serious Fraud Office in consequence of this Act are to be paid into the Consolidated Fund; and
   (b) any sums received by the Director of Public Prosecutions for Northern Ireland in consequence of this Act are to be paid to the Secretary of State.'

142 Omit Schedule 1 (the Assets Recovery Agency).

PART 7
AMENDMENTS TO OTHER ENACTMENTS

Parliamentary Commissioner Act 1967 (c. 13)

143 (1) Schedule 2 to the Parliamentary Commissioner Act 1967 (departments etc. subject to investigation) is amended as follows.

(2) Omit the entry for 'The Director of the Assets Recovery Agency.'.

(3) After the entry for 'Sentencing Guidelines Council' insert 'The Serious Organised Crime Agency.'.

(4) Omit the paragraph in the Notes headed 'Assets Recovery Agency'.

(5) After the paragraph in the Notes headed 'Ministry of Justice' insert—

'Serious Organised Crime Agency
In the case of the Serious Organised Crime Agency, an investigation may be conducted only in respect of the exercise of functions vested in it by virtue of a notice served on the Commissioners for Her Majesty's Revenue and Customs under section 317(2), 321(2) or 322(2) of the Proceeds of Crime Act 2002 (c. 29) (Revenue functions).'

Criminal Appeal Act 1968 (c. 19)

144 In section 33 of the Criminal Appeal Act 1968 (right of appeal to House of Lords) omit subsection (1A).
145 In section 51(1A) of that Act (interpretation) omit, 'subject to section 33(1A) of this Act,'.

Criminal Appeal (Northern Ireland) Act 1980 (c. 47)

146 (1) Section 31 of the Criminal Appeal (Northern Ireland) Act 1980 (right of appeal to House of Lords) is amended as follows.
     (2) Omit subsection (1A).
     (3) In subsection (3) omit, 'subject to subsection (1A) above,'.

Limitation Act 1980 (c. 58)

147 (1) Section 27A of the Limitation Act 1980 (actions for recovery of property obtained through unlawful conduct etc.) is amended as follows.
     (2) In subsection (2) for 'Director's' substitute 'relevant person's'.
     (3) In subsection (4) for 'Director's' substitute 'relevant person's'.
     (4) After subsection (7) insert—

         '(8) In this section "relevant person" means—
               (a) the Serious Organised Crime Agency,
               (b) the Director of Public Prosecutions,
               (c) the Director of Revenue and Customs Prosecutions, or
               (d) the Director of the Serious Fraud Office.'

Legal Aid, Advice and Assistance (Northern Ireland) Order 1981 (S.I. 1981/228 (N.I.8))

148 (1) Paragraph 2A of Part 1 of Schedule 1 to the Legal Aid, Advice and Assistance (Northern Ireland) Order 1981 (Crown Court proceedings under the Proceeds of Crime Act 2002 (c. 29)) for which legal aid may be given under Part 2 of the Order) is amended as follows.
     (2) In sub-paragraph (1)(a) omit 'or 204(3)'.
     (3) In sub-paragraph (1)(c) for 'to 201' substitute 'to 199'.

Prosecution of Offences Act 1985 (c. 23)

149 In section 3(2) of the Prosecution of Offences Act 1985 (functions of the Director of Public Prosecutions), after paragraph (fe), insert—

     '(ff) to discharge such duties as are conferred on him by, or in relation to, Part 5 or 8 of the Proceeds of Crime Act 2002 (c. 29) (civil recovery of the proceeds etc. of unlawful conduct, civil recovery investigations and disclosure orders in relation to confiscation investigations);'.

Bankruptcy (Scotland) Act 1985 (c. 66)

150 In section 31A(1)(b) of the Bankruptcy (Scotland) Act 1985 (property subject to restraint order)—
    (a) omit '52,'; and
    (b) for, '198 or 200' substitute 'or 198'.

Insolvency Act 1986 (c. 45)

151 In section 306A(1)(b) of the Insolvency Act 1986 (property subject to restraint order)—
    (a) omit '52,'; and
    (b) for, '198 or 200' substitute 'or 198'.

Criminal Justice Act 1987 (c. 38)

152 After section 1(6) of the Criminal Justice Act 1987 (functions of the Director of the Serious Fraud Office) insert—

   '(6A) The Director has the functions conferred on him by, or in relation to, Part 5 or 8 of the Proceeds of Crime Act 2002 (c. 29) (civil recovery of the proceeds etc. of unlawful conduct, civil recovery investigations and disclosure orders in relation to confiscation investigations).'

Limitation (Northern Ireland) Order 1989 (SI 1989/1339 (N.I.11))

153 (1) Article 72A of the Limitation (Northern Ireland) Order 1989 (actions for recovery of property obtained through unlawful conduct etc.) is amended as follows.
    (2) In paragraph (2) for 'Director's' substitute 'relevant person's'.
    (3) In paragraph (4) for 'Director's' substitute 'relevant person's'.
    (4) After paragraph (7) insert—

       '(8) In this Article "relevant person" means—
           (a) the Serious Organised Crime Agency,
           (b) the Director of the Serious Fraud Office, or
           (c) the Director of Public Prosecutions for Northern Ireland.'

Insolvency (Northern Ireland) Order 1989 (SI 1989/2405 (N.I.19))

154 In Article 279A(1)(b) of the Insolvency (Northern Ireland) Order 1989 (property subject to restraint order)—
    (a) omit '52,'; and
    (b) for, '198 or 200' substitute 'or 198'.

Police Act 1996 (c. 16)

155 (1) Section 97 of the Police Act 1996 (police officers engaged on service outside their force) is amended as follows.
    (2) In subsection (1) omit paragraph (ce).
    (3) In subsection (6)(a) omit '(ce),'.
    (4) In subsection (8) omit '(ce),'.

Police (Northern Ireland) Act 1998 (c. 32)

156 (1) Section 27 of the Police (Northern Ireland) Act 1998 (members of the Police Service of Northern Ireland engaged on other police service) is amended as follows.

(2) In subsection (1) omit paragraph (ca).

(3) In subsection (5)(b) omit '(ca),'.

(4) In subsection (7) omit '(ca),'.

157 After section 60ZA(6) of that Act (SOCA) insert—

'(7) An agreement or order under this section must not provide for procedures in relation to so much of any complaint or matter as relates to any functions of the Agency mentioned in section 2A of the Serious Organised Crime and Police Act 2005 (c. 15) (functions as tothe recovery of assets).'

Northern Ireland Act 1998 (c. 47)

158 (1) In section 75(4A) of the Northern Ireland Act 1998 (statutory duty on public authorities) after 'offences' insert 'or any of the functions conferred on him by, or in relation to, Part 5 or 8 of the Proceeds of Crime Act 2002 (c. 29) (civil recovery of the proceeds etc. of unlawful conduct, civil recovery investigations and disclosure orders in relation to confiscation investigations)'.

(2) After section 76(10) of that Act (discrimination by public authorities) insert—

'(11) The reference in subsection (1) to the functions of the Director of Public Prosecutions for Northern Ireland does not include any of the functions conferred on him by, or in relation to, Part 5 or 8 of the Proceeds of Crime Act 2002 (c. 29) (civil recovery of the proceeds etc. of unlawful conduct, civil recovery investigations and disclosure orders in relation to confiscation investigations).'

Access to Justice Act 1999 (c. 22)

159 (1) Paragraph 3 of Schedule 2 to the Access to Justice Act 1999 (advocacy in Crown Court proceedings under the Proceeds of Crime Act 2002 (c. 29) which may be funded as part of the Community Legal Service) is amended as follows.

(2) In sub-paragraph (1)(b) omit 'or 56(3)'.

(3) In sub-paragraph (1)(d) for 'to 53' substitute 'to 51'.

Police Reform Act 2002 (c. 30)

160 After section 10(8) of the Police Reform Act 2002 (general functions of the Independent Police Complaints Commission) insert—

'(9) Nothing in this Part shall confer any function on the Commission in relation to so much of any complaint, conduct matter or DSI matter as relates to—

(a) any functions of the Serious Organised Crime Agency mentioned in section 2A of the Serious Organised Crime and Police Act 2005 (c. 15) (functions as to the recovery of assets); or

(b) the functions of the National Policing Improvement Agency under section 3 of the Proceeds of Crime Act 2002 (c. 29) (accreditation and training of financial investigators).'

161 After section 26A(4) of that Act (SOCA) insert—

'(4A) An agreement under this section must not provide for procedures in relation to so much of any complaint, conduct matter or DSI matter as relates to any functions of the Agency mentioned in section 2A of the Serious Organised Crime and Police Act 2005 (c. 15) (functions as to the recovery of assets).'

162 After section 26B(4) of that Act (National Policing Improvement Agency) insert—

'(4A) An agreement under this section must not provide for procedures in relation to so much of any complaint, conduct matter or DSI matter as relates to the functions of the Agency under section 3 of the Proceeds of Crime Act 2002 (c. 29) (accreditation and training of financial investigators).'

Access to Justice (Northern Ireland) Order 2003 (S.I. 2003/435 (N.I.10))

163 (1) Paragraph 3 of Schedule 2 to the Access to Justice (Northern Ireland) Order 2003 (representation in Crown Court proceedings under the Proceeds of Crime Act 2002 (c. 29) which may be funded by the Northern Ireland Legal Services Commission) is amended as follows.

(2) In sub-paragraph (1)(a) omit 'or 204(3)'.

(3) In sub-paragraph (1)(c) for 'to 201' substitute 'to 199'.

Commissioners for Revenue and Customs Act 2005 (c. 11)

164 In section 21(1)(b) of the Commissioners for Revenue and Customs Act 2005 (disclosure to prosecuting authority)—

(a) omit 'or' at the end of sub-paragraph (i); and

(b) after sub-paragraph (ii) insert, 'or

'(iii) in the case of the Director of Revenue and Customs Prosecutions, to exercise his functions under, or in relation to, Part 5 or 8 of the Proceeds of Crime Act 2002 (c. 29).'

165 After section 35(4) of that Act (functions of the Director of Revenue and Customs Prosecutions) insert—

'(4A) The Director has the functions conferred on him by, or in relation to, Part 5 or 8 of the Proceeds of Crime Act 2002 (c. 29) (civil recovery of the proceeds etc. of unlawful conduct, civil recovery investigations and disclosure orders in relation to confiscation investigations).'

166 In section 37(1) of that Act (prosecutors) after 'section 35' insert '(excluding any function mentioned in subsection (4A) of that section)'.

167 (1) Section 40 of that Act (confidentiality) is amended as follows.

(2) In subsection (2) (exceptions to confidentiality restrictions), after paragraph (c), insert—

'(ca) does not apply to a disclosure made for the purposes of—

(i) the exercise of any functions of the prosecutor under Parts 2, 3 and 4 of the Proceeds of Crime Act 2002 (c. 29),

(ii) the exercise of any functions of the Serious Organised Crime Agency under that Act,

(iii) the exercise of any functions of the Director of Public Prosecutions, the Director of the Serious Fraud Office, the Director of Public

Prosecutions for Northern Ireland or the Scottish Ministers under, or in relation to, Part 5 or 8 of that Act,

   (iv) the exercise of any functions of an officer of Revenue and Customs or a constable under Chapter 3 of Part 5 of that Act, or

   (v) investigations or proceedings outside the United Kingdom which have led or may lead to the making of an external order within the meaning of section 447 of that Act,

  (cb) does not apply to a disclosure of information obtained in the exercise of functions under the Proceeds of Crime Act 2002 (c. 29) if the disclosure is made for the purposes of the exercise of a function which the Secretary of State thinks is a public function and which he designates by order,'.

(3) After subsection (10) insert—

  '(10A) An order under subsection (2)(cb)—

    (a) may include transitional or incidental provision,

    (b) shall be made by statutory instrument, and

    (c) shall not be made unless a draft has been laid before, and approved by a resolution of, each House of Parliament.'

168 In section 41(1) of that Act (disclosure of information to Director of Revenue and Customs Prosecutions) after 'prosecution' insert 'or for the purpose of the exercise by the Director of his functions under the Proceeds of Crime Act 2002 (c. 29)'.

Serious Organised Crime and Police Act 2005 (c. 15)

169 After section 2 of the Serious Organised Crime and Police Act 2005 (functions of SOCA as to serious organised crime) insert—

'2A Functions of SOCA as to the recovery of assets
SOCA has the functions conferred on it (whether directly or through its staff) by the Proceeds of Crime Act 2002 (c. 29) (functions relating to the recovery of assets).'

170 (1) Section 5 of that Act (SOCA's general powers) is amended as follows.

    (2) In subsection (2)(d) after 'or 3' insert 'or mentioned in section 2A,'.

    (3) In subsection (3) after '3' insert 'or mentioned in section 2A'.

    (4) In subsection (4) after 'section' insert '2A or'.

171 After section 19(4) of that Act (charges by SOCA and other receipts) insert—

  '(4A) Subsection (3) is subject to any provision made by the Proceeds of Crime Act 2002 (c. 29).'

172 (1) Section 33 (disclosure of information by SOCA) of that Act is amended as follows.

    (2) In subsection (2) after paragraph (c) insert—

  '(ca) the exercise of any function of SOCA mentioned in section 2A (functions relating to the recovery of assets);

  (cb) the exercise of any functions of the prosecutor under Parts 2, 3 and 4 of the Proceeds of Crime Act 2002 (c. 29);

  (cc) the exercise of any functions of the Director of Public Prosecutions, the Director of Revenue and Customs Prosecutions, the Director of the Serious Fraud Office, the Director of Public Prosecutions for Northern Ireland or the Scottish Ministers under, or in relation to, Part 5 or 8 of that Act;

(cd) the exercise of any functions of an officer of Revenue and Customs or a constable under Chapter 3 of Part 5 of that Act;

(ce) investigations or proceedings outside the United Kingdom which have led or may lead to the making of an external order within the meaning of section 447 of that Act;'.

(3) After subsection (2) insert—

'(2A) Subsections (1) and (2) do not apply to information obtained by SOCA in connection with the exercise of its functions under Part 6 of the Proceeds of Crime Act 2002 (c. 29) (Revenue functions).

(2B) But such information may be disclosed by SOCA—

(a) to the Commissioners;

(b) to the Lord Advocate for the purpose of the exercise by the Lord Advocate of his functions under Part 3 of that Act (confiscation: Scotland).

(2C) Information disclosed to the Lord Advocate under subsection (2B)(b) may be further disclosed by him only to the Scottish Ministers for the purpose of the exercise by them of their functions under Part 5 of that Act (civil recovery of the proceeds etc. of unlawful conduct).

(2D) Subsections (1) and (2), so far as relating to disclosure for the purposes of the exercise of any functions of the Lord Advocate under Part 3 of the Proceeds of Crime Act 2002 (c. 29) or of the Scottish Ministers under, or in relation to, Part 5 of that Act, do not apply to information obtained by SOCA in connection with the exercise of any of its functions other than its functions under that Act.'

173 After section 35(1) of that Act (restrictions on further disclosure) insert—

'(1A) Subsection (1) does not apply to—

(a) information disclosed by SOCA under section 33 to the Lord Advocate for the purpose of the exercise of any of his functions under Part 3 of the Proceeds of Crime Act 2002; or

(b) information disclosed by SOCA under section 33 to the Scottish Ministers for the purposes of the exercise of any of their functions under, or in relation to, Part 5 of that Act;

but see instead section 441 of the Proceeds of Crime Act 2002.'

174 In paragraph 8 of Schedule 1 to that Act (SOCA's staff) after sub-paragraph (1), insert—

'(1A) SOCA must appoint one of its employees as a person with responsibilities in relation to the exercise of SOCA's functions in Northern Ireland under the Proceeds of Crime Act 2002 (c. 29).'

175 In paragraph 21(1) and (2) of Schedule 5 to that Act (persons specified for the purposes of protection) omit 'is or'.

Gambling Act 2005 (c. 19)

176 In Part 2 of Schedule 6 to the Gambling Act 2005 (exchange of information: enforcement and regulatory bodies)—

(a) omit the entries relating to the Director and staff of the Assets Recovery Agency, the Director General and staff of the National Crime Squad and the Director General and staff of the National Criminal Intelligence Service; and

(b) after the entry for the Serious Fraud Office insert—

'The Serious Organised Crime Agency'.

Police and Justice Act 2006 (c. 48)

177 (1) Schedule 1 to the Police and Justice Act 2006 (National Policing Improvement Agency) is amended as follows.

(2) In paragraph 1 (the objects of the Agency)—

(a) after paragraph (e), insert—

'(ea) the carrying out of its functions under section 3 of the Proceeds of Crime Act 2002 (c. 29) (accreditation and training of financial investigators);'; and

(b) in paragraph (f) for '(e)' substitute '(ea)'.

(3) After paragraph 4(5) (consultation: Scotland or Northern Ireland) insert—

'(6) This paragraph does not apply to any exercise of the Agency's power under paragraph 2(1) which is for the purposes of attaining the object mentioned in paragraph 1(ea) (accreditation and training of financial investigators).'

(4) After paragraph 6(4) (strategic priorities) insert—

'(4A) Before determining strategic priorities for the Agency in relation to its functions under section 3 of the Proceeds of Crime Act 2002 (c. 29) (accreditation and training of financial investigators), the Secretary of State must (in addition to those required above) consult such other persons as the Secretary of State considers appropriate.'

(5) In paragraph 35 (payments by Agency to police authorities) after 'objects' insert '(other than the object mentioned in paragraph 1(ea): accreditation and training of financial investigators)'.

Corporate Manslaughter and Corporate Homicide Act 2007 (c. 19)

178 In Schedule 1 to the Corporate Manslaughter and Corporate Homicide Act 2007 (list of government departments etc.) omit 'Assets Recovery Agency'.

SCHEDULE 9   Section 74(3)

TRANSFERS TO SOCA OR NPIA

Interpretation

1 In this Schedule—

'the Agency' means the Assets Recovery Agency;

'the Director' means the Director of the Assets Recovery Agency;

'NPIA' means the National Policing Improvement Agency; and

'transfer scheme' means a scheme made by the Secretary of State under this Schedule.

Director and staff of Agency

2 (1) A transfer scheme may provide for a person who is the Director or a member of staff of the Agency to become an employee of SOCA or NPIA.

(2) If the person had a contract of employment before becoming an employee of SOCA or NPIA, the scheme may provide for that contract to have effect (subject to any

304

necessary modifications) as if originally made between him and SOCA or (as the case may be) NPIA.

(3) If the person did not have a contract of employment, the scheme may provide for the terms and conditions of his appointment or service to have effect (subject to any necessary modifications) as the terms and conditions of his contract of employment with SOCA or (as the case may be) NPIA.

3 (1) A transfer scheme may provide—
(a) for any secondment by virtue of which a person serves as the Director or a member of staff of the Agency to have effect as a secondment to SOCA or NPIA; and
(b) for him to serve as a member of the staff of SOCA or (as the case may be) NPIA.

(2) The scheme may make provision as to the terms and conditions which are to have effect as the terms and conditions of his secondment to SOCA or (as the case may be) NPIA.

4 (1) A transfer scheme may provide—
(a) for the transfer to SOCA or (as the case may be) NPIA of the rights, powers, duties and liabilities of the employer under or in connection with the contract of employment of a person who becomes a member of the staff of SOCA or NPIA by virtue of the scheme;
(b) for anything done before that transfer by, or in relation to, the employer in respect of such a contract or the employee to be treated as having been done by, or in relation to, SOCA or (as the case may be) NPIA.

(2) Sub-paragraph (1) applies with the necessary modifications in relation to a person who before becoming a member of the staff of SOCA or NPIA—
(a) did not have a contract of employment; or
(b) held an appointment by virtue of a secondment.

(3) A transfer scheme may make provision for periods before a person became an employee of SOCA or NPIA to count as periods of employment with SOCA or (as the case may be) NPIA (and for the operation of the scheme not to be treated as having interrupted the continuity of that employment).

5 (1) A transfer scheme may provide for a person who—
(a) is the Director or a member of staff of the Agency; and
(b) would otherwise become a member of the staff of SOCA or NPIA by the operation of the scheme; not to become a member of the staff of SOCA or (as the case may be) NPIA if he gives notice objecting to the operation of the scheme in relation to him.

(2) A transfer scheme may provide for any person who would be treated (whether by an enactment or otherwise) as being dismissed by the operation of the scheme not to be so treated.

6 (1) A transfer scheme may provide for the termination of an appointment as the Director or a member of staff of the Agency.

(2) The Secretary of State may make a payment of such amount (if any) as he may determine to the person who held the appointment.

Property, rights and liabilities etc.

7 (1) A transfer scheme may provide for the transfer to SOCA or NPIA of property, rights and liabilities of the Director or the Agency.

(2) The scheme may create rights, or impose liabilities, in relation to property, rights and liabilities transferred by virtue of the scheme.

(3) The scheme may provide for things done by or in relation to persons to whom sub-paragraph (4) applies to be—

    (a) treated as done by or in relation to SOCA or members of the staff of SOCA or (as the case may be) NPIA or members of the staff of NPIA;

    (b) continued by or in relation to SOCA or members of the staff of SOCA or (as the case may be) NPIA or members of the staff of NPIA.

(4) This sub-paragraph applies to—

    (a) the Director;

    (b) members of staff of the Agency.

(5) The scheme may, in particular, make provision about the continuation of legal proceedings.

8 A transfer scheme may provide for SOCA or NPIA to make any payment which—

    (a) before a day specified in the scheme could have been made by the Director or a member of staff of the Agency; but

    (b) is not a liability which can be transferred by virtue of paragraph 7.

Supplementary

9 (1) A transfer scheme may contain—

    (a) further provision in connection with any of the matters to which paragraphs 2 to 8 relate;

    (b) the provision mentioned in sub-paragraph (3).

(2) The provision which may be made under sub-paragraph (1)(a) includes provision as to the consequences of the termination of a person's appointment or employment by or by virtue of the scheme.

(3) The provision mentioned in this sub-paragraph is provision—

    (a) for the Secretary of State, or any other person nominated by or in accordance with the scheme, to determine any matter requiring determination under or in consequence of the scheme; and

    (b) as to the payment of fees charged, or expenses incurred, by any person nominated to determine any matter by virtue of paragraph (a).

10 Before making a transfer scheme which contains any provision relating to the Director or the members of staff of the Agency, the Secretary of State must consult such bodies appearing to represent the interests of the persons concerned as he considers appropriate.

11 A transfer scheme is not an order of the Secretary of State for the purposes of section 89.

SCHEDULE 10   Section 77

DETAINED CASH INVESTIGATIONS: FURTHER PROVISION

Amendments to the Proceeds of Crime Act 2002

1 The Proceeds of Crime Act 2002 (c. 29) (investigations) is amended as follows.

2 In section 342(1) (offences of prejudicing investigation) after 'a civil recovery investigation' insert, 'a detained cash investigation'.

3 In section 343(3) (judges) after 'a civil recovery investigation' insert 'or a detained cash investigation'.

4 In section 344(b) (courts) after 'a civil recovery investigation' insert 'or a detained cash investigation'.

5 In section 350(5)(b) (government departments) after 'a civil recovery investigation' insert 'or a detained cash investigation'.

6 In section 351(8) (supplementary) after 'a civil recovery investigation' insert 'or a detained cash investigation'.

7 (1) Section 352 (search and seizure warrants) is amended as follows.
   (2) In subsection (3)(c) after '(7)' insert, '(7A), (7B)'.
   (3) After subsection (5)(b) insert—

   '(c) a constable or an officer of Revenue and Customs, if the warrant is sought for the purposes of a detained cash investigation.'

8 (1) Section 353 (requirements where production order not available) is amended as follows.
   (2) In subsection (5)(a) after '(7)' insert, '(7A), (7B)'.
   (3) After subsection (10)(b) insert—

   '(c) a constable or an officer of Revenue and Customs, if the warrant is sought for the purposes of a detained cash investigation.'

9 (1) Section 356 (further provisions: civil recovery) is amended as follows.
   (2) In the heading after 'civil recovery' insert 'and detained cash'.
   (3) In subsection (1) after 'civil recovery investigations' insert 'or detained cash investigations'.
   (4) In subsection (6) after 'If' insert, 'in the case of civil recovery investigations,'.
   (5) In subsection (10) for the words from 'if' to 'reasonable' substitute 'if the appropriate person has reasonable'.
   (6) After subsection (10) insert—

   '(11) The appropriate person is—
      (a) the Director, if the warrant was issued for the purposes of a civil recovery investigation;
      (b) a constable or an officer of Revenue and Customs, if the warrant was issued for the purposes of a detained cash investigation.'

10 In section 357(2) (investigations to which disclosure orders do not apply) after 'to a' insert 'detained cash investigation or a'.

11 In section 363 (customer information orders) after subsection (1) insert—

   '(1A) No application for a customer information order may be made in relation to a detained cash investigation.'

12 In section 370 (account monitoring orders) after subsection (1) insert—

   '(1A) No application for an account monitoring order may be made in relation to a detained cash investigation.'

13 In section 378 (officers) after subsection (3) insert—

   '(3A) In relation to a detained cash investigation these are appropriate officers—
      (a) a constable;
      (b) an officer of Revenue and Customs.'

14 In section 380(2) (sheriff in Scotland to act in exercise of civil jurisdiction in making production orders in certain cases) after 'a civil recovery investigation' insert 'or a detained cash investigation'.

15 In section 385(4)(b) (government departments: Scotland) after 'a civil recovery investigation' insert 'or a detained cash investigation'.

16 In section 386(3)(b) (rules of court in connection with production orders and orders to grant entry: Scotland) after 'a civil recovery investigation' insert 'or a detained cash investigation'.

17 In section 387(2) (sheriff in Scotland to act in exercise of civil jurisdiction in issuing search warrants in certain cases) after 'a civil recovery investigation' insert 'or a detained cash investigation'.

18 In section 388(5)(a) (requirements where production order not available: Scotland) after '(7)' insert, '(7A), (7B)'.

19 (1) Section 390 (further provisions: confiscation, civil recovery and money laundering: Scotland) is amended as follows.

    (2) In the heading after 'civil recovery' insert, 'detained cash'.

    (3) In subsection (1) after 'civil recovery investigations' insert, 'detained cash investigations'.

    (4) In subsection (5) after 'a civil recovery investigation' insert 'or a detained cash investigation'.

    (5) In subsection (6) after 'a civil recovery investigation' insert 'or a detained cash investigation'.

    (6) In subsection (7) after 'a civil recovery investigation' insert 'or a detained cash investigation'.

20 In section 391(2) (investigations to which disclosure orders do not apply: Scotland) after 'to a' insert 'detained cash investigation or a'.

21 In section 397 (customer information orders: Scotland) after subsection (1) insert—

    '(1A) No application for a customer information order may be made in relation to a detained cash investigation.'

22 In section 404 (account monitoring orders: Scotland) after subsection (1) insert—

    '(1A) No application for an account monitoring order may be made in relation to a detained cash investigation.'

23 (1) Section 412 (interpretation: Scotland) is amended as follows.

    (2) In the definition of 'appropriate person', in paragraph (b), after 'a civil recovery investigation' insert 'or a detained cash investigation'.

    (3) In the definition of 'proper person', in paragraph (b), after 'a civil recovery investigation' insert 'or a detained cash investigation'.

24 (1) Section 416 (other interpretative provisions) is amended as follows.

    (2) In subsection (1) after 'confiscation investigation: section 341(1)' insert— 'detained cash investigation: section 341(3A)'.

    (3) After subsection (7) insert—

        '(7A) "Unlawful conduct" has the meaning given by section 241.'

25 In section 450(1)(a) (pseudonyms: Scotland) after 'a civil recovery investigation' insert 'or a detained cash investigation'.

Other amendments

26 In section 18(2)(f) of the Civil Jurisdiction and Judgments Act 1982 (c. 27)—

    (a) after 'a civil recovery investigation' insert 'or a detained cash investigation'; and

    (b) for 'meaning' substitute 'meanings'.

27 In section 64(3)(aa) of the Criminal Justice and Police Act 2001 (c. 16) after 'a civil recovery investigation' insert 'or a detained cash investigation'.

28 In Schedule 2 to the Commissioners for Revenue and Customs Act 2005 (c. 11) (functions of Commissioners and officers: restrictions etc.), after paragraph 13, insert—

'13A The powers conferred on an officer of Revenue and Customs by virtue of section 352(5)(c), 353(10)(c), 356(11)(b) or 378(3A)(b) of the Act of 2002 (powers in relation to search and seizure warrants and production orders) are exercisable only in relation to cash seized in accordance with paragraph 13 above by an officer of Revenue and Customs under section 294 of that Act.'

SCHEDULE 11   Section 79
POWERS TO RECOVER CASH: FINANCIAL INVESTIGATORS

Amendments to Chapter 3 of Part 5 of 2002 Act

1 Chapter 3 of Part 5 of the Proceeds of Crime Act 2002 (c. 29) (recovery of cash in summary proceedings) is amended in accordance with paragraphs 2 to 13.

2 (1) Section 289 (powers to search for cash) is amended as follows.

   (2) In subsection (1)—

      (a) for 'or constable who' substitute, 'a constable or an accredited financial investigator'; and

      (b) after 'premises', where it first appears, insert 'and'.

   (3) In subsection (2) for 'or constable' substitute, 'a constable or an accredited financial investigator'.

   (4) In subsections (3) and (4) for 'or constable' substitute, 'constable or accredited financial investigator'.

   (5) In subsection (5), after paragraph (b), insert—

      '(c) are exercisable by an accredited financial investigator only in relation to premises or (as the case may be) suspects in England, Wales or Northern Ireland.'

3 (1) Section 290 (prior approval by senior officer) is amended as follows.

   (2) In subsection (4), after paragraph (b), insert—

      '(c) in relation to the exercise of the power by an accredited financial investigator, an accredited financial investigator who falls within a description specified in an order made for this purpose by the Secretary of State under section 453.'

   (3) In subsection (6) for 'or constable' substitute, 'constable or accredited financial investigator'.

4 In section 291(2) (report on exercise of powers) for 'or constable' substitute, 'constable or accredited financial investigator'.

5 (1) Section 292 (code of practice) is amended as follows.

   (2) In subsection (1) after 'constables' insert 'and accredited financial investigators'.

   (3) In subsection (6) for 'or constable' substitute, 'a constable or an accredited financial investigator'.

6 (1) Section 294 (seizure of cash) is amended as follows.

(2) In subsections (1) and (2) for 'or constable' substitute, 'a constable or an accredited financial investigator'.

(3) After subsection (3) insert—

'(4) This section does not authorise the seizure by an accredited financial investigator of cash found in Scotland.'

7 (1) Section 295 (detention of seized cash) is amended as follows.

(2) In subsection (1) for 'or constable' substitute, 'constable or accredited financial investigator'.

(3) In subsection (4)(a) for 'or a constable' substitute, 'a constable or an accredited financial investigator'.

8 In section 296(2) (release of part of cash seized) for 'or constable' substitute, 'constable or accredited financial investigator'.

9 In section 297(4) (release of detained cash) after 'constable' insert 'or accredited financial investigator'.

10 In section 298(1)(a) (power to apply for forfeiture) before 'or' insert, 'an accredited financial investigator'.

11 After section 302(7) insert—

'(7A) If the cash was seized by an accredited financial investigator who was not an officer of Revenue and Customs or a constable, the compensation is to be paid as follows—

(a) in the case of an investigator—

(i) who was employed by a police authority in England and Wales under section 15 of the Police Act 1996 (c. 16) and was under the direction and control of the chief officer of police of the police force maintained by the authority, or

(ii) who was a member of staff of the City of London police force,

it is to be paid out of the police fund from which the expenses of the police force are met,

(b) in the case of an investigator who was a member of staff of the Police Service of Northern Ireland, it is to be paid out of money provided by the Chief Constable,

(c) in the case of an investigator who was a member of staff of a department of the Government of the United Kingdom, it is to be paid by the Minister of the Crown in charge of the department or by the department,

(d) in the case of an investigator who was a member of staff of a Northern Ireland department, it is to be paid by the department,

(e) in any other case, it is to be paid by the employer of the investigator.

(7B) The Secretary of State may by order amend subsection (7A).'

12 (1) Section 302A (powers for prosecutors to appear in proceedings) (as inserted by section 84(1) above) is amended as follows.

(2) In subsection (1)—

(a) after 'constable', in the first place where it appears, insert 'or an accredited financial investigator'; and

(b) after 'constable', in the second place where it appears, insert 'or (as the case may be) an accredited financial investigator'.

(3) After subsection (3) insert—

'(4) The references in subsection (1) to an accredited financial investigator do not include an accredited financial investigator who is an officer of Revenue and Customs but the references in subsection (2) to an officer of Revenue and Customs do include an accredited financial investigator who is an officer of Revenue and Customs.'

13 After section 303 insert—

'303A Financial investigators

(1) In this Chapter (apart from this section) any reference in a provision to an accredited financial investigator is a reference to an accredited financial investigator who falls within a description specified in an order made for the purposes of that provision by the Secretary of State under section 453.

(2) Subsection (1) does not apply to the second reference to an accredited financial investigator in section 290(4)(c).

(3) Where an accredited financial investigator of a particular description—
   (a) applies for an order under section 295,
   (b) applies for forfeiture under section 298, or
   (c) brings an appeal under, or relating to, this Chapter,
   any subsequent step in the application or appeal, or any further application or appeal relating to the same matter, may be taken made or brought by a different accredited financial investigator of the same description.'

Other amendments to 2002 Act

14 In section 438(1)(f) of the Proceeds of Crime Act 2002 (c. 29) (disclosure of information by the Director of the Assets Recovery Agency) before 'or' insert, 'an accredited financial investigator'.

15 (1) Section 459 of that Act (orders and regulations) is amended as follows.

(2) In subsection (4)(a) (exceptions to negative procedure) after '292(4),' insert '302(7B),'.

(3) In subsection (6)(a) (powers subject to affirmative procedure) after '292(4),' insert '302(7B),'.

(4) After subsection (6) insert—

'(6A) If a draft of an order under section 302(7B) would, apart from this subsection, be treated as a hybrid instrument for the purposes of the standing orders of either House of Parliament, it shall proceed in that House as if it were not a hybrid instrument.'

Amendments to other enactments

16 In section 40(2)(ca)(iv) of the Commissioners for Revenue and Customs Act 2005 (c. 11) (confidentiality) (as inserted by Schedule 8) after 'Customs' insert, 'an accredited financial investigator'.

17 In section 33(2)(cd) of the Serious Organised Crime and Police Act 2005 (c. 15) (disclosure of information by SOCA) (as inserted by Schedule 8) after 'Customs' insert, 'an accredited financial investigator'.

SCHEDULE 12   Section 88
REVENUE AND CUSTOMS: REGULATION OF INVESTIGATORY POWERS

Police Act 1997 (c. 50)

1 In section 93 of the Police Act 1997 (authorisations to interfere with property, &c.)—
   (a) in subsection (1B) for 'customs officer' substitute 'an officer of Revenue and Customs';
   (b) in subsection (3)(d) for 'a customs officer' substitute 'an officer of Revenue and Customs'; and
   (c) for subsection (5)(h) substitute—

      '(h) an officer of Revenue and Customs who is a senior official within the meaning of the Regulation of Investigatory Powers Act 2000 and who is designated for the purposes of this paragraph by the Commissioners for Her Majesty's Revenue and Customs;'.

2 In section 94(2)(f) of that Act (urgency) for 'by a customs officer designated by the Commissioners of Customs and Excise' substitute 'by an officer of Revenue and Customs who is a senior official within the meaning of the Regulation of Investigatory Powers Act 2000 and who is designated by the Commissioners for Her Majesty's Revenue and Customs'.

3 In section 107(4)(c) of that Act (supplementary) for 'the Commissioners of Customs and Excise.' substitute 'the Commissioners for Her Majesty's Revenue and Customs.'

4 In section 108(1) of that Act (interpretation) omit the definition of 'customs officer'.

Regulation of Investigatory Powers Act 2000 (c. 23)

5 The Regulation of Investigatory Powers Act 2000 is amended as follows.

6 In section 6(2)(h) (application for issue of interception warrant) for 'the Commissioners of Customs and Excise' substitute 'the Commissioners for Her Majesty's Revenue and Customs'.

7 In section 21(5)(c) (acquisition of data, &c.) for 'customs officers).' Substitute 'officers of Revenue and Customs).'

8 In the definition of 'relevant public authority' in section 25(1) (communications data: interpretation) for paragraphs (d) and (e) substitute—

      '(d) Her Majesty's Revenue and Customs;'.

9 In section 27(4)(c) (lawful surveillance, &c.) for 'customs officers).' substitute 'officers of Revenue and Customs).'

10 For section 32(6)(m) (authorisation of intrusive surveillance) substitute—

      '(m) an officer of Revenue and Customs who is a senior official and who is designated for the purposes of this paragraph by the Commissioners for Her Majesty's Revenue and Customs;'.

11 In section 33 (surveillance: authorisation)—
   (a) for subsection (2) substitute—

      '(2) A person who is a designated person for the purposes of section 28 or 29 by reference to office, rank or position in Her Majesty's Revenue and Customs shall not grant an authorisation under that section except on an application made by an officer of Revenue and Customs.';

312

(b) for subsection (4) substitute—

'(4) A person who is a senior authorising officer by virtue of a designation by the Commissioners for Her Majesty's Revenue and Customs shall not grant an authorisation for the carrying out of intrusive surveillance except on an application made by an officer of Revenue and Customs.'; and

(c) in subsection (5)(a) for 'a customs officer' substitute 'an officer of Revenue and Customs';

(and in the italic cross-heading before section 33 for 'customs' substitute 'Revenue and Customs').

12 In section 34 (grant of authorisation in senior officer's absence)—

(a) in subsection (1) for 'a customs officer;' substitute 'an officer of Revenue and Customs;';

(b) in subsection (2)(a) for 'the Commissioners of Customs and Excise,' substitute 'the Commissioners for Her Majesty's Revenue and Customs,'; and

(c) in subsection (4)(l)—

(i) for 'the Commissioners of Customs and Excise,' substitute 'the Commissioners for Her Majesty's Revenue and Customs, and

(ii) after 'if he is' insert 'a senior official'.

13 In section 35 (intrusive surveillance authorisation: notification)—

(a) in subsection (1) for 'customs' substitute 'Revenue and Customs';

(b) in subsection (10) for 'customs' substitute 'Revenue and Customs'; and

(c) in subsection (10)(b) for 'the Commissioners of Customs and Excise,' substitute 'the Commissioners for Her Majesty's Revenue and Customs;'.

14 In section 36 (approval required for authorisation of intrusive surveillance to take effect)—

(a) for subsection (1)(d) substitute—

'(d) an officer of Revenue and Customs;'; and

(b) for subsection (6)(g) substitute—

'(g) where the authorisation was granted by an officer of Revenue and Customs, the officer of Revenue and Customs for the time being designated for the purposes of this paragraph by a written notice given to the Chief Surveillance Commissioner by the Commissioners for Her Majesty's Revenue and Customs;'.

15 For section 37(1)(d) (quashing authorisations) substitute—

'(d) an officer of Revenue and Customs;'

(and in the heading to that section for 'customs' substitute 'Revenue and Customs').

16 For section 40(d) (information) substitute—

'(d) every officer of Revenue and Customs,'.

17 In section 46(3) (Scotland: restrictions) for paragraph (e) substitute—

'(e) the Commissioners for Her Majesty's Revenue and Customs;'.

18 In section 48(3)(c)(ii) (interpretation) for 'customs officers).' Substitute 'officers of Revenue and Customs).'

19 In section 49(1)(e) (encrypted data: disclosure: permission) for 'the customs and excise' substitute (in each place) 'Her Majesty's Revenue and Customs'.

20 In section 51 (cases where key required)—
   (a) for 'the customs and excise' (in each place) substitute 'Her Majesty's Revenue and Customs'; and
   (b) for 'the Commissioners of Customs and Excise' (in each place) substitute 'the Commissioners for Her Majesty's Revenue and Customs'.

21 In section 54(3) (secrecy) for 'the customs and excise' substitute (in each place) 'Her Majesty's Revenue and Customs'.

22 For section 55(1)(c) (general duty in relation to encrypted data) substitute—

   '(c) the Commissioners for Her Majesty's Revenue and Customs;'.

23 In section 56(1) (interpretation) omit the definition of 'the customs and excise'.

24 For section 65(6)(f) (the Tribunal) substitute—

   '(f) the Commissioners for Her Majesty's Revenue and Customs;'.

25 In section 71(2)(c) (codes of practice) for 'customs and excise' substitute 'Her Majesty's Revenue and Customs'.

26 In section 76A(11) (foreign surveillance operations) for paragraph (d) of the definition of 'United Kingdom officer' substitute—

   '(d) an officer of Revenue and Customs.'

27 In section 81(1) (interpretation) omit the definition of 'customs officer'.

28 In Schedule 1 (surveillance authorisation: relevant authorities) for paragraphs 7 and 8 substitute—

'Revenue and Customs

7 Her Majesty's Revenue and Customs.'

29 (1) In paragraphs 2(3) and (5), 4(2) and 5(3)(b) of Schedule 2 (encrypted data: disclosure: permission) for 'customs and excise' or 'the customs and excise' (in each place) substitute 'Her Majesty's Revenue and Customs'.
   (2) In paragraph 6(4) of that Schedule—
     (a) for 'A person commissioned by the Commissioners of Customs and Excise' substitute 'An officer of Revenue and Customs';
     (b) for 'those Commissioners themselves' substitute 'the Commissioners for Her Majesty's Revenue and Customs';
     (c) for 'their department' substitute 'Revenue and Customs'; and
     (d) for 'they' substitute 'the Commissioners'.

Commissioners for Revenue and Customs Act 2005 (c. 11)

30 The following paragraphs of Schedule 2 to the Commissioners for Revenue and Customs Act 2005 (which restrict the class of functions in connection with which certain powers may be used) shall cease to have effect—
   (a) paragraph 1 (Wireless Telegraphy Act 2006 (c. 36), s. 48); and
   (b) paragraph 11 (Regulation of Investigatory Powers Act 2000 (c. 23), ss. 6(2)(h), 32(6)(m), 49(1)(e) and 54 and Sched. 2, paras. 2(3) and 4(2)).

31 Nothing in section 6 or 7 of the Commissioners for Revenue and Customs Act 2005 (initial functions) restricts the functions in connection with which Her Majesty's Revenue and Customs may exercise a power under an enactment amended by this Schedule.

SCHEDULE 13   Section 91(1)
TRANSITIONAL AND TRANSITORY PROVISIONS AND SAVINGS

Serious crime prevention orders

1   In deciding for the purposes of paragraph (a) of section 1(1) or (2) whether a person has been involved in serious crime, the court may take account of conduct before the coming into force of that provision as well as conduct after the coming into force of that provision.

2   (1) Section 19, 20 or 21 does not apply to a person who is being dealt with on or after the coming into force of the section in relation to an offence of which the person was convicted before the coming into force of the section.

     (2) Sub-paragraph (1) does not prevent an application to the High Court for a serious crime prevention order in connection with the offence concerned.

3   In the application of section 23(2) or 24(5) before the commencement of paragraph 1(1) of Part 1 of Schedule 11 to the Constitutional Reform Act 2005 (c. 4) (citation of acts and rules), the reference to the Senior Courts Act 1981 (c. 54) is to be read as a reference to the Supreme Court Act 1981 (c. 54).

4   In the application of section 25(2)(a)—

     (a) in England and Wales, in relation to an offence committed before the commencement of section 282(1) of the Criminal Justice Act 2003 (c. 44) (increase in sentencing powers of magistrates' court from 6 to 12 months for certain offences triable either way); and

     (b) in Scotland, until the commencement of section 45(1) of the Criminal Proceedings etc. (Reform) (Scotland) Act 2007 (asp 6) (increase in sentencing powers from 6 to 12 months);

     the reference to 12 months is to be read as a reference to 6 months.

Encouraging or assisting crime

5   (1) Nothing in any provision of Part 2 affects the operation of—

     (a) any rule of the common law; or

     (b) any provision made by or under an Act or Northern Ireland legislation;

     in relation to offences committed wholly or partly before the commencement of the provision in Part 2 concerned.

     (2) For the purposes of sub-paragraph (1), an offence is partly committed before commencement if—

     (a) a relevant event occurs before commencement; and

     (b) another relevant event occurs on or after commencement.

     (3) In this paragraph 'relevant event', in relation to an offence, means any act or other event (including any consequence of an act) proof of which is required for conviction of the offence.

6   (1) This paragraph applies where, in any proceedings—

     (a) a person ('D') is charged in respect of the same act both with an offence under section 44 and with the common law offence of inciting the commission of another offence;

     (b) the only thing preventing D from being found guilty of the offence under section 44 is the fact that it has not been proved beyond reasonable doubt that the time when the act took place was after the coming into force of that section; and

    (c) the only thing preventing D from being found guilty of the common law offence is that it has not been proved beyond reasonable doubt that that time was before the coming into force of section 59.

  (2) For the purpose of determining D's guilt it shall be conclusively presumed that the time when the act took place was before the coming into force of section 44.

7 In relation to any time before the coming into force of section 27(1) of the Justice (Northern Ireland) Act 2002 (c. 26), the reference in section 53(b) to the Advocate General for Northern Ireland is to be read as a reference to the Attorney General for Northern Ireland.

Data-sharing

8 In the application of section 70(1)(a)—

  (a) in England and Wales, in relation to an offence committed before the commencement of section 282(1) of the Criminal Justice Act 2003 (increase in sentencing powers of magistrates' court from 6 to 12 months for certain offences triable either way); and

  (b) in Scotland, until the commencement of section 45(1) of the Criminal Proceedings etc. (Reform) (Scotland) Act 2007 (asp 6) (increase in sentencing powers from 6 to 12 months);

the reference to 12 months is to be read as a reference to 6 months.

Data matching

9 In relation to an offence committed before the commencement of section 282(1) of the Criminal Justice Act 2003 (c. 44) (increase in sentencing powers of magistrates' court from 6 to 12 months for certain offences triable either way), the reference to 12 months in each of the following provisions is to be read as a reference to 6 months—

  (a) section 32D(8)(b) of the Audit Commission Act 1998 (c. 18) (as inserted by paragraph 2 of Schedule 7 to this Act);

  (b) section 64D(8)(b) of the Public Audit (Wales) Act 2004 (c. 23) (as inserted by paragraph 4 of that Schedule).

SCHEDULE 14   Section 92
REPEALS AND REVOCATIONS

Title	*Extent of repeal or revocation*
Parliamentary Commissioner Act 1967 (c. 13)	In Schedule 2— (a) the entry for 'The Director of the Assets Recovery Agency.'; (b) the paragraph in the Notes headed 'Assets Recovery Agency'.
Criminal Appeal Act 1968 (c. 19)	Section 33(1A). In section 51(1A), the words ', subject to section 33(1A) of this Act,'.
Criminal Law Act 1977 (c. 45)	Section 5(7).

Title	*Extent of repeal or revocation*
Magistrates' Courts Act 1980 (c. 43)	Section 32(1)(b). Section 45. In Schedule 1, paragraph 35.
Criminal Appeal (Northern Ireland) Act 1980 (c. 47)	In section 31— (a) subsection (1A); (b) in subsection (3), the words ', subject to subsection (1A) above,'.
Legal Aid, Advice and Assistance (Northern Ireland) Order 1981 (S.I. 1981/228 (N.I.8))	In paragraph 2A(1)(a) of Part 1 of Schedule 1, the words 'or 204(3)'.
Magistrates' Courts (Northern Ireland) Order 1981 (S.I. 1981/1675 (N.I.26))	Article 60(1).
Criminal Attempts and Conspiracy (Northern Ireland) Order 1983 (S.I. 1983/1120 (N.I.13))	Article 13(8).
Bankruptcy (Scotland) Act 1985 (c. 66)	In section 31A(1)(b), the word '52,'.
Insolvency Act 1986 (c. 45)	In section 306A(1)(b), the word '52,'.
Public Order Act 1986 (c. 64)	In section 12(10), the words from 'notwithstanding' to the end. In section 13(13), the words from 'notwithstanding' to the end. In section 14(10), the words from 'notwithstanding' to the end. In section 14B(7), the words from 'notwithstanding' to the end.
Insolvency (Northern Ireland) Order 1989 (S.I. 1989/2405 (N.I.19))	In Article 279A(1)(b), the word '52,'.
Computer Misuse Act 1990 (c. 18)	Section 6(3). Section 7(4). In section 8(3), the words 'or by virtue of section 7(4) above'. Section 9(2)(d). In section 16(4), the words from 'and any reference' to the end.
Police Act 1996 (c. 16)	In section 97— (a) subsection (1)(ce); (b) in subsections (6)(a) and (8), the word '(ce),'.
Police Act 1997 (c. 50)	In section 108(1), the definition of 'customs officer'.

Title	Extent of repeal or revocation
Police (Northern Ireland) Act 1998 (c. 32)	In section 27— (a) subsection (1)(ca); (b) in subsection (5)(b), the word '(ca),'; (c) in subsection (7), the word '(ca),'.
Access to Justice Act 1999 (c. 22)	In paragraph 3(1)(b) of Schedule 2, the words 'or 56(3)'.
Regulation of Investigatory Powers Act 2000 (c. 23)	In section 56(1), the definition of 'the customs and excise'. In section 81(1), the definition of 'customs officer'.
International Criminal Court Act 2001 (c. 17)	Section 55(3). Section 62(3).
Proceeds of Crime Act 2002 (c. 29)	Sections 1 and 2. Section 3(6) and (8). Sections 4 and 5. In section 6(3)(a), the words 'or the Director'. In section 11(7), paragraph (b) and the word 'or' before it. In section 14(7)(b), the words 'or the Director (as the case may be)'. In section 16— (a) in subsection (1), the words 'or the Director (as the case may be)'; (b) in subsection (3), the words 'or the Director (as the case may be)' and 'or the Director'; (c) in subsection (4), the words 'or Director'; (d) in subsection (5), the words 'or the Director (as the case may be)' and 'or the Director'; (e) in subsection (6), the words 'or the Director'. In section 17(1), the words 'or the Director'. In section 18(6), the words 'or the Director (as the case may be)'. In section 19(1)(c), the words 'or the Director'. In section 20— (a) subsection (3); (b) in subsection (4), the words from 'If the court' to 'to do so,' and, in paragraph (b), the words 'or the Director'. In section 21(1)(b), (c) and (d), the words 'or the Director'. In section 22(2), paragraph (b) and, in paragraph (c), the words 'or 52'. In section 23(1)(b), the words 'or 52'. In section 26— (a) in subsection (1)(b), the words 'or the Director'; (b) in subsection (2), in paragraph (a), the words 'or the Director (as the case may be)' and, in paragraph (b), the words 'or the Director'.

Title	Extent of repeal or revocation

In section 27—
(a) in subsection (3)(a), the words 'or the Director';
(b) in subsection (5)(b), the words 'or the Director (as the case may be)';
(c) in subsection (7), the words 'or the Director'.

In section 28—
(a) in subsection (3)(a), the words 'or the Director';
(b) in subsection (5)(b), the words 'or the Director (as the case may be)'.

In section 31—
(a) in the heading, the words 'or Director';
(b) in subsections (1) and (2), the words 'or the Director'.

In section 33(2)—
(a) in paragraph (a), the words '(if the prosecutor appealed under section 31)';
(b) paragraph (b).

Section 34.

In section 35(1), paragraph (b) and the word 'and' before it.

Sections 36 and 37.

Section 39(6).

In section 40—
(a) in subsections (4)(a), (5)(a) and (6)(a), the words 'or the Director';
(b) in subsection (8)(b), the words 'or the Director (as the case may be)'.

Section 42(2)(b).

Sections 52 and 53.

Sections 56 and 57.

Section 60.

In section 63(1)(b), the words from 'or', where it first appears, to 'Director'.

In section 64—
(a) in subsection (1)(b), the words from 'or' to 'section 52';
(b) subsection (3).

In section 65—
(a) in subsections (1) and (2), the words 'or section 53';
(b) in subsection (5)(a), the words from 'or', where it first appears, to 'Director'.

Section 67(4)(c).

In section 74(1)—
(a) in paragraph (b), the words 'or the Director';
(b) in paragraph (c), the words 'or the Director (as the case may be)'.

Title	*Extent of repeal or revocation*
	In section 156(3)(a), the words 'or the Director'.
	In section 161(7), paragraph (b) and the word 'or' before it.
	In section 164(7)(b), the words 'or the Director (as the case may be)'.
	In section 166—
	(a) in subsection (1), the words 'or the Director (as the case may be)';
	(b) in subsection (3), the words 'or the Director (as the case may be)' and 'or the Director';
	(c) in subsection (4), the words 'or Director';
	(d) in subsection (5), the words 'or the Director (as the case may be)' and 'or the Director';
	(e) in subsection (6), the words 'or the Director'.
	In section 167(1), the words 'or the Director'.
	In section 168(6), the words 'or the Director (as the case may be)'.
	In section 169(1)(c), the words 'or the Director'.
	In section 170—
	(a) subsection (3);
	(b) in subsection (4), the words from 'If the court' to 'to do so,' and, in paragraph (b), the words 'or the Director'.
	In section 171(1)(b), (c) and (d), the words 'or the Director'.
	In section 172(2), paragraph (b) and, in paragraph (c), the words 'or 200'.
	In section 173(1)(b), the words 'or 200'.
	In section 176—
	(a) in subsection (1)(b), the words 'or the Director';
	(b) in subsection (2), in paragraph (a), the words 'or the Director (as the case may be)' and, in paragraph (b), the words 'or the Director'.
	In section 177—
	(a) in subsection (3)(a), the words 'or the Director';
	(b) in subsection (5)(b), the words 'or the Director (as the case may be)';
	(c) in subsection (7), the words 'or the Director'.
	In section 178—
	(a) in subsection (3)(a), the words 'or the Director';
	(b) in subsection (5)(b), the words 'or the Director (as the case may be)'.
	In section 181—
	(a) in the heading, the words 'or Director';
	(b) in subsections (1) and (2), the words 'or the Director'.

Title	Extent of repeal or revocation
	In section 183(2)—
	(a) in paragraph (a), the words '(if the prosecutor appealed under section 181)';
	(b) paragraph (b).
	Section 184.
	Section 186.
	Section 188(6).
	In section 189—
	(a) in subsections (4)(a), (5)(a) and (6)(a), the words 'or the Director';
	(b) in subsection (8)(b), the words 'or the Director (as the case may be)'.
	Section 191(2)(b).
	Sections 200 and 201.
	Sections 204 and 205.
	Section 208.
	In section 210(2)(b) and (3), the words 'or 200'.
	In section 211(1)(b), the words from 'or', where it first appears, to 'Director'.
	In section 212—
	(a) in subsection (1)(b), the words from 'or' to 'section 200';
	(b) subsection (3).
	In section 213—
	(a) in subsections (1) and (2), the words 'or section 201';
	(b) in subsection (5)(a), the words from 'or', where it first appears, to 'Director'.
	Section 215(4)(d).
	In section 430(2)—
	(a) in paragraph (b), the words 'or 52';
	(b) in paragraph (d), the words 'or 200'.
	Section 436(5)(b) and (ga).
	Section 438(2) to (4).
	Section 449(5).
	Schedule 1.
	In Schedule 8, the words from 'The Director', where it first appears, to 'by law.", where it first appears.
	In Schedule 11, paragraphs 2, 4(2), 9(3), 30(1) and (2) and 34(1) and (2).
	In section 222(1)—
	(a) in paragraph (b), the words 'or the Director';
	(b) in paragraph (c), the words 'or the Director (as the case may be)'.
	Section 313.
	Section 325(1).

Title	Extent of repeal or revocation
	Section 356(6).
	Section 376.
	Section 378(7).
	In section 417(2)—
	(a) in paragraph (b), the words 'or 52';
	(b) in paragraph (d), the words 'or 200'.
	In section 419(2)(b), the word '52,'.
	In section 420(2)—
	(a) in paragraph (b), the words 'or 52';
	(b) in paragraph (d), the words 'or 200'.
	In section 422(2)(b), the word '52,'.
	In section 423(2)—
	(a) in paragraph (b), the words 'or 52';
	(b) in paragraph (d), the words 'or 200'.
	In section 425(2)(b), the word '52,'.
	In section 426(2)—
	(a) in paragraph (b), the words 'or 52';
	(b) in paragraph (d), the words 'or 200'.
	In section 427(3)(b), the word '52,'.
	In section 428(2)—
	(a) in paragraph (b), the words 'or 52';
	(b) in paragraph (d), the words 'or 200'.
	In section 429(3)(b), the word '52,'.
Crime (International Cooperation) Act 2003 (c. 32)	In Schedule 5, paragraphs 82 and 83.
Access to Justice (Northern Ireland) Order 2003 (S.I. 2003/435 (N.I.10))	In paragraph 3(1)(a) of Schedule 2, the words 'or 204(3)'.
Commissioners for Revenue and Customs Act 2005 (c. 11)	In section 21(1)(b), the word 'or' at the end of sub-paragraph (i).
	Paragraphs 1 and 11 of Schedule 2.
	Paragraph 98 of Schedule 4.
Serious Organised Crime and Police Act 2005 (c. 15)	Section 99(4).
	In Schedule 4—
	(a) in paragraph 82(2), paragraph (b) and the word 'and' at the end of paragraph (b);
	(b) paragraphs 169, 176 and 178.
	In Schedule 5, in paragraph 21(1) and (2), the words 'is or'.
Gambling Act 2005 (c. 19)	In Part 2 of Schedule 6, the entries relating to the Director and staff of the Assets Recovery Agency, the Director General and staff of the National Crime Squad and the Director General and staff of the National Criminal Intelligence Service.

Title	Extent of repeal or revocation
Wireless Telegraphy Act 2006 (c. 36)	In Schedule 7, paragraph 38.
Police and Justice Act 2006 (c. 48)	Section 35(2).
	In section 36, in the section to be substituted for section 3 of the Computer Misuse Act 1990 (c. 18), in subsection (2), paragraph (d) and the word 'or' preceding it.
	Section 38(1).
	In Schedule 14, paragraphs 19(2) and 29(2).
Tribunals, Courts and Enforcement Act 2007 (c. 15)	In Schedule 13, paragraph 145.
Corporate Manslaughter and Corporate Homicide Act 2007 (c. 19)	In Schedule 1, the words 'Assets Recovery Agency'.

Index

QM LIBRARY
(MILE END)